EERDMANS COMMENTARIES ON THE DEAD SEA SCROLLS

The Eerdmans Commentaries on the Dead Sea Scrolls series marks a milestone in scroll studies. The sixteen volumes in the ECDSS series, each one written by a world-renowned scholar, bring together for the first time expert translations, critical notes, and line-by-line commentary for every translatable manuscript found at Qumran. Produced with scholarly rigor yet accessible to students and non-specialists, these volumes are essential to the study of the Dead Sea Scrolls and also provide crucial background for research into both the New Testament and rabbinical Judaism.

EERDMANS COMMENTARIES ON THE DEAD SEA SCROLLS

EDITORS
Martin G. Abegg Jr. and Peter W. Flint

Rules and Laws I • Charlotte Hempel

Rules and Laws II • Lawrence H. Schiffman

The Temple Scroll • Florentino García Martínez

The Thanksgiving Scroll • TBA

Psalms and Hymns • Peter W. Flint

*Liturgical Works • James R. Davila

Calendrical Texts • Uwe Glessmer

Paraphrased Torah I • Moshe Bernstein

Paraphrased Torah II • George J. Brooke

Paraphrased Prophets • James C. VanderKam and Monica Brady

Pesharim • Craig A. Evans

The War Scroll • Martin G. Abegg Jr.

Eschatology • John J. Collins

*Wisdom Literature • John Kampen

The Copper Scroll • Albert M. Wolters

Enochic Writings • John C. Reeves

*Now available

WISDOM LITERATURE

John Kampen

WILLIAM B. EERDMANS PUBLISHING COMPANY

GRAND RAPIDS, MICHIGAN / CAMBRIDGE, U.K.

Published 2011 by
Wm. B. Eerdmans Publishing Co.
2140 Oak Industrial Drive N.E., Grand Rapids, Michigan 49505 /
P.O. Box 163, Cambridge CB3 9PU U.K.

Printed in the United States of America

17 16 15 14 13 12 11   7 6 5 4 3 2

Library of Congress Cataloging-in-Publication Data

Kampen, John.
Wisdom literature / John Kampen.
p.   cm. — (Eerdmans commentaries on the Dead Sea scrolls)
Includes bibliographical references and index.
ISBN 978-0-8028-4384-5 (pbk.: alk. paper)
1. Dead Sea scrolls. 2. Wisdom literature —
Criticism, interpretation, etc.   I. Title.

BM487.K347   2011

296.1′55 — dc22

2010043283

www.eerdmans.com

To Ben Zion Wacholder,
who taught me to
רז נהיה דרוש והתבונן בכל דכרי אמת
("Search the mystery of existence and
gain understanding in all ways of truth")
4Q416 (Instruction) 2iii:17

Contents

Preface

When I began work on these wisdom texts less than a decade after the majority of them became known to the scholarly world and prior to the official publication of most of them in the DJD series, very few people were aware of them and of their potential significance. However, the magic attendant the exploration of this unknown material, the captivating nature of their content, and the significance of the concepts developed and utilized throughout their fragments have made these texts the center of an astounding amount of academic research in the past decade. This commentary attempts to provide for the reader a summary of a good deal of the major research as well as make a contribution to the study of individual texts and to advance our understanding of their contribution to the changing picture of the lives and beliefs of Jews in the latter portion of the Second Temple period. As this new and enhanced picture of Jewish life of that era comes into clearer focus, we acquire a better understanding of the origins of Judaism and Christianity. Of equal significance, we get a clearer picture of the changes in the intellectual and religious life that accompany a society in a period of rapid transition.

I am deeply indebted to those many fellow academics who have been engaged in the study of these texts with me. Most of them are cited in the bibliographies and footnotes of this volume. Many of them launched their academic careers with a study of these wisdom texts. Much of the tremendous amount of effort expended on this wisdom literature in the past decade has been accomplished by persons barely known or even unknown to the academic community before the turn of the millennium. I continue to learn from so many of them. To the many colleagues in the Qumran section of the Society of Biblical Literature and the International Organization of Qumran Studies who heard and responded to my many papers as I worked through the various issues necessary to produce this commentary I offer my admiration for their endurance and my gratitude for their attention and comments.

Given the present state of research and study, we are left with a large body of work yet adequately to be synthesized and incorporated into this larger portrait to which each of us contributes in our own way and from our particular expertise and vantage point. The reader of this commentary can anticipate continuing change and growth in our understanding of specific texts and even certain terms. This means that our understanding of major concepts and their contexts as well as their significance will continue in a state of flux. For many working in the field, the desire to fill out this picture is a goodly portion of the allure that drew us to the field and impels our efforts. I recognize that many persons utilizing this commentary from ancillary fields will not be used to, and perhaps less tolerant of, the tenuous and changing nature of the results of our labors.

Throughout the work on these texts and this publication I have been the beneficiary of significant institutional support. A sabbatical from Bluffton University provided the block of time necessary to do the initial work on this volume. I am grateful to Lee Snyder, then president, who made it possible. An NEH grant from the Albright Institute of Archaeological Research in Jerusalem permitted my work to proceed in the rich academic environment of that city. The Institute has been integral to my continuing growth as a scholar of Second Temple Judaism; its director Sy Gitin has been an indispensable source of advice and support throughout much of my academic career. When I came to the Methodist Theological Seminary in Ohio (MTSO), presidents Norman Dewire and Jay Rundell permitted me to take precious blocks of time away from my administrative responsibilities in order that I might continue this research and publication. Student assistants at MTSO who contributed to the production of this volume include Chris Gardener with research and Mark Schanely with indexing. Christina Fetheroff checked citations.

The editors of this series, Peter Flint and Martin Abegg, were an ongoing source of support throughout the research and writing of this volume. I am very grateful to them for the initial invitation to undertake it. Marty's editorial guidance in earlier phases of the work and his careful reading of the manuscript were invaluable and saved me from both mistakes and infelicities. In spite of his best efforts, some of my errors remain. Allen Myers, Senior Editor at Eerdmans, provided encouragement and advice on an ongoing basis. Jennifer Hoffman, Associate Managing Editor, assisted with editorial work on a complicated manuscript. I am very grateful to both of them.

Work on this volume would have been much more arduous had it not been for the active interest and continuing support of my loving wife, Carol Lehman.

This volume is dedicated to Ben Zion Wacholder, my teacher. One morning in the fall of 1978 he called and asked me to stop on the way to his house to pick up a new volume that had come into the library the previous day. This volume was the original Hebrew publication of the Temple Scroll by Yigael Yadin. That day changed both of our lives. He began research on the Temple Scroll, and Qumran texts dominated the remainder of his academic career. My work with him on *The Dawn of Qumran* brought me into this field. The experience of daily study over a number of years with a man who reveres all texts and has an encyclopedic knowledge of so many of them set the tone and direction of my own studies. Even though the wisdom texts were never part of our work together, this commentary would not have been possible without those years of study. It is my hope that it reflects some evidence of his labors.

Abbreviations and Sources

The texts used in this commentary follow the ordering of fragments and line numbers as they are found in their publication in the Discoveries in the Judaean Desert (DJD) series. For the most part this is also the text to be found in *DSSSE* and *DSSR*, vol. 4. References to the text of 1QH[a] *(Hodayot[a])* and associated MSS follow their publication as found in DJD 40. Citations of the Hebrew Bible and translations of that text, unless noted otherwise, are from the NRSV.

Qumran Manuscripts

Listed below are the sigla and titles of some of the MSS from Qumran that I refer to throughout this commentary. The MS numbers for each of the wisdom compositions are listed in the introduction to this volume (see p. 10 below) as well as in the introduction to each chapter.

CD   *Damascus Document* MSS from the Cairo Genizah
1QH   *Hodayot* MSS from Cave 1 *(Thanksgiving Hymns)*
1QM   *War Scroll* MS from Cave 1 (1Q33)
1QS   *Community Rule* MSS from Cave 1 *(Serek ha-yaḥad)*
1QSa   *Rule of the Congregation*
4QD   *Damascus Document* MSS from Cave 4
4QH   *Hodayot* MSS from Cave 4 *(Thanksgiving Hymns)*
4QM   *War Scroll* MSS from Cave 4
4QS   *Community Rule* MSS from Cave 4 *(Serek ha-yaḥad)*

Other Abbreviations

The following are used in addition to the standard SBL abbreviations.

DSSANT Michael Wise, Martin Abegg Jr., and Edward Cook. *The Dead Sea Scrolls: A New Translation.* San Francisco: HarperSanFrancisco, 2005.

DSSB Martin Abegg Jr., Peter Flint, and Eugene Ulrich. *The Dead Sea Scrolls Bible: The Oldest Known Bible Translated for the First Time into English.* San Francisco: HarperSanFrancisco, 1999.

DSSC Martin G. Abegg Jr. *The Dead Sea Scrolls Concordance.* Volume 1: *The Non-Biblical Texts from Qumran.* One volume in 2 parts. Leiden: Brill, 2003.

DSSCat Stephen A. Reed and Marilyn J. Lundberg. *The Dead Sea Scrolls Catalogue: Documents, Photographs and Museum Inventory Numbers.* SBLRBS 32. Atlanta: Scholars Press, 1994.

DSSEL Emanuel Tov, ed. *The Dead Sea Scrolls Electronic Library.* Rev. ed. Leiden: Brill; Provo: Brigham Young University, 2006.

DSSR Donald W. Parry and Emanuel Tov, eds. *The Dead Sea Scrolls Reader.* 6 vols. Leiden: Brill, 2004-5.

DSSSE Florentino García Martínez and Eibert J. C. Tigchelaar. *The Dead Sea Scrolls: Study Edition.* 2 vols. Leiden: Brill; Grand Rapids: Eerdmans, 1997-98.

EDSS Lawrence H. Schiffman and James C. VanderKam, eds. *Encyclopedia of the Dead Sea Scrolls.* 2 vols. Oxford: Oxford University Press, 2000.

HDSS Elisha Qimron. *The Hebrew of the Dead Sea Scrolls.* HSS 29. Atlanta: Scholars Press, 1986.

IBHS Bruce K. Waltke and M. O'Connor. *An Introduction to Biblical Hebrew Syntax.* Winona Lake, Ind.: Eisenbrauns, 1990.

PAM Palestine Archaeological Museum (photograph accession numbers)

PEUDSS Ben Zion Wacholder, Martin G. Abegg, and James Bowley. *A Preliminary Edition of the Unpublished Dead Sea Scrolls: The Hebrew and Aramaic Texts from Qumran.* 4 vols. Washington, DC: Biblical Archaeology Society, 1991-96.

Full publication information for many of the works cited in the notes of this commentary is available in the bibliographies found either at the conclusion of the introduction to this volume or at the conclusion of the introduction of each chapter.

Introduction

The First Forty Years of Research

The study of wisdom and wisdom literature at Qumran has a fascinating history.[1] An overview of that history is a necessary introduction to the study of the texts currently considered to be representatives of that literary corpus. Present conceptions of these texts and their place within the changing formulations of the social circles in which they originated inform a continuing reappraisal of the social and intellectual history of Second Temple Judaism.

In 1965 when James Sanders published the *Psalms Scroll* from Cave 11, he noted that "no work has been done, to my knowledge, on Wisdom thinking generally in Qumrân literature."[2] While he did note the presence of wisdom vocabulary in other documents such as 1QS and 1QH, he likened their context to usage in the canonical psalms. Elsewhere he is quoted as stating that "the Sapiential is not a Qumran characteristic."[3] In a later survey article W. Loundes Lipscomb in conjunction with Sanders summarized the state of research with regard to wisdom at Qumran and concluded that while the major Cave 1 texts do contain ample evidence of wisdom vocabulary, they are not to be regarded

---

1. Portions of this introduction are adapted from my survey article, "The Diverse Aspects of Wisdom in the Qumran Texts," in *The Dead Sea Scrolls after Fifty Years: A Comprehensive Assessment* (ed. James C. VanderKam and Peter Flint; 2 vols.; Leiden: Brill, 1998-99), 1:211-43. Some topics covered in this introduction receive more extensive treatment there. This introduction also refers to work on the topic since that article was published.

2. J. A. Sanders, *The Psalms Scroll of Qumrân Cave 11 (11QPsᵃ)* (DJD 4; Oxford: Clarendon, 1965), 69 n. 1.

3. Attributed to him in John E. Worrell, "Concepts of Wisdom in the Dead Sea Scrolls" (diss., Claremont Graduate School, 1968), 115.

as sapiential: "While the Essene texts contain wisdom vocabulary and expressions, a concern for knowledge and instruction, and an ethical dualism characteristic of the wisdom literature, these elements are external to and superimposed upon the basically apocalyptic fabric of Qumran thought."[4] As wisdom compositions included among the texts of unknown authorship they listed 4Q184 and columns from 11QPsª. For them texts of unknown authorship were those that do not include Essene vocabulary, that is, do not contain evidence of sectarian authorship. These claims reflect the evaluation of the majority of scholars of Qumran literature concerning the question of wisdom at the end of the first two to three decades of research. On the fortieth anniversary of the initial discovery of the scrolls, Sarah Tanzer in her dissertation on 1QH reached a similar conclusion with regard to the state of research: "The presence of Wisdom at Qumran, and especially in 1QH, has never been thoroughly investigated."[5] She noted in the research material a presupposition that Qumran must be regarded exclusively as either an apocalyptic or a wisdom community.[6] Her dissertation was a subtle push to begin to frame the question(s) in a different manner.

These summary observations are interesting in light of early publications that identified the presence of wisdom terminology in these newly discovered texts. The earliest surveys of this material noted the extensive presence of terminology related to דעת ("knowledge") in these texts: "'Knowledge' is one of the prominent words of CDC and it is used primarily with reference to the divine law."[7] In his more comprehensive work a few years later Millar Burrows noted the use of the verb "know" and the noun "knowledge" also in 1QS and 1QHª. He pointed to the frequent appearance of the synonyms "'wisdom,' 'prudence,' 'understanding,' 'insight,' and the like" in the scrolls available to him at the time, indicating a vocabulary similar to Proverbs.[8] Using "knowledge" as the key term along with its cognates, W. D. Davies organized the passages from the major

---

4. W. Loundes Lipscomb with James A. Sanders, "Wisdom at Qumran," in *Israelite Wisdom: Theological and Literary Essays in Honor of Samuel Terrien* (ed. John G. Gammie, Walter A. Brueggemann, W. Lee Humphreys, and James M. Ward; Missoula, Mont.: Scholars Press, 1978), 280.

5. Sarah Tanzer, "The Sages at Qumran: Wisdom in the *Hodayot*" (Ph.D. diss., Harvard University, 1987), 12.

6. Ibid., 12-14.

7. M. Burrows, "The Discipline Manual of the Judaean Covenanters," *OtSt* 8 (1950): 156-92, esp. 168-71 (quote from p. 168); cf. A. Dupont-Sommer, *The Dead Sea Scrolls: A Preliminary Survey* (trans. E. Margaret Rowley; Oxford: Blackwell, 1952 [orig. 1950]), 42, 65 n. 1. CDC (Cairo Genizah Document of the Damascus Covenanters), now abbreviated as CD (Cairo Damascus), refers to the *Damascus Document*.

8. Millar Burrows, *The Dead Sea Scrolls* (New York: Viking, 1955), 253-55.

Cave 1 scrolls dealing with the question of "knowledge" into six major groupings: intelligent discernment, those passages associated with the law, expressed or implied secret knowledge, the interpretation of events or passages of eschatological significance, knowledge of an intimate or personal kind, and knowledge as mediated.[9] He identified eschatology and ethics as features that distinguish the Qumran materials. In his classification he highlighted the connection of "knowledge" in these texts with law. He did note that they "seem to have placed a greater emphasis upon the concept of knowledge, whatever its exact connotation, than the more strictly Jewish circles, whose literature across the centuries is preserved in the Old Testament."[10] Clearly he recognized the importance of "knowledge" for the sectarian authors of these Cave 1 documents.

Of particular interest to these early researchers was the relationship of these new materials to the texts of Gnosticism, given the extensive use of wisdom terminology within the latter. Kurt Schubert held that 1QS iii:13–iv:26 was the oldest gnostic text presently available.[11] K. G. Kuhn argued that they were not gnostic texts, but that a "gnostic" understanding of knowledge lay behind them. Qumran represented a gnostic pattern of thought, but its literature did not contain gnostic literary allusions and references.[12] The discussions of "knowledge" by Burrows and Davies noted above also were attempts to address this question. This issue was driven not primarily by the recently discovered Nag Hammadi materials but rather by those theories that discerned a gnostic influence in the NT documents, referred to as "Hellenistic Gnosticism" by Davies.[13] While noting some interest in cosmological speculation in those scrolls, he saw the major interest reflected therein to be the interpretation of the events of world history, of prophecy.[14] He also noted the connection of knowledge with law, an ethical nuance not always characteristic of Hellenistic *gnosis*.[15] The recognition of the ethical and religious dimensions of the dualism present in the Qumran documents was an attempt to differentiate it from Gnosticism.

9. W. D. Davies, "'Knowledge' in the Dead Sea Scrolls and Matthew 11:25-30," *HTR* 46 (1953): 113-39.

10. Ibid., 135.

11. Schubert, "Der gegenwärtige Stand der Erforschung der in Palästina neu gefundenen hebräischen Handschriften, 25: Der Sektkanon von En Feshcha und die Anfänge der jüdischen Gnosis," *TLZ* 78 (1953): 502.

12. K. G. Kuhn, "Die in Palästina gefundenen hebräischen Texte und das Neue Testament," *ZTK* 47 (1950): 203-5.

13. Davies, "Knowledge," 113.

14. Ibid., 133-34. These similarities are also denied by Burrows, "Discipline Manual," 168; idem, *Dead Sea Scrolls,* 252-59.

15. Davies, "Knowledge," 135.

The attempt to understand the particular dualism related to these Cave 1 documents focused on the "Treatise on the Two Spirits" (1QS iii:13–iv:26). An extensive literature contrasts the psychological dimensions, based on the treatise's connections with wisdom literature, to the cosmic and cosmological references within that and related texts.[16] While noting the influence of Gerhard von Rad with his thesis that apocalyptic conceptions of time and history had their origins in wisdom circles, Tanzer observed that the attempts to understand the dualism of these new texts were based upon the presupposition that their origins were to be ascribed exclusively to either apocalyptic or wisdom circles.[17] The extensive debates on this particular question came to a conclusion in an article by John Gammie in which he cataloged the varieties of dualism that had been put forth up to that time and then argued that the ethical dualism advanced in the biblical wisdom literature is both internalized into a psychological dualism and externalized into a cosmic dualism within the Qumran materials.[18]

One of the reasons that connections with the biblical wisdom materials were not as clearly established on a substantial basis as we now might expect was the relative scarcity of the term "wisdom" in these materials from Cave 1. For example, in K. G. Kuhn's concordance published in 1960, which includes the major Cave 1 texts, we find 13 references to the term "wisdom" and 5 to the adjective "wise," whereas 42 appearances of "knowledge" are noted and another 16 places use a variant Hebrew form of the term (דעה and דעות), which includes references such as the "God of knowledge." This observation is buttressed by 117 appearances of the verb "know" (ידע) in these same texts. In his dissertation, John Worrell attributed the relative infrequency of the term "wisdom" in these compositions to the sectarian opposition to the hermeneutical authorities of the day — the Pharisees.[19] Evidence for such a formulation of the historical situation in the second century B.C.E. is lacking. In her summary, Tanzer concluded that the explanation for the relative scarcity of the term is the particularization of the character of wisdom at Qumran.[20] While this rationale could imply a level of intentionality to the shift in vocabulary not supported by the evidence, the argument is instructive as we ponder subsequent developments in the study of this remarkable material.[21]

16. For a summary see Kampen, "Diverse Aspects," 213-18.

17. Tanzer, "Sages at Qumran," 12-14.

18. J. G. Gammie, "Spatial and Ethical Dualism in Jewish Wisdom and Apocalyptic Literature," *JBL* 93 (1974): 356-85.

19. Worrell, "Concepts of Wisdom," 119, 406.

20. Tanzer, "Sages at Qumran," 179.

21. For a more extensive discussion of the wisdom vocabulary in the Dead Sea Scrolls, see my forthcoming article.

The Corpus of Wisdom Literature

In the fall of 1991 the fragments of the numerous texts from Cave 4 that had previously been unavailable for study to the majority of those scholars interested in their contents were opened up to researchers by the Israel Antiquities Authority. The story of the events of that fall is too long to narrate here, but worthy of notice.[22] Among the texts that became available at that point were a number that proved to be related to wisdom, transforming our understanding of this literary tradition within the Qumran texts and in Second Temple Judaism. We can now advance our study of wisdom in Second Temple Judaism informed by this expanded circle of available texts.

The Hebrew Bible

The difficulties associated with the identification and classification of a new and potentially amorphous collection of wisdom texts begins already with the definition of this corpus of literature within the more established traditions of the HB. The most obvious criterion for the identification of wisdom texts is the employment of the term "wisdom" (חכמה) within them. The various forms of the root for "wisdom" (חכם) appear 318 times in the HB,[23] with 183 of those occurrences within the books of Proverbs, Job, and Qohelet (Ecclesiastes). When we add to this list the Wisdom of Solomon and Ben Sira (Sirach or Ecclesiasticus) with their use approximately 120 times of the Greek terms *sophia* and *sophos,* we have compiled the roster of biblical books normally considered to constitute the wisdom corpus.[24] James Crenshaw suggests that these five books "retain a mysterious ingredient that links them together in a special way," and elsewhere speaks of their "certain indescribable quality."[25] Both

22. A good summary of these events can be found in the chapter entitled "Scroll Wars" in James C. VanderKam and Peter Flint, *The Meaning of the Dead Sea Scrolls: Their Significance for Understanding the Bible, Judaism, Jesus, and Christianity* (San Francisco: HarperSanFrancisco, 2002), 381-403.

23. Another 22 references occur in the Aramaic texts of Ezra and Daniel.

24. Before entering into an extensive discussion of the issue of description and definition, Roland E. Murphy begins with the assumption that these five books are the starting point (*The Tree of Life: An Exploration of Biblical Wisdom Literature* [2d ed.; Grand Rapids: Eerdmans, 1996], 1).

25. For the former see James L. Crenshaw, *Old Testament Wisdom: An Introduction* (Atlanta: John Knox, 1981), 17; for the latter, 25. He attributes the phrase to Archer Taylor, who used it as a description of the proverb, *The Proverb, and an Index to the Proverb* (repr. Hatboro, Pa.: Folklore Associates, 1962), 3. Crenshaw presents his book as an attempt to clarify that "indescribable quality."

Crenshaw and Roland Murphy, prominent interpreters of this biblical literature, also note its variety of literary forms or genres.[26] An initial description of biblical wisdom begins with an identified corpus of literature rather than a common definition.

A few common themes in the biblical literature bear mention prior to our examination of Qumran literature. The first of these is the manner in which the viewpoints developed in this literature are rooted in the belief that there is a basic sense of order and that it is established in creation: "The central assumption of all the books is that God made the world, an order within which the human race must learn to live. That order was given privileged expression on the day of creation."[27] In antiquity cosmogonies were foundational statements about the nature of human societies: "Elements of the universe were given their purpose on the day of creation; the origin of a reality was its essence."[28] Thus in biblical wisdom, "The Lord by wisdom founded the earth, by understanding he established the heavens."[29] Creation has its basis in divine order, which is sometimes entitled "wisdom" in this literature.

This emphasis on creation is contrasted with the historical and covenantal emphases usually considered central to biblical (and Jewish) literature.[30] The stories of the patriarchs, Moses, and the exodus are absent from this literature. Other than some clearly identifiable sections in the later compositions, Wisdom of Solomon 11–19 and Sirach 44–50, and the identification of wisdom with the Torah in Sirach 24, historical recital and salvation history do not play a part. This does not mean that wisdom is understood in an ahistorical manner. Wisdom instruction is very frequently rooted in everyday experience; it regularly deals with concrete behavior: what persons should do, when they should do it, why. It is based on the recognition of a very dynamic relationship between human beings and their environment. The created world is used as both example and inspiration by the sages (e.g., Prov 25:11–26:28; Job 38–41). Within this dynamic relationship creation is a visible manifestation of wisdom, which has its basis in the Creator. Thus knowledge based on human observation and encounter is not simply secular, in the manner in which we define it in the modern world, but rather is integrally related to experience with the Divine.

26. Crenshaw, *Old Testament Wisdom*, 36-39; Murphy, *Tree of Life*, 7-13. See also the following survey articles: J. L. Crenshaw, "Wisdom in the Old Testament," *IDBSup* 952-56, esp. 953-54; Roland E. Murphy, "Wisdom in the OT," *ABD* 6:920-31, esp. 921; Richard J. Clifford, "Introduction to Wisdom Literature," *NIB* 5:1-16, esp. 7-8.

27. Clifford, "Introduction to Wisdom Literature," 8-9.

28. Ibid., 9.

29. Prov 3:19. See also Prov 8:22-31 and Job 38–41.

30. On this section see Murphy, *Tree of Life*, 111-31.

The notion of order is central to this literature. Wisdom literature has sometimes been labeled as secular knowledge because it is discernible from experience. It is probably more accurate to say that the knowledge gained by experience is the manner in which the fundamental order of the universe becomes apparent. It is creation that is available to human experience. It is the window to the order on which it is established. The reason of the universe is unlocked by human observation and experience. There is a certain autonomy to creation and its activities. The discovery of its events, patterns, and laws is integral to the acquisition of wisdom, thereby laying the foundation for lessons concerning the wise human life and related rules or laws of conduct. Ultimately the Creator provides the rationale and sanction for the life lived according to wisdom.

It is with this understanding of creation and order that another central theme of wisdom literature begins to make sense: "the fear of the Lord is the beginning of wisdom."[31] It is this recognition that validates the experiential basis of wisdom within this corpus of literature. Herein we see the fundamental "religious" reality that undergirds this literature, whether dealing with theological issues such as the nature of evil or passing on traditional wisdom about the proper handling of situations in everyday life. The fear of the Lord underlies the ability of the human being to appropriate an understanding of creation and of the order that lies behind it. In Ben Sira this is ultimately equated with the law: "The whole of wisdom is fear of the Lord, and in all wisdom there is the fulfillment of the law" (19:20 NRSV). That this statement is solidly rooted in the wisdom tradition can be seen in its placement following the poem in praise of God for the creation of humankind in Sirach 17, the mercy and compassion of God for the created human in Sirach 18, and resultant injunctions about living the good life.

It is apparent that human beings are viewed as morally responsible agents in this literature, which reflects great concern about the consequences of human action upon the individual and the community. There is a strong affirmation that the actions of human beings have consequences, whether good or evil. Those consequences are experienced within a person's lifetime. This framework provides a context for a viewpoint frequently articulated, particularly in Proverbs and Ben Sira, that there are two ways to live. One is evil and one is good (Prov 2:13, 20); one is the way of wisdom and the paths of uprightness, the

---

31. Prov 9:10 (cf. Job 28:28; Ps 111:10; Prov 15:33; Prov 1:7 might be better translated, "the fear of the Lord is the origin [or 'best part'] of knowledge"). See also Prov 31:30, where the woman or capable wife is praised for her "fear of the Lord" in the concluding verses of this composition in which Lady Wisdom is a major character.

other the path of the wicked and the way of evildoers (4:11, 14). The way of evil is contrasted with the way of righteousness (8:13, 20), and the way of the wicked with the path of righteousness (12:26, 28). In the latter reference there is life in the path of righteousness, and "in walking that path there is no death." The promise of wisdom is life. Similarly, the book of Deuteronomy also articulates the two ways, most memorably in Deut 30:15-20.[32] This section follows the blessings and curses stated in covenantal language in chap. 28. The results of righteous living are probed in the book of Job and even more extensively in Qohelet, which raises questions about this perspective within the wisdom tradition. The questions, however, assume that it is part of the wisdom tradition, frequently recommending that fearing God is important, even though God is a mysterious entity, and constantly referring to the term "wisdom," which is regarded as a precious asset that provides access to the understanding of all life, even when it is unknowable and desperately hard to attain.

One remarkable attempt to portray the power of the two ways can be seen in their personification as Lady Wisdom and Dame Folly.[33] The vivid portrayal of wisdom as a seductive woman in Proverbs 1–9, Sirach 24, Bar 3:9–4:4, and Wisdom 7–9 provides a literary image for the choices faced by humankind (note also 1 Enoch 42). While Job 28 is sometimes mentioned, the depiction in vv. 12 and 20 is more abstract. She speaks for herself on the basis of her own authority in three major pericopes in which she appears (Prov 1:20-33; 8:1-36; 9:1-6, 10-12). She was the first thing created by God and was with God during the entire act of creation, thereby possessing divine status. She calls out to men,[34] since through her they are able to "understand the fear of the Lord and find the knowledge of God" (2:5). She will save them from Dame Folly ("the foolish woman"), who is identified as the "strange woman," "the alien woman[35] with her smooth words," in Prov 2:16 and 7:5. In Sirach 24 Wisdom is a divine being who seeks a dwelling place on earth among humans. In this passage she also is identified with the Torah.

This is obviously a very complex literature with a variety of themes within

---

32. Murphy, *Tree of Life*, 104-6.

33. Sidnie White Crawford, "Lady Wisdom and Dame Folly at Qumran," *DSD* 5 (1998): 355-66. An ongoing debate with regard to the biblical texts on Lady Wisdom concerns whether the personification relates to an actual person (divine or hypostasis) or is a literary device. For a summary on this point see Judith Hadley, "Wisdom and the Goddess," in *Wisdom in Ancient Israel: Essays in Honour of J. A. Emerton* (ed. John Day, Robert P. Gordon, and H. G. M. Williamson; Cambridge: Cambridge University Press, 1995), 234-43.

34. As noted by Crawford, the addressees here appear to be exclusively male ("Lady Wisdom," 356 n. 1).

35. "Alien woman" here is a better rendering of נכריה than NRSV "adulteress."

each composition in addition to those elements that are common to more than one of them. The skepticism concerning the possibilities of wisdom itself that is also present and receives greatest expression in Qohelet could also be described.[36] This overview has concentrated on those features most central to the interpretation of the wisdom texts from Qumran.

The Texts from Qumran

The most recent attempt to identify the wisdom texts from the Qumran corpus is in the classification of texts from the Judean Desert according to content and literary genre in volume 39 of the DJD series.[37] While pointing to the difficulties inherent in the definition of the genre of wisdom literature, Armin Lange includes in the listing compositions that attest to a sapiential genre, sapiential vocabulary, and sapiential thinking. The general nature of this commentary does not permit an examination of the variety of genres or literary forms represented within these texts.[38] The Qumran texts included in the DJD listing (DJD 39:140) appear on page 10, classified according to their sapiential subgenres.

The most notable absence from this list is 4Q420-421 *(Ways of Righteousness)*. In my introduction to that text I discuss the manuscript issues related to the publication of 4Q264a *(Halakha B)* that affect its classification. This led both Armin Lange and Charlotte Hempel no longer to consider 4Q420-421 as a wisdom text.[39] But the removal of the composition from the listing of wisdom literature seems premature. John Strugnell had proposed that we have either three copies of the same composition that comprises both legal and wisdom elements, or that 4Q421 combines fragments from two distinct compositions.[40]

---

36. Martin A. Shields, *The End of Wisdom: A Reappraisal of the Historical and Canonical Function of Ecclesiastes* (Winona Lake, Ind.: Eisenbrauns, 2006).

37. Armin Lange with Ulrike Mittmann-Richert, "Annotated List of the Texts from the Judaean Desert Classified by Content and Genre," in DJD 39:115-64.

38. The bibliography for introductory surveys of the biblical material can be found in nn. 24-26 above.

39. Lange, "Die Weisheitstexte aus Qumran: Eine Einleitung," in *Wisdom Texts from Qumran and the Development of Sapiential Thought* (ed. C. Hempel, A. Lange, and H. Lichtenberger; BETL 159; Leuven: Leuven University Press/Peeters, 2002), 7; Hempel, "The Qumran Sapiential Texts and the Rule Books," in *Wisdom Texts from Qumran,* ed. Hempel et al., 283. Within the publications, neither Lange nor Hempel indicates knowledge of Eibert Tigchelaar, "More on 4Q264A (4QHalakha A or 4QWays of Righteousness^c?)," *RevQ* 19 (2000): 453-56.

40. John Strugnell, "The Smaller Hebrew Wisdom Texts Found at Qumran: Variations, Resemblances, and Lines of Development," in *Wisdom Texts from Qumran,* ed. Hempel et al., 44-45.

Sapiential Instructions

Instruction (1Q26; 4Q415-418; 4Q418a; 4Q418c; 4Q423)

Book of Mysteries (1Q27; 4Q299-300; 4Q301?)

Ben Sira (2Q18; Masıh)

4QSapiential-Didactic Work A (4Q412)

4QSapiential-Hymnic Work A (4Q426)*

4QBeatitudes (4Q525)

Collection of Proverbs

4QInstruction-Like Composition B (4Q424)

Didactic Speeches

Treatise on the Two Spirits: 1QS iii:13–iv:26 par. 4QpapS^c (4Q257) v–vi‡

4QSapiential Work (4Q185)

4QCryptA Words of the Maskil to All Sons of Dawn (4Q298)

Sapiential Poetic Text

4QSapiential Hymn (4Q411)*

Sapiential Texts Too Fragmentary for Further Classification

4QWiles of the Wicked Woman (4Q184)

4QpapAdmonitory Parable (4Q302)†

4QMeditation on Creation A (4Q303)†

4QMeditation on Creation C (4Q305)†

4QComposition Concerning Divine Providence (4Q413)†

4QSapiential-Didactic Work B (4Q425)†

4QThe Two Ways (4Q473)†

---

* These hymnic or poetic compositions are not included in the texts discussed in this commentary.

† The limited fragments of these compositions did not warrant treatment in this commentary and can be found in DJD volumes.

‡ Since this passage is part of the texts of the *Community Rule,* it does not receive treatment in this commentary.

He favored the latter. In his argument advocating the renaming of 4Q264a as *Ways of Righteousness*[c], Eibert Tigchelaar prefers the former.[41] In either case, the classification of 4Q420 and the majority of 4Q421 as wisdom literature remains a reasonable possibility.[42] The extensive presence of wisdom vocabulary suggests greater similarity with *Instruction* than with the *Community Rule*.

Also missing from this list is 4Q419 *(Instruction-Like Composition A)*. While initially considered a wisdom composition entitled *Sapiential Work B*, the evidence for this identification has not been convincing. In this extremely fragmentary composition the identification was largely based on the use of the phrase in 8ii:7, "if he will close his hand then the spirit of all flesh will be gathered in," with wording identical to 4Q416 2ii:2//4Q417 2ii:4//4Q418 8.[43] Subsequent examination has demonstrated that the context for its usage is very different in the two compositions, with it being related to the issue of creditors in *Instruction* while in 4Q419 it appears in a column discussing the visitation of God in judgment. The employment of the phrase in *Instruction* appears to be based on Deut 15:7, which concerns the response to those in need. This connection is not evident in 4Q419. The fragmentary evidence provides only hints of parenetic material, inadequate for literary classification.

The difficulties encountered in the classification of many of these texts also are due to the somewhat arbitrary criteria we as modern scholars have to develop in order to engage in substantive study that will increase our understanding of this literature from antiquity. This problem is already identified in the discussion of the related material from the Cave 1 texts above. In this case we have texts that have a great deal of interest in knowledge and truth, but do not contain the term "wisdom" in an extensive manner, nor does the literary structure resemble other known wisdom literature. Another example of the difficulty can be seen in the text of *Aramaic Levi*, which includes an extensive section extolling wisdom in the testament that has Levi anointed as a priest forever and contains instruction about presiding over the temple.[44] The importance of and rewards for advancing wisdom, for being a sage, are developed in a very ample manner in the text, similar to those known to us in texts such as Ben Sira.

---

41. Tigchelaar, "More on *4Q264A*," 456.

42. Note the documented presence of wisdom vocabulary in these texts charted by Strugnell, "Smaller Hebrew Wisdom Texts," 56-60.

43. I remind readers that until its appearance in DJD 34 (1999) *Instruction* was called *Sapiential Work A*.

44. 4Q213 1-4 (DJD 22:5-22). For another reconstruction also including the Genizah copy of *Aramaic Levi* see Robert A. Kugler, *From Patriarch to Priest: The Levi-Priestly Tradition from Aramaic Levi to Testament of Levi* (SBLEJL 9; Atlanta: Scholars Press, 1996), 118-30.

The order of the treatment of the compositions in this commentary begins with *Instruction* because it is the most comprehensive and presumably influential nonbiblical wisdom text within the circles that utilized these writings,
based on the number of copies that were identified among the fragments. Some
of the topics covered in this introduction also concentrate on this text since
there is considerably more of it available for an initial analysis of significant
questions concerning wisdom in the Qumran texts than is available for the
other exemplars of this literature. This is followed by *Mysteries,* the writing that
most resembles *Instruction* to the point that some scholars have considered
them manuscripts of the same composition. The remainder of the texts then
follow in the order of the manuscript numbers that were assigned to them. The
list concludes with the fragments of Ben Sira from the Dead Sea collection.

Wisdom and Apocalyptic

Literary Form and Genre

While Gerhard von Rad posited that apocalyptic conceptions of time and history had their origins in wisdom circles, these two bodies of literature have
been viewed and studied as two distinct and even opposing entities.[45] Even
those who accepted his thesis tended to view it as a question of origins rather
than a case of interrelated literary activity carried out within communities
struggling with issues of meaning, identity, and community cohesion within a
larger Hellenistic ethos. In light of the additional texts from the Dead Sea
Scrolls and changes within the disciplines related to their exploration, perceptions of the nature of both of these bodies of literature and of their respective
development have changed. Enhanced attempts at the classification of these
genres of literature in light of the new evidence were the first step. Apocalyptic
literature received more attention in the earlier phases.[46] Scholars have been
quite willing to speak of a genre of apocalyptic literature as they have attempted
to define it. There have been significant advances in the study of biblical wisdom literature during this time period. Summary works by major scholars in

45. Gerhard von Rad, *Old Testament Theology* (trans. D. M. G. Stalker; 2 vols.; New York:
Harper & Row, 1962-65), 2:301-8; idem, *Wisdom in Israel* (trans. J. D. Martin; Nashville:
Abingdon, 1972), 263-83.
46. The best-known attempt at classification was the definition of "apocalyptic" ad-
vanced in the volume edited by John Collins, *Apocalypse: The Morphology of a Genre* (*Semeia* 14;
Missoula, Mont.: Scholars Press, 1979).

the field have already been listed.[47] It has been less clear that wisdom literature even within the biblical literature can be defined as a genre. In the outline of the Qumran literature cited above we find listed a variety of literary forms. A good deal of the wisdom literature from Qumran became available even to specialists in the field only after 1991. As a body of literature it has received limited attention, and comprehensive analyses have just begun to emerge. While significant, attempts at more precise classification and description have resulted in further questions, without in most cases definitive results.

This very good work at classification and analysis has also resulted in efforts to challenge the assumed autonomy of the two bodies of literature. While we speak of the impact of the study of the Dead Sea Scrolls on the study of apocalyptic literature and apocalypticism, there are no apocalypses, as that genre has come to be defined, among the Qumran manuscripts.[48] The reader of this commentary will quickly find perceptions normally associated with eschatology in the HB and vocabulary familiar from apocalyptic literature distributed broadly throughout this wisdom literature. The very documents that initially advanced our analysis have led us to questions concerning the categories employed in their study.

A recent attempt to examine these issues is summarized in the volume *Conflicted Boundaries in Wisdom and Apocalypticism*, a collection of essays from the SBL working group on Wisdom and Apocalypticism.[49] In an introductory essay for that project, begun in 1994, George Nickelsburg states the problem: "The thesis of this paper is that the entities usually defined as sapiential and apocalyptic often cannot be cleanly separated from one another because both are the products of wisdom circles that are becoming increasingly diverse in the Greco-Roman period."[50] The availability of the wisdom texts from the Qumran corpus vividly demonstrates the accuracy of this observation since many of these compositions are characterized by the integration of eschatological and apocalyptic perspectives and vocabulary into literature clearly

---

47. See nn. 24-26 above.

48. See now the argument for the *Genesis Apocryphon* as an apocalypse in the dissertation of Daniel Machiela, "The Genesis Apocryphon (1Q20): A Reevaluation of Its Text, Interpretive Character, and Relationship to the Book of Jubilees" (University of Notre Dame, 2007).

49. Benjamin G. Wright III and Lawrence M. Wills, eds., *Conflicted Boundaries in Wisdom and Apocalypticism* (SBLSymS 35; Atlanta: SBL, 2005). Note also the extensive collection of essays that emerged from the 51st Colloquium Biblicum Lovaniense: F. García Martínez, ed., *Wisdom and Apocalypticism in the Dead Sea Scrolls and in the Biblical Tradition* (BETL 168; Leuven: Leuven University Press/Peeters, 2003).

50. George W. E. Nickelsburg, "Wisdom and Apocalypticism in Early Judaism: Some Points for Discussion," in *Conflicted Boundaries*, ed. Wright and Wills, 20.

identified with the wisdom tradition. Instructive is the conclusion of John Collins that wisdom is not to be identified with a single worldview nor does it constitute one set literary form. He suggests that it is "most satisfactorily defined as instructional material."[51] While this may be too broad to be significantly helpful in determining classification, it is a meaningful description of its essence. It is important to be able to identify this new wisdom literature in the manner suggested earlier, as having continuity with the body of biblical books so recognized, whose common essence admittedly was difficult to delineate. I would amend his definition to suggest that it is instructional material that can be identified with the biblical tradition of wisdom, while not limited by it in form or content. It is with that vague delineation of wisdom literature that we begin to understand the relationship of wisdom and apocalypticism in Second Temple Judaism.[52]

A number of the major themes in biblical wisdom literature identified earlier in this introduction are also characteristic of apocalyptic literature. Interest in the nature of creation is significant in apocalyptic literature. In his extensive comparison Randal Argall concluded that the conceptual frameworks for the treatment of creation in *1 Enoch* and Ben Sira are remarkably similar.[53] In both cases they teach the importance of obedience. In both cases the created order is enlisted in support of their own beliefs and practices. In both cases creation is structured in such a manner that judgment will fall on those who deviate from these practices grounded in the structure of creation. The related issue of order finds a similar coherence. The calendrical issues as developed in the Astronomical Book of *1 Enoch* demonstrate the interest in order. Within the structure of *1 Enoch* the Astronomical Book and the apocalypses provide an ideological framework for the strong polarity between the fools and the wise, the rich and the righteous, in the concluding Epistle. The polarity that characterized human existence is part of the order of the universe. We also note, with the exception of Ben Sira, the relative absence of history, Torah, and covenant in the biblical wisdom books. In addition, we observe that an appeal to the Torah does not characterize *1 Enoch*. While the portions of Genesis related to cre-

---

51. John J. Collins, "Wisdom Reconsidered, in Light of the Scrolls," *DSD* 4 (1997): 281.

52. Note the further attempt to describe this literature by John J. Collins, "The Eschatologizing of Wisdom in the Dead Sea Scrolls," in *Sapiential Perspectives: Wisdom Literature in Light of the Dead Sea Scrolls. Proceedings of the Sixth International Symposium of the Orion Center, 20-22 May, 2001* (ed. Collins, Gregory E. Sterling, and Ruth A. Clements; STDJ 51; Leiden: Brill, 2004), 49-65.

53. Randal A. Argall, *1 Enoch and Sirach: A Comparative Literary and Conceptual Analysis of the Themes of Revelation, Creation and Judgment* (SBLEJL 8; Atlanta: Scholars Press, 1995), 99-164.

ation and the watchers are very important in *1 Enoch,* the foolish and the rich are not judged for disobedience to the law. The watchers defy the order of creation, not the Mosaic law. Nickelsburg has pointed out the all-encompassing nature of wisdom in that composition: "Law and its interpretation are embodied in the notion of revealed 'wisdom.'"[54] The parenetic aspects in the Epistle of Enoch are developed through the description of the two ways, similar to wisdom literature. Walking on the right paths is just as important in *1 Enoch* as in Proverbs. So we find, just as in wisdom literature, an approach to the manner in which knowledge of the divine will is appropriated by human society and by which human beings determine the character of the "good" life that does not begin with the Torah. Notice that these remarks about the Torah apply only to certain representatives of wisdom literature. Ample evidence of the use and centrality of the Torah for other types of literature in the Qumran corpus is adequately attested, and the manner in which it intertwines with understandings of the meaning of wisdom in some other genres is apparent.[55] We find exceptions even within the wisdom literature from Qumran.

The most notable link of the Torah and wisdom is to be found in 4Q525 *(Beatitudes).* See the introduction to that text for a discussion of this aspect. In this text the stipulations for the good life do become explicitly linked to the Torah. This theme is developed in Jewish medieval literature. The text that has received some attention with regard to Qumran studies is the wisdom text from the Cairo Genizah.[56] It is not to be considered a composition directly related to other Qumran writings or the evidence concerning the Essenes in the Second Temple period.[57]

---

54. Nickelsburg, *1 Enoch 1: A Commentary on the Book of 1 Enoch, Chapters 1–36; 81–108* (Hermeneia; Minneapolis: Fortress, 2001), 50. Note also idem, "Enochic Wisdom: An Alternative to the Mosaic Torah?" in *Hesed Ve-Emet: Studies in Honor of Ernest S. Frerichs* (ed. Jodi Magness and Seymour Gitin; BJS 320; Atlanta: Scholars Press, 1998), 123-32.

55. Georg Sauer, "Weisheit und Tora in qumranischer Zeit," in *Weisheit ausserhalb der kanonischen Weisheitsschriften* (ed. Bernd Janowski; Gütersloh: Gütersloher Verlagshaus, 1996), 107-27.

56. Klaus Berger, *Die Weisheitsschrift aus der Kairoer Geniza: Erstedition, Kommentar und Übersetzung* (2d ed.; TANZ; Tübingen: Francke, 1996); G. Wilhelm Nebe, *Text und Sprache der hebräischen Weisheitsschrift aus der Kairoer Geniza* (HOS 25; Frankfurt am Main: Peter Lang, 1993).

57. G. Wilhelm Nebe, "Die wiederentdeckte Weisheitsschrift aus der Kairoer Geniza und ihre 'Nähe' zum Schrifttum von Qumran und zu Essenern," in *New Qumran Texts and Studies: Proceedings of the First Meeting of the International Organization for Qumran Studies, Paris 1992* (ed. George J. Brooke; STDJ 15; Leiden: Brill, 1994), 241-54.

Social Contexts

The interrelationship of wisdom and apocalypticism is an issue that appears within the context of our study of Second Temple Judaism, most notably in our analysis of literature composed between the beginning of the Hellenistic era in 330 B.C.E. and the end of the Bar Kokhba revolt in 135 C.E. The aforementioned volume on this issue, *Conflicted Boundaries*, includes an examination of the social context of these texts and the social location of the persons who produced them. Analysts of both bodies of literature very quickly determined that all of these compositions originated among educated members of a scribal class.[58] In his examination of selected wisdom and apocalyptic writings from the second century B.C.E., Richard Horsley had determined: "There must have been four different scribal circles in Jerusalem, therefore, in the early second century."[59] He identifies them with four bodies of literature: *1 Enoch*, Daniel, Ben Sira, and proto-Qumran. (The last group is presumed but not developed in his essay.) A brief analysis of these groups helps establish a social context for some of the wisdom texts of this commentary.

John Collins describes the *maskilim* ("sages" or "wise") as that group central to the book of Daniel who constitute the circle from which the final form of the Hebrew and Aramaic text emanated.[60] The sages or "wise" are the only ones who "understand" the nature and inevitable outcome of human history, hence are the exclusive holders of the knowledge of salvation.[61] They are the heroes of the time of persecution who are not destroyed but resurrected at the end of time. Philip Davies has identified the central features of this scribal group, arguing that the values reflected in the text are those of an educated elite, a scribal community.[62]

---

58. This was recognized already by Jonathan Z. Smith, "Wisdom and Apocalyptic," in *Religious Syncretism in Antiquity: Essays in Conversation with Geo Widengren* (ed. B. A. Pearson; Series on Formative Contemporary Thinkers 1; Missoula, Mont.: Scholars Press, 1975), 131-56; repr. in *Map Is Not Territory: Studies in the History of Religion* (SJLA 23; Leiden: Brill, 1978), 67-87. See also Nickelsburg, "Wisdom and Apocalypticism," 34-35. On the class basis of sectarianism in general, see Seth Schwartz, *Imperialism and Jewish Society, 200 B.C.E. to 640 C.E.* (Princeton: Princeton University Press, 2001), 91-99.

59. Richard A. Horsley, "The Politics of Cultural Production in Second Temple Judea: Historical Context and Political-Religious Relations of the Scribes Who Produced *1 Enoch*, Sirach, and Daniel," in *Conflicted Boundaries*, ed. Wright and Wills, 145. This approach also is evident in his monograph, *Scribes, Visionaries, and the Politics of Second Temple Judea* (Louisville: Westminster John Knox, 2007).

60. John J. Collins, *Daniel* (Hermeneia; Minneapolis: Fortress, 1993), 66-67.

61. Dan 11:33, 35; 12:3, 10. Note also the introduction of Daniel and his friends in 1:4 already as "wise in all knowledge."

62. Philip R. Davies, "The Scribal School of Daniel," in *The Book of Daniel: Composition*

Daniel is trained in the wisdom of the Chaldeans and functions in the royal court. Some assume that religious insight is an intellectual matter. While mantic (i.e., related to divination) wisdom predominates, this is assumed to be knowledge. These sages are concerned with correct behavior, based on enlightenment about the manner in which the world works. Stefan Beyerle points to their high social position, designating them as members of a Jewish "upper class," a highly educated intellectual elite.[63] He directs attention to Dan 1:4 and 17, which use terms such as "understanding," "wisdom," and "knowledge."

In *1 Enoch* we find a very negative portrayal of the wealthy and powerful.[64] This attitude is most explicit in the Epistle of Enoch, where the rich are the focus of many of the woes:

> Woe to those who build their houses with sin;
> . . . by the sword they will fall.
> And those who acquire gold and silver in judgment will quickly perish.
> Woe to you, rich, for in your riches you have trusted;
> and from your riches you will depart,
> because you have not remembered the Most High in the days of your riches.
> You have committed blasphemy and iniquity;
> and you have been prepared for the day of bloodshed
> and the day of darkness and the day of great judgment.[65]

As noted by Nickelsburg, the wealthy are never spoken of in a positive manner in the Epistle of Enoch.[66]

This appears to be the experience of the circle of authors represented throughout *1 Enoch,* most clearly in the Book of the Watchers and the Book of the Luminaries.[67] The most visible evidence that this world is characterized by profound evil and radical injustice is its total dominance by the rich and power-

---

and Reception (ed. John J. Collins and Peter W. Flint; 2 vols.; VTSup 83; Leiden: Brill, 2001), 1:247-65.

63. Stefan Beyerle, "The Book of Daniel and Its Social Setting," in *Book of Daniel,* ed. Collins and Flint, 1:205-28.

64. Nickelsburg, "Revisiting the Rich and Poor in *1 Enoch* 92–105 and the Gospel According to Luke," *SBLSP* 37 (2 vols.; Atlanta: Scholars Press, 1998), 2:579-95.

65. *1 En.* 94:7-9; Nickelsburg, *1 Enoch 1,* 460. Cf. also 97:8-9; Nickelsburg, "Revisiting," 581-87.

66. Nickelsburg, "Revisiting," 587.

67. Ibid., 592. On the continuity of the intellectual tradition in *1 Enoch* see Patrick A. Tiller, *A Commentary on the Animal Apocalypse of I Enoch* (SBLEJL 4; Atlanta: Scholars Press, 1993), 117-19, 123-26.

ful. The contrast to the rich and powerful developed within the texts of *1 Enoch* is not with the poor but with the righteous:

> Do not say, you who are righteous and pious in life:
> "In the days of our tribulation we toiled laboriously;
> and every tribulation we saw, and many evils we found.
> We were consumed and became few, and our spirits, small;
> and we were destroyed and there was no one to help us with word
> and deed;
> we were powerless and found nothing.
> We were crushed and destroyed." (*1 En.* 103:9-10)[68]

The closest parallel to the "sages" in the Enochic works is in the Epistle, *1 En.* 98:9 and 99:10.[69] In this section the fools do not listen to the wise, hence they face judgment. They practice idolatry, they are "those who worship stones — and who carve images of silver and gold and wood and stone and clay and worship phantoms and demons and abominations and evil spirits and all errors, not according to knowledge; no help will you find from them" (99:7).[70] These same fools "alter the true words and pervert the holy covenant" (99:2). In this section those who listen to the words of the wise are the ones who "learn to do the commandments of the Most High and walk in the paths of his righteousness" (99:10). As noted above, this does not mean an explicit emphasis on covenant and the Torah.[71] The term "wisdom" is used in significant contexts throughout all five sections of *1 Enoch,* including the introduction to the Book of Parables.[72] For example, the Epistle of Enoch is introduced as a revelation of the wisdom of Enoch to his children and "to the last generations who will observe truth and peace."[73] While wisdom is from God and one can know it only through revelation, it is knowledge of that revelation which distinguishes the "chosen" and the "righteous." Enoch is referred to as a scribe rather than a "sage," sometimes the "scribe of righteousness" or the "scribe of truth."[74]

---

68. Nickelsburg, *1 Enoch 1,* 512.

69. Ibid., 484, 493.

70. From here on, unless otherwise noted, all translations of *1 Enoch* are from George W. E. Nickelsburg and James C. VanderKam, *1 Enoch: A New Translation, Based on the Hermeneia Commentary* (Minneapolis: Fortress, 2004).

71. Cited above is Nickelsburg, *1 Enoch 1,* 50; see also idem, "Enochic Wisdom," 123-32.

72. *1 En.* 5:8; 32:6 (Book of the Watchers); 37:1-2 (Book of Parables); 82:1-3 (redactional bridge to the Epistle); 92:1; 98:9; 99:10; 104:12 (the Epistle); 93:10 (including the Apocalypse of Weeks and perhaps 89:28 and 90:6 in the Animal Apocalypse that identify the opening of the eyes); see Nickelsburg, *1 Enoch 1,* 50-52.

73. *1 En.* 92:1; Nickelsburg, *1 Enoch 1,* 430-31.

74. *1 En.* 12:4; 15:1. See Nickelsburg, *1 Enoch 1,* 65-67.

The scribal identification in Ben Sira is clear, beginning with the description in Sir 39:1: "He seeks out the wisdom of all the ancients and is concerned with prophecies." The sage or scribe requires leisure time in order to become wise.[75] The term γραμματεύς ("scribe") appears only twice in the text, in 10:5 and in the very significant identification of 38:24, "the wisdom of the scribe depends upon the opportunity of leisure; only the one who has little business can become wise." The synonyms for "wisdom," "knowledge," and "understanding" are ubiquitous throughout the Greek text, as well as their adjectival usages, so the designation as "scribe/sage" seems appropriate.[76] We also see that in the exaltation of Simeon, the high priest, the author has a political perspective to advance among the competing allegiances present in Jerusalem at the beginning of the second century B.C.E..[77] Benjamin Wright III attempted to address the issue of the social location of the author of Ben Sira by comparing it with *1 Enoch*.[78] The circles in which these two texts originated had contrasting views of the temple, priests and priesthood, the origin and basis of wisdom, and the value of dreams and visions. Yet there is evidence of some similarity in the social location of the authors of these texts. In both cases the primary identification is as scribe/sage. Both texts reflect communities that "care about the priesthood primarily because all apparently were priests or were closely connected with them."[79] Throughout *1 Enoch* we find a criticism of the existent temple and priesthood from a member of the scribal

75. Sir 38:24; Daniel J. Harrington, "The Wisdom of the Scribe According to Ben Sira," in *Ideal Figures in Ancient Judaism* (ed. George W. E. Nickelsburg and John J. Collins; SBLSCS 12; Chico, Calif.: Scholars Press, 1980), 181-88.

76. Benjamin G. Wright III, "The Discourse of Riches and Poverty in the Book of Ben Sira," *SBLSP* 37 (2 vols.; Atlanta: Scholars Press, 1998), 2:570 n. 24; Benjamin G. Wright III and Claudia V. Camp, "'Who Has Been Tested by Gold and Found Perfect?' Ben Sira's Discourse of Riches and Poverty," *Henoch* 23 (2001): 162-63 n. 21. Richard Horsley and Patrick Tiller are credited with the proposal.

77. James K. Aitken, "Biblical Interpretation as Political Manifesto: Ben Sira in His Seleucid Setting," *JJS* 51 (2000): 191-208.

78. Benjamin G. Wright III, "Putting the Puzzle Together: Some Suggestions Concerning the Social Location of the Wisdom of Ben Sira," in *Conflicted Boundaries*, ed. Wright and Wills, 133-49; idem, "'Fear the Lord and Honor the Priest': Ben Sira as Defender of the Jerusalem Priesthood," in *The Book of Ben Sira in Modern Research: Proceedings of the First International Ben Sira Conference, 28-31 July 1996, Soesterberg, Netherlands* (ed. Pancratius C. Beentjes; BZAW 255; Berlin: de Gruyter, 1997), 189-223. See now also Richard A. Horsley, "Social Relations and Social Conflict in the *Epistle of Enoch*," in *For a Later Generation: The Transformation of Tradition in Israel, Early Judaism, and Early Christianity* (ed. Randal A. Argall, Beverly A. Bow, and Rodney A. Werline; Harrisburg: Trinity Press International, 2000), 100-115.

79. Wright, "Fear the Lord," 218. Note also the wisdom ascribed to Levi in Kugler, *From Patriarch to Priest*, 118-38.

class, presumably related in some manner to the priesthood.[80] The exalted roles of Aaron in Sir 45:6-22 and of Simon, the high priest, in 50:1-21 are well-known features of that composition. Strong opinions on the temple and priesthood from authors self-described as scribes characterize the social setting for both compositions.

In his comparison of *1 Enoch* and Ben Sira, Argall concludes that "when one takes account of the unique authorial viewpoints and the disparate concepts of judgment present in each book, the hypothesis becomes feasible that the authors are referring to the same wealthy class at about the same time in history."[81] Using a very different form of literary expression, the authors of these three diverse literary compositions address the disparity of wealth and power in the Jewish community of the second century B.C.E. and propose different responses. These responses are developed in the context of Jewish life in the Greek and Roman empires.

The extensive, disparate, and fragmentary nature of the Qumran literature does not permit a simplistic or univocal description of the authors of these documents or their social setting.[82] After a clear identification between the first seven major scrolls and the site of Qumran had been established, most academic work proceeded on the assumption that these were sectarian compositions related to the *yaḥad* ("community" or "communal organization"). Subsequent research impelled especially by the additional publications after 1991 demonstrated the inadequacies of such an approach to this corpus.[83] Two primary approaches emerged to work at this issue, one historical and the other sociological. On the historical side, Florentino García Martínez and Adam S. van der Woude proposed a pre-Qumranic phase of intellectual development reflected in some of the literature, followed by a sectarian phase also present in the archeo-

---

80. George W. E. Nickelsburg, "Social Aspects of Palestinian Jewish Apocalypticism," in *Apocalypticism in the Mediterranean World and the Near East: Proceedings of the International Colloquium on Apocalypticism, Uppsala, August 12-17, 1979* (ed. David Hellholm; Tübingen: Mohr [Siebeck], 1983), 641-54; idem, "The Epistle of Enoch and Qumran Literature," *JJS* 33 (1982): 333-48; idem, "Revisiting," 579-605; idem, *1 Enoch 1*, 62-67.

81. Argall, *1 Enoch and Sirach*, 254.

82. For a comprehensive summary of this literature see VanderKam and Flint, *Meaning of the Dead Sea Scrolls*, 209-38.

83. Problems were identified with this approach long before 1991. Note, for example, the work of Michael Stone on the fragments of *Enoch*: "Lists of Revelated Things in the Apocalyptic Literature," in *Magnalia Dei, the Mighty Acts of God: Essays on the Bible and Archaeology in Memory of G. Ernest Wright* (ed. Frank Moore Cross, Werner E. Lemke, and Patrick D. Miller; Garden City, N.Y.: Doubleday, 1976), 414-51; idem, "The Book of Enoch and Judaism in the Third Century B.C.E.," *CBQ* 40 (1978): 479-92; idem, "Enoch, Aramaic Levi and Sectarian Origins," *JSJ* 19 (1988): 159-70.

logical evidence at the Qumran site.[84] García Martínez has continued to develop this approach, dubbed the "Groningen hypothesis." He distinguishes features for the classification of nonbiblical texts that divides them into four groups: (a) sectarian works, representing the thought or halakah of Qumran in its most developed and typical form; (b) works of the formative period, presenting a vision still not so clearly differentiated from the Essenism that is its ultimate source, but containing indications of future development and an already characteristic halakah; (c) works that reflect Essene thought and accord with what classical sources teach us; and (d) works belonging to the apocalyptic tradition that gave rise to Essenism and was considered part of the common heritage.[85] There are and continue to be other hypotheses developed to account for the more complex literary record, as well as new interpretations of the archeological evidence.[86] The historical questions related to the study of this literature at present only become more complex. What the Groningen hypothesis points to is the clear evidence that some literature within the corpus is nonsectarian, sometimes dubbed pre-Qumranic, but was considered important and was valued by the sectarians. Devorah Dimant in particular points to "the uniform nature of the entire collection. All the caves contain the same types of works in more or less the same proportions."[87] We approach the wisdom literature with the recognition that there is a coherence in the collection but that cohesiveness does not center in a sectarian identity. The literature rather represents certain ideological streams that we are only beginning to identify. This approach is apparent in Lange's introduction to

84. F. García Martínez, "Qumran Origins and Early History: A Groningen Hypothesis," *Folia Orientalia* 25 (1988): 113-36; F. García Martínez and A. S. van der Woude, "A 'Groningen' Hypothesis of Qumran Origins and Early History," *RevQ* 14 (1989-90): 521-41.

85. Note also Florentino García Martínez, "The Origins of the Qumran Movement and of the Essene Sect," in *The People of the Dead Sea Scrolls: Their Writings, Beliefs and Practices* (ed. García Martínez and Julio Trebolle Barrera; trans. Wilfred G. E. Watson; Leiden: Brill, 1995), 77-96.

86. One of the best known of the former is Gabrielle Boccaccini, *Beyond the Essene Hypothesis: The Parting of the Ways Between Qumran and Enochic Judaism* (Grand Rapids: Eerdmans, 1998). For the latter see Jodi Magness, *The Archaeology of Qumran and the Dead Sea Scrolls* (Grand Rapids: Eerdmans, 2002). For a collection of various perspectives on the archeological issues see Katharina Galor, Jean-Baptiste Humbert, and Jürgen Zangenberg, eds., *Qumran: The Site of the Dead Sea Scrolls: Archaeological Interpretations and Debates* (STDJ 57; Leiden: Brill, 2006). Note the most recent appraisals of the evidence: Alison Schofield, *From Qumran to the Yaḥad: A New Paradigm of Textual Development for* The Community Rule (STDJ 77: Leiden: Brill, 2009); John J. Collins, *Beyond the Qumran Community: The Sectarian Movement of the Dead Sea Scrolls* (Grand Rapids: Eerdmans, 2010).

87. Devorah Dimant, "The Qumran Manuscripts: Contents and Significance," in *Time to Prepare the Way in the Wilderness* (ed. Devorah Dimant and Lawrence H. Schiffman; STDJ 16; Leiden: Brill, 1995), 35. Note also VanderKam and Flint, *Meaning of the Dead Sea Scrolls,* 209-38.

these texts.[88] We then see attempts to place individual compositions into some schema of intellectual and historical development.

Qumran scholars also looked to the discipline of sociology to determine the social context for these texts. An important issue is how to determine whether a literary work reflects a sectarian orientation. Carol Newsom developed a case study on this question during her work on the *Songs of the Sabbath Sacrifice*.[89] She proposed three possibilities for what might be meant by referring to a text as sectarian: (1) it had been written by a member of the Qumran community; (2) the manner in which it was read; and (3) a way of describing content or rhetorical stance.[90] She noted that the first area is much more complicated than it might appear on the surface. Given the present level of ambiguity and dispute regarding the relationship of site and text noted above, this is an important observation.[91] Using the third category, she proposed: "A sectarian text would be one that calls upon its readers to understand themselves as set apart within the larger religious community of Israel and as preserving the true values of Israel against the failures of the larger community."[92] I will not review the extensive literature available on this subject, but note that work on this issue has been evaluated more recently by Jutta Jokiranta.[93] In the summary of her analysis of previous attempts she identified three areas that are the best candidates for helping us identify sectarian texts: (a) tension with the sociocultural environment; (b) the tendency to view oneself as uniquely legitimate; and (c) the tendency to set up boundaries against others.[94] The wisdom literature at Qumran provides significant material for the discussion of both the historical and sociological questions outlined here. The discussion of these questions is an integral part of identifying the social context of any of the wisdom texts from Qumran.

88. Lange, "Weisheitstexte," 3-30.

89. Carol A. Newsom, "'Sectually Explicit' Literature from Qumran," in *The Hebrew Bible and Its Interpreters* (ed. W. H. Propp, B. Halpern, and D. N. Freedman; Winona Lake, Ind.: Eisenbrauns, 1990), 167-87.

90. Another case study utilizing slightly different criteria was published by Esther G. Chazon, "Is *Divrei Ha-Me'orot* a Sectarian Prayer?" in *The Dead Sea Scrolls: Forty Years of Research* (ed. Devorah Dimant and Uriel Rappaport; STDJ 10; Leiden: Brill, 1992), 3-17.

91. See n. 86 above.

92. Newsom, "'Sectually Explicit' Literature," 178-79.

93. Jutta M. Jokiranta, "'Sectarianism' of the Qumran 'Sect,' Sociological Notes," *RevQ* 20 (2001): 223-39; idem, "Learning from Sectarian Responses: Windows on Qumran Sects and Emerging Christian Sects," in *Echoes from the Caves: Qumran and the New Testament* (ed. Florentino García Martínez; STDJ 85; Leiden: Brill, 2009), 177-209.

94. Two more recent studies should also be consulted: Eyal Regev, *Sectarianism in Qumran: A Cross-Cultural Perspective* (Berlin: de Gruyter, 2007); David J. Chalcraft, ed., *Sectarianism in Early Judaism: Sociological Advances* (London: Equinox, 2007).

From the perspective of such an analysis I find that most of the wisdom compositions are not sectarian. Evidence for such an argument can be found in the introduction to each of the works discussed in the commentary. The only exceptions in this collection are 4Q298 (*4QCryptA Words of the Maskil to All Sons of Dawn*), 4Q412 (*Sapiential-Didactic Work A*), and 4Q420-421 (*Ways of Righteousness*). Such a proposal also suggests that these compositions are presectarian, preceding the development of this sectarian social group.[95] This evidence points to a particular trajectory of wisdom literature in Second Temple Judaism that was used by the sectarian adherents and their authors along with other genres of literature available to them. The particular nature of this wisdom literature lent itself well to sectarian interpretation and development. In addition to the wisdom compositions, we find an extensive use of terms related to this tradition such as "wisdom," "knowledge," and "insight" in compositions of other genres within the sectarian corpus of literature. This also means that the particular conjunction of wisdom and apocalyptic elements characteristic of this literature does not represent a conflation that emerged out of a sectarian self-consciousness. That conjunction was already existent when the particular sectarian identity characteristic of some of the Qumran literature was developed.

Instruction and Issues of Social Location

The issue of social location has emerged as significant in the discussion of the wisdom texts from Qumran due to the literary and ideological shifts identified by and within the study of this literature. This has been particularly true in the study of the developments regarding the conjunction of wisdom and apocalyptic literature. Within the study of Qumran literature this research has found focus in the investigation of the fragments of *Instruction*, since it is the most substantial wisdom composition found in the corpus.[96] The study of social location has been identified by Benjamin Wright in his study of Ben Sira as "the attempt to identify the person, people, groups, or communities (if they were gathered into such coherent social bodies) responsible for a text or to find the place in the social landscape where a text most likely originated."[97] A noteworthy feature of *Instruction* has been identified as the apparent poverty of the circles connected with this composition and the

---

95. Michael A. Knibb, "The Book of Enoch in the Light of the Qumran Wisdom Literature," in *Wisdom and Apocalypticism*, ed. García Martínez, 199. Taking a different view is Menahem Kister, "Wisdom Literature at Qumran," in *The Qumran Scrolls and Their World* (ed. Menahem Kister, 2 vols.; Jerusalem: Yad Ben-Zvi, 2009), 1:299-320 (Hebrew).

96. See the introduction to *Instruction* in this volume for a discussion of the date of composition prior to the sectarian texts.

97. Wright, "Putting the Puzzle Together," 89.

implications of this observation for the determination of social location.[98] This emphasis is in stark contrast to the social location of the scribes in Daniel, *1 Enoch,* and Ben Sira already discussed above. In contrast to *1 Enoch,* the rich and powerful are not held up as the persons responsible for an unjust and immoral society. The only concern with regard to the rich is how one handles them, particularly with regard to debt. The circles of the addressee are regarded as the poor in *Instruction* in contrast to *1 Enoch,* where they are referred to as the righteous and the holy. The nature of the knowledge imparted to the addressee is then very different. In the Epistle of Enoch there is a more explicit and advanced dualism at the social level.[99]

In Ben Sira we seem to find a fairly open attitude to the subject of wealth.[100] Ben Sira is not poor but does support the poor. In his role as counselor and educator of the powerful, he takes a good deal of responsibility for training the elite with regard to their responsibilities for justice, for treatment of the poor. The author does not consider himself poor but he also is not among the wealthy. Indeed, he counsels people to be wary of the rich and their motives: "A rich person will exploit you if you can be of use to him, and if you are in need he will abandon you. . . . When he needs you he will deceive you, and will smile at you and encourage you; he will speak to you kindly and say, 'What do you need?'"[101] Caution in dealing with the rich and powerful is also apparent in texts such as 4:1-3: "My child, do not cheat the poor of their living and do not keep needy eyes waiting. Do not grieve the hungry or anger one in need. Do not add to the troubles of the desperate, or delay giving to the needy."[102] These injunctions, however, appear to be academic education for associates in professional roles rather than community organizing on behalf of the poor. This knowledge of the world combined with a sense of justice rooted in a schooled spirituality seems to characterize Ben Sira's response to poverty.

In contrast to Ben Sira, the apparent poverty of the addressee in *Instruc-*

---

98. E. J. C. Tigchelaar, "The Addressees of 4QInstruction," in *Sapiential, Liturgical and Poetical Texts from Qumran: Proceedings of the Third Meeting of the International Organization for Qumran Studies, Oslo 1998, Published in Memory of Maurice Baillet* (ed. Daniel K. Falk, F. García Martínez, and Eileen M. Schuller; STDJ 35; Leiden: Brill, 2000), 62-75; Catherine M. Murphy, *Wealth in the Dead Sea Scrolls and in the Qumran Community* (STDJ 40; Leiden: Brill, 2001), 163-209; Matthew J. Goff, *The Worldly and Heavenly Wisdom of 4Q Instruction* (STDJ 50; Leiden: Brill, 2003), 127-67; Benjamin G. Wright III, "The Categories of Rich and Poor in the Qumran Sapiential Literature," in *Sapiential Perspectives,* ed. Collins et al., 109-23; Benjamin G. Wold, *Women, Men and Angels: The Qumran Wisdom Document 'Musar leMevin' and Its Allusions to Genesis Creation Traditions* (WUNT 2/201; Tübingen: Mohr Siebeck, 2005), 24-30.

99. Goff, *Worldly and Heavenly Wisdom,* 229.

100. Wright, "Discourse of Riches and Poverty," 559-78.

101. Sir 13:4-7; Wright, "Discourse of Riches and Poverty," 573.

102. See also Sir 4:1-10; 13:15-24.

tion is assumed.[103] While Wold's argument that a multivalent understanding of the meaning of poverty in *Instruction* is necessary, there is clear evidence that the addressees are dealing with very real concerns about debt, a prominent issue for native peoples within the Hellenistic empires.[104] The multivalent nature of the poverty and need addressed in the composition reframes the issues in light of the heavenly and temporal realities in a manner familiar to us from apocalyptic literature. Indeed, to use a contemporary term to illustrate the point, it would appear that the *mevin* is being empowered within the state of his or her real or potential poverty. Note the contrast between Sir 13:4-7, in which the apprentice scribe is warned about potential exploitation and manipulation by the rich person, and 4Q416 2ii:6, where the servant is enjoined not to lose his personhood and his essential religious core: "And in your affairs do not downplay your own spirit. For any amount of money do not trade the spirit of your holiness." In this case the addressee in poverty is addressed as an ethically responsible person.[105] Such an insight provides another reason for understanding why this particular wisdom literature would have been of interest to sectarians who were departing from the support of conventional social structures.

The "Sage" in Qumran Wisdom Literature

The sage *(maskil)* is a recurring figure in a variety of Qumran texts, including the wisdom compositions. There is a limited consistency in usage across the varieties of texts available, so a survey is necessary to establish a context of understanding even for the wisdom texts. The role of the sage is most clearly defined in some of the sectarian texts. As noted by Newsom, the sage in the *Community Rule* is the crucial figure who provides the basic instruction about the nature of the community, its origins and theology, and then also is in charge of admitting prospective candidates for membership in the sect and ranking its hierarchy.[106] Perhaps the *Community Rule* was composed as a guide for the *maskil,* "who was charged with a crucial role in the admission, instruction, and advancement of the members of

103. While the article of Tigchelaar is instructive on a number of points, I do not find the argument for the conditional nature of the interest in poverty to be compelling ("Addressees of 4QInstruction," 69-71).

104. Wold, *Women, Men and Angels,* 235.

105. Murphy (*Wealth in Dead Sea Scrolls,* 208) notes the manner in which *Instruction* favors terms relating to lack and poverty from among the typical lexicon of economic terms normally employed in wisdom literature.

106. See Carol A. Newsom, "The Sage in the Literature of Qumran: The Functions of the *Maśkil,*" in *The Sage in Israel and the Ancient Near East* (ed. John G. Gammie and Leo G. Perdue; Winona Lake, Ind.: Eisenbrauns, 1990), 373-82.

the society."[107] In the introduction to the "Treatise on the Two Spirits" it is the sage "who shall instruct all the sons of light and shall teach them the nature of all the children of men according to the kind of spirit which they possess" (1QS iii:13-14). This "sage" as teacher again receives emphasis in 1QS ix:12–x:5. He is "concerned with the formation of the community, both through his admission and regulation of members and through his instruction in the knowledge that the community shares in common, yet that separates it from outsiders."[108] This knowledge is related to the Torah and, perhaps even more significantly, provides the rationale for the particular practices based on the community's interpretation of it: "he should conceal his own insight into the Law when among perverse men. He shall save reproof — itself founded on true knowledge and righteous judgment — for those who have chosen the Way, treating each as his spiritual qualities and the precepts of the era require. He shall ground them in knowledge" (1QS ix:17-18; *DSSANT* 139-40). Sections of the *Hodayot* associated with the *maskil* have similarities with the language and themes related to this figure in 1QS, and the speaker of 1QH^a vi:19-33 attributes to himself the same role of establishing the hierarchical order of the community as is ascribed to him in 1QS ix:14-16.[109] We may find within the compositional history of the *Community Rule* (*Serek*, S) materials evidence of an earlier usage of this figure that predates the sectarian understanding reflected in this latter section of 1QS.[110]

While it is clear that this term describes a significant position in the sectarian hierarchy attested in these citations, it does not appear yet to have that designation in *Instruction*. Hence it occurs as both noun and participle in that composition. This is also true of 4Q421 1ii:10, 12. The apprentice nature of the role of the "man of discernment" (discussed below in the introduction to *Instruction*) is highlighted in 4Q417 1i; in line 25 he is referred to as the "son of a sage." In 4Q416 2ii:13-15 and parallel passages the "man of discernment" is referred to as the "servant of a sage," as well as a "firstborn son." Evidence of the role of sage as teacher can be found in 4Q418 81+81a:17, even though in this case it is plural: "gain in understanding and from the hand of each of your *maskilim* grasp even more."[111] It is with regard to basic issues of theology and history that

---

107. Carol A. Newsom, *The Self as Symbolic Space: Constructing Identity and Community at Qumran* (STDJ 52; Leiden: Brill, 2004), 102.

108. Newsom, "Sage," 375.

109. Newsom, *Self*, 277-79, 299.

110. For an insightful development of the use of this term within the compositional history of the S documents see Charlotte Hempel, "*Maskil(im)* and *Rabbim*: From Daniel to Qumran," in *Biblical Traditions in Transmission: Essays in Honour of Michael A. Knibb* (ed. Hempel and Judith M. Lieu; JSJSup 111; Leiden: Brill, 2006), 133-56.

111. Perhaps also in 4Q418 238 1.

the sage instructs the "son of discernment" in *Instruction*. In other words the sages in *Instruction* are the teachers of the "men of discernment," the major addressees of that composition. This is the place designated for them in the extant fragments. The innovative nature of this portrayal is perhaps clearer when contrasted with Proverbs, where the son is addressed by the father as the guide for the wise life.[112] There does appear to be some continuity between this elemental role for the sage in *Instruction* and the central authoritative place of the sage in the *Community Rule*. Hints of that latter role can be found in the texts already mentioned above. We do already have in *Instruction* evidence that the relationship of teacher and student is a significant link in advancing the understanding of the "mystery of existence" (a phrase also discussed in the introduction to *Instruction*). The plural reference suggests that it is perhaps in the circle of these teacher-sages that the people of discernment are introduced to these mysteries. However, we note that within the limitations of the fragmentary evidence available to us, there is no role for the sage beyond that of teacher. Perhaps "teacher" would be an even better translation of the term in this composition than "sage."[113]

Other texts also mention the sage. The term is significant in 4Q298 (*Words of the Maskil [Sage] to the Sons of Dawn*) 1-2i:1, 4Q400-407 (*Songs of the Sabbath Sacrifice,* six times), and 4Q510-511 (*Songs of the Sage*). There are also scattered references in other texts. The limited fragments of 4Q298 do not permit the development of an understanding of the role of the "sage" that would be suggested by the potential of the title ("Words of the Sage to the Sons of Dawn"). The long list of epithets describing the addressees suggests sectarian adherents who are receiving instruction similar in nature to that of 1QS and 1QH[a] identified above. Within the preserved materials we note that these adherents are to "increase in the knowledge of the appointed times whose interpretations I will recount in order that you might gain understanding of the end of the ages and the former times you would consider in order to know . . ." (4Q298 3-4ii:8-10; see translation below). This is consistent with the type of instruction the *maskil* is responsible for in 1QS and 4Q510-511 as well as the kind of knowledge that undergirds it, as we find in *Instruction* and other wisdom texts from Qumran. Strugnell points out that the frequent use of the sage as author in Qumran texts, and the absence of the sage as author in biblical texts, help to establish the common sectarian provenance of these compositions.[114]

---

112. Benjamin G. Wright III, "From Generation to Generation: The Sage as Father in Early Jewish Literature," in *Biblical Traditions in Transmission,* ed. Hempel and Lieu, 309-32.

113. See also Strugnell, "Smaller Hebrew Wisdom Texts," 43 n. 16.

114. Ibid., 43.

This same figure is the subject of 4Q510-511 *(Songs of the Sage[a,b])*.[115] Here the sage writing in the first person is the one who "makes known the splendor of his beauty, in order to frighten and ter[rify] all the spirits of the angels of destruction."[116] Newsom notes the manner in which the sage refers to the divine gift of knowledge that he has received.[117] In this case, however, the "sage" has the further role to keep the "spirits of the angels of destruction" at bay.[118] For the sage this knowledge is the source of the authority and power necessary to gain victory within the dualistic struggle in which the "community" is engaged. This figure also constitutes the heading for each composition in the *Songs of the Sabbath Sacrifice* (4Q400-407). While not necessarily a sectarian composition, its influence is demonstrated by the literary dependence of 4Q510-511 on it.[119] Thus we can see the manner in which a title for an office with roots in the accepted biblical tradition is developed in the literary traditions of the wisdom texts into an accepted office attested within the sectarian literature of the Qumran corpus.

The New Testament

The greatest contribution that the fragments of Qumran have made to the study of the NT and Christian origins is to enhance our understanding of the developments within Jewish history during the latter portion of the Second Temple era. Here we examine specific connections between the texts of the NT and early Christianity with the Qumran fragments within the context of perspectives on Jewish history enhanced by the study of the latter. The relationship of wisdom and apocalyptic, the association of wisdom and the Torah, as well as the varied and changing understandings of wisdom within the development of sectarian movements in Second Temple Judaism are topics of considerable significance for an understanding of the treatment of wisdom within the materials of the NT and early Christianity. Noteworthy is the recent monograph of Grant Macaskill, who provides an integrative perspective on wisdom and apocalyptic in a study including both *Instruction* and Matthew.[120] He finds in both *1 Enoch*

---

115. M. Baillet, DJD 7:215-62; B. Nitzan, "Hymns from Qumran — 4Q510-4Q511," in *Dead Sea Scrolls: Forty Years,* ed. Dimant and Rappaport, 53-63.

116. 4Q510 1:4-5; trans. from Newsom, "Sage," 381, from which this discussion of 4Q510-511 is drawn. See also Tanzer, "Sages at Qumran," 165-67.

117. She cites 4Q511 18ii:7-9 as an example.

118. See also Nitzan, "Hymns from Qumran," 55.

119. Newsom, "'Sectually Explicit' Literature," 180-81; idem, "Sage," 381.

120. Grant Macaskill, *Revealed Wisdom and Inaugurated Eschatology in Ancient Judaism and Early Christianity* (JSJSup 115; Leiden: Brill, 2007).

and *Instruction* an "inaugurated eschatology" in which the revealing of wisdom to a select group set apart from the remainder of Israel is a key factor in explaining the relationship of these two literary traditions. He then identifies the same phenomenon in Matthew. The explanation of this relationship, basic for the study of *Instruction* as well as the wisdom elements throughout the Qumran evidence, has crucial implications for the study of many NT texts and the historical questions encountered in the exploration of Christian origins. Most significantly, the possibility that the acquisition of wisdom and knowledge could be confined to the adherents of a particular sect within Second Temple Judaism provides a context within which first-century adherents of groups centered in Jesus Christ could make similar claims. This clarifies a Palestinian Jewish environment as a potential context for the claims in some NT compositions regarding wisdom. Further research will be required to fill out this picture. A few aspects of these developments are treated here as examples.

The Gospel that is most explicit in proposing connections between Jesus and wisdom is Matthew. The most significant section of the work to refer to Jesus as wisdom is in Matthew 11. We see in v. 19: "the Son of Man came eating and drinking, and they say, 'Look, a glutton and a drunkard, a friend of tax collectors and sinners!' Yet wisdom is vindicated by her deeds." Wisdom here is clearly identified with Jesus, the man who performed these deeds. While the text is from Q, here the allusion is back to the beginning of the chapter in response to the question of the disciples of John the Baptist, "Are you the one who is to come, or are we to wait for another?" The author has Jesus reply with a list of items primarily from the book of Isaiah listing occurrences at that future time when God will intervene on behalf of the righteous and that this author has applied to Jesus. In contrast to Luke 7:35, "yet wisdom is justified by all her children," Matt 11:19 states, "yet wisdom is justified by her deeds." In this case the author wants to establish that it is the deeds that justify the identification of Jesus with wisdom and that provide the basis for the claim made by the author of this Gospel later in the chapter. The emphasis on deeds makes the connection to the messianic era and establishes Jesus as the authoritative representative of God ("son of God") who will preside over the period of God's reign. While the connection of Jesus with wisdom is clearly established, the author also provides a very particular definition for the connection, not simply an identification of Jesus with wisdom tradition(s). In this case Jesus is not portrayed as an exponent of or envoy for wisdom but is rather wisdom herself.[121] It is Jesus/wisdom who is then rejected in the following texts, where we find the woes upon Bethsaida and Chorazin.

---

121. Celia Deutsch, *Lady Wisdom, Jesus, and the Sages: Metaphor and Social Context in Matthew's Gospel* (Valley Forge: Trinity Press International, 1996), 2.

The use of the figure of Lady Wisdom follows immediately at the end of chap. 11,[122] a section that has frequently played a role in Christian diatribes against Jews: "Come to me, all you that are weary and are carrying heavy burdens, and I will give you rest. Take my yoke upon you, and learn from me, for I am gentle and humble in heart, and you will find rest for your souls. For my yoke is easy and my burden is light." The parallels with Sir 51:23-27 have long been noted. The reader is entreated to "acquire wisdom for yourself without money"; and the author notes, "I have labored but little and found for myself much serenity." The reader also is to "put your neck under her yoke," a theme already developed in Sir 6:23-31.[123] The connection between "yoke" and "wisdom" is even more explicit in the Hebrew text of Ben Sira than in the Greek version. The image of the yoke is common in rabbinic literature, with a statement of Rabbi Nechuniah (Nehunya) ben Hakanah in m. 'Abot 3:5 an important reference point: "Whoever accepts the yoke of the Torah, then the yoke of the kingdom and the yoke of daily life shall be removed from him." Interestingly we now have in 4Q421 1aii-b:10 a reference to the yoke of wisdom. In 4Q421 this man who is a sage and possesses understanding is to "carry the yoke of wisdom." He will receive admonition and "walk in the ways of God." While there are many similarities between these passages and Matt 11:29, the identification of Jesus with the yoke differentiates the latter passage. Wisdom imagery abounds throughout this section, but it is distinguished by the fact that Jesus is its personification.

Two trends within the wisdom literature of Second Temple Judaism provide a context for this Matthean usage. We of course have ample evidence of the hypostatization of wisdom in Jewish literature. This is already suggested in Proverbs 1–9, especially chap. 8, where Wisdom is present at creation. This is developed in Ben Sira and leads to the declaration in chap. 24 that wisdom is the Torah. Note also Bar 3:9–4:4. The Wisdom of Solomon also declares that Wisdom is a divine being, present at creation (9:9, cf. 8:3-4). In 1 Enoch 37–71 we find the basis for the proposed identification of wisdom with the Son of Man.[124] In these

---

122. Ibid., 54-60.

123. Cf. D. Hagner, Matthew 1–13 (WBC 33a; Dallas: Word, 1993), 321, who rejects the argument that Matt 11:25-30 is based on the Moses typology proposed by D. C. Allison Jr., "Two Notes on a Key Text: Matthew 11:25-30," JTS 39 (1988): 477-85; and adopted in the commentary Allison coauthored with W. D. Davies, A Critical and Exegetical Commentary on the Gospel According to Saint Matthew (3 vols.; ICC; Edinburgh: T & T Clark, 1988-97), 2:272-93. Note the argument of Robert Gundry: "At most, therefore, the passage in Sirach exercised an indirect and vague influence on Matthew" (Matthew: A Commentary on His Literary and Theological Art [Grand Rapids: Eerdmans, 1982], 220).

124. Deutsch, Lady Wisdom, 18-19.

parables the Son of Man is preexistent, both hidden and revealed; he is a wisdom figure given the spirit of wisdom, understanding, and might. He also is the revelation of God's wisdom, the source of the "secrets of wisdom," and apocalyptic judge. Significant for our passage is the withdrawal of wisdom in *1 En.* 42:1-2. Lady Wisdom here goes forth from the heavens to take her dwelling among humankind but, finding no habitation, she returns to the heavens.[125] A biblical basis for this withdrawal is noted in Prov 1:28-31. Then in *1 En.* 42:3 iniquity seeks a home among humankind and finds it. Lady Wisdom cannot dwell with people because she cannot find a home, thereby permitting the deployment of evil in the world. In Matthew 11 the calls for repentance on the part of the Son of Man, rejected by the citizens of Chorazin and Bethsaida, give a place for evil in the world, even though in this case vengeance is reserved for the day of judgment. Within the Qumran texts we find the vivid personification of Dame Folly in 4Q184 and the apparent description of Lady Wisdom in 4Q185 1-2, even though she is not named in the fragments. While illuminating, the occurrence of personification is not adequate to explain the developments within Matthew.

Just as significant for our purposes is the growth in the sectarian identification of wisdom. Within the use of notions of wisdom in the literature from Qumran we see the manner in which a sectarian movement could adapt and co-opt wisdom imagery that had been influential in its development to the point that it becomes totally identified with the beliefs and way of life advocated by those sectarians. It is this type of use of wisdom imagery that the author of the book of Matthew uses in the identification of Jesus with wisdom. It is this history that explains the "wisdom greater than Solomon" in 12:42 and the wisdom that astounds the people in the synagogue of his hometown in 13:54. Since we now know of other instances in Second Temple Judaism where the prospects for the attainment of wisdom and knowledge were tied to membership in an exclusive sectarian entity, the idea of Jesus as the exclusive source of wisdom for his followers appears in a broader context. The identification of Jesus with wisdom also provides a context for understanding the association of Jesus with the Torah. In addition to Sir 24:23 and Bar 4:1, we see this developed throughout the text entitled *Beatitudes* and stated most explicitly in 4Q525 2ii+3:3-10. It is also apparent in the fragmentary evidence of 4Q185 1-2ii. This development in the inherited wisdom traditions of Second Temple Judaism provides a context for the authoritative legal claims attributed to Jesus in the antitheses of Matthew 5 following the beatitudes of that text. The followers of Jesus can make claims to the exclusive source of wisdom in the same manner that other groups made similar assertions. We are dealing with the beliefs and

---

125. Ibid., 18.

way of life that the followers of Jesus advocated within the Jewish community of which they were a part. In other words Jesus is wisdom for the community of his followers as well as the hermeneutical principle for its interpretation. The wisdom texts from Qumran have now clarified the nature and possibility of this option in Second Temple Judaism.

This same possibility lies behind the identification of Jesus Christ with wisdom in the writings of Paul, evident in passages such as 1 Cor 1:30: "He is the source of your life in Christ Jesus, who became for us wisdom from God" (see also 1 Cor 1:24). In 1 Cor 8:6 Paul points to a preexistent wisdom present at creation that either was Christ or whose representation he inherited. Both wisdom's preexistence and role in creation are evident in the MSS of *Instruction* and in the related texts. Note, for example, the assumption of the preexistence of the "mystery of existence" in 4Q417 1i:1-12//4Q418 43,44,45i:1-9 (see discussion in the introduction to *Instruction*), where wisdom is present for the action of creation performed by the God of knowledge. This assumption of the preexistence of wisdom as a phenomenon rooted in the biblical texts and interpreted through the wisdom traditions of Qumran is not exclusive to these texts. We note how Philo and other Judeo-Greek writers developed this on the basis of Greek literature. Gnostic texts provide evidence of another interpretive tradition. Mystery cults such as that of Isis also had an impact on the interpretation of this phenomenon in Jewish texts. What this evidence does demonstrate is the manner in which such assumptions were also present and developed in the texts of portions of Palestinian Judaism composed in Hebrew (and Aramaic).

A similar observation can be made about the dichotomy of flesh and spirit pervasive in the writings of Paul. The particularly negative view of "flesh" that is evidenced in those compositions finds a context in these wisdom texts. In 4Q418 81+81a:1-2 we read, "For he has separated you from all the spirit of flesh. You, keep separate from all that he hates and abstain from all of the abominations of the soul." Here the spirit of flesh is associated with a sphere that is in opposition to the will of God. In 4Q416 1:10-13 "every spirit of flesh will be laid utterly bare," in contrast to what will happen with the sons of heaven. Other passages throughout *Instruction* support this understanding of "flesh" as describing a sinful reality in opposition to God in a manner similar to its usage in Paul in passages such as Gal 5:17 or Rom 8:5-8. The negative portrayal of flesh provides a context for this contrast with spirit.[126]

---

126. This has been developed most convincingly by Jörg Frey, "Die paulinische Antithese von 'Fleisch' und 'Geist' und die palästinisch-jüdische Weisheitstradition," *ZNW* 51 (1999): 45-77; idem, "The Notion of 'Flesh' in 4QInstruction and the Background of Pauline Usage," in *Sapiential, Liturgical and Poetical Texts*, ed. Falk et al., 197-226; idem, "Flesh and Spirit in the

Less clear is Collins's proposal that an immediate connection is to be made between this distinction in *Instruction* and the differentiation of immortality of the soul from the mortal body attributed to Philo and possibly the Wisdom of Solomon.[127] Tigchelaar's proposal that this could be an early form of the distinction between "spirit" and "soul" is no more convincing.[128] However, Collins's basic argument that two types of humanity are developed in 4Q417 1i:13-17 by contrasting Gen 1:27 with 2:7 is an insightful contribution to the discussion. Similarly, Tigchelaar's concluding words on the meaning of the same passage are significant: "obedience to His words is a prerequisite for receiving the full ability of understanding one's place in the predestined plan of history."[129] I discuss this passage further in the commentary below.

We might expect that four areas of NT studies, among others, will receive further development in light of this additional material regarding wisdom in Second Temple Judaism. First, a body of research suggests a wisdom core for Q, that hypothesized source used by the authors of the Gospels of Matthew and Luke. That source would have included eschatological warnings while also portraying Jesus as a wisdom teacher.[130] Further research is necessary to determine whether the particular traditions of wisdom in the Qumran documents contribute to that discussion.[131] Second, the Gospel of John portrays Jesus as incarnate preexistent wisdom, one who is able to differentiate the light from the darkness, life from death, and flesh from spirit for those who believe in him. Early research identified commonalities in the dualism of this Gospel and that found in some of the sectarian scrolls. Further work is now to be expected on the more nuanced views of wisdom and apocalyptic evident in these wisdom traditions from Qumran. Third, the Letter of James is a collection of wisdom

---

Palestinian Jewish Sapiential Tradition and in the Qumran Texts: An Inquiry into the Background of Pauline Usage," in *Wisdom Texts from Qumran,* ed. Hempel et al., 367-404. See also Eibert Tigchelaar, "'Spiritual People,' 'Fleshly Spirit,' and 'Vision of Meditation': Reflections on *4QInstruction* and 1 Corinthians," in *Echoes from the Caves,* ed. García Martínez, 103-18.

127. John J. Collins, "The Mysteries of God: Creation and Eschatology in 4QInstruction and the Wisdom of Solomon," in *Wisdom and Apocalypticism,* ed. García Martínez, 299-303.

128. Tigchelaar, "Spiritual People," 109-13.

129. Ibid., 116.

130. John S. Kloppenborg, *The Formation of Q: Trajectories in Ancient Wisdom Collections* (Philadelphia: Fortress, 1987); idem, *Excavating Q: The History and Setting of the Sayings Gospel* (Minneapolis: Fortress, 2000).

131. Note the manner in which Macaskill introduces his study as a response to Kloppenborg (*Revealed Wisdom,* 1-9). See also Matthew J. Goff, "Discerning Trajectories: 4QInstruction and the Sapiential Background of the Sayings Source Q," *JBL* 124 (2005): 657-73; George J. Brooke, "The Pre-Sectarian Jesus," in *Echoes from the Caves,* ed. García Martínez, 43-44.

instructions. Earlier attempts to identify elements within the composition related to the sectarian scrolls from Qumran found incidental but not significant connections. We do find the familiar use of the two ways ideology in Jas 3:13–4:8. Fourth, just as in James, we can expect other sections with injunctions on how to live to receive more attention. One example is the household codes of Eph 5:21–6:6 and Col 3:18–4:1.[132] Further work on connections with the more extensive wisdom traditions represented in the Qumran texts is warranted.

Bibliography

Collins, John J. *Jewish Wisdom in the Hellenistic Age*. OTL. Louisville: Westminster John Knox, 1997.

———. *Seers, Sibyls and Sages in Hellenistic-Roman Judaism*. JSJSup 54. Leiden: Brill, 1997.

Collins, John J., Gregory E. Sterling, and Ruth A. Clements, eds. *Sapiential Perspectives: Wisdom Literature in Light of the Dead Sea Scrolls. Proceedings of the Sixth International Symposium of the Orion Center, 20-22 May, 2001*. STDJ 51. Leiden: Brill, 2004.

Falk, Daniel K., F. García Martínez, and Eileen M. Schuller, eds. *Sapiential, Liturgical and Poetical Texts from Qumran: Proceedings of the Third Meeting of the International Organization for Qumran Studies, Published in Memory of Maurice Baillet*. STDJ 35. Leiden: Brill, 2000.

García Martínez, Florentino, ed. *Wisdom and Apocalypticism in the Dead Sea Scrolls and in the Biblical Tradition*. BETL 158. Leuven: Leuven University Press/Peeters, 2003.

Goff, Matthew J. *Discerning Wisdom: The Sapiential Literature of the Dead Sea Scrolls*. VTSup 116. Leiden: Brill, 2007.

Harrington, Daniel J., S.J. *Wisdom Texts from Qumran*. London/New York: Routledge, 1996.

Hempel, Charlotte, and Judith M. Lieu, eds. *Biblical Traditions in Transmission: Essays in Honour of Michael A. Knibb*. JSJSup 111. Leiden: Brill, 2006.

Hempel, C., A. Lange, and H. Lichtenberger, eds. *The Wisdom Texts from Qumran and the Development of Sapiential Thought*. BETL 159. Leuven: Leuven University Press/Peeters, 2002.

---

132. See commentary to 4Q416 2iii:19-iv:13 below. Note also Jean-Sébastien Rey, "Family Relationships in *4QInstruction* and in Eph 5:21-6:4," in *Echoes from the Caves*, ed. García Martínez, 231-55.

Lange, Armin. *Weisheit und Prädestination: Weisheitliche Urordnung und Prädestination in den Textfunden von Qumran.* STDJ 18. Leiden: Brill, 1995.

————. "Wisdom and Predestination in the Dead Sea Scrolls." *DSD* 2 (1995): 340-54.

Woude, A. S. van der. "Wisdom at Qumran." In *Wisdom in Ancient Israel: Essays in Honour of J. A. Emerton.* Ed. John Day, Robert P. Gordon, and H. G. M. Williamson, 244-56. Cambridge: Cambridge University Press, 1995.

Wright, Benjamin G., III, and Lawrence M. Wills, eds. *Conflicted Boundaries in Wisdom and Apocalypticism.* SBLSymS 35. Atlanta: SBL, 2005.

Instruction (1Q26, 4Q415-418, 423)

Introduction

Content

This extraordinary text, noteworthy for the significance of its content, its size, and its influence, contains a combination of instructional material similar to that of the wisdom injunctions found in biblical books such as Proverbs and Ben Sira, and eschatological literature rooted in Hebrew prophecy and best known to us from the book of *1 Enoch*. As in the case of Ben Sira, the work as a whole takes the form of instruction from a senior sage to a junior (or juniors) being groomed for some significant educational or leadership role. The implications of the instruction rendered far exceed the consequences for the individual being instructed and rather extend to the entire people with whom these individuals are affiliated. While it is to be assumed that this people is Israel, never is that term used in these extensive fragments,[1] nor is any other formal name employed throughout.

Universal judgment is a theme throughout a number of the fragments. A role for a heavenly host is included in these descriptions as the sons of truth face the consequences of righteous judgment. The hope that an epoch of truth will be realized is also part of this description. Gaining an understanding that this is the nature and lot of humankind is a common task for the junior sage as well as the entire people addressed throughout this composition. Individuals will be judged according to their spirit. The younger sage and presumably those

---

1. It is found in 4Q417 24:1, but this fragment is not to be regarded as coming from *Instruction*, in part because of the unusual nature of its terminology (see DJD 34:207).

who are judged worthy of participation in the epoch of truth with the heavenly host have had their ear uncovered to understand the "mystery of existence." This mystery was present in the act of creation, is operative at the time of the writer, and is the key to understanding the future of the world and the fate of its inhabitants. Those who understand and accept this mystery of existence walk in perfection, righteousness, and truth. Instructions on how to live are rooted in this worldview and are integral to the understanding to be developed by the "sons of truth." Given the frequent instructions addressed to those in poverty, we can presume that this was the condition of many persons addressed in this work. A good deal of instruction concerning borrowing money, the necessity for speedy repayment, and relationships with the creditor are covered. Instruction for marriage is also found in this text. One section addresses the female members of the intended audience. Instruction regarding the work of craftsmen and farmers also is present in these fragments. Practical advice on harvest as well as obligations concerning the festivals and the injunctions against the mixing of diverse kinds in biblical law are examined. Making restitution for damage done by one's animals is also mentioned. What distinguishes this text is the rationale provided for this instruction in a literary piece in which both present and future receive extensive treatment.

This composition does stand in marked contrast to the semi-autonomous and even personified portrayal of wisdom advanced in Proverbs, particularly in chaps. 1–9. There are no hints within *Instruction* of the personification of wisdom that enlivens those chapters. While we might appreciate the manner in which the attraction of wisdom and the seduction of its opponent could have formed a significant background for the reader attempting to make a decision related to the wisdom advanced in these works, such an image finds no mention in the text.[2] It is the worldview advocated in the text rather than a female figure known as Wisdom that receives mention here. Wisdom in this literary piece then does not get equated with Torah as in Sirach 24 either, since it has no existence independent of perspectives advanced within the work.

---

2. For example, note the manner in which Roland Murphy concludes his summary of biblical wisdom literature with a chapter entitled "Lady Wisdom" (*The Tree of Life: An Exploration of Biblical Wisdom Literature* [ABRL; New York: Doubleday, 1990], 133-49). These compositions do not even receive mention in the article by Sidnie White Crawford, "Lady Wisdom and Dame Folly at Qumran," *DSD* 5 (1998): 355-66. Note also the conclusion of James L. Crenshaw's chapter on Proverbs in *Old Testament Wisdom: An Introduction* (rev. ed.; Louisville: Westminster John Knox, 1998), 80-82.

Manuscripts

Prior to its publication in DJD 34 in 1999, this text was named *4QSapiential A.* At least eight copies of *Instruction,* which form the basis of this commentary, can be identified among the Qumran fragments.[3] The text of 1Q26 is found in DJD 1, the remainder in DJD 34, which also includes a reedition of 1Q26. The existence of this fragment from Cave 1 means that its title should be *Instruction* rather than *4QInstruction,* as it is frequently called in the literature discussing this significant work. The largest copy is 4Q418 with about three hundred fragments.[4] It is estimated that 4Q418 in its original form would have been as long as the most lengthy of the presently available texts from Qumran, 11Q19 *(Temple*a*).* Its length is 8.148 meters (about 26 feet), estimated by Yigael Yadin to have been about 9 meters (29-30 feet) in the original. The most substantial consecutive body of text is 4Q416 2, which has the remains of 4 columns, some of them rather full. Another composition, 4Q414, is found on the verso of 4Q415. The latter was probably written first and then reused.[5] Evidence of other copies is also available.

Additional evidence of *Instruction* has more recently been presented. One more fragment has been identified by Émile Puech and Annette Steudel.[6] Esther and Hanan Eshel have drawn attention to another fragment, which they have labeled 4Q416 23, found in an American exhibit collection and its catalog.[7]

The evaluation of the fragments for the text of 4Q418 1-2+2a-c is a complicated question. Eibert Tigchelaar has proposed that they form the basis for a

3. John Strugnell and Daniel J. Harrington, S.J., *Qumran Cave 4, XXIV: Sapiential Texts, Part 2* (DJD 34; Oxford: Clarendon, 1999), 1-2, 501; Eibert J. C. Tigchelaar, *To Increase Learning for the Understanding Ones: Reading and Reconstructing the Fragmentary Early Jewish Sapiential Text 4QInstruction* (STDJ 44; Leiden: Brill, 2001), 15-17, 167-69.

4. Note that this total is according to fragment number, and a few fragments have been reclassified, hence the total is slightly less than 303.

5. DJD 34:41; *To Increase Learning,* 28-30.

6. Émile Puech and Annette Steudel, "Un nouveau fragment du manuscrit *4QInstruction* (*XQ7 = 4Q417* ou *418*)," *RevQ* 19 (2000): 623-27. This was originally published by Armin Lange as XQ7 (Unidentified Text) in DJD 36:492-93.

7. Esther and Hanan Eshel, "A Preliminary Report on Seven New Fragments from Qumran," in *Meghillot: Studies in the Dead Sea Scrolls V-VI* (ed. Moshe Bar-Asher and Emanuel Tov; Jerusalem: Bialik Institute/Haifa University Press, 2007), 277-78. They cite this fragment containing two Hebrew words from the catalog of Lee Biondi, *From the Dead Sea Scrolls to the Bible in America: A Brief History of the Bible from Antiquity to Modern America Told Through Ancient Manuscripts and Early European and American Printed Bibles* (n.p.: Biblical Arts of Arizona, 2004), 13. In this catalog it is identified as a fragment of 4Q418. The words on the photograph of the fragment are to be found in 4Q418 148, 5. The identification of the Eshels seems more accurate on paleographic grounds.

separate MS from the remainder of 4Q418, thereby adding to the total number of available MSS.[8] There are paleographic grounds to question the relationship of 4Q418 1-2 to the remainder of 4Q418. They are copied in a discernibly different though contemporary hand. Whether these fragments provide evidence of another copy of *Instruction* or were a repaired beginning of 4Q418 is an open question, even though I accept the arguments of Daniel J. Harrington and John Strugnell that incline toward the latter (see DJD 34:226-27). Of the utmost importance is the recognition that these fragments do aid our reconstruction of 4Q416 1 (see next paragraph below), but provide no further content for *Instruction*, whether they belong to 4Q418 or another copy. Note that frags. 3, 4, and 5 are close to frags. 1 and 2 in color and preparation of the surface, but also could belong to frags. 6-303. I have also accepted the use of frags. 2a-c in this reconstruction (DJD 34:83, 225).[9] Note also the utilization of scattered fragments of 4Q418 to aid in the reconstruction of 4Q416 1:9-17.[10]

A systematic reconstruction of a unified text incorporating all of the fragments is not possible. The wide margin on the right-hand side of 4Q416 1 indicates that it was the beginning of the parchment and of this copy of *Instruction*. An overlap in text with 4Q418 1 lends support to the hypothesis that this column was the beginning of the composition as attested in the extant copies. While in his original reconstruction Torleif Elgvin rejected this proposal, he appears to have changed his stance.[11] The monograph of Tigchelaar, *To Increase Learning*, needs to be consulted on textual readings on a regular basis along with the DJD 34 publication. The other monographs on this text also contain extensive comments on detailed readings of these fragmentary MSS. Whether they all represent substantially similar texts, or whether some constitute subsequent editions of this work, has not been determined in a reliable manner.[12] The major issue for discussion is whether 4Q417 represents an earlier stage of composition than 4Q416 and 4Q418.[13]

Since 4Q416 1 is the longest copy of consecutive columns available and

---

8. Tigchelaar, *To Increase Learning*, 17, 61-69. Note the response to Elgvin's earlier proposals of this nature in DJD 34:226-27.

9. See also Tigchelaar, *To Increase Learning*, 42-49, 61-69.

10. See ibid., 66-69, 74-75.

11. T. Elgvin, "The Reconstruction of Sapiential Work A," *RevQ* 16 (1995): 566-67. But note the comments by Matthew J. Goff, *Worldly and Heavenly Wisdom of 4QInstruction* (STDJ 50; Leiden: Brill, 2003), 5 n. 19.

12. See the summary in Tigchelaar, *To Increase Learning*, 155-71.

13. Frey, "'Flesh' in 4QInstruction and Pauline Usage," in *Sapiential, Liturgical and Poetical Texts from Qumran: Proceedings of the Third Meeting of the International Organization for Qumran Studies, Published in Memory of Maurice Baillet* (ed. Daniel K. Falk, Florentino García Martínez, and Eileen M. Schuller; STDJ 35; Leiden: Brill, 2000), 212 n. 69.

also marks the beginning of at least one copy of the text, I have chosen to place it at the beginning of the MSS of *Instruction* discussed in this commentary. The remainder then follow in numerical order according to MS number. This arrangement provides the student of this literary work an opportunity to begin inquiry with a substantive original introduction to the text.

Historical Context and Review of Research

The dates of the MSS provide the terminus ad quem for determining the time of composition of this work. From the perspective of paleographic development, 4Q416 is regarded as the earliest MS, dating from the transitional period between the late Hasmonean and the earliest Herodian type, that is, 50-25 B.C.E. 4Q418 is considered slightly later in that transitional period, 40-20 B.C.E.; 4Q418a may also be from that time, 50-1 B.C.E.; but 4Q415, 4Q417, 4Q418b, and 4Q418c are labeled as representing the early Herodian formal hand (30-1 B.C.E.). The rustic semiformal hand of the early or middle Herodian period of 1Q26 also emerges from the latter dates. 4Q423 is a sample of a middle or late Herodian formal hand, dated between 10 B.C.E. and 50 C.E.[14] These MSS point to the widespread use of the text in the second half of the first century B.C.E., a period of extensive activity at the Qumran site and in the development of Jewish sectarian movements in Judea.

The publishers of the editio princeps propose that the number of available MSS points to the significance of this composition for the inhabitants of the Qumran site. The quantity suggests that it apparently was copied rather frequently, and regarded as "'authoritative' or even perhaps considered 'canonical,'" according to Strugnell and Harrington. However, it "does not reflect a specific or closed community like that of Qumran, nor an earlier quasi-sectarian group."[15] They view it as a bridge document between Proverbs and Ben Sira, thereby making it a third-century B.C.E. text.

While casting it in a considerably different thematic framework, Armin Lange proposes a similar date of composition. On the basis of the use of certain Persian loanwords not found in Biblical Hebrew such as רז and כשר, as well as the Hiphil participle of the root בין (i.e., מבין) and the infinitive construction התהלכו עם, he argues the terminus ad quem for its date of composition is toward the end of the third or the beginning of the second century B.C.E.[16] Since

---

14. The introduction to each MS in DJD 34 describes its place in the paleographic development. Note also the summary chart by Brian Webster in DJD 39:351-446.

15. Strugnell and Harrington, DJD 34:22.

16. Lange, *Weisheit und Prädestination*, 47.

he is working with the thesis of Gerhard von Rad that wisdom is rooted in apocalyptic, he sees the sapiential motifs of *Instruction* as "a theology which can no longer be described as wisdom and which is on its way to apocalypticism."[17] In his monograph Tigchelaar builds on a similar approach with slightly different chronological results. He is primarily interested in the variety of issues associated with the reconstruction of the text. Building on similarities between *Instruction* and the "Treatise on the Two Spirits" in 1QS, also noted by Lange, he argues that the terminus ad quem for its composition is somewhere in the second century B.C.E.[18]

While developing in detail the connections with the sectarian creations in the Qumran corpus, Elgvin argues for a presectarian provenance for *Instruction,* positing a date of composition in the mid-second century B.C.E.[19] His argument for the author's use of *1 Enoch,* particularly the Epistle of Enoch (*1 Enoch* 91–107), leads him to posit a date for the authorship of the discourses of *Instruction* in the middle of the second century B.C.E., hence the date of the work as a whole.[20] While the proposed dating is in line with proposals advanced by others, the dependence on *1 Enoch* is more difficult to substantiate. The similarities are much more likely to emerge out of a common tradition-historical milieu.[21] Noteworthy throughout this portion of his study (as well as elsewhere in his publications) is the focus in his comparative literary evaluation on the apocalyptic and sectarian traditions rather than on wisdom literature. He posits two literary stages, the first of which is composed of traditional sapiential material. A later portion is a proto-Essene layer, which is composed of apocalyptic thought. Conclusions on the historical setting for the document's authorship are drawn on the basis of its place within those traditions. In a more recent publication he posits the origin of the literary work to the first quarter of the second century B.C.E., but also is open to a late-third-century possibility.[22]

Daryl Jefferies views *Instruction* as a sectarian composition. Working

---

17. Lange, "Wisdom and Predestination," 348, with reference to the Treatise on the Two Spirits in 1QS 3:15–4:26.

18. Tigchelaar, *To Increase Learning,* 247-48.

19. Elgvin, "An Analysis of 4QInstruction" (Ph.D. diss., Hebrew University, 1997), 167-68. He also posits an earlier alternative in the first two decades of the same century, recognizing that the majority of his arguments could support either date (188-89).

20. Ibid., 168-72, 176-87.

21. Loren T. Stuckenbruck, "4QInstruction and the Possible Influence of Early Enochic Traditions: An Evaluation," in *Wisdom Texts from Qumran,* ed. Hempel et al., 245-61.

22. Torleif Elgvin, "Priestly Sages? The Milieus of Origin of 4QMysteries and 4QInstruction," in *Sapiential Perspectives: Wisdom Literature in Light of the Dead Sea Scrolls. Proceedings of the Sixth International Symposium of the Orion Center, 20-22 May, 2001* (ed. John J. Collins, Gregory E. Sterling, and Ruth A. Clements; STDJ 51; Leiden: Brill, 2004), 83-84.

from a form-critical analysis of the admonitions, he finds that the traditional wisdom forms known from the HB and Ben Sira are present, but then are directed toward sectarian ends.[23] However, he differentiates it from those works most commonly accepted as a product of the Qumran community.[24] Thus he argues it is "extra-Qumranic," perhaps applied to those who lived in the camps throughout Israel.[25] From such a perspective, he prefers a mid-second-century date for its creation (150-100 B.C.E.).[26]

After a rather comprehensive summary of the available research, Matthew Goff arrives at a date similar to many of those already mentioned.[27] He points to the lack of any hints of the Maccabean crisis or other evidence of the type of eschatological urgency that emerged as a more prominent element in Jewish life after the events of the reign of Antiochus IV Epiphanes (175-164 B.C.E.); however, he does not regard that as definitive evidence of dating. He does consider this work as prior to the sectarian literature, while recognizing that there is continuing debate about these issues. He concludes that several factors argue for an early-second-century B.C.E. date; however, the evidence is not definitive: "A safe conclusion is that *Instruction* was written in the second century B.C.E."[28] He explicitly pays attention to the relationship of wisdom and apocalyptic in the work. This is also the interest of Benjamin Wold. He argues that the creation "represents a single genre that combines elements of wisdom with themes associated with apocalyptic literature."[29] With this argument he places his viewpoint closer to that of Strugnell and Harrington, portraying it as a particular expression within the development of wisdom literature. Recent monographs have incorporated and built on the perspectives developed by Goff.

Among the most recent studies, Samuel Adams does not find that the text reflects different layers, but rather an attempt to "associate righteous behavior with access to the heavenly realm and wickedness with eternal punishment."[30]

23. See Jefferies, *Wisdom at Qumran: A Form-Critical Analysis of the Admonitions in 4QInstruction* (Piscataway, N.J.: Gorgias, 2002), 319-24, for a summary of conclusions.

24. Ibid., 57-77, 323-24.

25. This option is considered but rejected by Elgvin, "Analysis," 176-77. Jefferies argues that *Instruction* is "specifically directed to the needs of the community without concern for the broader wisdom tradition" (*Wisdom at Qumran*, 323).

26. Jefferies, *Wisdom at Qumran*, 77.

27. Goff, *Worldly and Heavenly Wisdom*, 228-32.

28. Ibid., 231.

29. Wold, *Women, Men and Angels* (WUNT 2/201; Tübingen: Mohr Siebeck, 2005), 19-20.

30. Adams, *Wisdom in Transition: Act and Consequence in Second Temple Instructions* (JSJSup 125; Leiden: Brill, 2008), 220.

In contrast to traditional wisdom teaching, worldly success does not come to virtuous individuals. The addressee must rather learn and adopt a particular view of the universe in order to be saved from destruction. In its outlook it has a good deal of similarity with the Epistle of Enoch.[31] He adopts Goff's view that this work reflects a group setting in which there is evidence of a membership of subsistence and moderate means. For its date of creation, it follows the Epistle of Enoch and Daniel, but precedes the *Hodayot* and the "Treatise on the Two Spirits," hence late second century B.C.E.[32]

For Grant Macaskill the eschatological viewpoint developed in *Instruction* is neither entirely future nor entirely realized, but rather inaugurated. While not discussing the date of composition, his handling of the concepts and literary developments is consistent with the many scholars who have advocated a second-century B.C.E. date. This is associated with an idea of revealed wisdom, in this case related to the mystery of existence (see "Key Terms" below for a discussion of this expression). This wisdom is inaugurated in the sense that it is the province of and related to existence within an eschatological community described and anticipated within the text.[33] Here the cosmological discourse serves a paranetic function. The righteous person is to emulate the heavenly bodies by carrying out one's own allotted position in life and performing the associated tasks, as is true for the heavenly bodies. This is the way to be eliminated from the coming judgment or to be judged favorably. But this orientation is rooted in creation, not simply in projections of the future. It is based in the structure and order of the universe.

It is my belief that we need to resist the temptation to limit the creativity of those associated with the developing literary traditions within Israel to the second century B.C.E., hence a late-third or early-second-century B.C.E. date is quite possible. In addition to the significant number of copies of *Instruction* found in the Qumran corpus, we also see that two of the copies of this work were rolled up in the less usual way with the beginning of the text on the inside of the scroll.[34] This feature points to its active use at the time of the abandonment of the site. Also significant is the presence of a copy in Cave 1, where apparently the most significant texts related to sectarian existence were stored. The argument for this document's influence can be demonstrated both for a number of the more recently published wisdom texts and for the sectarian texts familiar to us over a longer period of time. The composition with the greatest

31. Ibid., 236-37.

32. Ibid., 37-45.

33. Macaskill, *Revealed Wisdom and Inaugurated Eschatology in Ancient Judaism and Early Christianity* (JSJSup 115; Leiden: Brill, 2007), 72-114.

34. 4Q415 and 416; Elgvin, "Analysis," 10, 13-14.

similarities to *Instruction* in literary styles, themes, and vocabulary is *Mysteries*.[35] All the evidence points to *Instruction* as an early and significant work in a particular trajectory of wisdom literature in Second Temple Judaism.

Literary Questions

Introductory Section (4Q416 1)

The wide margin on the right-hand side of this fragment indicates that it was the beginning of this copy of *Instruction* (note the discussion of "Manuscripts" above). It is fortunate that we have this evidence from 4Q416 1 because scholars would not have expected this column to be first in a work that is predominantly of a wisdom nature, since there is no precedent in Jewish wisdom literature for a composition that begins in this manner. Noteworthy in addition to its content is the third person narration in this column within a work that is predominantly in the second person singular, a frequent literary characteristic of wisdom works.

The cosmological and eschatological character of this column sets an extraordinary context for this particular literary creation. The cosmological setting for the work is developed first (lines 1-9), with the fragments providing evidence of the role of the luminaries, with regard to both the calendar and the created order, even its political divisions. Such an extensive and important role for the luminaries suggests some ideological similarities with *1 Enoch*, particularly the first section (chaps. 1–36) and the Astronomical Book (chaps. 72–82). Already in line 4 we also have reference to judgment, suggesting that this is an integral part of the construction of the universe. The judgment of those in "the service of wickedness" and of "the sons of his truth" is explained in lines 9-13. The implications of this judgment for the end of world history are then developed. Fragmentary evidence of the importance of being able to distinguish between good and evil, presumably within the world, can be found in line 15. The author has provided a cosmological framework for an eschatology and a resultant ethic that will be developed throughout the remainder of the composition, a cosmology known to us from more familiar Qumran works such as the section of the *Community Rule* designated the "Treatise on the Two Spirits" (1QS iii:13–iv:26).

A tentative proposal by Tigchelaar would place 4Q418 238 at the top of

---

35. See the summary of this evidence by John Strugnell, "The Smaller Hebrew Wisdom Texts Found at Qumran: Variations, Resemblances, and Lines of Development," in *Wisdom Texts from Qumran*, ed. Hempel et al., 47-49.

the column of 4Q416 1i in order to place the term מַשְׂכִּיל ("sage") at the beginning of the literary work. This is based on the physical similarity of that fragment to 4Q418 229, a text that he identifies with a parallel to 4Q416 1i:2.[36] In the
discussion of his hypothetical reconstruction, however, he suggests that this
would then identify the addressee of the document as the sage in a manner similar to the sections of sectarian creations that are addressed לַמַּשְׂכִּיל ("to the
sage").[37] A literary analysis of the fragments suggests rather that the מֵבִין ("man
of discernment") is the addressee of this text (see below). In that case there is no
basis for arguing that 4Q418 238 constitutes the first line of the original text of
4Q416, even if it is found in the first column.

Literary Connections with the Treatise on the Two Spirits

Early in the research on *Instruction,* similarities with the "Treatise on the Two
Spirits" (1QS iii:13–iv:26) and 1QH[a] v-vi were identified by Armin Lange.[38] This
section of the *Community Rule* was identified as being possibly of earlier provenance than the remainder of the composition relatively early in the process of
its literary analysis since it did not appear to contain typical sectarian references such as the term יחד ("community") and similar indicators. Of particular
significance to Lange were the references to the אל הדעות ("God of knowledge") as the creator of the order of the world that were common to the two
works (1QS iii:15; 4Q299 [Myst[a]] 35:1; 73:3; 4Q417 1i:8//4Q418 43,44,45i:6; 4Q418
55:5 — the close relationship of *Mysteries* to *Instruction* is discussed in the introduction to that text).[39] He also notes that this order is described using the term
מחשבה ("intention")[40] and argues that all three literary pieces originated in the
same presectarian circles. Other terms also can be identified such as "truth and
iniquity," "children of iniquity," "sons of heaven," "epoch of peace," and "all the
epochs of eternity."[41]

Tigchelaar proposes two stages for the authorship of the "Treatise on the
Two Spirits" and suggests that the second or later stage (1QS iii:13-18 and iv:15-
26) originated from the same circles as *Instruction.*[42] He bases this conclusion

36. Tigchelaar, *To Increase Learning*, 69, 161, 183.
37. Ibid., 183.
38. Lange, *Weisheit und Prädestination*, 148-70; idem, "Wisdom and Predestination," 346-
48.
39. This designation is also found in sectarian texts elsewhere in 1QH[a] ix:28; xx:13 (see
note to that line in DJD 40:256); xxi:32; xxii:34; xxv:32-33.
40. See the commentary on 4Q416 2iii:14 below.
41. *To Increase Learning*, 196-98.
42. Ibid., 194-203.

on his expansion of the list of vocabulary items that are common to the "Treatise on the Two Spirits" and *Instruction* but that are rarely found in other texts or that share a particular meaning within those two texts, such as "cast the lot," "ways of truth," "eternal joy," "eternal pit," "dark places," and "according to a man's inheritance in the truth." These common features are concentrated in the introductory and concluding sections of the "Treatise." He also notes the absence from these lines of the light-darkness terminology that is at the center of the dualism developed in the "Treatise." Since the evidence does not permit as clear a division of the material as this summary suggests, and since the hypothesis depends on the supposition of a relationship between the circles that produced *Instruction* and this particular piece of the text, the proposal should be treated with caution.[43] This is not to deny that the similarities noted are striking and beg for explanation.

Tigchelaar also evaluates the proposal of Elgvin that there are parallels between 4Q417 1i and 1QH[a] v-vi.[44] Vocabulary items include the "mysteries of the wonders of God," "all epochs forever," and "assignment for eternity." While Tigchelaar adds terms to the list such as "eternal glory," "eternal foundations," and "spirit of flesh," he suggests that the hymn of 1QH[a] v-vi was influenced by *Instruction* and the "Treatise," rather than emerging from the same circles.

Key Terms

There are distinctive terms in *Instruction,* sometimes with occasional appearances in other Qumran wisdom texts, that require definition and explanation. The task of providing clear explanation for this terminology is formidable. The difficulty, of course, is lodged precisely in the terms' uniqueness, hence their lack of attestation in comparable sources. This task is one portion of the attempt to provide adequate identification and classification of various aspects of this newly identified addition to the collection of wisdom literature.

רז נהיה *("mystery of existence")*

This is a very difficult term to translate. The word רז as "mystery" is a Persian loanword that appears in Hebrew in Qumran texts and in Aramaic in Daniel. In Daniel it is related to dream interpretation and includes revelations from God concerning the future course of human history. In Greek translation,

---

43. See the review by Matthew Goff in *RBL* (online edition), 5/7/2005.
44. *To Increase Learning,* 203-7.

μυστήριον continues to be used in the NT to designate a riddle as well as the divine plan and sometimes points to the promised future (eschatological) action of God. Somewhat similar to the following description of the use of the phrase in the Qumran texts, we see the declaration in Mark 4:11, "to you has been given the mystery of the kingdom of God." In later Jewish mystical literature, the term רז is replaced by סוד.[45]

Most translators have preferred to bring the predominant eschatological context for the use of the term in *Instruction* into its translation. Translations such as "the mystery to come," "the mystery that is to be/come," "the mystery that is to be," or "the mystery that was coming into being" could suggest that the author(s) of *Instruction* was (were) interested rather exclusively in the prediction of the future.[46] It is not clear to me that this is justified; such an understanding could hamper our comprehension of this composition. Rather, within *Instruction* the reader or adherent can only expect to understand the future as one understands the creation and its purposes as well as the development of history and its direction: "*raz* refers to the mysteries of creation, that is, the natural order of things, and to the mysteries of the divine role in the historical processes. The source of these mysteries is divine wisdom."[47] García Martínez emphasizes the comprehensive nature of this revelation:

> In my view, this implies that the author of 4QInstruction considered all the knowledge he communicated, be it of an apocalyptic nature or similar to traditional biblical wisdom, as the same kind of knowledge. By also presenting his "secular" teachings as being included within the רז נהיה, he gave them the same authority he gives to the other "mysteries" about which he instructed the "one seeking understanding." He used the same strategy

45. Gershom G. Scholem, *Jewish Gnosticism, Merkabah Mysticism, and Talmudic Tradition* (New York: Jewish Theological Seminary, 1965), 3 n. 3.

46. For the first see Torleif Elgvin, "Wisdom and Apocalypticism in the Early Second Century BCE — The Evidence of 4QInstruction," in *The Dead Sea Scrolls Fifty Years After Their Discovery: Proceedings of the Jerusalem Congress, July 20-25, 1997* (ed. Lawrence H. Schiffman, Emanuel Tov, and James C. VanderKam; Jerusalem: Israel Exploration Society, 2000), 235; idem, "The Mystery to Come: Early Essene Theology of Revelation," in *Qumran Between the Old and New Testaments* (ed. F. H. Cryer and T. L. Thompson; JSOTSup 290; Sheffield: Sheffield Academic Press, 1998), 131. For the second see Daniel J. Harrington, S.J., "The Rāz Nihyeh in a Qumran Wisdom Text," *RevQ* 17 (1996): 551; DJD 34:32. For the third see John J. Collins, "Wisdom Reconsidered, in Light of the Scrolls," *DSD* 4 (1997): 272-74. For the last see Lawrence H. Schiffman, *Reclaiming the Dead Sea Scrolls: The History of Judaism, the Background of Christianity, the Lost Library of Qumran* (Philadelphia: Jewish Publication Society, 1994), 207.

47. Schiffman, *Reclaiming the Dead Sea Scrolls*, 206. The most extensive study rooting the mystery of existence within an understanding of creation is found in Wold, *Women, Men and Angels*, 20-24, 244-45.

of legitimation of this authority for the whole composition, without distinguishing between heavenly and worldly wisdom. His instructions' most worldly concerns were also presented as "revealed" wisdom.[48]

The comprehensive view of time articulated in *Instruction* is demonstrated in 4Q417 1i:2-6//4Q418 43,44,45i:2-4, the astounding column that begins with the injunction to the "man of discernment" (for a discussion of this term, see below): "consider [the mystery of existence and the deeds of old, whatever was (נהיה) and whatever will be (נהיה) with them . . . for]ever [. . . for whatever is (הויא) and for whatever will be (נהיה) with them . . .] in all [. . .] every de[ed . . . day and night meditate upon the mystery of ex]istence and search daily." A similar use of the verb is evident in the "Treatise on the Two Spirits" in the *Community Rule,* "From the God of knowledge comes all which is and will be" (1QS iii:15). The use of the term נבט in the Hiphil form ("behold" or "consider") in conjunction with the "mystery of existence" is also found in both constructions. In 4Q418 123i:3 נהיה appears to be the form of the verb that designates the past in a line that speaks of past, present, and future.[49] All of this is involved in the study of the רז נהיה and attempts to order one's life in accordance with it. Informative is the manner in which Benjamin Wold has anchored this concept solidly within an understanding of creation.[50] The future unfolds as one begins to understand the natural world and the course of human history, which itself is developing in light of an inevitable future. While the composition we have called *Instruction* has a great deal of interest in the future, that interest is developed within the context of a more comprehensive understanding of the past, present, and future reflected in this particular term.[51] Thus in this commentary I employ the translation, "mystery of existence."[52]

---

48. F. García Martínez, "Wisdom at Qumran: Worldly or Heavenly?" in *Wisdom and Apocalypticism,* ed. García Martínez, 12-14. While emphasizing the apocalyptic nature of the work, Elgvin also emphasizes the comprehensive nature of this term in "Wisdom and Apocalypticism," 235.

49. This term also appears in 1QS xi:4-6.

50. Wold, *Women, Men and Angels,* 20-24, 234-35.

51. See Matthew J. Goff, "The Mystery of Creation in 4QInstruction," *DSD* 10 (2003): 165-74; idem, "Wisdom, Apocalypticism, and the Pedagogical Ethos of 4QInstruction," in *Conflicted Boundaries,* ed. Wright and Wills, 61-63.

52. *DSSSE* 1:97; 2:859, and other places where this phrase is translated. Attempts to capture the comprehensive nature of this phrase can be found in *PEUDSS* 2:xii; and in Lange, *Weisheit und Prädestination,* 97 ("Geheimnis des Werdens"); idem, "Wisdom and Predestination in the Dead Sea Scrolls," *DSD* 2 (1995): 341 n. 4, where he states a preference for "mystery of becoming" rather than "mystery of being." Note also Jörg Frey, "Different Patterns of Dualistic Thought in the Qumran Library: Reflections on Their Background and History," in *Legal Texts*

The content of the "mystery of existence" is a topic of speculation and debate. Injunctions to study it and to live one's life in accordance with it suggest a specific composition or corpus. Attempts to identify it with a specific literary unit have not been successful, however, and may be misguided. Actual references to the title outside *Instruction* are found only in 4Q300 3:3-4//1Q27 1i:3-4 and 1QS xi:3-4. The very fragmentary text 4Q418 184:2 that mentions "by the hand of Moses" in the line prior to the reference to the "mystery of existence" is too oblique and singular to propose a direct connection with the Torah.[53] Lange has proposed and developed this understanding of the term.[54] While there are allusions to legal points in the text, there is no reference to "Torah" in the extensive fragments and no rhetorical argumentation for its authority or usage. While Adams's caution about an argument that sees the "mystery of existence" as a replacement for Torah has some merit, it is not clear that one needs to posit some relationship between Torah and mystery.[55] While statements or principles from the Torah may be incorporated into the mystery, the pursuit of the addressee is to be focused on the "mystery of existence." Though interesting and suggestive, there is nothing that would argue for a direct connection to the specific text of the "Treatise on the Two Spirits" (1QS iii:13–iv:26), even though the content might fit much of the description implied in the references throughout the *Instruction* texts. Clearly a more extensive literature (and perhaps, concept) is implied. It is much more likely that this title is at least in part self-referential, suggesting the study of *Instruction* itself, as well as *Mysteries* and similar texts that share some understanding of the nature of this knowledge. It is important to recognize that at its root this knowledge is a mystery and it seems doubtful that the authors of any of these texts believed that the entire mystery was contained within any one text. Mysteries of this magnitude and significance could not adequately be explained and studied in such a manner. The word "mystery" rather suggests the exploration, appropriation, and development of a unique, comprehensive worldview of which the authors of

---

and Legal Issues: Proceedings of the Second Meeting of the International Organization for Qumran Studies, Published in Honour of Joseph M. Baumgarten (ed. Moshe J. Bernstein, Florentino García Martínez, and John Irwin Kampen; STDJ 23; Leiden: Brill, 1997), 298-99; Goff, *Discerning Wisdom*, 15.

53. Daniel J. Harrington, S.J., "The *Rāz Nihyeh* in a Qumran Wisdom Text (1Q26, 4Q415-418, 423)," *RevQ* 17 (1976): 549-53; Torleif Elgvin, "Wisdom With and Without Apocalyptic," in *Sapiential, Liturgical and Poetical Texts*, ed. Falk et al., 24-26.

54. Armin Lange, "In Diskussion mit dem Temple: zur Auseinandersetzung zwischen Kohelet und weisheitlichen Kreisen am Jerusalemer Tempel," in *Qohelet in the Context of Wisdom* (ed. A. Schoors; BETL 136; Leuven: Leuven University Press/Peeters, 1998), 113-59.

55. Adams, *Wisdom in Transition*, 245-56.

these texts only provided hints and clues, leaving the reader and/or adherent free to delve further into the revelation of the mystery.[56] The continuous injunction in this composition is the pursuit of the רז נהיה. It "is not so much concealed from the addressees as it is revealed within the instruction of the document. The addressee is exhorted to persevere in grasping the mystery and is to live according to it."[57]

For a discussion of the related term סוד ("council" or "mystery"), see the commentary to 4Q417 1i:8.

אוט ("inner desire")

It is surprising that this enigmatic term has not occasioned more discussion (see DJD 34:31-32, 332). Outside *Instruction* it is found only in 4Q424 1:6. Based on frequency of usage its most significant appearance is in 4Q418 126ii, one of the more philosophical portions of this composition. An analysis of these references supports some relationship of the term to the idea of "mystery" as proposed by Strugnell and Harrington,[58] and does not suggest the feasibility of any translation such as "goodness" (*DSSANT* 487) or "kindness" (*DSSANT* 493; *DSSSE* 2:851, on 4Q416 2ii:12) based on the usage of the term אט and לאט in the HB (BDB 31; *HALOT* s.v. אט). While the proposal that it represents a form of the *nota accusativi* (את) is not convincing (*PEUDSS* 4:xi), it does seem in some manner to relate directly and personally to the addressee. A similar context is evident for the term in 4Q418 81+81a:16. Its partial reconstruction in 4Q418 103ii:6, however, illustrates the more specific contexts in which it can appear (see commentary to that text). Many of the references are in conjunction with the terms חפץ ("requirement" or "desire") or מחסור ("poverty"), frequently of the addressee.[59] This observation leads Goff to understand it as a material term.[60] The material nature of the term is also supported by Wold.[61] I do not

---

56. In addition to the previous notes, the following references permit further exploration of this subject: Lange, "Wisdom and Predestination," 341 n. 3; Torleif Elgvin, "'The Mystery to Come': Early Essene Theology of Revelation," in *Qumran Between the Old and New Testaments*, ed. Cryer and Thompson, 113-50; Goff, *Worldly and Heavenly Wisdom*, 30-79; idem, "Mystery," *EDSS* 1:588-91; DJD 34:32.

57. Wold, *Women, Men and Angels*, 245.

58. DJD 34:31-32. The translation "secret" is also accepted by Jefferies, *Wisdom at Qumran*, 172-73.

59. Overlooked in the listings of the use of the term is 4Q418 138:4, based upon the reading of Tigchelaar and supported by the photographs. Here it also appears in the context of חפץ. See the translation of that fragment below.

60. Goff, *Worldly and Heavenly Wisdom*, 152-53 n. 104.

61. *Women, Men and Angels*, 219. Further, though not convincing, evidence is to be found

find the contexts to be related solely to material issues in a manner that justifies such an interpretation. It is for these reasons that I choose to translate the term "inner desire," thereby attempting to capture the essence of a term that reflects something intensely personal about the addressee(s) and relates to material issues on the basis of the inner disposition or resolve of the human being, hence is in part hidden or even unknown. In 4Q416 2ii:12//4Q418 8:13 we may find a reflection that God also has an "inner desire" and a suggestion concerning the value for the human being to conform to that "inner desire" of the Divine. This translation is preferable to "secret" in 4Q424 1:6.[62]

מבין ("man of discernment")

This handbook of wisdom identifies two persons involved in the instructional task, the משכיל ("sage") and the מבין ("man of discernment"). The addressee in this text is the "man of discernment." Strugnell and Harrington propose for the title of the composition מוסר למבין ("Instruction for the man of discernment"; DJD 34:3). The repeated form of address throughout the text is "and you, O man of discernment."[63] While it appears most frequently in the singular, we also find it employed in plural form.[64] As noted by Goff, the singular is employed as a rhetorical device to enhance direct engagement with the reader.[65] This suggests that there is a body of persons addressed in this text. In 4Q418 123ii:4 we learn that it is to an understanding of the ages "that God uncovered the ear of those who understand (מבינים) through the mystery of existence." The next line begins with the injunction, "You, O man of discernment, when you observe all these things. . . ." In 4Q417 1i:18 it is the individual בן מבין ("son of discernment") who is enjoined to consider the "mystery of existence" (for the discussion of this term, see above); however, within the rhetoric of the document this is an injunction for all the men of discernment. When the man of discernment has absorbed this kind of understanding, then "you will know the difference between the good and evil according to their deeds," arguing that

---

in the recent argument for the term's etymology from the use of אט in Gen 33:14: Tzvi Novick, "The Meaning and Etymology of אוט," *JBL* 127 (2008): 339-43.

62. See DJD 36:339. On the term note also the observations of A. Schoors, "The Language of the Qumran Sapiential Works," in *Wisdom Texts from Qumran*, ed. Hempel et al., 77-78.

63. 4Q416 4:3; 4Q417 1i:1, 13-14, 18; 4Q418 81+81a:15; 102a+b:3; 123ii:5; 168:4; 176:3. The title appears without context in 4Q299 *(Mysteries)* 34:3; 4Q417 1iii:10; 4Q418 117:2; 158:4; 227:1; 273:1; 4Q418a 7:2, 3. 4Q418 17:2 may be a reference to the בן מבין ("son of discernment").

64. 4Q415 11:5; 4Q416 1:16//4Q418 2+2a-c:8; 4Q418 123ii:4; 4Q418 221:3.

65. Goff, *Worldly and Heavenly Wisdom*, 220.

this knowledge is the basis of ethics. Then we learn that "the God of knowledge is the base of truth and with the mystery of existence He spread out her foundation and her deeds" (4Q417 1i:8-9).

To "uncover" or "reveal" is also important in other Qumran texts. We note the leading lines from the initial sections of the *Damascus Document:* "And now, listen, all who know righteousness and understand the deeds of God" (i:1-2); "And now, listen to me, those who enter the covenant, and I will uncover your ear to the ways of the wicked" (ii:2-3); and "And now, sons, listen to me and I will uncover your eyes to see and to understand the deeds of God" (ii:14-15). Apparent is the relationship of this form of address to the phrase from Prov 5:7, 7:24, and 8:32: "And now, sons, listen to me." In Prov 8:32-33 it is "instruction" that the sons are supposed to hear when they are enjoined to listen to God. In 4Q525 14ii:18 we see a glimpse of both *Instruction* and the *Damascus Document* in the line, "And now, man of discernment, listen to me. . . ." In these texts the מבין as addressee is approached in a manner rooted in the wisdom tradition and is dispatched wisdom with a foundation in eschatology, thereby forming the basis for a new direction in wisdom teaching whose influence can be discerned from other compositions now available to us in the Qumran corpus.[66]

For a discussion of the "sage" *(maskil),* a significant figure in a number of Qumran texts, see the introduction to this volume.

חכמה *("wisdom")*

We note some differences between the use of the term חכמה within *Instruction* and in Proverbs. Most apparent is the use of the term to designate the acquisition of a certain skill level, evident in the phrase חכמת ידים ("craftsmanship") found in 4Q418 81+81a:15, 19; 102a+b:3; 137:2; 139:2. With 5 of the 10 references to the term utilized in this manner, they constitute a sizable proportion of the appearances. This phrase is not found in the HB, but is employed in Sir 9:17 (MS A) in an adjectival form, "skilled craftsmen." When we look at the other references we find evidence of other dissimilarities with the term's use in Proverbs. The term also occurs in *Mysteries,* that work most closely related to *Instruction,* in which the largest number of references point to mysteries and hidden wisdom, a connection not apparent in the biblical book. Here we find an understanding of wisdom that is characterized as eternal mysteries that were sealed and available only when one opens the vision, a description that is more

---

66. On the rhetorical significance of this figure see Benjamin G. Wright III, "From Generation to Generation: The Sage as Father in Early Jewish Literature," in *Biblical Traditions in Transmission,* ed. Hempel and Lieu, 309-32.

familiar to us from apocalyptic literature than Proverbs. Of equal significance is the castigation of the reader, perhaps Israel, for not having paid attention to the eternal mysteries. We also find the term used in conjunction with the even more elusive term, **אוט**, which I have discussed above and translate as "inner desire" (4Q416 2ii:12//4Q418 8:13). This term appears to represent a very specific concept unattested in other extant Hebrew literature, hence peculiar to this composition. The role of wisdom in creation and in the fate of the created order is spelled out in 4Q417 1i and in 4Q418 126:4-5. We note the manner in which wisdom in these references is attached to the very specific worldview developed in this composition.

מחסור ("poverty")

The term most characteristic of *Instruction* with regard to the topic of poverty is **מחסור**, attested 25 times in the extant fragments according to the reconstruction of Strugnell and Harrington. This term is almost totally absent from the remainder of the Qumran corpus, and Strugnell cites its use in *Mysteries* and 4Q424 as evidence of literary contacts between these three wisdom compositions.[67] In the HB it is most commonly found in Proverbs.[68] Within Proverbs it is used to designate the poverty that results from laziness or excessive living (6:11; 14:23; 21:5, 17; 22:16; 24:34). However, other terms are used to speak of responsibilities one might have toward the poor (e.g., **ענוים**, 14:21; **דל**, 14:31), those whose social location is defined by poverty. It is almost exclusively a wisdom term in that composition. It is this wisdom term that is used to convey the situation of the addressees in *Instruction*. When offering practical advice with regard to property, marriage, and borrowing money, it is employed to designate the addressee whose social location is one defined by want. The reversal of the use of this central term coupled with the direct address of the person in need is a very surprising development within the wisdom tradition.

מחשבה ("intention")

This is a significant term found in a number of compositions throughout the Qumran corpus. As noted by Lange, in both the "Treatise on the Two Spirits" (1QS iii:13–iv:26) and *Instruction*, the order of creation is derived from **חדעות**

---

67. Strugnell, "Smaller Hebrew Wisdom Texts," 47. Its other occurrences are in 1QH[a] vii:29; 4Q299 (*Mysteries*[a]) 65:3; 4Q424 (*Instruction-Like Composition B*) 1:8. The last two are wisdom texts closely related to *Instruction*.

68. J. David Pleins, "Poor, Poverty: Old Testament," *ABD* 5:407.

אל ("the God of knowledge") and is described using the term מחשבה to designate the "intention" of God in creation.[69] Carol Newsom has pointed to the
semiotic nature of the understanding of God implied in the use of this phrase; it
is not the act of God in creation that gives meaning to the world, it is the God of
knowledge who gives the phenomena of the world meaning through his
מחשבה.[70] See the further note on the "God of knowledge" under the commentary to 4Q417 1i:8 below. This understanding of the relationship of wisdom and
creation is shared between the two documents.[71] While *Instruction* can speak
of the "intention" of God in creation and also address questions of "intention"
to the addressee emerging from the context of God's desire for creation, the
"Treatise on the Two Spirits" has developed this into a more definitive
worldview where the term would more accurately be translated as "plan" rather
than "intention."

התהלך *("walk")*

The Hitpael form of "walk" is common in the HB, but bears a particular ethical
significance in a limited number of compositions in the Qumran corpus, particularly apparent in this composition. This term in this form is attested at least
34 times in the fragments of *Instruction*. Characteristic of its use in this composition is 4Q416 2iii:10//4Q418 9+9a-c:9: "Walk in righteousness so that God will
cause his countenance to shine on all your ways." It is prominent in both the
Community Rule (12 times) and the *Damascus Document* (12 times) as well as in
their Cave 4 MSS (4 times and 7 times, respectively), including lines such as
1QS i:8: "To be united in the assembly of God and to walk before him perfectly,"
or iii:17-18: "He created man to rule the world. He arranged two spirits for him
by which to walk." In 4Q525 it appears 7 times, with leading phrases such as in
2ii+3:3-4: "he shall walk in the law of the Most High."

69. The only reference to the title in HB is 1 Sam 2:3. See 4Q417 1i:8-12//4Q418 43, 44,
45i:6-9; 4Q418 55:5; 4Q299 35:1; 73:3 (on מחשבה see 4Q299 1:5; 3aii-b:5, 10, 11, 13; 10:11; 4Q300
5:1); 1QS iii:15-18; Lange, *Weisheit*, 129; idem, "Wisdom and Predestination," 348.

70. Carol A. Newsom, "Knowing and Doing: The Social Symbolics of Knowledge at
Qumran," *Semeia* 59 (1992): 139-53. See also Martin Hengel, *Judaism and Hellenism* (trans. John
Bowden; 2 vols.; Philadelphia: Fortress, 1974), 1:219.

71. As noted by Lange, "The theology of the Teaching of the Two Spirits is a logical development of the dualism which characterizes the idea of the pre-existent order in 4QSap A" ("Wisdom and Predestination," 348). It is in this light that we must understand his other claim that
they were composed by the same circles. Note also Frey, "Dualistic Thought," 299.

The Addressees and Social Location

The poverty of the circles associated with *Instruction* and the implications of this for the determination of social location have already received attention in the introduction to this volume. In that discussion I developed the distinction between this composition and some other literary exemplars in Second Temple Judaism with regard to the issue of social location. This handbook of wisdom identifies two persons involved in the instructional task, the משכיל ("sage") and the מבין ("man of discernment"). While receiving limited mention in the extant fragments, the "sage" appears to be an important figure in this composition.[72] While there is good evidence that the term designates a significant position in the hierarchy attested in other compositions from the Qumran corpus that are considered sectarian texts, here it would be more accurate to characterize its use as descriptive rather than official. Hence it appears as both noun and participle in this composition. While the man of discernment is referred to as a "son of a sage" in 4Q417 1i:25, he has already been addressed as the "son of the man of discernment" in line 18, there employing the formulaic introduction, ואתה בן מבין ("and you, son of the man of discernment"), found elsewhere throughout the composition without the term "son."[73] In line 18 he is to "consider . . . the mystery of existence and know," and in line 25 he is to "gain in the understanding of your mysteries and in the foundation . . .)." Already he has received notice in line 2 that "you shall be wise to the [fearful] mysteries of the wonde[rs of God]." Evidence of the role of sage as teacher can be found in 4Q418 81+81a:17, even though in this case it is plural: "gain a great deal in understanding and from the hand of every sage grasp even more." Note the use of the same verb, התבונן ("gain in understanding"), in both cases. Since the addressee in this column is identified in the singular, the designation of every sage, suggesting the plural, is a significant indicator of the author's understanding that this is a distinct group or body of persons. However, we note that within the limitations of the fragmentary evidence available to us, there is no role for the "sage" beyond that of teacher.

It is in the term "man of discernment" that we find the primary identification of the addressees in this text. While it appears most frequently in the singular, we also find it employed in plural form.[74] As noted by Goff, the singular is employed as a rhetorical device to enhance direct engagement with the reader.[75]

---

72. Note the discussion of "The 'Sage' in Qumran Wisdom Literature" in the introduction to this volume, 25-28.

73. The reference to בן מבין in line 18 is the only time this phrase appears in the fragments of *Instruction*.

74. 4Q415 11:5; 4Q416 1:16//4Q418 2+2a-c:8; 4Q418 123ii:4; 4Q418 221:3.

75. Goff, *Worldly and Heavenly Wisdom*, 220.

This suggests that there is a body of persons addressed in this text. It is noteworthy that the title some scholars give to this text is מוסר למבין ("Instruction for the man of discernment") (DJD 34:3).[76] Unattested as a title within the text, the more significant designation is found in the repeated form of address throughout the text, ואתה מבין ("and you, man of discernment").[77]

We note that this identification is established in 4Q417 1i, near the beginning of that copy of the composition.[78] While we do not know the relationship of this column to 4Q416 1i,[79] which clearly is the beginning of one manuscript of the text, we do note that there is considerable overlap between 4Q416 2i-ii and 4Q417 2i-ii. The most significant column identifying the social status of the man of discernment is 4Q416 2iii. It is in this column that the addressee is most explicitly given advice about coming to terms with poverty. The significance of this column for the topic has been recognized by Benjamin Wold.[80] At the very beginning of this column in line 2 the addressee is enjoined, "and remember that you are poor." In line 19 the injunction begins, "and if you are poor." Before this conditional statement in this same column we twice read, "you are needy" (lines 8, 12). In the first instance the paragraph introduced by this phrase reads:

> Needy are you. Do not lust after (anything) beyond your inheritance. Do not be consumed by it lest you will remove your boundary. If he will restore you to glory, walk in it and in the mystery of existence search for its birth times. Then you will know his inheritance. Walk in righteousness so that God will cause his countenance to shine on all your ways. Give honor to him who glorifies you and praise his name daily, for he raised your head from poverty. Among the princes he seated you and over an inheritance of glory he gave you authority. Seek his will daily.[81]

76. The appropriateness of the title מוסר למבין could be called into question since the term מוסר is found in the texts of *Instruction* only four times, with two of those references to a parallel text (4Q416 2iii:13//4Q418 9+9a-c:13) and one in a text so fragmentary that it is the only term identified (4Q418 297:1).

77. 4Q416 4:3; 4Q417 1i:1, 13-14, 18; 4Q418 81+81a:15; 102a+b:3; 123ii:5; 168:4; 176:3. The title appears without context in 4Q299 34:3; 4Q417 1ii:10; 4Q418 117:2; 158:4; 227:1; 273:1; 4Q418a 7:2, 3. 4Q418 17:2 may be a reference to the בן מבין ("son of discernment"). In the plural it is found in 4Q415 11:5; 4Q418 2+2a-c:8; 123ii:4; 221:3. The translation of this phrase is mine, based upon an attempt to differentiate the various synonyms for wisdom and knowledge within *Instruction*. Here I translate בינה as "understanding" and "man of discernment" for the phrase under discussion here. For the biblical phrase see Prov 5:7; 7:24; 8:32-33. The Proverbs phrase itself is evident in 4Q525 13:6; 31:1.

78. Note parallels in 4Q418 43,44,45i + 4Q418a:11.

79. Note parallels in 4Q418 1-2+2a-c.

80. "Metaphorical Poverty in 'Musar leMevin,'" *JJS* 58 (2007): 146-48.

81. 4Q416 2iii:8-12//4Q418 9-10 (see commentary for textual details).

Here we find advice from the teacher helping the man of discernment to come to terms with being in need. The advice is not to spend your days lusting after wealth that is not immediately available to you. If you do so, the effort will consume you and you "will remove your boundary," that is, change your aspirations. Your material fate is in the hands of God. You as a man of discernment are enjoined to "walk in righteousness." God will give you your place of honor and raise your head from poverty, even in your state of need. The second paragraph follows immediately:

> Needy are you. Do not say, "I am poor," so I will not seek knowledge. Put your shoulder to all instruction. With all [. . .] refine your heart and with an abundance of understanding your intentions. Search the mystery of existence and gain understanding in all the ways of truth. All the roots of unrighteousness consider and then you will know what is bitter to a man and what is sweet to a fellow.[82]

In this case the student is enjoined not to use poverty as an excuse to abandon the quest for knowledge. Nowhere in biblical or early postbiblical wisdom literature do we find such a direct address to persons in poverty. This form of direct address contradicts Wold's attempt to argue that the interest of *Instruction* in poverty is metaphorical, related to spiritual lack and need.[83]

In both of the texts just cited, the ביון ("poor") is enjoined to "search the mystery of existence." Later in the same column the addressee in poverty is enjoined to search the mystery of existence (a subject discussed among the "Key Terms" above) for the proper treatment of his father and mother and what to do when he takes a wife. The term most characteristic of *Instruction* with regard to the topic of "poverty" is מחסור (also discussed in the list of "Key Terms"). As noted earlier in the introduction to this chapter, the man of discernment in poverty is addressed as an ethically responsible person.[84]

In 4Q418 81+81a, a fragment that is under debate with regard to the priestly associations of the circle of addressees,[85] we read: "You, man of discernment, if he has given you authority over craftsmanship and knowled[ge . . .] . . . From there you will attend to your sustenance . . . gain in understanding and

---

82. 4Q416 2iii:12-15//4Q418 9-10 (see commentary for textual details).

83. Wold, "Metaphorical Poverty."

84. Catherine M. Murphy (*Wealth in the Dead Sea Scrolls and in the Qumran Community* [STDJ 40; Leiden: Brill, 2002], 208) notes the manner in which *Instruction* favors terms relating to lack and poverty from among the typical lexicon of economic terms normally employed in wisdom literature.

85. Tigchelaar, "Addressees of 4QInstruction," in *Sapiential, Liturgical and Poetical Texts*, ed. Falk et al., 73-74.

from the hand of every sage grasp even more" (lines 15-17). In 4Q418 102a+b: 3-4 ["you,] man of discernment, in truth from the skill of all your craftsmanship . . . you walk about and then he will seek your will, for all who inquire of it."[86] Here we find the man of discernment is addressed as craftsman. The injunctions to the farmer and rural landholder are explicitly embedded in the mystery of existence (4Q423 3-5). The relationship of the man of discernment and the craftsman or farmer stands in stark contrast to the portrayal in Sir 38:24-34, where their work is respected but it is not considered the proper work of the scribe/sage and is actually a hindrance to the fulfillment of the scribe's duties and advance in knowledge. The poor addressed in this composition include craftsmen and farmers who have inherited or adopted the outlook advocated therein.

Instruction also includes women as morally responsible agents. 4Q415 2ii is written in the second person feminine, thereby explicitly including female addressees. A feminine addressee, with the exception of some form of hypostatized wisdom, is rather rare in wisdom literature.[87] Strugnell and Harrington suggest a female associate of the man of discernment addressed throughout Instruction (DJD 34:48). Such a proposal misses the corporate nature of the body addressed in the text. The question is not, What is the relationship of the material in this column to the man of discernment? The issue is to determine what the evidence in this column tells us about the nature of that group here addressed as being men of discernment. While the instructions throughout this composition carefully delineate the role of men and women, with the women clearly holding a subordinate place in the social hierarchy, they are addressed as ethical agents who take responsibility for their own actions. The level of their inclusion throughout the composition, then, is rather remarkable.

Within Instruction we find very limited evidence of interest in the temple and priesthood.[88] The major subject under discussion in 4Q423 3-5 is the farmer and his obligations with regard to the sacrificial system. The reference to Korah in frag. 5 does suggest some allusion to the priesthood. The elusive reference in line 1a, added by a later scribal hand, "lest you return to Levi the priest," requires more adequate context for interpretation. The reference to the judgment of Korah and his company in the next line could continue some theme about the criteria for judging the priesthood. The story in Numbers 16 here provides a basis for making judgment upon leading figures. Korah is also

86. See also 4Q418 137:2; 139:2.
87. Wold, Women, Men and Angels, 199-202.
88. Elgvin, "Priestly Sages." This is in contrast to Lange, "In Diskussion mit dem Tempel," 131, 137-40.

referred to in 4Q418a 3:3. While the destruction of Korah and his company would have stirred the imagination of an author who envisioned eternal destruction for those who were of the spirit of flesh, there is no reason to regard it as a reference to some significant division in the sectarian history related to Qumran, as proposed by James M. Scott.[89] In 4Q418 81+81a we find evidence of a viewpoint that is to empower these economically deprived adherents. With the references to having your lot cast with the "holy ones" and the emphasis on "your very great glory," Elgvin's favorable comparison with the *maskilim* in Dan 12:3 who will shine like the sun and with the righteous in *1 En.* 104:2-6 who will shine like the lights of heaven (already discussed above) is viable.

Thus within the circle of the מבינים are farmers, craftsmen, women, slaves, and persons burdened with debt and usury. When we compile this picture we see how different this composition is from the other texts attributed to scribal circles.[90] At the center of this identity is a group addressed as the *mevinim*. Since the center of this group's existence is around an unwritten body of knowledge known as the "mystery of existence," elements of which are explained within *Instruction* but which rely on a continuing oral tradition passed on by "teachers" within the group, this is not public knowledge available to anyone. It is rather an exclusive body of knowledge available only to those who make the commitment to join this group, the first step in appropriating the knowledge of the mystery of existence.[91] Within this group were collected members who do not fit any of the social structures or statuses known to us from extant sources. It does, however, fit within and provide a reframing of the issues for native peoples experiencing the dislocation of urbanization, increasing levels of social stratification, and progressive consolidation of land ownership that characterized the advance of the Hellenistic empires into the Near East.

Bibliography

Note also the bibliography in the introduction to this volume. The periodical literature on this text is vast. Some attempt has been made to include substantial portions of it in the footnotes.

89. Scott, "Korah and Qumran," in *The Bible at Qumran: Text, Shape, and Interpretation* (ed. Peter W. Flint; Grand Rapids: Eerdmans, 2001), 182-202.
90. The multiple addressees included in the second person masculine singular form of address as well as the feminine form and the variety of topics is noted by Tigchelaar ("Addressees of 4QInstruction," 73) and Goff (*Worldly and Heavenly Wisdom*, 219).
91. Tigchelaar, "Addressees of 4QInstruction," 75; note that Elgvin also uses the term "democratization" with regard to 4Q418 81 ("Priestly Sages," 83).

Adams, Samuel L. *Wisdom in Transition: Act and Consequence in Second Temple Instructions.* JSJSup 125. Leiden: Brill, 2008.

Elgvin, Torlief. "An Analysis of 4QInstruction." Ph.D. diss., Hebrew University, 1997.

———. "Priestly Sages? The Milieus of Origin of *4QMysteries* and *4QInstruction.*" In *Sapiential Perspectives: Wisdom Literature in Light of the Dead Sea Scrolls. Proceedings of the Sixth International Symposium of the Orion Center, 20-22 May, 2001.* Ed. John J. Collins, Gregory E. Sterling, and Ruth A. Clements, 67-87. STDJ 51. Leiden: Brill, 2004.

Goff, Matthew J. *The Worldly and Heavenly Wisdom of 4QInstruction.* STDJ 50. Leiden: Brill, 2003.

Jefferies, Daryl F. *Wisdom at Qumran: A Form-Critical Analysis of the Admonitions in 4QInstruction.* Piscataway, N.J.: Gorgias, 2002.

Macaskill, Grant. *Revealed Wisdom and Inaugurated Eschatology in Ancient Judaism and Early Christianity.* JSJSup 115. Leiden: Brill, 2007.

Tigchelaar, Eibert J. C. *To Increase Learning for the Understanding Ones: Reading and Reconstructing the Fragmentary Early Jewish Sapiential Text 4QInstruction.* STDJ 44. Leiden: Brill, 2001.

Wold, Benjamin J. *Women, Men and Angels.* WUNT 2/201. Tübingen: Mohr Siebeck, 2005.

Instruction[b] (4Q416)

Frag. 1 + 4Q418 1,2,2a-c

[1]every spirit [. . .] [2]to determine his desire [. . .] [3]festival by festival [. . .] [4]according to their host for every [dominion . . . for every] [5]kingdom, for every [state, for every man . . .] [6]according to the poverty of their host. [The judgment of all of them is his . . .] [7]The host of the heavens he appointed ov[er . . . and luminaries . . .] [8]for omens of them and signs for their fes[tivals . . . day of his decree] [9]one after another. All the assignment of them [. . .] they shall recount [. . .] [10]in the heavens he will pronounce judgment upon the service of wickedness. All the sons of his truth will be acceptable to [. . .] [11]its end and they will be terrified. All who defiled themselves by it will cry out for the heavens will be afraid [. . .] [12][s]eas and the depths are terrified. Every spirit of flesh shall be laid utterly bare and the sons of the heav[ens . . . on the day of] [13]its [judg]ment and all injustice will cease forever. The epoch of tr[uth] will be realized [. . .] [14]in all

the epochs of eternity, for he is the God of truth and from before the years of [iniquity . . .] [15]so that the righteous can distinguish between good and evil [. . .] every judgme[nt . . .] [16]it is the [in]clination of the flesh. Men of comprehen[sion . . .] [17]his [v]isions for [. . .]

Notes

See the discussion of the evaluation of the fragments for the text of 4Q418 1-2,2a-c under "Manuscripts" in the introduction to this chapter. On the various small fragments which could contribute to our reading of this column, particularly lines 9-16, see Tigchelaar, *To Increase Learning*, 69, 74-75.

Line 2: "desire" — חפץ means desire in the sense of what gives God pleasure or delight. The closest parallel to this nonbiblical phrase is found in 4Q424 1:11, where the human being rather than God is the subject. In that case it would seem to designate what God "desires [or 'requires'] if the human being is to live a life of wisdom." It occurs 22 times in the fragments of *Instruction* as well as in various sectarian compositions such as CD, 1QS, and 1QHᵃ. In 4Q525 2iii:3 and in 1QM v:6, 9, 14; xii.13 it is used to describe "precious" or perhaps "pleasing" stones.

Line 4: "host" — צבא is primarily a military term, designating a retinue or an army. It appears 486 times in the HB, mostly in the plural and most often as a divine epithet associated with Yahweh. This is probably related to the understanding that Yahweh led the armies of Israel. It is also common in the phrase "host of heaven" to refer to heavenly bodies, both in personified form and as celestial entities. The heavenly beings constitute a company of beings under the sovereignty of Yahweh, his heavenly army. In this text, as in a good deal of other Second Temple literature, the reference is to the place of these beings in the company of Yahweh that is believed to reflect the created order. This order in heaven reflects the רצון ("desire" or "will") of God in a more immediate manner than the created earthly order.

Lines 4-5: "for every [dominion . . . for every] kingdom, for every [state, for every man . . .]" — While the text is fragmentary and the reconstruction hypothetical (see DJD 34:84), its meaning would appear to be "for each kingdom, each state, each man." See *IBHS* §7.2.3.

Lines 8-9: "[day of his decree] one after another" — This reconstruction is based on 1QS x:7. In that account the rotation of the heavenly bodies in conjunction with the created order and the festival calendar is described as being in order "one after another" (זה לזה), a phrase also found in 1QS x:4. This phrase is rare both in biblical and Qumran texts. Given the subject matter of this column I find this reconstruction preferable to "they shall proclaim" (יגידו) in DJD 34:81, 85.

Line 10: "in the heavens" — Tigchelaar proposes Hebrew בשמים rather than משמים, as found in DJD 34:81 (*To Increase Learning,* 44).

Line 11: "its end" — Although קצה could be "the end," the *Instruction* texts have a strong preference for the use of קץ over the longer קצה. In this case the same third feminine singular suffix would also be the cause of the defilement indicated in the phrase "by it" later in the same line. In both cases the fragmentary text does not permit us to know what that antecedent actually is.

Line 11: "will be terrified" — The meaning of יראו is hard to determine. While it could also be based on the Hebrew root ראה ("to see"), the root ירא ("to fear") seems more likely in context.

Line 13: "its [judg]ment" — The reconstruction of the well-attested noun in this phrase rather than the less frequent Niphal infinitive seems a more likely possibility (DJD 34:86).

Line 14: "from before the years of [iniquity . . .]" — This reconstruction seems more likely than "eternity" (DJD 34:81). In 4Q228 1i:5 we find a reference to the עתי עולה ("times of iniquity") and in 4Q265 7:10 to the קצי עולה ("periods of iniquity"). The proposed reconstruction argues for the antiquity of the God of truth who precedes the limited period of iniquity envisioned in the latter text.

Line 16: "Men of comprehen[sion . . .]" — While other options are available for the reconstruction of this text, it seems most advisable to rely on 4Q418 2,2a-c:8 at this point.

Line 17: "his [v]isions" ([מ]ראתיו) — So little remains of this line as well as of what precedes and follows it that a reconstruction is very difficult. "Creatures" (DJD 34:83) is based on the Niphal participle of ברא ("create"), a relatively rare construction. "Visions" appears to be consistent with the material in the remainder of the column.

Commentary

For a general discussion of the content and significance of this fragment see the introduction. On the description of the judgment see commentary to 4Q418 69.

Line 3: This is apparently a reference to the festal cycle of the Jewish year, but the fragmentary context does not permit us to understand the point of the reference.

Lines 4-5: "according to their host for every [dominion . . .]" — The root of the verb "reign" and the noun "dominion" is probably related to the word *sar* ("official, ruler, leader"; see *HALOT* s.v. שׂרה and שׂרר), a term sometimes employed for the ruling angels in the heavenly host. In this case these lines most likely mean that the ruling heavenly hosts are given areas of jurisdiction in such a way that every kingdom, every state, and every man are under some appointee's jurisdiction in this cosmic scenario. These lines demonstrate the universal nature of the judgment. Note the importance of this perspective for Macaskill (*Revealed Wisdom*, 72-114).

Line 6: "according to the poverty (מחסור) of their host" — The majority of the 26 appearances of this term in the *Instruction* texts and the two references in the *Mysteries* texts apply to the human addressee(s). The cosmological viewpoint of this fragment suggests an integral relationship between the luminaries who have authority to rule creation and humankind that later in the column also faces judgment. The apparent "poverty" or "lack" of the heavenly host may be the result of human activity. Since the hosts of the heavens have dominion, the inverse may also be true; they may bear some responsibility for the "poverty" of the human addressee(s).

Line 9: "All the assignment of them (פקודותם)" — While the most obvious translation would be "their visitation" (cf. DJD 34:83), it is not clear what this would mean. In this literature God is the one who does the visitation in the context of judgment, with the result that there is some "assignment" of their future fate with eternal consequences, hence this translation. Such an interpretation of פקודותם is evident in 4Q287 6:4; in 4Q418 43,44,45i:5//4Q417 1i:7; and in the biblical usage of the phrase "time of their visitation" in passages such as Jer 8:12; 10:15; 46:21; 50:27; 51:18, which always results in calamity or death. This is more likely than projecting some judicial role for the heavenly bodies. See commentary on line 6 above. The "assignment" of their fate is also fundamental to the deterministic viewpoint of the human situation in the important description of Qumran dualism in 1QS (iii:14, 18; iv:6, 11, 19, 26). In some cases, then, the term פקודה should be translated "punishment," reflecting the occasion of God's visitation and judgment.

Line 10: "service of wickedness" (עבודת רשעה) — Harrington and Strugnell prefer the translation "work of wickedness" (DJD 34:83, 85). Since the cosmological viewpoint of this column presumes a realm of good and evil, it is then appropriate to speak about being in service to the realm of evil, the apparent intent of this passage.

Line 12: "sons of the heav[ens . . .]" — For commentary on the significance of these references to the angels, see 4Q418 69.

Line 13: "epoch of tr[uth]" — See DJD 34:86-87 for a discussion of this reconstruction. 'Emet ("truth") is a very common term in this composition, appearing 49 times. There are a total of 221 references to the term in the Cave 4 fragments, more than in the entire HB. This term is ubiquitous in 1QS (43 appearances in *DSSC*) and 1QH[a] (71 appearances in *DSSC*), pointing to its basic significance for sectarian ideology. While unattested elsewhere in the Qumran corpus, the "age of truth" here is an important designation, coupled with the "God of truth" in line 14 and "all the sons of his truth" in line 10, all indications of the importance of the term "truth" to the ideology underlying this composition.

Line 15: "so that the righteous can distinguish between good and evil" (צדיק בין טוב לרע להבין) — This reading is based on the parallel text for this line found in 4Q418 2, 2a-c:7, which in my judgment represents the more likely intent of the passage. The other potential meaning of the passage is "to establish righteousness (in order to determine the difference) between good and evil" (contra DJD 34:87-88).

To "distinguish between good and evil" is not a common biblical phrase but is well attested in Qumran literature found within or related to the wisdom materials (1QH[a] vi:22-23; 4Q300 3:2; 4Q367 3:10; 4Q370 ii:4; 4Q417 1i:8, 17-18; 4Q418 43,44,45i:14). The only biblical reference is significant for wisdom literature, since in 1 Kgs 3:9 Solomon asks God for the ability "to distinguish between good and evil," the exact wording of 4Q418 2, 2a-c:7. This phrase could well lie behind 4Q300 3:2-3//1Q27 1i:2-3: "in order that they would know (the difference) between g[ood and evil, and between falsehood and truth, and that they might understand the mysteries of transgression . . .] all their wisdom." Perhaps the viewpoint developed in this wisdom literature helps to establish the ideological foundation whereby the author of the *Damascus Document* is able "to distinguish (להבדיל) between the clean and the unclean, and to make known the difference between the holy and the common" (CD vi:17-18). This text then provides an instance of where this unique wisdom tradition is altered in the sectarian tradition with its emphasis on purity.

Line 16: "[in]clination of the flesh" (בשר צר[י]) — See the commentary on 4Q417 1ii:12.

Frag. 2, col. i

Since the state of preservation of 4Q417 2i is considerably better than the text of 4Q416 2i:1-20, I will use it as the basic text for this translation and discussion. See the text there with accompanying notes and commentary.

4Q416 2i:21-22+4Q417 2ii:1

(These two lines are the portion of the column that does not have a parallel in 4Q417 2i.)
²¹[. . .] in anger. If you will quickly extend your hand ²²[not to send forth . . . to] ask for your food, for he

Notes

Line 21: "anger. If" — 4Q418 7b:12.

Line 22: "to ask for your food" — 4Q418 7b:13.

Commentary

It is very hard to determine the general topic being discussed. Whether this concerns borrowing and its consequences, the subject that immediately follows these lines, is not clear.

Frag. 2, col. ii + 4Q417 2ii + 4Q418 + 4Q418a (various fragments noted)

¹He opened [his] merc[y . . . to fil]l all the po[verty of his inner desire and to give food] ²to all life. Not [. . . if] he will close his hand then the spirit of all flesh will be gathered in. ³Not [. . . he will stumble by it and] with [his] reproach you will cover your face and with his folly ⁴from imprisonment. However much [money the creditor will charge in interest . . . quickly] repay and you will be equal to him. If a bag ⁵containing your valuables you leave in the [charge of your creditor for the sake of your friend you have giv]en all of your life to him. Quickly give that which ⁶belongs to him and take back [your] bag.

And in your words do not downplay your own spirit. For any amount of money do not exchange the spirit of your holiness, ⁷for there is no price equal [to it. . . . Do not permit any ma]n to turn you aside. With favor eagerly seek his presence and speak according to his language. ⁸Then you will find what you desire [. . . for your reproach you shall not trade him.] Your statutes you shall not abandon, and pay [very careful] attention to your mysteries.

⁹If he will appoint you to his service [there is no rest for you and] no rest for your eyes until you have done ¹⁰[his] command[s. . . . do n]othing additional and if there is something to set [aside . . .] and do not let (anything) remain for him, even money, without ¹¹[. . . lest he will say, "He despised me and fallen . . ."] See how great is the jealousy ¹²[of man and deceitful the heart from all . . .] Also within his desire you grasp hold of service to him and the wisdom of his inner desire ¹³[. . .] you will advise him [and you will be] to him a firstborn son and he will have compassion on you as a man on his only child. ¹⁴[For you are his servant and] his [select]ed.

You, do not trust whatever you hate. Do not be concerned over your distress. ¹⁵[You, be for him as a wi]se [slave.] Also do not debase yourself for someone who is not equal with you. Then you will be ¹⁶[a father to him. . . .] Anyone who does not possess your strength do not strike lest you stumble and your reproach will be very great. ¹⁷[Do not s]ell yourself for money. It is better that you be a servant in spirit. Freely you will serve your taskmasters but for a price ¹⁸you will not sell your honor. You will not pledge away your inheritance lest he take possession of your body. Do not overindulge in food ¹⁹when without clothing. Do not drink wine when without food. Do not seek out luxuries when you ²⁰are lacking bread. Do not glorify yourself in your poverty when you are poor lest ²¹you show disdain for your own life.

Also do not treat with contempt the vessel of your [bo]som.

Notes

Line 1: "all the po[verty]" — 4Q418 7b:14.

Line 2: "[. . . if] he will close" — 4Q418 8:1.

Line 3: "and with [his] reproach" — 4Q418 8:2.

Line 4: "[money]" — 4Q418 8:3.

Line 4: "you will be" — 4Q418 8:4.

Line 5: "containing your valuables you leave in the [charge]" — 4Q418 8:4.

Line 5: "all of your life" — 4Q418 8:5.

Lines 5-6: "that which belongs to him and take back (לו וקח) [your] bag" — Note the alternative reading here in 4Q418 8:5: "so that he will not take (לוא יקח) [your] bag."

Lines 6-7: "For any amount of money do not exchange the spirit of your holiness" — In 4Q418 8:6 this line reads, "For any amount of money do not let the spirit of your holiness speak." The latter text contains the verb "speak" (תאמר), rather than "trade" (מור) (see DJD 34:93, 98). The term מור ("trade, exchange") is not found elsewhere in the fragments of *Instruction*. The text closest in meaning is found in 1QH[a] vi:31: "I will not exchange your truth for money." Those engaged in the process of gaining understanding are enjoined to retain their integrity and their own spiritual identity, regardless of the physical circumstances they are encountering. The implication would be that in this case the "holy spirit" is something resident in each person, at least all those engaged in the process of learning discernment.

Line 7: "you aside. With favor eagerly seek his presence" — 4Q418 8:7.

Line 7: "presence" — Literally "face."

Line 8: "[your reproach]" — This term is in 4Q417 2ii:11, but not reconstructed here in 4Q416. See also the reconstruction of Tigchelaar (*To Increase Learning*, 56, 76-77).

Lines 8-9: "pay [very careful] attention to your mysteries" — The reconstruction of מאדה ("very careful") as an adverb at the beginning of line 9 is based on the proposal of Tigchelaar (*To Increase Learning*, 47, 76). This adverb follows the Hebrew term השמר ("guard" or "pay attention") in 4Q418 123ii:7 and 177:7.

Line 11: "your eyes" — This reconstruction in the middle of the lacuna after "fallen" as found in DJD 34:90, 93, is questioned on good grounds by Tigchelaar (*To Increase Learning*, 46-47, 76) and not included in this translation.

Line 12: "Also" — Following 4Q417 2ii:16, rather than "if."

Line 14: There is no indication in the manuscript at this point of a paragraph break and there continues to be some continuity of argument from the previous section. But I put in this paragraph break to conform to the expectations of English usage.

Lines 14-15: Note that 4Q418 21 has been incorporated into the reconstruction of 4Q418 8 as 8c.

Line 16: "[father]" — This is reconstructed on the basis of 4Q418a 19:3. 4Q417 2ii:20 rather appears to read [לע]בד ("a ser[vant]").

Line 18: "not pledge away" — 4Q417 2ii:23 adds "money" (הון).

Lines 19-21: The right margin of each of these lines moves further to the left, suggesting that either there was a hole in the leather already in antiquity or that it was unsuitable for writing (DJD 34:92). Thus the lines are shorter but letters are not missing.

Tigchelaar proposes that 4Q418 11 overlaps with this text and should be incorporated into the reconstruction of 4Q418 8-9.

Line 21: Tigchelaar notes that the Hebrew preposition ל ("to" or "for") in the phrase "for your own life" is missing from the text in DJD 34:90 (*To Increase Learning*, 47).

Commentary

Line 1: "[inner desire]" — See the discussion of אוט in the "Key Terms" in the introduction to this chapter.

Line 2: "[. . . if] he will close his hand" — See Deut 15:7, in which this expression applies to the אביון ("needy") in the community. In Deut 15:8 the injunction is that you are rather to "open" your hand to meet the need (or "poverty"), whatever it might be. Perhaps this provides the background for the allusion to "poverty" in line 1. In this case we find here some continuation of the concern for the needy (אביון) discussed in the previous column. See commentary to line 16 there.

Line 2: "then the spirit of all flesh will be gathered in" — This appears to be a reference to death (cf. Ps 104:29). The spirit of flesh is a common reference to human beings, also found in line 12 below (cf. 4Q418 2,2a-c:4), presumably its meaning in 4Q417 1i:17 (cf. 4Q418 43,44,45i:13) and 4Q418 81+81a2 (cf. 4Q423 8:1). If these two lines reflect any interest in community maintenance, then the closing of the hand in an economically marginal community can mean death for others. This particular phrase appears elsewhere only in 4Q419 8ii:7.

Line 3: "folly" — אולת is a particular concern in *Instruction* (4Q415 9:5; 4Q417 1i:7; 4Q418 220:3; 243:2; 4Q423 5:7) and in Proverbs, also found in 4Q525 2ii+3:2.

Lines 3-4: "with [his] reproach you will cover your face and with his folly from imprisonment" — This is a difficult sentence to understand. The last word could refer to a prisoner or imprisonment. In Mishnaic Hebrew the term refers to obligation. "To bind" or "to confine" is a frequent meaning of the term in Biblical Hebrew and in the Qumran texts. If it relates to the consequences of indebtedness, imprisonment is a real possibility.

Line 4: "However much [money the creditor will charge in interest . . . quickly] repay" — Deut 23:19-20 forbids charging interest of any kind to "your brothers" (אחיך), but not to foreigners. This would have been an important question for sectarian legislation, where the role of the "brother" or "fellow" was so important. The Talmud qualifies this by permitting the payment of interest, an issue not addressed in the biblical text (*b. B. Metzia* 70b). Due to the lacuna in the text it is difficult to determine whether the injunction for repayment applies directly to this stipulation.

Lines 5-6: It is unclear what the role of the "friend" in this line is. It seems more likely that the meaning of בעד ("for the sake of") suggests borrowing to help out a friend rather than borrowing money from someone because he is your friend (*DSSANT* 486-87).

Lines 6-13: Whether the "man of discernment" here is receiving instructions with regard to the treatment of a human or divine superior is perhaps an open question (DJD 34:11). Harrington and Strugnell see the divine referent in lines 6-9, and then change to a human superior in the rest of the section.[92]

Line 7: "speak according to his language" — This interesting allusion perhaps finds explanation in particular attention to issues of language in some of the Qumran literature.[93] Jefferies points to the requirement of the "overseer" to "master the language," stated in CD xiv:9-10 (*Wisdom at Qumran*, 175-76).

Line 8: "Then you will find what you desire" — The Hebrew term חפץ has the more common translation of "desire," but here "require" may more adequately reflect the context. It refers to the "desires" of God, what is pleasing to God or reflects in the will of God. So here when it refers to a human being it seems better to translate it to refer to what God desires of humans. For the term in a judicial context see Isa 58:1-2. For a similar use in CD xiv:12, see Jefferies (*Wisdom at Qumran*, 145-46).

Lines 8-9: "Your statutes you shall not abandon, and pay [very careful] attention to your mysteries" — We must remember that this is instruction for the "man of discernment." This would appear to be an injunction that the "son of discernment" not abandon his own principles (i.e., of God, perhaps in a manner similar to the stories of Daniel) in the service of his superior (see DJD 34:99-100).

Line 12: "wisdom of his inner desire" — See discussion of both "wisdom" and "inner desire" under "Key Terms" in the introduction to this chapter.

Line 14: "Do not be concerned over your distress" — This is a very difficult phrase to translate because of two rather rare words in it, שקד and מדהבה. The closest parallel to the phrase as a whole is in 4Q267 (D[b]) 9iv:6, which Baumgarten translates, "watch over . . . in their distress (DJD 18:108). This interpretation follows a frequent reading of the term מדהבה in Isa 14:4 as מרהבה on the basis of 1QIsa[a] (e.g., note *HALOT* s.v. מדהבה). As Eileen Schuller points out, however, other Qumran texts also have the same consonants as are present here: 4Q427 7ii:3; 4Q431 2:2; 1QH[a] xi:26; xx:21; 4Q418 176:3 and CD xiii:9 (DJD 29:105). The translation as "oppressor" (DJD 29:99) is more comprehensive,

92. DJD 34:93, 97-105; *DSSANT* 487. Note also Jefferies, *Wisdom at Qumran*, 175-76.
93. William M. Schniedewind, "Qumran Hebrew as an Antilanguage," *JBL* 118 (1999): 235-52.

even though it may include the "oppressive tax-gatherer" (DJD 34:93). Since the term is so elusive, a biblical *hapax legomenon* in Isa 14:4, it seems better here to translate it with a more general meaning.[94] The term מדהבה also occurs in 4Q418a 16:3.

Line 15: "[wi]se [slave]" rather than "slave of a sage" — See also Sir 7:21; 10:25.

Line 16: "lest you stumble" — כשל is rather significant among the sectarian writings from Qumran.[95]

Line 17: "your taskmasters" (נוגשיכה) — This term is also found in Isa 14:4. See my commentary to line 14 above.

Line 18: "You will not pledge away your inheritance lest he take possession of your body" — Presumably the meaning of this line is that if you give your inheritance as collateral on something like a loan, you may have endangered your future welfare, for if you are unable to repay the loan, your inheritance becomes the property of another. This may be a reference to slavery as the result of indebtedness during the Greco-Roman era.

Line 20: "poor" — The Hebrew terms רוש (verb) and ריש (noun) are found throughout *Instruction,* but appear elsewhere in the wisdom corpus from Qumran only at 4Q525 15:1 in the noun form and in other Qumran texts as verbs at 1QH[a] x:36; xiii:16, 22; 4Q372 1:17. See the discussion of "Social Location" above.

Line 21: "Do not treat with contempt the vessel of your [bo]som (כלי הכקיח)." Pierre Benoit suggested (orally, DJD 34:109) that this reference contributes to the solution for understanding 1 Thess 4:4: "to take control of his own vessel (τὸ ἑαυτοῦ σκεῦος κτᾶσθαι) with sanctity and honor," the meaning of which has been the subject of debate throughout Christian history. In the wake of the identification of the similarity of this Qumran passage to the Pauline verse, two major interpretations still hold sway. Strugnell and Harrington argue that the

94. This is the case in *DSSSE* (1:167) for 1QH[a] xi:25 (xi:26 in DJD 40); see DJD 34:104; Jefferies, *Wisdom at Qumran,* 178. On this term in the Qumran materials see also Catherine Murphy, *Wealth,* 40-44, 180-82.

95. Esther G. Chazon, "Is *Divrei Ha-Me'orot* a Sectarian Prayer?" in *The Dead Sea Scrolls: Forty Years of Research* (ed. Devorah Dimant and Uriel Rappaport; STDJ 10; Leiden: Brill, 1992), 14-15; James E. Harding, "The Wordplay between the Roots כשל and שכל in the Literature of the Yahad," *RevQ* 19 (1999): 69-82.

"vessel" refers to the wife and concerns all matters that fall under the heading of honor, not just the prohibition of contempt or sexual misuse (DJD 34:108-9).[96] On the basis of the use of the word "vessel" (כלי) in 1 Sam 21:5 and postbiblical literature, Elgvin argues that it refers to the male sexual organ.[97] The point then is to wear proper clothing that covers the "vessel" in a modest manner. While I am more inclined to accept the second argument, the most important point is the recognition that the question needs to be resolved in such a way that it acknowledges the similarity of and possible connection between the two passages.

Frag. 2, col. iii + 4Q418 9-10

[2]Remember that you are poor [. . .] and your want [3]you shall not find. In your disloyalty [. . .] designate you [4]you shall not stretch forth your hand for it lest it be scorched and with its fire your body will be consumed. Ju[st as you to]ok it, so return it. [5]J . . . oy to you if you are innocent of it.

Also, from any man whom you do not know, do not take money [6]lest he will add to your poverty. If he places it on your head, assume responsibility for it to the point of death but do not let your spirit be corrupted [7]by it. Then you will lie with the truth and in your death your memory will blo[om for]ever and after you [i.e., your death] you will inherit [8]joy.

Needy are you. Do not lust after (anything) beyond your inheritance. Do not be consumed by it lest you will remove [9]your boundary. If he will restore you to glory, walk in it and in the mystery of existence search for its birth times. Then you will know [10]his inheritance. Walk in righteousness so that God will cause his countenance to shine on all your ways. Give honor to him who glorifies you [11]and praise his name daily, for he raised your head from poverty. Among the princes he seated you and over an inheritance [12]of glory he gave you authority. Eagerly seek his desire daily.

Needy are you. Do not say, "I am poor," so I [13]will not seek knowledge. Put your shoulder to all instruction. With all [. . .] refine your heart and with an abun

96. See here also J. Strugnell, "More on Wives and Marriage in the Dead Sea Scrolls: (4Q416 2 ii 21 [Cf. 1 Thess 4:4] and 4QMMT § B," *RevQ* 17 (1996): 537-47. Note also the excursus in DJD 34:109-10.

97. Torleif Elgvin, "'To Master His Own Vessel': 1 Thess 4.4 in Light of New Qumran Evidence," *NTS* 43 (1997): 604-19.

dance of understanding [14]your intentions. Search the mystery of existence and gain understanding in all the ways of truth. All the roots of unrighteousness [15]consider and then you will know what is bitter to a man and what is sweet to a fellow.

Honor your father in your poverty [16]and your mother with the little you have, for as God is to a man, thus is his father, and as angels are to a young man, thus his mother. For [17]they are the furnace of your conception. Just as he gave them authority over you and formed (you) according to the spirit, so serve them. Just as [18]he has uncovered your ear to the mystery of existence glorify them for the sake of your own glory [. . .] honor before them [19]for the sake of your life and the length of your days.

If you are poor as [. . .] [20]without statute. If you take a wife in your poverty, take the birth [times . . .] [21]from the mystery of existence in your union. Walk together with the helpmate of your flesh [. . .]

Notes

Line 3: "designate you" — Some term relating to a loan or pledge probably precedes this (DJD 34:114).

Line 5: "J . . . oy" — There is apparently a *vacat* in the middle of the word. Harrington and Strugnell indicate that this was due to an unsuitable writing surface (DJD 34:111).

Line 8: "Do not be consumed by it" — The Hebrew verb בלע can mean either "to swallow, engulf, destroy" or "to confuse," in the passive voice, "to be confused" (respectively, *HALOT* s.v. I, III). A play on these two meanings can be found in Hos 8:7-8, where we find that "strangers devour it" in v. 7 and "Israel is confused [or 'bewildered']" in v. 8. Here in the text under consideration, the context suggests the paralyzing effects of lust, which are more likely to result in "being consumed" than in "being confused." The only other place in the Qumran texts where the root is employed in the Hitpael form is 1QH[a] xi:15 and a parallel text. This reference appears to have its basis in Ps 107:27, in which it refers to "being confused" (see DJD 40:155 for this translation). In *Instruction* the term is also used in this sense in 4Q417 2i:3//4Q418 9+9a-c:7. While the term also appears in 4Q418 16:4 in the DJD version, see my notes there for a different reading.

Line 9: "to glory, walk in it" — In this fragment the preposition and pronoun בה ("in it") are attached directly to the word "to glory," an unusual construction and presumably a scribal error. They apparently are identified as two words in the parallel text, 4Q418 9+9a-c:8, even though only small dots remain for the letters on the line at that point.

Line 11: The term for "poverty" here is ראש rather than the more common ריש. This orthography is also found in the parallel text, 4Q418 9+9a-c:11, as well as in 4Q416 2i:4.

Line 16: "with the little you have" — The reading of this term is based on the parallel in 4Q418 9+9a-c:17. The Hebrew term is מצער ("little, few"), rather than מצעד ("footstep") (contra DSSSE 2:852-53; cf. DJD 34:110, 112).

Line 16: "for as God is to a man" — A literal translation of this text would be "for as a father is to a man." Presumably the mention of "father" in this case is a reference to God. Such a reading is confirmed by the parallel text of 4Q418 9+9a-c:17.

Line 16: "as angels are to a young man" — The insightful proposal that the term אדנים means "angels" rather than "masters" or "gods" is advanced by Wold (*Women, Men and Angels,* 149-55).

Commentary

Line 2: "poor" — The Hebrew terms רוש (verb) and ריש (noun) occur in this column in lines 2, 6, 11, 12, 15, 19, 20, and throughout *Instruction,* but appear elsewhere in the Qumran wisdom corpus only at 4Q525 15:1 in the noun form and as a verb at 1QH[a] x:36; xiii:16, 22; 4Q372 1:17. See the discussion of "Social Location" above.

Lines 3-5: This instruction not to touch money entrusted to one appears to be contradicted in the NT, where Jesus, in the parable of the talents, appears to teach the opposite (Matt 25:14-30; Luke 19:11-27).[98]

---

98. George J. Brooke, *The Dead Sea Scrolls and the New Testament* (Minneapolis: Fortress, 2005), 23; idem, "The Pre-Sectarian Jesus," in *Echoes from the Caves: Qumran and the New Testament* (ed. Florentino García Martínez; STDJ 85; Leiden: Brill, 2009), 47-48.

Line 8: "Needy" — On אביון see commentary to 4Q417 2i:16, 17 below.

Lines 8-9: "remove your boundary" — Injunctions against moving the boundary of a neighbor are noted in Deut 19:14, because one is tampering with the inheritance that God established with the "first" to inherit the land. This injunction receives further warrant in Deut 27:17 when anyone who removes the boundary of his neighbor is cursed. The author of *Instruction* probably adopted the phrase from Prov 22:26-28 and 23:10-11, where it appears in the context of discussions of the responsibilities related to wealth and poverty. Note the well-known use of the phrase in CD v:20, where the "removers of the boundary" appear at the time of destruction and cause Israel to go astray. In CD "the boundary" has become a metaphor used to designate the religious and cultural legacy with its attendant prescriptions of a proper way of life rather than the literal markers designating the legacy of plots of land. In *Instruction* the concern about removing the boundary has to do with the religious and personal effects of lusting after something that is beyond you or not yours. This is seen as a degradation or removal of your true inheritance, the religious birthright that is the concern of the author.

Lines 9, 12, 18: "glory" — See commentary to 4Q417 2i:11 below.

Lines 9, 10, 21: "walk" — This use of the verb הלך in the Hitpael form is common throughout *Instruction* and appears to relate to the particular way of life being taught in the text. Elsewhere it is found most frequently in the manuscripts of the *Community Rule* and the *Damascus Document,* as well as in 5Q525, all with a similar meaning. See discussion of "Key Terms" in the introduction to this chapter.

Lines 9, 14, 18, 21: "mystery of existence" — See the introduction.

Line 9: "birth times" — See the commentary to 4Q417 2i:11 below.

Line 11: "princes" — The נדיבים are attested elsewhere in the fragments of *Instruction* and in CD vi:4, 8, as well as scattered throughout other Qumran texts. In *Instruction,* whether they are "noblemen" by virtue of political power or by advanced knowledge is not clear. The verbal root, appearing most commonly in 1QS and 4QS texts in the Hitpael form, refers to voluntary or exclusive dedication. The Greek translation of this same root is also found in 1 Macc 2:42 with regard to the Hasideans.

In this particular passage, "princes" or "noblemen" may be used in a metaphorical sense (see 4Q417 2i:5 below) to designate the nature of the fate of the addressees who adhere to the "mystery of existence." In this case their head will be raised from poverty and over an "inheritance of glory" they have been given authority. This appears to point to the manner in which the lot of the righteous is shared with the angels. Their spirit shares in the eternal lot of the angels in the presence of the Divine. This suggests an understanding of some form of eternal existence for the righteous without the concept of resurrection.[99]

Line 12: "Eagerly seek his desire daily" — This reference to Hebrew חפץ refers to the "desire" or "will" of God in terms of what God wants from human beings, hence designating in this text the nature of wisdom.

Line 14: "intentions" — The Hebrew term מחשבות is very important in some significant Qumran texts. It is well attested throughout *Instruction* as well as in the *Mysteries* texts. It also is present in sectarian texts such as the *War Scroll* and the *Hodayot,* and especially in the section of the *Community Rule* known as the "Treatise on the Two Spirits" (1QS iii:13–iv:26). These "intentions" are rooted in God's plan for creation and for the role of humankind within it. The future of creation and of each individual is rooted in God's "intention" for creation. In "The Treatise on the Two Spirits" this preexistent order for creation determines the lot of each individual.[100]

Lines 15-16: "Honor your father in your poverty and your mother with the little you have, for as God is to a man, thus is his father, and as angels are to a young man, thus his mother" — This injunction to honor both father and mother betrays similarities to the penalties listed in 4Q270 (Dᵉ) 7i:13b-15a in which "murmuring against" the fathers results in permanent expulsion from the community while the same action with regard to the mothers results in ten days of punishment.[101]

Lines 15-19: This section on family relationships, more specifically on the fifth commandment, has certain similarities to the NT teachings on the topic, most

---

99. Goff, *Worldly and Heavenly Wisdom,* 206-14. For an extensive analysis of the role of the relationship of the addressees and the angels in creation, in life, and in the future, see Wold, *Women, Men and Angels,* 124-82. For commentary on the significance of these references to the angels see 4Q418 69.

100. On this term see Lange, *Weisheit,* 126-32; idem, "Wisdom and Predestination," 346-48; DJD 34:171-72.

101. Cecilia Wassen, *Women in the Damascus Document* (SBLAcBib 21; Atlanta: SBL, 2005), 184-97.

apparently in the household codes as found in Eph 5:21–6:9 and Col 3:18–4:1.[102] In his study Jean-Sébastian Rey notes the manner in which this section in *Instruction* is a literary unit, bracketed by a quotation from Deut 5:16, with connections to Eph 6:1-4.[103] He observes that this usage is peculiar to *Instruction* and to Eph 6:1-4, but absent from Col 3:20-21, a likely source for the Ephesians passage. Common to their usage of the passage from Deuteronomy is the omission of the reference to "the land which God gives you."

Line 16: "for as God is to a man, thus is his father, and as angels are to a young man, thus his mother" — The suggestion that this section of the composition is based on an interpretation of Gen 1:26 has been advanced and developed by Wold (*Women, Men and Angels*, 149-55). In this case the plural form in Gen 1:26, "let us make humankind in our image," quite possibly refers to angels participating with God in creation.

Line 18: "uncovered your ear to the mystery of existence" — This phrase also appears in 1Q26 1:4; 4Q418 10a-b:1; 123ii:4; 184:2; 190:2; 4Q423 5:1, the first part ("uncovered your ear") in 4Q299 8:6. The phrase "to uncover your ear" is found in Isa 22:14, with regard to revelation concerning the consequences of the iniquity of Israel. In Job 33:16 and 36:10 the revelation concerns מוסר ("instruction" or "discipline"). In Job 36:15 God "opens their ear" by oppression or affliction. See the introduction for a discussion of the "mystery of existence."

Lines iii:19–iv:6: The precise content of this fragmentary section is difficult to determine. Its exegetical base is Gen 2:18, 24. While there is no direct evidence that this text relates to the legislation concerning polygamy and divorce in 11Q19 lvii:17-19 and CD iv:12-v:11, the remaining fragments do not provide a clear explanation for the apparent emphasis. The reference in iv:6, "removed a boundary over his life," suggests the legal importance of this section. As noted in the commentary to lines 8-9 above, the concern here is about the boundary of the religious and personal life of the addressee as a member of Israel, hence metaphorical, rather than a statement about an inheritance of land. In the history of Jewish law the Qumran texts contain legislation prohibiting divorce, in contrast to the evidence from the early rabbinic tradition. While we do not find evidence of the practice of polygamy in these same rabbinic materials, we also do not find texts prohibiting it. Thus the Qumran texts demonstrate a different

---

102. Jean-Sébastian Rey, "Family Relationships in *4QInstruction* and in Eph 5:21–6:4," in *Echoes from the Caves*, ed. García Martínez, 231-55.

103. Ibid., 233-42.

legislative tradition concerning divorce and polygamy within the Jewish community at the turn of the eras. This same prohibition of divorce appears in the NT as well. Gen 2:24 is used as the exegetical basis for the prohibition of divorce in Matt 19:5-6, also cited in 1 Cor 6:16 and Eph 5:31.

Line 20: "birth [times . . .]" — See commentary to 4Q417 2i:11 below.

Line 21: "together" — This term, יחד, used as an adverb throughout *Instruction* (at least 12 times), becomes a self-designation for the sect, translated "community," in the manuscripts of the *Community Rule, Rule of the Congregation,* and other compositions emerging from the sectarian life described in some of the Qumran scrolls. See discussion under "Literary Questions" in the introduction to 4Q525. The phrase "walk together" is also found in 4Q525 14ii:15.

Line 21: "Walk together with the helpmate of your flesh" — In his study Rey discusses the relationship of this section (iii:19–iv:13) to Eph 5:21-33.[104] He notes that this emphasis on the unity of the couple, interpreted much more broadly than in sexual terms, is accentuated by mention that they become one flesh (iv:1, 4), a reference to Gen 2:24, and also used in Eph 5:31. This unity also finds mention in iv:5, "You shall be together with the wife of your bosom, for she is the flesh of your nak[edness]," thereby placing this literary section in the context of the story of the creation of woman in Gen 2:21-25, especially 2:23. A similar reference to this story can be found in Eph 5:28c-31. Also found in Eph 5:32 is the word μυστήριον ("mystery"), a suggestive allusion to the "mystery" or "mystery of existence" of *Instruction.*

Frag. 2, col. iv + 4Q418 10

¹his father [and] his mother and cli[ng to his wife and they will be one flesh.] ²He has given you authority over her [. . . her father] ³he did not give authority over her. From her mother he separated her and for you [is her longing. She shall be] ⁴to you as one flesh. Your daughter he shall separate for another and your sons [. . .] ⁵You shall be together with the wife of your bosom, for she is the

104. Ibid., 242-55. Also note the discussion of this section by Menahem Kister, "Divorce, Reproof, and Other Sayings in the Synoptic Gospels: Jesus Traditions in the Context of 'Qumranic' and Other Texts," in *Text, Thought, and Practice in Qumran and Early Christianity: Proceedings of the Ninth International Symposium of the Orion Center for the Study of the Dead Sea Scrolls and Associated Literature, Jointly Sponsored by the Hebrew Center for the Study of Christianity* (ed. Ruth A. Clements and Daniel R. Schwarz; STD 84; Leiden: Brill, 2009), 195-229, see 203-7.

flesh of your nak[edness . . .] ⁶Whoever has authority over her besides you, he has removed a boundary of his life.

Over [her spirit] ⁷he has given you authority to walk according to your desire and not to increase the vow or the freewill offering. ⁸Turn her spirit to your desire and every binding oath, every v[ow . . .] ⁹nullify by the utterance of your mouth. According to your desire restrain [her . . . the utterance] ¹⁰of your lips. Forgive her [. . .] for your sake do not let her increase [. . .] ¹¹your glory in your inheritance [. . .] ¹²with your inheritance lest [. . .] ¹³wife of your bosom and reproach [. . .]

Notes

Line 1: While there is a good possibility that this line is based on Gen 2:24, Tigchelaar notes that the reconstruction is even more hypothetical than the text in DJD 34:123 would suggest (*To Increase Learning*, 48).

Line 8: "her spirit" — Strugnell and Harrington propose an emendation from the apparent reading of "your spirit" based on the parallel to lines 6-7, found in full form in 4Q418 10a-b:8 (see DJD 34:129).

Line 10: "your lips" — An emendation to "her lips" is similarly proposed for this text, also based on the reading in Num 30:13.

Commentary

Line 1: "his father [and] his mother and cli[ng to his wife and they will be one flesh]" — Gen 2:24 is not cited in those sections of the scrolls that deal with prohibitions of polygamy and perhaps divorce, such as 11Q19 lvi:18; lvii:15-19; CD iv:19-v:2. It is cited in NT passages dealing with these issues: Matt 19:5-6; Mark 10:8; 1 Cor 6:16; Eph 5:31.[105]

Lines 2-7: "He has given you authority over her" — This repeated theme in these lines is noteworthy and brings Gen 3:16 into this section in conjunction with Gen 2:21-25, especially 2:24 (see commentary to iii:21 above). A specific issue here is the husband's obligation to take on the vows and oaths of the wife, or to permit her to make them, thereby giving him responsibility for carrying out

---

105. See Lutz Doering, "Marriage and Creation in Mark 10 and CD 4-5," in *Echoes from the Caves*, ed. García Martínez, 142.

those obligations. It is worthwhile to look at this section in conjunction with Eph 5:21-24 and Col 3:18, the household codes of the NT.[106]

Line 5: "together" — See discussion in the introduction to 4Q525 under "Literary Questions."

Line 6: "removed a boundary" — See commentary to iii:9 above.

Lines 6-13: This section finds its biblical basis in Num 30:3-15 concerning vows made by women, with particular reference to v. 13. There is no hint in the fragments of the biblical limitation on the stipulation that the father or the husband can nullify the woman's vow only if acting immediately on hearing of it. The authority of the husband is more absolute in *Instruction* than in the biblical text. In line 10 note that the injunction to forgive has replaced the biblical expression that "the Lord will forgive her" in Num 30:12. In 11Q19 liii:16–liv:3 the biblical injunction is for the most part repeated. Then in 11Q19 liv:4-5 the particular cases of the widow and divorcee are mandated. In this case their vows are valid, presumably affirming their independent legal status. In CD xvi:10-12 the husband may annul the oath, but only if he is aware of its nature and able to evaluate it.

Line 7: "walk" — See commentary to 4Q416 2iii:9 and 4Q417 19:4.

Frag. 3

[1][...] your welfare and with your inheritance [...] [2][...] for from him is the inheritance of all life. By his hand is the visit[ation ...] [3][...]not be at peace until wickedness has come to an end. For there is wrath in every a[ge ...] [4][...] distress will not perish, for great is the loving-kindness of God. There is no end [...] [5][...] your [na]me praise very [...] [6][...] in everything that [...] [7][...] with the host [...]

Commentary

Line 4: "great is the loving-kindness of God" — See also 4Q417 1ii:8.

106. Rey, "Family Relationships," 248-52.

Frag. 4

¹ti[me of] wrath, for he who loves [. . .] ²anger for against them the furnace will
be stoked [. . .]

³You, man of discernment, rejoice in the inheritance of truth [. . .]

Notes

Line 1: "ti[me of] wrath" — Both the singular קץ and the plural קצי ("times")
are attested in the Qumran fragments, so it is difficult to determine the original
reading in this reconstruction.

Commentary

Line 3: "man of discernment" — On this frequent designation see the introduction to this chapter.

Line 3: "truth" — The term אמת appears 45 times in the fragments of *Instruction*. It also is found a number of times in the very limited fragments of 4Q420-
421. Elsewhere in the Qumran documents it is ubiquitous throughout 1QS, CD,
and 1QH, along with the accompanying fragments of their multiple MSS. These
three compositions are primary descriptions of the sectarian life and thought
attested among the Qumran scrolls and the presence of this term constitutes
one piece of evidence for the continuation of the centrality of wisdom themes
in that literature.

Frag. 5, col. i

This fragment has a few letters in a second column.
¹[. . .] which is appointed[. . .] ²[. . .] who does not appoint you ³[. . .] if it does
not increase

Commentary

Line 3: It is impossible to determine the topic of this fragment. Thus whether it
is a person or an object, such as money, that does not increase cannot be determined.

Frag. 6

[1][. . .] with your judgments thus he desires [. . .]

Frag. 7

See 4Q418 77:2-4.

Frag. 8

[1][. . .] his [he]art and to pros[per . . .]

Frag. 9

[1][. . .] when she is pregnant [. . .]

Frag. 10

[1][. . .] and also [. . .]

Frag. 11

[1][. . .] and you will be [. . .]

Notes

While this verb is written in the perfect form, it is more likely to be future in context, though that is extremely difficult to determine.

Frag. 14

[2][. . .] to all [. . .]

Frag. 16

[2][. . .] by the spirit [. . .]

Frag. 17

²[. . .] your favor ³[. . . myst]ery of existence. Know ⁴[. . .] your house [. . .] ⁵[. . .] utterance of your mouth [. . .]

Notes

Line 5: For this reading see DJD 34:138 and Tigchelaar (*To Increase Learning,* 49).

Frag. 18

²[. . .] and the fruit of his tongue [. . .] ³[. . .] when you go out [. . .] ⁴[. . .] their deeds [. . .]

Notes

Only isolated words can be found on the remaining frags. 19-22.

Frag. 23

¹knowledge of your service [. . .]

Notes

These words are found in a fragment from an American museum catalog identified and classified by Esther and Hanan Eshel as 4Q416 23.[107] The same phrase is found in 4Q418 148ii:5. See the discussion of "Manuscripts" in the introduction to this chapter for details.

---

107. Esther and Hanan Eshel, "A Preliminary Report on Seven New Fragments from Qumran," in *Meghillot,* ed. Bar-Asher and Tov, 277-78.

Instruction[a] (4Q415)

Frag. 1, col. i

³[. . .] to whomever ⁴[. . .] you will find ⁵[. . .] and [your] reproach [. . .]

Notes

The placement of the order in which these fragments should appear is enhanced by the MS of the verso, 4Q414. The ink of the verso is apparent on the photographs of some of the fragments of 4Q415, even though quite faint.

Line 5: "[your] reproach" — This reconstruction is based on a possible overlap with 4Q418 178 (Tigchelaar, *To Increase Learning*, 31).

Frag. 1, col. ii and Frag. 2, col. i

Each of these two fragments appears to contain portions of one original column. My line numbers follow frag. 2, since that contains the more substantial portion of the preserved text.
¹[. . .] a[l]l ²[. . .]measure of his deeds ³[. . .] his [wa]ys when he walks in perfection ⁴[. . .] forever and the seed of ⁵your holiness not [. . . f]or your seed will not depart ⁶from the inheritance of [. . .] You will rejoice in the fruit of ⁷[. . .] princes ⁸[. . . for al]l times it will sprout ⁹[. . .] and be renewed

Notes

Lines 4-9: Tigchelaar has proposed 4Q418 14, 234, 235, and 236 as parallels to 4Q415 1ii-2i:4-9 (*To Increase Learning*, 31-32, 225-30).

Line 5: "will not depart" — It is impossible to determine on paleographic grounds whether this is the Qal form ("depart") or the Hiphil form ("remove") of the verb מוש, given the similarity of the *yod* and the *waw* in this MS.

Commentary

Line 3: "walks in perfection" — This is a common phrase in Qumran texts, particularly in 1QS to speak about adherence to the sectarian lifestyle. תמים ("perfection") appears at least eight times in 11Q19, emphasizing its significance for the ideological basis of the legislation in that composition. Also see commentary to 4Q416 2iii:9 and 4Q417 19:4.[108]

Line 5: "holiness" — This term is much less common in the Qumran scrolls than in the biblical and rabbinic materials. Tigchelaar suggests its placement here is evidence of the sacerdotal interests expressed in certain sections of this composition (*To Increase Learning*, 225-30, 235-36).

Line 7: "princes" — See commentary to 4Q416 2iii:11 above, where I discuss the relationship of this term to some angelic status.

Frag. 2, col. ii

¹like a father honor [. . .] ²do not cease in your heart [. . .] ³all the day and in his bosom [. . .] ⁴lest you will break the hol[y] covenant [. . .] ⁵and you will be an enemy to your own soul [. . .] ⁶[. . .] until [. . .] ⁷in the house of [your ori]gin and with your covenant [. . .] ⁸ praise [. . .] all men [. . .] ⁹[. . .] from the placement of birth times

Notes

Line 1: Both Strugnell and Harrington (DJD 34:47) and Tigchelaar (*To Increase Learning*, 33) propose reading "father-in-law" later in this line.

Line 4: "break" — This use of the verb פרע in this sense is common in Rabbinic Hebrew.

Line 5: "you will be an enemy to your own soul" — This unusual Hebrew construction could be a reversal of the stated expectation in Exod 23:22, "if . . . you do all that I say, then I will be an enemy to your enemies and a foe to your foes."

---

108. See Brent A. Strawn with Henry W. Morisanda Rietz, "(More) Sectarian Terminology in the *Songs of the Sabbath Sacrifice*: The Case of תמימי דרך," in *Qumran Studies: New Approaches, New Questions* (ed. Michael Thomas Davis and Brent A. Strawn; Grand Rapids: Eerdmans, 2007), 53-64.

Commentary

This column is unusual in that the limited fragments suggest a female addressee. Strugnell and Harrington suggest a female associate of the "man of discernment" who is addressed throughout *Instruction* (DJD 34:48). This column is significant since the female addressee is being instructed as a morally responsible individual capable of making her own decisions and responsible for her own actions. The apparent call for loyalty and the dangers of breaking the holy covenant suggest a theme that could have been important to sectarian leaders.

Line 9: "placement of birth times" — See commentary to 4Q417 2i:11 below.

Frag. 4

¹[. . .] the[ir] deeds [. . .] ²[. . .] because [. . .]

Frags. 5 + 3

¹young she[ep . . .] ²in all the pa[ths . . .]

Notes

Lines 1-2: The reconstruction in this line is based on the proposed parallel with 4Q418 172:6 (Tigchelaar, *To Increase Learning*, 33-34). The relatively rare Hebrew term עשתרות, attested in Deut 7:13; 28:4, 18, 51, in that context designates the "offspring" of the flock, included as part of the livestock and in parallel construction with the cattle. It is doubtful that the name of the goddess Astarte (עשתרת) would be found here in this fragment.

Line 2: "pa[ths]" — This reconstruction is based on the comments of Tigchelaar (*To Increase Learning*, 33-34).

Frag. 6

¹[. . .] the council of me[n . . .]
    ²Needy are you and king[s . . .] ³your poverty with your council [. . .]

⁴with the mystery of existence examine these and [. . .] ⁵from the house of [. . .] and with the meas[ure . . .] ⁶[co]uncil of men [. . .]

Commentary

Lines 1, 6: "council of me[n . . .]" — The reconstruction סוד ("council, counsel") is more likely than יסוד ("foundation") since the phrase is also attested in CD xiv:10 and 4Q512 36-38iii:13 and makes more sense in this context. The term סוד is amply attested in the corpus of nonbiblical Qumran literature (101 times), much more frequently than in the HB (21 times). It is most prominent in 1QS, 1QHᵃ, the *Songs of the Sabbath Sacrifice*, 5Q510-511, and 4Q512. It also has the meaning of "mystery" and "foundation" in other Qumran texts. In this column we find evidence of two terms used for "council," both of which appear frequently in the manuscripts of the *Community Rule*.

Line 2: "needy" — See commentary to 4Q417 2i:16 below.

Line 3: "poverty" — The Hebrew terms רוש (verb) and ריש (noun) are found throughout *Instruction,* but appear elsewhere in the wisdom corpus from Qumran only at 4Q525 15:1 and in other Qumran texts at 1QHᵃ x:36; xiii:16, 22; and 4Q372 1:17. See the discussion of "Social Location" above.

Line 3: "with your council" — בעצתכה is the most likely reconstruction here since there is space for the letters and this term is very common in the Qumran sectarian texts such as 1QS and its parallels, 1QSa, 1QSb, and 1QHᵃ. Columns such as this one help explain the popularity of *Instruction* among authors of the sectarian compositions. See commentary to line 1 above.

Line 6: "[co]uncil" — See commentary to line 1 above.

Frag. 7

²and your bars are bron[ze . . .] ³the entrance is strong and

Notes

Line 3: "strong" — Tigchelaar prefers חוק ("statute") to חזק ("strong") (*To Increase Learning,* 34).

Commentary

The only biblical reference to bronze bars is in 1 Kgs 4:13. The reference to the "entrance" (ביאה) also is rare, found only in Ezek 8:5. These would suggest references to the temple, but we cannot say more than that. The term ביאה ("entrance") is used in different contexts in 3Q15 *(Copper Scroll)* and 4Q322-324a, 332-333 *(Mishmarot, Calendrical Documents)*, the other places where it is found.

Frag. 8

²[. . .] you shall not mix ³[. . .] fruit

Commentary

It is impossible to determine whether the verb in line 2 refers to giving a pledge, a concern expressed elsewhere in *Instruction,* or is related to the injunctions against mixing of categories, a theme of concern in Second Temple literature, such as is found in 11Q19 xxxv:12; xxxvii:11; xlv:4. The latter is a more likely explanation if it is related to the previous fragment and if we can determine that this was the subject of discussion there.

Frag. 9

¹[. . .] you will linger [. . .] ²so that your womb conceive for [. . .] ³[. . .] ⁴men [. . .] ⁵with folly, she shall not be equal to a leader [. . .] ⁶with her he has established it, for it is the plan [. . .] ⁷together, the male has authority over the fe[male . . .] ⁸her spirit, to have authority over her [. . .] ⁹their poverty, one from ano[ther . . .] ¹⁰According to this [. . .] ¹¹female and according to [accurate] scales [. . .]

Notes

Lines 2-3: Tigchelaar proposes some alternative readings for these lines. They do not affect the portions of the lines translated in this text (*To Increase Learning,* 35).

Commentary

This fragment appears to have a theme similar to frag. 2, col. ii above. The authority of the male over the female appears to have its warrant in God's plan for the world.

Line 5: "folly" — אולת is a particular concern in *Instruction* (4Q416 2ii:3; 4Q417 1i:7; 4Q418 220:3; 243:2; 4Q423 5:7) and in Proverbs, also found in 4Q525 2ii+3:2.

Line 6: "plan" (תכון) — This term meaning "design" or "plan" is used in the *Community Rule* to describe the plan that God has designated for the life of the sect and its members: v:3, 7; vi:4, 8, 9, 10, 22; vii:21; viii:4, 13, 19; ix:2, 3, 7, 12, 18, 21; x:5, 7, 9. In some cases this plan is so specific and preordained that it refers to the fate or "lot" of the individual. The plan for the sect is rooted in God's design of the world. In these wisdom texts this concept is referred to with the phrase תכון חבל ("plan of the world"), found in 1Q27 1i:6-7 (see reconstruction of 4Q299 1:07 in this commentary) and 4Q418 159ii:7, where Strugnell and Harrington understand this same form to be the third feminine singular inflection of כון ("the earth is established") (DJD 34:384). The fragmentary nature of this column does not permit a definitive interpretation. A similar meaning is possible in 4Q418 127:6 and in other sapiential texts: 4Q299 6ii:16; 20:1; 4Q298 3-4i:6, 8.

Line 7: "together" — See discussion in the introduction to 4Q525 under "Literary Questions."

Line 8: "her spirit, to have authority over her" — It is difficult to determine the grammatical relationships of this fragmentary line. In view of line 7, it is doubtful that "her spirit" would be given authority in this line.

Line 11: "[accurate] scales" — This reconstruction is based on parallels with 4Q418 127:6; 167a,b:2.

Frag. 10, cols. i + ii

No full words are discernible in this fragment. Tigchelaar has proposed the reconstruction ובאאהבתו ("and with his love") for line 3, based on a possible overlap with 4Q418 169:3. While the reconstruction of this term at this point seems plausible, it does not follow that the text is an overlap with 4Q418 169+170:3, since that text reads וּבְאַהֲבַת חֶסֶד ("and with loving kindness"), a construction that is incompatible with the third person singular pronoun found in our text (*To Increase Learning*, 35).

Frag. 11 + <u>4Q418 167a + b</u> + 4Q418a 15 + 13

[01][... her measure in all ...] [02][...] [03][... with them for according to accurate scales ...] [04][... they will not be with them for one will go up and the other down] [2][... each one for their measure and that is not ...] [3][ephah by eph]ah, omer by omer [...] [4]which are not together [... their spirit for her beauty ...] [5][...] men of discernment for according to the spirits they will be me[asured ... you together have measured their spirit ...] [6][ev]ery blemish of her recount to him and help [him] discern her bodily defects [... when he strikes] [7]in darkness [...] she will [not] be for him a stumbling block before him [...] [8][...] send [...] strike him and his anger is kindled against [...] [9]with a weight she measures their spirit [...] [10]he will n[o]t stumble because of her and if he will strike [...] [11]and if she is separated when she is pregnant by you, take [her] off[spring] ... [12]when she walks about gain greatly in understanding. Whether it is male [or female ...] [13]her dwelling you will not find. In these things examine her [...]

Notes

Lines 01-3 are reconstructed and arranged according to the additional observations of Tigchelaar (*To Increase Learning*, 36-38).

Line 3: The very limited evidence of 4Q418a 15:4 has "ephah" and "omer" in reverse order.

Commentary

It is difficult to determine the content of this column and its related fragments. It appears to concern instructions to the man of discernment with regard to the selection and treatment of a wife or, as has been suggested, the selection of a husband for a daughter (see reference to Qimron in DJD 34:59). It is certainly possible that lines 1-3 concern interactions in the marketplace. The theme seems to be careful consideration in the choice of a wife, both with regard to ideological compatibility and the considerations involved in raising a family. Its fragmentary nature prohibits more precise conclusions concerning the injunctions. Certain common vocabulary suggests some thematic connection with 4Q416 2iii:19–iv:6.

Line 3: "[ephah by eph]ah, omer by omer" — This construction is most similar to Deut 25:14 and Prov 20:10. In both cases they are injunctions against the unjust use of different measures for various purposes, a tactic for fraudulent dealing. Note also Ps 62:10. The ephah and omer were used for measuring the capacity of dry goods such as grain. The omer, a Hebrew word also meaning "sheaf," is the amount designated as the daily ration of bread in Exod 16:13-36. An omer was one-tenth of an ephah.

Line 4: "together" — See discussion in the introduction to 4Q525 under "Literary Questions."

Line 5: "[together]" — The translation of ביחד here is the least clear example of its adverbial use, found in the previous line and amply attested throughout *Instruction*. Here it comes the closest to its use as a name in the sectarian texts and could be translated "in common."

Line 5: "[their spirit . . .]" — The most significant statement concerning the nature of humankind within creation is found in the "Treatise on the Two Spirits" in 1QS iii:13–iv:26. In this treatise the *maskil* ("sage") is instructed to teach all of the sons of light about the nature and fate of humankind within creation. They are to understand that humankind was created to rule over the world and that it was given two spirits within which to walk until the time appointed for God's visitation, the spirits of truth and falsehood.

Line 6: "bodily defects" — גויתיה may also refer to the internal condition of the body. This is the manner in which the term is used in *m. Miqw.* 10:7 in which it indicates that food and drink can make the "body" unfit.

Line 6: "[strikes]" — While this may refer to striking his foot or stubbing his toe, as in Ps 91:12 and Prov 3:23 (see DJD 34:61-62), this identification is by no means certain.

Line 11: "off[spring]" — מולדי elsewhere is translated as "birth times." See commentary to 4Q417 2i:11 below.

Line 12: "gain greatly in understanding" — This unusual phrase is also found in 4Q417 3:3; 4Q418 81+81a:17; as well as in Jer 2:10.

Frag. 12

²your spir[it . . .] ³and know [. . .]

Frag. 13

³[. . .] he who acts treacherously with his flock [. . .] ⁴[. . .] they established with all [. . .] ⁵[. . .] like a resting place [. . .]

Notes

Line 4: It is impossible to determine whether the first word visible in this line is "they established," "establish him," or "his foundation."

Frag. 15

¹[. . .] your [in]heritance [. . .]

Frag. 17

²[. . .] reprove [. . .]

Frag. 18

²[. . .] your inner desire [. . .]

Commentary

Line 2: "inner desire" — For discussion of אוט see the introduction to this chapter.

Frag. 19

²[. . . ju]dg[me]nts of [. . .] ³[. . .] strike [. . .]

Frag. 21

²whose fruit [. . .] ³if you see [. . .]

Frag. 22

²[. . .] he will not cea[se . . .]

Frag. 23

¹[. . .] his [de]eds and know [. . .]

Frag. 24

¹[. . .] with the mystery of ex[istence . . .] ²[. . .] his spirit [. . .]

Frag. 25

¹[. . . mystery of ex]istence in [. . .]

Frag. 28, col. ii

¹wine [. . .] ²with [. . .]

Frag. 31

² [. . .] truth [. . .]

Frag. 32

²[. . .] without right[eousness . . .] ³[. . .] man [. . .]

Notes

Line 2: בלא ("without") rather than the proposed כלא ("withhold" or "imprison [the righteous]").

Commentary

The small fragments above have no value except that we continue to find the presence of words central to the self-understanding of *Instruction* such as "deeds," "mystery of existence," "spirit," "truth," and "righteousness."

Instruction^c (4Q417)

Frag. 1, col. i + 4Q418 43,44,45i + 4Q418a 11

¹[...] you, man of discer[nme]nt [...] ²[...] consider, [you shall be wise to the fearful] mysteries of the wonders of [God. The origin ...] ³[...] to him [...] and consider [the mystery of existence and the deeds of old, for what was and what will be] ⁴[with them ... for]ever [... for what ⁵is and for what will be with them ...] in all [...] every de[ed ...] ⁶[... day and night meditate on the mystery of ex]istence and search daily and then you will know truth and perversity, wisdom ⁷[and foll]y [...] dee[d] in all their ways with their assignment for all epochs forever and the assignment ⁸for eternity. Then you will know the difference between the [go]od and [evil according] to [their] deeds. For the God of knowledge is the base of truth and with the mystery of existence ⁹he spread out her foundation and her deeds[.... with all wis]dom and with all [...] he fashioned her. The dominion of her deeds ¹⁰is for a[l]l [... He ex]pounded for their under[st]anding all of her d[eed]s, how to walk ¹¹in [the inclination of] their understanding. He expounded [...] and with the disposition for understanding present [...] of his intention are made kn[own] ¹² with those who walk perfectly [in all] his [d]eeds. These things diligently seek daily and consider carefully [al]l ¹³their consequences. Then you shall know the glory of [his] stren[gth with] the mysteries of [his] wonde[rs and the mig]ht of his deeds.

You, ¹⁴man of discernment, inherit your reward with the et[ernal] memorial [for it will] come. Engraved is your statute and inscribed is every assignment,

¹⁵for engraved is that which is inscribed by God concerning all the in[iquities of] the sons of perdition. The memorial book is written before him ¹⁶for those who keep his word. It is the vision of insight for the memorial book. They shall give it as an inheritance to humankind (in company with) a people of spirit, f[o]r ¹⁷after the pattern of the holy ones he formed it. Yet he did not give this insight to the spirit of flesh, for it could not distinguish between ¹⁸[go]od and evil according to the judgment of his [sp]irit.

You, son of discernment, consider [. . .] the mystery of existence and know ¹⁹[. . .] all life and its way of walking that is assigned concerning the deeds of [. . .] ²⁰[und]erstanding between the great and small, and with your counsel [. . .] ²¹[. . .] with the mystery of existence [. . .] ²²[. . .] every vision [k]now [. . .] and with all [. . .] ²³you shall be strengthened daily. You shall not be touched by unrighteousness [. . . for anyone who touches] ²⁴it will not be innocent. In accordance with his inheritance in it, he shall be dec[lared guilty . . .]

²⁵Son of a sage, gain in the understanding of your mysteries and in the foundation[s . . .] ²⁶[be] established in you al[l . . .] with the reward of [. . .] ²⁷Do not seek out the desires of you[r] heart and your e[y]es [. . .]

Notes

Line 2: "[you shall be wise to the fearful] mysteries of the wonders of [God]" — The conjunction ו ("and") is not found in the parallel text as reconstructed in 4Q418 43,44,45i:1, hence I see no need to reconstruct it here (contra DJD 34:151, 153; Tigchelaar, *To Increase Learning*, 52).

Line 9: The lacuna in the middle of the line is reconstructed as [ע]רמה ("[cle]verness") in DJD 34:151, but rejected by Tigchelaar as not fitting the space or the traces of the available letters (*To Increase Learning*, 52-53).

Line 12: "with those who walk perfectly" — See commentary below. Tigchelaar raises questions about this reconstruction based on the amount of space available. While rare in the wisdom texts, the same phrase is found in 4Q415 2i+1ii:3 and 4Q417 1ii:5. A reference to those who walk in perfection is also found in 4Q525 5:11.

Line 16: "(in company with) a people of spirit" — The Hebrew word עם can either be a noun meaning "people" or a preposition designating "with." In the MS of this text the word appears twice in consecutive order, but the second usage is supralinear and appears to be added by a later scribe. Without the supralinear addition, I read the phrase "people of spirit" as standing in apposition to and hence defining "humankind."

Commentary

Line 2: "mysteries of the wonders" — This is a common theme in sectarian compositions such as the *Hodayot* (H) and *Serek* (S, *Community Rule*) texts, though "wonders" is used as an abstract singular noun in those instances, hence the most frequent translation is "wondrous mysteries."

Line 3: "[mystery of existence]" — See the introduction, especially the discussion under "Key Terms."

Line 3: "[for what was and what will be]" — The same Hebrew construction consisting of ל ("to, for") and ו ("and") with a distributive meaning is used here as it is in 4Q416 1:4-5.

Line 6: "wisdom" — See discussion of חכמה under "Key Terms" in the introduction to this chapter.

Line 6: "meditate" — The verb הגה also appears in 4Q525 2ii+3:6; 14ii:19. It appears to reflect the same root as the חזון הגוי ("vision of *insight*") "for the memorial book" found below in lines 15-16, or the ספר הגוי ("book of *insight*") referred to in CD x:6; xiii:2; xiv:7-8; 1QSa i:7.

Line 7: "assignment" — See commentary to 4Q416 1:9.

Line 8: "God of knowledge" — The importance of this title, אל הדעות, for sectarian literature bears mention. It appears in the HB only in 1 Sam 2:3, "for the Lord is a God of knowledge" (without the article), but it is found throughout the Qumran manuscripts. Significant is its location in the introduction to the "Treatise on the Two Spirits" in 1QS iii:15: "From the God of knowledge is all that is and that will be. Before they were, he established their entire intention." The importance of this title is attested by its use in 1QH[a] ix:28; xx:13 (see note to that line in DJD 40:256); xxi:32; xxii:34; xxv:32-33. In the wisdom texts it is found also in 4Q299 73:3; 4Q418 43,44,45i:6; 55:5. It is present in 4Q504 4:4// 4Q506 131-132:9. Closely related is 4Q402 4:12, מאלוהי דעת ("from the God of knowledge"), a text that also emphasizes the role in the conception of the world. This title also appears in 4Q510 1:2 and 4Q511 1:7-8.

Line 8: "base of truth" (סוד אמת) — This phrase, also found in the parallel text 4Q418 43,44,45i:6 and in 4Q418a 12:2, is a significant term in other Qumran literature, most notably in the texts of the *Hodayot:* 1QH[a] vi:32 (partially reconstructed); ix:29; x:12; xiii:11, 28 // 4Q429 (H[c]) 2:7; xviii:6; xix:7, 12, 15 (partially reconstructed), 19. It is also to be found in 4Q286 (Berakhot[a]) 1ii:7, a work with similarities in vocabulary to both wisdom and sectarian texts. The term occurs thirty times in 1QH[a] and parallel texts and is used liberally throughout many of the sectarian texts such as the S *(Serek, Community Rule)* and D *(Damascus Document)* MSS. As noted by both Qimron *(HDSS* §500.3) and Strugnell and Harrington (DJD 34:158), this term is interchanged with יסוד throughout these texts. In Biblical Hebrew the former term סוד means "council" and "counsel," or in some cases "mystery," referring perhaps to what had been determined in the council of God. In the Qumran literature the latter usage becomes more frequent and is associated with *raz* ("mystery") and *nistarot* ("hidden things"). In later rabbinic usage it replaces the term for "mystery."[109] The latter יסוד more often is the architectural term used for a "foundation wall" or "base" as found in Exod 29:12 and Lev 4:7, 18, 25, 30, 34. In some instances such as 1QH[a] ix:29 the construct relationship probably designates an adjectival meaning such as "true counsel" (see DJD 40:131). In the sectarian literature it is frequently used to designate organizational structure; see 4Q415 6:1, 6 and commentary there. We also find references to the "council of the gods" in 4Q418 69ii:15 and elsewhere and the "council of the holy ones" in 1QH[a] xii:26 and elsewhere.

Lines 8-9: The pivotal role of wisdom in the act of creation is described in these lines, as in 4Q418 126ii:4-5. Note its role in the discussion of the term "intention" (מחשבה) in line 12 under "Key Terms" in the introduction to this chapter. In these lines the role of wisdom in creation is ascribed to the רז נהיה ("mystery of existence"), also discussed among the "Key Terms" above.

Line 9: "[wis]dom" — See discussion of חכמה under "Key Terms" in the introduction to this chapter.

Lines 10, 12, 19: "walk" — See commentary to 4Q416 2iii:9 and 4Q417 19:4.

Line 11: "[inclination]" — יצר is an important term. Its manifold usages in Hebrew literature are rooted in Gen 6:5 in a portrayal of the wickedness of human-

---

109. Scholem, *Jewish Gnosticism,* 3 n. 3.

kind ("every inclination of the thoughts of their hearts was only evil continually" [NRSV]). In rabbinic literature it reflects the constant struggle within every human being to do either good or evil. In Qumran literature, consonant with Gen 6:5 it is frequently linked with some form of מחשבה, translated "thought" or "intention." For this term see commentary on 4Q416 2iii:14.

Line 11: "understanding" — מבינה is attested at least six times in *Instruction*, but is relatively rare in the remainder of the Qumran scrolls and is not found in Biblical Hebrew. The equivalent biblical term appears to be תבונה, also attested in other Qumran compositions (4Q365 10:4; 4Q411 1ii:9; 4Q446 2:3).

Line 11: "disposition for" — This translation of כושר is an attempt to capture the sense of the act of will that is necessary to gain the understanding discussed in *Instruction*. This is not simply available through the cultivation of a superior intelligence; this understanding is acquired only through the development of deliberate attitudes and probably even actions. This is the same Hebrew term for the rabbinic concept of "kosher," hence it means "fitting, ritually permitted" (see DJD 34:159).

Line 12: "walk perfectly" — A rare phrase in the HB, found in Ps 15:2 and Prov 28:18, but rather important to sectarian compositions from Qumran. The language of perfection is common in the *Damascus Document* and pervades the *Community Rule* as well as the Cave 4 fragments of both compositions. Its presence in the *Temple Scroll*, a composition that is not necessarily sectarian, demonstrates even more clearly its centrality for the legal traditions valued in the literature of the Qumran corpus. References to the "perfect of the way," also found in Prov 11:20, and to walking in perfection appear to be significant in the *Songs of the Sabbath Sacrifice.*[110] See also the notes to this line above.

Line 13: "mysteries of [his] wonde[rs]" — See commentary to line 2 above.

Line 14: "et[ernal] memorial" (זכרון הע[ולם]) — This reconstruction departs from that of Harrington and Strugnell, "Remembering the re[quital]" (DJD 34:154-55), and Jefferies, "the peaceful remembrance" (*Wisdom at Qumran,* 266, 271), both reconstructing בזכרון הש[לום]; and Elgvin, "when you remember the st[ylus]" ("Analysis," 258) and Lange, "im Gedächtnis der Zeit" ("in remembrance of the time"; *Weisheit und Prädestination,* 53), both reconstructing בזכרון הע[ת]. Neither reconstruction is convincing nor has any parallel attes-

---

110. Strawn with Rietz, "(More) Sectarian Terminology."

tations. While the term העולם is not common, it does appear in 4Q221 7:7 ("the eternal tablets") and 11Q13 1,2i,3i,4ii:20 ("ages of the world") as well as in Jer 28:8; Joel 2:2; Pss 28:9; 41:13; 106:48; 133:3; Eccl 3:11; Dan 12:7; Neh 9:5; 1 Chr 16:36; 17:14. The idea of an eternal memorial more adequately fits the literary context than the other proposals.[111]

Lines 14 and 15: "engraved" — The biblical *hapax legomenon* חרות is found in the HB in Exod 32:16: "The tablets were the work of God, and the writing was the writing of God, *engraved* upon the tablets." This is a reference to the two tablets of the covenant that Moses brought down from Mount Sinai, direct communication from God to the Israelites. It is this authority that the author claims for this composition, referring both to the fate that has been determined for humankind and to the injunctions to search the mystery of existence for knowledge concerning daily life. The parenetic material is anchored in revelation about the nature of the created world and the fate of humankind.

Line 14: "assignment" — See commentary to 4Q416 1:9.

Line 15: "that which is inscribed" — The best-known use of this term in the Qumran scrolls is the reference to the *mehoqeq* ("rod") in the exegesis of Num 21:18 in CD vi:3-11. As found in the passive Pual form in our text *(mehuqqaq)*, it can refer to something that is decreed. In the active Poel form, as found in CD, it can also refer to the ruler who has the power to decree or to the staff that he holds. Hence in our text we see the reference in line 14 to the "statutes" *(hoq)*, a term related to the same root. A similar use of the Pual form can be found in Prov 31:5: "or else they will drink and forget *what has been decreed*, and will pervert the rights of all the afflicted." In all of these references, the term has a legal connotation.

Line 15: "sons of perdition" — This translation follows Elgvin's proposal ("Analysis," 88) that בני שית here refers to the citation from Num 24:17, quoted in CD vii:21, 4Q175 i:13, and 1QM xi:6, and read in the light of Lam 3:47, where שאת refers to "perdition." This is in contrast to those interpreters who translate this literally as the "sons of Seth."[112]

---

111. For an extensive discussion of the many issues in the section from lines 13-17, see Eibert Tigchelaar, "'Spiritual People,' 'Fleshly Spirit,' and 'Vision of Meditation': Reflections on 4QInstruction and 1 Corinthians," in *Echoes from the Caves*, ed. García Martínez, 103-18. On this phrase he accepts the reconstruction of Lange and Elgvin, but notes some of its grammatical difficulties (see pp. 106-7, 114).

112. Note also Goff, *Worldly and Heavenly Wisdom*, 102-5. This is also the conclusion of

Line 16: "It is the vision of insight for the memorial book" — In Mal 3:16 we read that "a memorial book ['book of remembrance' in NRSV, RSV, KJV] was written before him of those who revered the Lord and thought on his name." This text provides an appropriate backdrop for its use in 4Q417 1i.

The reference in this and the next line to הגי, "insight," appears to be related to the *sefer hagu* ("book of insight" — sometimes *hagy*), developed in 1Q28a 1:7; CD x:6; xiii:2, and restored in CD xiv:7-8 and in parallel texts of the *Damascus Document* (4Q266 8iii:5; 4Q270 6iv:17). While most translators understand the term to be related to its appearance in Ps 49:3 and thus translate it as "meditation," the verbal root appears to mean "speak, proclaim," hence here a passive formulation to refer to that which is spoken or proclaimed in a vision. Hence I have adopted the translation "insight," as proposed by Edward Cook (*DSSANT* 484).

Interpreters of these texts tended to understand *sefer hagu* as "the Torah of Moses" or as some reference to an esoteric, sectarian collection of rules, perhaps extant in compositions such as the *Temple Scroll* or the *Community Rule,* or unavailable to modern researchers.[113] What is clear in *Instruction* is the specificity of the vision: "He did not give the revelation to the spirit of flesh (1.17)." Furthermore, it is used as the basis of judgment for recording in the "memorial book." While its specific content is not spelled out, these lines suggest something other than the Torah of Moses. In keeping with an understanding of certain strands in apocalyptic thought, it is only the insiders, "those who understand," who know how God is making decisions of judgment. Hence it is denied to the spirit of flesh. Goff clarifies this picture by pointing out that the "key realization . . . that the addressee was to derive from the vision of Hagu pericope was that he is like the 'spiritual people.'"[114] This perspective is based on the argument that *Instruction* presents two contrasting types of humankind, the spiritual people and the fleshly spirit.[115] Note the parallel text in 4Q418 43,44,45i:12-13. The verbal root *hgh* is also employed in both noun and verbal forms in 4Q417 1i:6//4Q418 43,44,45i:4; 1QH^a xix:5, 24//4Q427 1:4; (xxvi:13//4Q427 7i:17 [reconstructed]), and 4Q525 (Beatitudes) 14ii:19.

Lines 16-18: "They shall give it as an inheritance . . . [go]od and evil according to the judgment of his [sp]irit." The obscurity of the content coupled with its

Wold in his extensive summary and analysis of these lines, including the interpretive alternatives for both אנוש and שת (*Women, Men and Angels,* 124-49).

113. Steven D. Fraade, *EDSS* 1:327. See Lange, *Weisheit und Prädestination,* 69-90; idem, "Wisdom and Predestination," 341-43.

114. *Worldly and Heavenly Wisdom,* 122.

115. Ibid., 80-123.

fragmentary nature make this section very difficult to interpret.[116] The Hebrew term אנוש could refer to Enosh, the son of Seth, or to humankind in general.[117] The present translation is influenced by the perspective of John Collins, who argues that "man" here refers to Adam and the tradition that the knowledge of good and evil originates with that first man. He cites 1QS iii:17 in the "Treatise on the Two Spirits": "He created *enosh* to rule the world." The man related to the "people of spirit" is formed after the pattern of the "holy ones," probably the angels or at least participants in a heavenly reality, while "the revelation" is not given to the "spirit of flesh." In this particular description the "spirit of flesh" is not even equated with humanity in general. In other words, "man [i.e., humankind] . . . of spirit" participates in the heavenly realm while the "spirit of flesh" is very earthly. Such a viewpoint is fundamental for the development of the dualism known in sectarian texts such as the *Community Rule,* the *Damascus Document,* and the *Hodayot* as well as the Cave 4 MSS of each. Participation in the angelic realm also pervades compositions such as the *Songs of the Sabbath Sacrifice.* For an extensive analysis of the role of the relationship of the addressees and the angels in creation, in life, and in the future see Wold (*Women, Men and Angels,* 124-82). For commentary on the significance of these references to the angels see 4Q418 69.

Line 25: "Son of a sage" — See the discussion of the terms מבין and משכיל in the introduction to this chapter.

Line 25: "your mysteries" — The fragmentary context makes even more difficult our comprehension of a difficult phrase. It would appear to point to a necessary internalization of the knowledge of the mysteries advanced throughout this column.

Line 25: "foundation[s . . .]" — See line 9 above.

Line 27: "Do not seek out the desires of you[r] heart and your e[y]es" — See Num 15:39, where the sentence continues, "so that you lust after them," using the verbal form of the word for "adultery." The relationship of loyalty to the

116. On this passage see Tigchelaar, "Spiritual People." See also the discussion of "The New Testament" in the introduction to this volume.

117. See DJD 34:163-65. On Enosh see Lange, *Weisheit und Prädestination,* 86-90. For Collins's view see *Jewish Wisdom,* 123-25. Note his earlier essay: "In the Likeness of the Holy Ones: The Creation of Humankind in a Wisdom Text from Qumran," in *The Provo International Conference on the Dead Sea Scrolls: Technological Innovations, New Texts, and Reformulated Issues* (ed. Donald W. Parry and Eugene Ulrich; STDJ 30; Leiden: Brill, 1999), 609-18.

new covenant and going astray using metaphors of adultery are common in CD i–viii.

Frag. 1, col. ii + 4Q418 123

³in the mystery of exist[en]ce [. . .] ⁴compassion [. . .] ⁵walk about in perfec[tion . . .] ⁶bless his name [. . .] ⁷from your rejoicing [. . .] ⁸great are the mercies of Go[d . . .] ⁹praise God and concerning every affliction, bl[ess . . .] ¹⁰in his will they will be. He is a man of discernment [. . .] ¹¹Assign all your ways [. . .] ¹²The intention of the evil inclination shall not deceive you [. . .] ¹³for truth you will search[. . . .] shall not deceive you [. . .] ¹⁴without the understandings of the flesh he has commanded[. . . .] shall not lead you astray [. . .] ¹⁵you shall not consider [. . .] you shall not say [. . .] ¹⁶thus [. . .]

Commentary

Line 5: "walk" — See commentary to 4Q416 2iii:9 and 4Q417 19:4.

Line 5: "walk about in [perfection . . .]" — A rare phrase in the HB, found in Ps 15:2 and Prov 28:18, but rather important to sectarian compositions from Qumran. The language of perfection is common in the *Damascus Document* and pervades the *Community Rule* as well as the Cave 4 fragments of both compositions. Its presence in the *Temple Scroll,* a composition that is not necessarily sectarian, demonstrates even more clearly its centrality for the legal traditions valued in the literature of the Qumran corpus. References to the "perfect of the way," also found in Prov 11:20, and to walking in perfection appear to be significant in the *Songs of the Sabbath Sacrifice.*[118]

Line 9: "affliction" — Most often used in contexts discussing purity, but there is very limited discussion of this subject in *Instruction* (see DJD 34:24-25).

Line 10: "in his will" — Sometimes translated "in his desire," this term is also common in discussions of purity.

Line 12: "intention of the evil inclination" — The "design" or "intent" of God for the entire created order and every piece within it is an integral part of the strict

---

118. Strawn with Rietz, "(More) Sectarian Terminology."

sectarian worldview found in passages such as 1QS iii:15-18 in the "Treatise on the Two Spirits." The Hebrew term מחשבה is found a number of times in *Instruction* as well as in other Cave 4 fragments, particularly the MSS of *Mysteries* and *4QBerakhot*. In addition to the *Community Rule* it is also common in the *Damascus Document* and its Cave 4 MSS. The "inclination" is also a common term scattered throughout wisdom and other texts in the Cave 4 fragments, as well as in the *Community Rule* and the *Damascus Document*. It is employed in conjunction with the term "intention" in other Qumran wisdom texts as well as the *Community Rule* and the *Damascus Document*. The "evil inclination" and the "good inclination" as integral to the description of the nature of humankind is integral to rabbinic anthropology. Also see commentary to 4Q416 2iii:14.

Line 14: "understandings of the flesh" — The intent of this strange phrase is probably to indicate that the intent of God for creation is the opposite of fleshliness. In this fragmentary column it appears in the section that lists the various ways that humankind can be deceived.[119]

Frag. 2, col. i + <u>4Q416 2i</u> + 4Q418 + 4Q418a *(various fragments noted)*

(Since the state of preservation of 4Q417 2i is considerably better than the text of 4Q416 for this column, I have used it as the basic text for translation and discussion. The text of <u>4Q416 2i:1-20</u> is underlined and the fragments of 4Q418 and 4Q418a are itemized in the notes. 4Q416 2:21-22 does not have a parallel in 4Q417, so I included it among the texts of 4Q416.)

[1]at any time lest he implore you. According to his spirit, speak with him lest [he will hate you. Also . . .] [2]without reproof of that which is proper, forgive him. He who is associated [with iniquity in the time of . . .] [3]Moreover, do not disturb his spirit, for in a whisper you have spok[en . . .] [4]and announce his reproof quickly. Do not overlook your own transgressions [for . . .] [5]he indeed will be as righteous as you. For he is a prince among prin[ces . . .] [6]he will do, for how exceptional he is in every deed, to <u>not</u> [. . .]

[7]Do not consider a man of perversity as a helper and also not an enemy [. . . to <u>not</u> . . .] [8]the wickedness of his deeds with his punishment. Know how you will walk with him [. . .] [9]Let it not depart from your heart.

---

119. DJD 34:172. Note the article by Jörg Frey, "Flesh and Spirit in the Palestinian Jewish Sapiential Tradition and in the Qumran Texts: An Inquiry into the Background of Pauline Usage," in *Wisdom Texts from Qumran*, ed. Hempel et al., 389.

Do not increase only for yourself [your appetite when you are in poverty . . .]
¹⁰For what is more insignificant than a poor man? Do not rejoice in your
mourning, lest you will toil unduly throughout your life. Consider the mystery
of ¹¹ existence, grasp the birth times of salvation and know who inherits glory or
perversity. Has not [. . . broken of spirit] ¹²and for those who mourn eternal joy.

Be an advocate for your own desires and do not [. . .] ¹³for all your deviations.
Decla[re] your judgments like a righteous ruler. Do not tak[e . . .] ¹⁴Do not
overlook your own [transgres]sions. Conduct yourself like a humble man in
your dispute, judgment [. . .] ¹⁵grasp, then God will see, he will turn his face and
he will overlook your sins, for before his face ¹⁶none can stand. Who will be declared righteous in his judgment? Without forgiveness [h]ow can [any] needy
man [stand up before him?]

¹⁷You, if you are in need of food, your poverty and your abundance [. . . br]ing
[. . . , i]f ¹⁸you have any that is left over carry it to the city of his will. Take your
portion from it and nothing mor[e . . .] ¹⁹If you are in need, your poverty
should not be for lack of money, for [his] treasury will not lack [. . . according]
²⁰to his word everything will be. Eat that which he will provide for food and
nothing more le[st . . . you shall shorten] ²¹your life.

If due to your poverty you borrow money from m[e]n, [there shall be no respite
for y]ou ²²day or night and there is no rest for your soul [until] you have repaid
[the loan of your] creditor. Do not lie ²³to him, lest you would bear guilt. Also
the reproach of [your] cred[itor. . . . Do not ev]er [entrust] his neighbor ²⁴so
that when you are in need he will close his hand like a fishhook [. . . and like
him borrow and know (your) lender. . . .] ²⁵If an affliction will strike you and
hasten [. . . pain do not conceal from your lender] ²⁶lest he will uncover your reproach [. . . ruler over him and then] ²⁷they will not smite with a staff [. . . and
nothing] ²⁸m[ore. And also you [. . .]

Notes

Line 1: "implore you" (ישבעכה) — It is much more likely that this verb is related to the root שבע ("to swear") than to שבע ("to satisfy"). Note CD ix:9, 11,
where this term appears in the midst of a folio whose central topic is reproof,
also true of this column (see commentary below). On this meaning see *HALOT*
s.v. שבע (Hiphil 2). I do not find the parallel with Prov 25:17 convincing (contra
Jefferies, *Wisdom at Qumran,* 120).

104

Lines 1-2: The reconstructions "[he will hate you. Also . . .]" at the end of line 1 and "[with iniquity in the time of . . .]" at the end of line 2 are based on 4Q417 26 (Tigchelaar, *To Increase Learning*, 55-56), along with the connection with Prov 25:17.

Line 2: "He who is associated [with]" (והנקשר) — I accept the hypothesis that these letters form one word (DJD 34:178). It is attested in fragmentary contexts apparently with this meaning in the texts of the *Damascus Document* (CD xiii:10, 19//4Q266 [Dᵃ] 9iii:10; 4Q266 [Dᵃ] 5i:10//4Q267 [Dᵇ] 5ii:3) and in 4Q364 10:1. See also Neh 4:6, "be joined together."

Line 5: "will be as righteous" (יצדק) — While the general context of these verses would suggest the legal definition of this term "declared innocent," that meaning does not fit the character of the simile in this line "as you."

Line 9: "Let it not depart from your heart" — The *vacat* after the אל ("not" or "God") could make it appear as though it were the last word of a sentence on the previous line. But the negation with the imperfect in line 9 is a more likely linguistic construction.

Line 9: "increase only for yourself [your appetite]" — Here I translate תרחב [נפשכה] as in Isa 5:14 and Hab 2:5 (cf. DJD 34:181; see also Ps 138:3 and Prov 22:23).

Line 9: "[when you are in poverty]" — This reconstruction from the parallel text of 4Q416 2i:4 has the unusual spelling of ראש rather than the more common ריש for the term "poverty." This spelling is also found in 4Q416 2iii:11//4Q418 9+9a-c:11.

Line 11: "grasp" (קח) — I have tried to capture the unusual sense of the verb "to take" in a manner that fits this context. A similar usage can be noted in other passages such as 4Q416 2iii:20 and 4Q418 77:2 (see DJD 34:182).

Lines 11-12: "[broken of spirit] and for those who mourn eternal joy" — Note the apparent similarity of this line to 1QHᵃ xxiii:16, also partially reconstructed at that point. On the basis of this parallel, "broken of spirit" is a plausible reconstruction at the end of line 11, though we still do not know how to reconstruct the beginning of that lacuna. Note the attempt of Strugnell and Harrington (DJD 34:182).

Line 12: "Be an advocate for" ([הי]ה ב[על ריב]) — 4Q418a 22:1.

Line 13: "righteous ruler. Do not tak[e . . .]" — 4Q418a 22:2.

Line 14: "humble man in your dispute, judgment" — 4Q418a 22:3.

Line 15: "God will see, he will turn his face and he will overlook" — 4Q418 7a:1.

Lines 15-16: "for before his face none" — 4Q418a 22:4.

Line 16: "declared righteous in his judgment? Without forgiveness [h]ow" — 4Q418 7a:2 and 4Q418a 22:5. The reconstruction of the fragmentary remnants of the latter line on the basis of this text is questioned by Tigchelaar (*To Increase Learning*, 132).

Line 17: "your poverty and your abundance [. . . br]ing [. . . , i]f" — 4Q418 64+199+66. A reconstruction of portions of lines 17-20 is proposed by Tigchelaar[120] and accepted in DJD 34:173, but note the discussion of 4Q418 199 in DJD 34:420. Note the translation in *DSSANT* 485.

Lines 20-21: "[. . . you shall shorten] your life" — 4Q418 7b:4.

Line 22: "night and there is no rest" — 4Q418 7b:5.

Line 23: "bear guilt. Also" — 4Q418 7b:6.

Line 24: "you are in need he will close" — 4Q418 7b:7.

Line 24: "like a fishhook" — See *DSSANT* 485. This word is more common in Mishnaic Hebrew, but occurs in Isa 19:8; Hab 1:15; Job 40:25.

Line 25: "If an affliction will strike you" — 4Q418 7b:8.

Line 25: The reconstruction of the end of this line is partially completed from 4Q416 2i:18, but the text of DJD 34:173, מנוגה ("one who strikes"), is highly un-likely on paleographic grounds since a *gimel* would not leave a trace of a letter on its upper right side. A *shin* would leave such a trace, hence the paleographically more plausible מנושה ("one who lends") of DJD 34:89.

120. E. J. C. Tigchelaar, "הבא ביחד in 4QInstruction (4Q418 64+199+66 par 4Q417 1 i 17-19) and the Height of the Columns of 4Q418," *RevQ* 18 (1998): 589-593; idem, *To Increase Learning*, 76-77.

Line 27: "they will not smite with a staff" — 4Q418 7b:10.

Line 28: "m[ore]" — 4Q418 7b:11. The letters עברה from 4Q418 7b:12 at the end of the line are included in 4Q416 2i:21.

Line 28: Following "you" the text's editors propose the reconstruction "son of discernment" (בן מבין). This seems doubtful because this address would normally begin a new paragraph, hence would not begin, "and also." There is no example in all of the extant *Instruction* texts where "also" occurs preceding "you, man of discernment," or "you, son of discernment."[121]

Commentary

Lines 1-6: This first section appears to reflect a tradition of the interpretation of Lev 19:17-18, the laws of reproof, that becomes rather important in the sectarian texts from Qumran. In this text the importance of the injunction is upheld while the caution of wisdom is enjoined in its execution. The fragmentary remains of 4Q286 13,14,20a,b and 4Q288 (Berakhot^c) 1 bear hints of the same attitude (DJD XI:40-43), where the reproof should be carried out "in proper meekness and in upright purpose [. . .] and will have mercy on him [. . .] with his compassionate love, and with the spirit of humility."[122] The importance of this tradition is attested in multiple references in the sect's legal literature: 1QS v:24–vi:1; CD vi:20–vii:3; ix:2-8; ix:16–x:3; xx:4-5; 4Q266 7i; 4Q267 9i; 4Q270 6iii-iv, as well as in the record of acts of reproof noted in 4Q477. It is important to understand that these texts suggest that reproof had a formal place within the discipline and the legal procedures of the sect. This tradition finds subsequent development in Matt 18:15-20, with a different stream of interpretation recorded in rabbinic texts.[123]

---

121. See also Tigchelaar, *To Increase Learning,* 76-77.

122. Bilhah Nitzan, "The Laws of Reproof in 4QBerakhot (4Q286-290) in Light of Their Parallels in the Damascus Covenant and Other Texts from Qumran," in *Legal Texts and Legal Issues,* ed. Bernstein et al., 159-60. See also Menahem Kister, "Divorce, Reproof, and Other Sayings," in *Text, Thought, and Practice,* ed. Clements and Schwarz, 220-22.

123. Recent studies of these texts include Lawrence H. Schiffman, *Sectarian Law in the Dead Sea Scrolls* (BJS 33; Chico, Calif.: Scholars Press, 1983), 89-109; James Kugel, "On Hidden Hatred and Open Reproach: Early Exegesis of Leviticus 19:17," *HTR* 80 (1987): 43-61; Esther Eshel, "4Q477: The Rebukes by the Overseers," *JJS* 45 (1994): 111-22; Florentino García Martínez, "Brotherly Rebuke in Qumran and in Mt 18:15-7," in García Martínez and Julio Trebolle Barrera, *The People of the Dead Sea Scrolls* (trans. Wilfred F. Watson; Leiden: Brill, 1995), 221-32; John Kampen, "Communal Discipline in the Social World of the Matthean Community," in *Commu-*

Line 2: "without reproof of that which is proper, forgive him" — This line is difficult to understand. The Hebrew term כשר ("kosher" in later Judaism) finds limited use in the HB, where it can mean "that which is pleasing" and refer to "noble conduct" (*HALOT* s.v. כשר). See DJD 34:178. It appears only three other times in the Qumran scrolls: 4Q200 1ii:3; 4Q417 1ii:11; 4Q418 77:2. Here in the context of this column, it would appear to suggest a clear definition of the object of reproof or a relative judgment of its significance and severity, that is, the person may be doing a number of things correctly and should not be reproved for those actions.

The phrase "forgive him" also is not straightforward. The Hebrew term עבר is best known to many of us with the meaning of "pass over" from the story of the exodus. The best-known usage with regard to transgressions or shortcomings is found in Amos 7:8; 8:2 (DJD 34:178; *HALOT* s.v. עבר). "To pass over transgressions" is the basis for the translation "forgive."[124]

Lines 5-6: "For he is a prince among prin[ces . . .] he will do, for how exceptional he is in every deed, to not [. . .]" — There are three possible interpretations of this fragmentary line: (1) One possible translation assumes that the good and special treatment of the person under consideration for reproof is based on a viewpoint that extols the particular and significant role of each human being: "For you are a prince among prin[ces . . .] he will act, for, how unique he is in every deed, without[. . . .]"[125] This translation assumes a more exalted role for the human being than is attested in the sectarian texts that emphasize the low estate of the human being, a viewpoint found in its most pronounced form in the *Hodayot*. García Martínez and Tigchelaar develop this viewpoint even further in their later translation, which no longer even includes the term "prince": "For he . . . is your next of k[in . . .] he will do. For how can he be keen in any affair without . . ." (*DSSSE* 2:855). (2) A different translation follows from the assumption that the third person singular reference here is to God: "For he is a prince among prin[ces . . . forgiveness] he will do, for how unique is he throughout creation, to not . . ." (DJD 34:179). While interesting, there is no compelling literary analogy that justifies such an approach. Note

nal Life in the Early Church: Essays Honoring Graydon F. Snyder (ed. Julian V. Hills; Harrisburg: Trinity Press International, 1998), 158-74; Kenneth L. Hanson, "The Law of Reproof: A Qumranic Exemplar of Pre-Rabbinic Thought," *HS* 47 (2006): 211-25.

124. See Prov 19:11; Jefferies, *Wisdom at Qumran*, 121-22.

125. Florentino García Martínez, *The Dead Sea Scrolls Translated: The Qumran Texts in English* (trans. Wilfred E. G. Watson; Leiden: Brill, 1994), 385. In both this text and the revised version that follows (*DSSSE* 2:854-57), the text follows the earlier order of the fragments, hence found as 4Q417 1i:5-6.

also 4Q418 140:4. (3) The translation adopted in this text assumes that it does apply to a "prince" (*DSSANT* 484-85). There are cases in Qumran literature where legislation that is written for the ruling official seems to apply to the group as a whole. An example can be found in CD v:1, which begins "concerning the prince (ועל הנשיא) it is written, 'He shall not multiply wives for himself.'" This statement appears in the context of a discussion of the ban on polygamy and divorce as well as the particular definition of incest. Such a case apparently applies here where the special treatment of the prince is actually used as an analogy for the stipulations of all of those who enter into the new covenant in the land of Damascus (CD vi:19). See commentary on 4Q416 2iii:11.

Line 8: "punishment" (also "assignment") — See commentary on 4Q416 1:9.

Lines 9-10: "[poverty]" and "poor man" — The Hebrew terms רוש (verb) and ריש (noun) are found throughout *Instruction,* but appear elsewhere in the wisdom corpus from Qumran only at 4Q525 15:1 in the noun form and in other Qumran texts as verbs at 1QH^a x:36; xiii:16, 22; 4Q372 1:17. See the discussion of "Social Location" above.

Line 10: "Do not rejoice in your mourning, lest you will toil unduly throughout your life." This appears to refer to the time when you should be in mourning, perhaps because of being in the state of poverty. When you have grasped the insights from the mystery of existence, then you will understand how mourning is turned into eternal joy (line 12). This may be helpful in understanding the meaning of the beatitude concerning mourning in Matt 5:4. While in that verse the response is that the mourners will be comforted, the injunction to rejoice in v. 12 concludes these beatitudes. In this case the text mentions a reward in heaven rather than eternal joy, as found here in line 12.

Line 11: "birth times" (מולדים) — Lawrence Schiffman in his treatment of the term in *Mysteries* (see commentary to 4Q299 1:4 and 4Q417 2i:4) proposes that the term בית מולדים ("house of birth times") refers "to the time of birth which is seen to affect the future and nature of the individual" (DJD 20:37). He finds such a use in *Tg. Onq.* to Gen 40:20 and in the use of this same term to designate the onset (or "birth") of the new moon in rabbinic literature (see Jastrow, 742). Matthew Morgenstern provides further evidence for this interpretation, which is rooted in the use of ancient horoscopes.[126] The term is used in 4Q186

---

126. Morgenstern, "The Meaning of בית מולדים in the Qumran Wisdom Texts," *JJS* 51 (2000): 141-44.

1ii:8 and 2i:8. Both Tigchelaar and Goff support this translation.[127] Note also the commentary to 4Q416 2iii:9 in DJD 34:117. It is possible, if the horoscope references are not as significant as here assumed, that this should then be translated as "origins" ("causes" in *DSSANT* 485). An understanding of the term as "birth times" is part of the manner in which the basic themes of both *Instruction* and *Mysteries* are rooted in an understanding of creation, that is, of "origins" (Wold, *Women, Men and Angels,* 88).

Line 11: "glory" (כבוד) — In the HB this term can be used to designate power and might, hence it comes to refer to the more abstract attributes of honor, dignity, and majesty. It can also refer to glory or splendor, particularly as it is attributed to God, for example in connection with God's appearance in the tabernacle (Exod 29:43; 40:34-35; Lev 9:6, 23; Num 14:10; 16:19; 16:42; 20:6). Some of the prophets, particularly Ezekiel, described the presence of the Lord in the Jerusalem temple in this manner by depicting the Lord as a blazing fire surrounded by a cloud (Ezek 1:4; 8:2; 9:3; 10:4, 18; 11:23; 43:2, 4). Other objects such as the temple (Hag 2:9), the throne (Isa 22:23; Jer 14:21; 17:12), and crowns (Job 19:9; Ps 8:5) have "glory" attributed to them. The manifestation of God's glory is a developing theme in prophetic eschatology (Isa 24:23), which takes on universal dimensions in the postexilic texts (Isa 58:8; 60:1-3; 62:1-2). This development can be seen to continue in apocalyptic literature, where we find references to the "great glory" (*1 En.* 14:20; 102:3; 104:1; *T. Levi* 3:4), described with vivid imagery in the ascent scene in *1 Enoch* 14 (see 14:16, 20, 21 for the use of the term "glory"). In this text, as in 4Q525 14ii:14, it is quite possible that the one "who inherits glory" is the one who gets to participate in the glory of God, presumably also eternal life.[128] In the Hebrew text of Sir 37:26, "the wise of the people will inherit glory, and his name will stand for life eternal" (Genizah MS D). These references to the participation in the glory of God also appear to explain the imagery of Dan 12:3 and Matt 13:43: "Then the righteous will shine like the sun in the kingdom of their Father."

Lines 11-12: "[broken of spirit] and for those who mourn eternal joy" — For the "broken of spirit" see Isa 66:2; Prov 15:13; 17:22; 18:14, as well as 1QM xi:10. On "those who mourn" see commentary to line 10 above. A similar idea with regard to pain or sorrow can be found in 2 Cor 6:10.

127. E. J. C. Tigchelaar, "Your Wisdom and Your Folly: The Case of 1-4QMysteries," in *Wisdom and Apocalypticism,* ed. García Martínez, 87; Goff, *Worldly and Heavenly Wisdom,* 195-96.

128. For the biblical materials see Moshe Weinfeld, "כָּבוֹד," *TDOT* 7:22-38. See also DJD 34:182.

Line 12: "Be an advocate for your own desires" — This fragmentary section seems to concern the responsibility of the man of discernment in making decisions about legal cases (DJD 34:10). If this is a correct assumption concerning the context, then this line does not make sense if the term בעל ריב (literally "master of dispute") means the same as the biblical איש ריב (literally "man of dispute"; Isa 41:11; Jer 15:10; Job 31:35), as proposed by Harrington and Strugnell (DJD 34:183) and implied in the translation of Cook (*DSSANT* 485). It is much more plausible that the man of discernment is here being enjoined to take charge of the case that he has been called on to arbitrate and to use his best instincts and judgments to arrive at a just conclusion.

The more common translation of חפץ is "desires," but here "requirements" could more adequately reflect the context. It is not meant to reflect the literal desires of humankind, but rather what would be expected of humans trying to meet the desires of or live according to the will of God. For an understanding of "desires" of God in a judicial context see Isa 58:1-2. For a similar use in CD xiv:12, see Jefferies (*Wisdom at Qumran*, 145-46).

Line 14: "humble man" — The translation of Hebrew עני is interesting in that it can designate either the humility associated with Hebrew ענוה or the wretched human effects of prolonged oppression.

Line 15: "God will see, he will turn his face and he will overlook your sins" — In this case the hiding of God is reversed, "God will be seen."[129] The presence of God will become apparent in the gracious act of forgiveness.

Line 16: "needy" (אביון) — This is actually the first Hebrew word on line 17, but the construction of a readable translation did not permit such a placement in this text. This Hebrew term is very significant in that it becomes an important self-designation for the authors of a number of the sectarian Qumran texts. In 4Q171 1-10:i:10 and 1-10iii:10 we find references to the "congregation (עדת) of the needy," and in fragments of the *War Scroll* (4Q491 11i:11) to the "council (עצת) of the needy." There are at least 40 different usages of this term in the scrolls, more than any of the other synonyms for this term used in the Qumran compositions. This word also provides the name for the later sect called "Ebionites."[130]

129. On the hiding of the face of God see Samuel E. Balentine, *The Hidden God: The Hiding of the Face of God in the Old Testament* (Oxford: Oxford University Press, 1983).

130. See Igor R. Tantlevskij, "Ebionites," *EDSS* 1:225-26. Note the article on this passage that places it within the context of the malicious effects of debt and slavery in Second Temple Judaism: Joshua Ezra Burns, "Practical Wisdom in 4QInstruction," *DSD* 11 (2004): 12-42. Rather

Lines 17-21: In this fragmentary section we appear to find an emphasis on moderation coupled with dependence on God and possible allusions to some community structure to supply subsistence needs.

Lines 17-18: "You, if you are in need of food, your poverty and your abundance [. . . br]ing [. . . , i]f you have any that is left over carry it to the city of his will. Take your portion from it and nothing mor[e. . . .]" This translation varies considerably from both DJD 34:173 and *DSSANT* 485. "Bring together" (הבא ביחד) is the expected meaning of this phrase in a text that does not yet know the *yaḥad* ("community") of the sectarian texts.[131] It does, however, suggest that within this wisdom text valued by the sectarians some idea of mutual dependence was already present. "The city of his will" (למחוז חפצו) is a very rare phrase, found in the HB only in Ps 107:30. In the biblical passage the pronoun is "their" rather than "his." I expect that this phrase already marks the elevation of the temple or Jerusalem as a symbolic center for the life of wisdom, later applied by the sect to the future or glorified temple described in the *Temple Scroll* and other documents, or to stipulations for the temple and/or the city of the temple such as those found in the new covenant in the land of Damascus or the community itself. It is a passage such as this that would become important when the community of goods becomes a literal requirement for membership in the sect (Josephus: *J. W.* 2.122-23, 126-27; *Ant.* 18.20; Philo: *Good Person* 12.77; *Hypothetica* 10.4, 11-12; 1QS i:11-12; v:1-2; vi:17-22).

Lines 19-20: "[. . . according] to his word" — This is presumably a reference to words (or commands) that proceed from the mouth of God (DJD 34:187-88). The argument would be that this is the source of all of the provisions for living.

Line 21: "[there shall be no respite for y]ou" — Reconstructed by Harrington and Strugnell on the basis of Ps 83:2 (DJD 34:188). Other options are available (see Elgvin, " Analysis," 197; Jefferies, *Wisdom at Qumran*, 160, 165, 169) that are no more certain but suggest the same theme.

Lines 21-27: Here is practical advice concerning loans: (1) only borrow when absolutely necessary (line 21); (2) repay as quickly as possible (lines 21-22); (3) do not lie to the lender (line 23); (4) do not rely on an intermediary to con-

---

than stressing the incongruous nature of this passage within *Instruction,* his article could be used to demonstrate the manner in which practical advice considered to be divine revelation characterizes the entire composition.

131. For the reconstruction of this line, see the notes to it above.

vey information or payment to the lender (lines 23-24); (5) do not try to hide a problem such as illness that could prevent timely repayment (lines 25-27).

Frag. 2, col. ii

See 4Q416 2i:21-22 and 2ii above.

Frag. 3

[1][. . .] death they will give with the man [. . .] [2][. . .] upon it according to the ruling. The flock [. . .] [3][. . . gain] greatly in the understanding of [. . .] [4][. . .] flesh with the affliction of [. . .] [5][. . .] it is and the length [. . .]

Commentary

Line 3: "[. . . gain] greatly in the understanding" — This same unusual phrase occurs in 4Q415 11:12 and 4Q418 81+81a:17.

Line 4: "affliction" — The fragmentary context prohibits a definitive reading. תענית is the name of a tractate in Mishnah and Talmud discussing the fasts in the Jewish calendar. A rabbinic composition entitled *Megillat Taanith* ("Scroll of Fasting") lists the holidays of celebration on which fasting was forbidden for rabbinic Jews. The Aramaic text appears to be a first-century or early-second-century C.E. composition. A day of fasting is also mentioned in CD vi:19 and a festival of fasting in 4Q508 2:3. The "affliction" of the sons of light receives mention in 4Q510 1:7-8//4Q511 10:4-6.

Frag. 4, col. ii

[1][. . .] cover [. . .] [2]impurity to be opened [. . .] [3]your name will flourish fore[ver. . .] [4]for your house devastation [. . .] [5][. . .] from judgment [. . .] [6][. . .] which [. . .]

Notes

The few letters remaining from col. i do not permit any meaningful reconstruction.

Frag. 5

See 4Q418 69ii:4-8.

Frag. 6

¹[. . .] and your mouth [. . .] ²[. . . al]l the statutes of Go[d . . .] ³[. . .] and not [. . .]

Notes

Line 3: The context is too fragmentary to determine whether this is the negative particle or a second reference to divinity.

Frag. 7

¹[. . .] for us and [. . .] ²[. . . al]l life and excep[t for . . .]

Frag. 11

²[. . .] for God [. . .] ³[. . .] his righteousness [. . .] ⁴[. . .] for [al]l [. . .]

Notes

Line 2: "God" — We again cannot determine whether this is a negation *('al)* or a reference to divinity *('el)*. It is doubtful that the negation would follow כי ("for").

Frag. 13

²He called their name [. . .] ³Thus you will do [. . .] ⁴the truth [. . .] ⁵the spirit [. . .] ⁶all [. . .]

Notes

Line 2: "He called their name" — This refers to the divine choice of or favor for a particular group, since the genitive form is in the plural. This familiar biblical idiom has two important forms, referring either to the human invocation of God or to the special divine choice of a human being (DJD 19:185, commenting on 4Q391 62ii:3). Only in Gen 5:2 does it appear in the latter sense in the plural, referring there to the creation of the male and the female. God calls the "righteous" by name in 4Q521 2ii+4:5 (see commentary in DJD 25:13). Note the sectarian adoption of this phrase ("those called by name") in texts such as CD iv:3-4 (perhaps similarly used in 4Q275 1:2); 1QSa ii:11, 13; 4Q491 19:4 (perhaps closely related is 1QM iv:10-11). In *Instruction* the phrase is also found in 4Q418 81+81a:12.

Frag. 14

³[. . .] with her walk in tr[uth. . .] ⁴[. . .] names God specified for [. . .] ⁵[. . .] in sorrow [. . .]

Notes

Line 3: "tr[uth . . .]" — Reconstruction according to Tigchelaar (*To Increase Learning*, 59).

Commentary

Line 3: "walk" — See commentary to 4Q416 2iii:9 and 4Q417 19:4.

Line 4: "names God specified" — While in frag. 13 we have language similar to CD iv:3 concerning those "called by name," this reference to specification is similar to CD iv:4.

Frag. 16

¹[. . .] for [. . .] ²[. . .] their wings lifting [. . .]

Commentary

Line 1: "for" — This unusual form of כיא appears quite often in the orthography of the Qumran texts (*HDSS* 21). It is also the only extant term that can be recognized in frag. 18.

Line 2: "their wings lifting" — Whether this is a reference to the wings of the cherubim in Ezek 10:16, 19; 11:22 or to the pentateuchal tradition of Exod 19:4 and Deut 32:11, also found in 4Q504 (DibHam^a) 6:7-8, is impossible to determine.

Frag. 19

²[...] righteousness [...] he will seek diligently [...] ³[...] with the bee. Is it not [...] with her wings [...] ⁴[...] for [every] commandment he will walk in righteousness with [his] neigh[bor...] ⁵[...] measure out her food and spare [her] produ[ce...]

Commentary

Line 4: "walk in righteousness with [his] neigh[bor...]" — The Hitpael (usually reflexive) form of הלך ("walk") is much more common in Qumran texts than in the HB. To "walk in righteousness" is also the theme of 4Q416 2iii:9-10// 4Q418 9,9a:8-10. It is quite significant in the sectarian texts, with ten references in 1QS (six of those in the two columns of the "Treatise on the Two Spirits"), one in 1QSa, two in 1QSb, and twelve in CD. In these texts it does relate to issues of sectarian worldview and lifestyle. While we cannot reconstruct the entire line, its presence in close proximity to the term "commandment" is also significant, indicating the connection with the postbiblical legal tradition. See also commentary to 4Q416 2iii:9.

Of equal importance is the presence of the term רעה ("neigh[bor...]"). This is a central term in the sectarian texts with 22 references in 1QS and 10 in CD, found in contexts dealing with the treatment of other members of the group.

Line 5: The context and meaning of this line are very difficult to determine. The unusual referent, "produce," for the verb חמל ("have compassion for, spare"), is closest to the same use of the verb in 4Q418 101ii:4 with regard to "wealth." In the HB it almost always refers to people and the subject is either God or person. In Jer 50:14, however, we read that the attackers on Babylon are to "spare no arrows."

Frag. 20

¹[...] you shall do [...] ²[... w]onders of God you shall be wise [...] ³[... eve]ry deed. Do not cease [...] ⁴[... fore]ver [and] ever [....] he kn[ows...] ⁵[...] truth and glory [...] ⁶[... according to the insig[ht...]

Notes

Line 1: "you shall do" — This reading of Tigchelaar (ועתשׂה) appears more likely, on the basis of the photograph, than הנעשׂה ("that which is done") proposed in DJD 34:205 (*To Increase Learning*, 59).

Commentary

Line 2: "you shall be wise" — The editors propose that the *samekh* in this verb is a substitution for a *sin*. While nowhere else in the available fragments of wisdom literature from Qumran is such a change made for the root שׂכל ("insight"), it seems to be the best fit for the immediate context.[132]

Line 4: "He kn[ows . . .]" — The root ידע ("to know") provides the basis for the most likely reconstruction here. Since this phrase is found in 1QS iv:25, that column could provide a clue for defining the context of this fragment, while acknowledging doubt that the fully developed dualism of the "Treatise on the Two Spirits" of 1QS iii–iv would be present here. Note the similar phrase in 1QHª xxi:27 and 4Q511 22:4; 48+49+51ii:6-7.

Notes

Fragments 21-26 are so fragmentary that a translation of isolated words is not helpful. Strugnell and Harrington suggest that frag. 24 should not be considered part of *Instruction* (DJD 34:207).

Frag. 27

¹[. . .] lovers of [. . .] ²[. . .] understanding [. . .]

Frag. 28

¹[. . . do no]t seek [. . .]

---

132. DJD 34:205. Note the discussion of Qimron, *HDSS* 28-30.

Frag. 29, col. i

¹[. . .] ears ²[. . .] ³[. . .] ⁴[. . .] ⁵[. . .] like the sun ⁶[. . .] for a tithe ⁷[. . .] his under-standing

Instruction^d (4Q418)

Frags. 1, 2, 2a, 2b, 2c

For translation and commentary, see 4Q416 1 above. These fragments represent a different scribal hand than frags. 6-303 of this MS. Since there is no case of a doublet between these two sections, however, they may still be part of the same manuscript., the former probably a repair to the outside of the scroll (DJD 34:227). These initial fragments could, of course, be evidence of a different MS, as has been argued by Elgvin.¹³³ The hides of frags. 3, 4, and 5 with only a few extant letters are similar in color and preparation of surface to those of frags. 1-2. See notes to 4Q416 1 above and the discussion of the "Manuscripts" in the introduction to this chapter.¹³⁴

Frag. 4

See 4Q418a 23.

Frag. 5

¹[. . . mystery] of existence [. . .]

Frag. 7

For translation and commentary see 4Q417 2i above. This includes both frags. 7a and 7b.

---

133. Elgvin, "The Reconstruction of Sapiential Work A," *RevQ* 16 (1995): 559-80.
134. See also Tigchelaar, *To Increase Learning,* 42-49, 61-69.

Frag. 8

For translation and commentary see 4Q416 2ii above. This also includes the extant letters from frags. 8a, 8b, 8c, and 8d.

Frag. 9

For translation and commentary see 4Q416 2iii above. This also includes the extant letters from frags. 9a, 9b, and 9c.

Frag. 10

For translation and commentary see 4Q416 2iii:17–iv. This includes both frags. 10a and 10b.

Frag. 11

¹[. . .] luxur[ies . . .] ²[. . .] ³[. . .] God [. . .]

Notes

It is difficult to place this fragment with any accuracy (DJD 34:238).

Tigchelaar proposes the above reading in line 1 rather than "[for] yo[ur] sake," as found in DJD 34:238. He proposes it to be part of the reconstruction of 4Q418 8-9, hence a parallel to 4Q416 2ii:19-21 (*To Increase Learning*, 81).

Frag. 12

¹[. . . t]hat not [. . .] ²[. . .] your [l]ife [. . .]

Notes

It is difficult to place this fragment with any accuracy (DJD 34:238), so it has been reclassified as 4Q418 8d.

Frag. 13

²[. . .] your mourning [. . .]

Notes

Perhaps this is another copy of 4Q417 2i:9-11, on which see the text there for translation and commentary.

Frag. 16

²[. . .] you [. . .] ³[. . .] your [po]verty [. . .] ⁴[. . .] his [int]ention to fill [. . .]

Notes

Line 4: "to fill" — למלא is the proposal of Tigchelaar (*To Increase Learning*, 82), in contrast to DJD 34:240-41: לבלע ("to confuse").

Commentary

Line 4: "[int]ention" — See commentary to 4Q416 2iii:14 and 4Q417 1ii:12.

Frag. 17

¹[. . .] assignment of ²[. . .] understand ³[. . .] seek him ⁴[. . .] mystery

Commentary

Line 1: "assignment of" — See commentary to 4Q416 1:9 above for this translation of קודת[פ].

Frag. 18

²[. . .] to you by him [. . .]

Commentary

Line 2: Too fragmentary to reconstruct meaning with any certainty.

Frag. 19

³[. . .] you will be equal [. . .] ⁴[. . .] your field [. . .]

Frag. 20

²[. . .] impurity, he had insight [. . .] ³[. . .] before [. . .]

Frag. 21

¹[. . .] his [sele]cted. You [. . .] ² [You, be for him] as a wise slave [. . .]

Commentary

This fragment corresponds to 4Q416 2ii:14-15 and 4Q417 2ii:18-19 and has been reclassified as 4Q418 8c. See commentary to the former text above.

Frag. 28

¹[. . .] for [. . .] ²[. . .] ³[. . .] You [. . .]

Frag. 29

¹[. . .] mixed ki[nds . . .]

Commentary

Whether the first visible letter is a *kap* is difficult to determine with certainty. If it is, it is the only reference to "mixed kinds" in *Instruction* aside from 4Q418

103ii:7-8. It is an important concept in biblical law, found in Lev 19:19 and Deut 22:9, and then developed in 4Q396 1-2iv:6-11//4Q397 6-13ii:13-15 with regard to mixing of priests and laity, a theme also utilized in 11Q19 xxxv:12 and xxxvii:11. It is also discussed with regard to marriage laws in 4Q269 9:2//4Q270 5:16//4Q271 3:10 and mentioned in 4Q481 1:2.

Frag. 33

¹[. . .] take one [. . .] ²[. . .] you shall [not] abandon lest ³[. . .] do not stre[tch] forth your hand ⁴[. . .] thus [. . .]

Notes

Line 2: The negation here is reconstructed.

Frag. 34

¹[. . .] lest [. . .] ²[. . .] the great wind storm [. . .] ³[. . .] wait for ca[lm . . .]

Notes

Line 1: The reading in DJD 34:250, "[his] judgment[s]," is rejected as problematic on paleographic grounds by Tigchelaar (*To Increase Learning*, 85).

Line 3: The reading פהכו, which would most likely be a metathesis for הפכו ("they changed"), is doubtful on the basis of the photographs (DJD 34:250). More consistent with the limited remains visible on the photographs is יחכו ("wait for"), proposed by Tigchelaar (*To Increase Learning*, 85).

Frag. 35

²[. . .] lest [. . .] ³[. . .] eagerly seek [his] presen[ce . . .] ⁴[. . .] bag [. . .] ⁵[. . .] for want of [. . .]

Notes

Line 2: "lest" — Reading פן, as proposed by Tigchelaar (*To Increase Learning*, 85).

Line 4: "bag" — כיס in DJD 34:250. The shape of the fragment does not permit a definite reading of this term. Tigchelaar proposes מוסר ("instruction") (*To Increase Learning*, 85).

Commentary

Line 3: See Prov 7:15. Note the phrase is also found in 4Q416 2ii:7; 4Q417 2ii+23:10; 4Q418 8(+8a-c)+8d:7.

Frag. 36

²[. . .] on account of your blood [. . .] ³[. . .] he will receive [. . .]

Frag. 37

²[. . .] be equal to it [. . .] ³[. . .] that which burns [. . .] ⁴[. . .] be separated [. . .] ⁵[. . .] to you [. . .]

Notes

Line 3: Both the letters and the context are difficult to determine.

Line 4: "be separated" — Tigchelaar reads נפרד, rather than תפרד ("you will separate"), as found in DJD 34:250-51.

Frag. 38

²[. . .] for [. . .] ³[. . .] and then [. . .]

Frag. 40

²[. . . forev]er and ev[er . . .]

Frags. 43,44,45, col. i

See 4Q417 1i for translation and commentary.

Frag. 45, col. ii

¹³he chose [. . .] ¹⁴truth [. . .] ¹⁵the time of [. . .] ¹⁶suppor[t of . . .]

Notes

The line numbers follow the placement of frag. 45i according to the reconstruction of frags. 43,44,45i.

Line 13: Based on the evidence of what he sees as the base strokes of two letters rather than one, Tigchelaar suggests נבחר ("he was chosen"), rather than בחר (*To Increase Learning,* 87-88).

Commentary

There are no links between the fragments of col. ii and 4Q417 1ii.

Line 16: "suppor[t of . . .]" — The term משען is scattered throughout the sectarian texts from Qumran: 1QS xi:4, 5; 1QHᵃ xviii:34; 1QM iv:13; xvii:4. It is also found in 4Q438 10:2. In Exod 21:19 it literally refers to a staff (for support).

Frag. 46

¹[. . .] you shall understand the intenti[ons of . . .] ²[. . .] you shall endure the weari[ness . . .] ³[. . .] for their desires and the w[ays of . . .]

Commentary

Line 1: "intenti[ons]" — See commentary to 4Q416 2iii:14 and 4Q417 1ii:12.

Line 2: The fragmentary context makes reconstruction almost impossible. The other lines in this fragment suggest a spiritual struggle with the will of God for creation rather than physical labor and agricultural produce proposed in DJD

34:259. The term "endure" (יכלכל) occurs six times in the fragments of the *Songs of the Sabbath Sacrifice.*

Frag. 47

¹[. . .] they will r]ule in their dominions [. . .] ²[. . .] their labor. Will he be idle for [. . . ?] ³[. . . wick]edness they shall walk from time to [time] ⁴[. . .] with all [their] descendants [. . .]

Commentary

Line 3: On "walk" see commentary to 4Q416 2iii:9 and 4Q417 19:4.

Line 4: "descendants" — This seems a more likely translation of צאצאים than "produce," the proposal in DJD 34:260-61, which was based on the presupposition of an agricultural context for this section.

Frag. 48

²[. . .] holy [. . .]

Frag. 55

³[. . .] with labor we delve into its ways, we will pause ⁴[. . .] vigilance shall be in our hearts [at all times] and trust in all our ways. ⁵[. . .] knowledge. They do not eagerly seek understandi[ng and the desire of God they do no]t choose. Is not the God of knowledge ⁶[. . .] upon truth, to establish all their ways on understanding? It is the portion for those who inherit truth. ⁷[. . .] vigilance in [. . .] deed. Is not peace and quiet ⁸[. . . Have] you [not kn]own, have you not heard that the holy angels are his in heaven ⁹[. . .] truth and they will pursue all of the sources of understanding. They will keep watch over ¹⁰[. . . acco]rding to their knowledge they will be glorified, one man more than his neighbor. According to his insight, he will multiply his honor. ¹¹[. . .] are they like a man, for he is lazy? Or the son of man for he will cease to be? Is he not ¹²[. . . for]ever. They will inherit an eternal possession. Have you not seen

Notes

Line 1: There is not enough material remaining in this line for the reading of either the editors (DJD 34:265) or Tigchelaar to be convincing (*To Increase Learning*, 89-90, 208).

Line 10: "[. . . accor]ding to" — Tigchelaar does not consider this reconstruction compatible with the traces of the remaining letters (*To Increase Learning*, 90).

Commentary

Particular features of this column are similar to those found in frag. 69ii. The use of both the first and second person plural forms is more extensive in these two texts than elsewhere in the composition. The rhetorical question is more commonly used in these columns than in the remainder of the composition, particularly when introduced by the interrogative ה, especially הלוא ("Is it not . . . ?"). There are also certain terms used in common. Five out of the ten appearances of the root שקד ("to keep watch") in *Instruction* are found in these two columns. The appearances of this word are rare in the remainder of the Qumran evidence. The term שקט ("silence") is only found in these columns within *Instruction*. The terms דעה and דעת ("knowledge") are also more common here than in the remainder of *Instruction*. Whether these two columns represent a distinct provenance different from other sections of *Instruction* has not yet been determined (*To Increase Learning*, 208-24).

Line 3: "delve into its ways" — The verb literally means "to dig," but this translation is substantiated by the parallel construction of 4Q525 5:12. The Hebrew term דרך ("way") is a rather common metaphor describing the way of life ordained by God in the sectarian texts.

Line 5: "the God of knowledge" — See commentary on 4Q417 1i:8.

Lines 8-9: "holy angels are his in heaven" — We can expect that the lacuna at the beginning of the next line refers to creatures on earth, a common juxtaposition in these lines, so line 9 picks up on the responsibilities of human beings. For an extensive analysis of the role of the relationship of the addressees and the angels in creation, in life, and in the future see Wold (*Women, Men and Angels*, 124-82). For commentary on the significance of these references to the angels see 4Q418 69.

Line 10: "[. . . acco]rding to their knowledge they will be glorified, one man more than his neighbor" — See 1Q28a (Sa) i:18 and 1QH^a xviii:29.

Line 12: "eternal possession" — In 1QS xi:7 the chosen are given as an eternal possession.

Frag. 58

¹[. . .] foolish of he[art . . .] ²[. . .] and every spirit of understanding [. . .] ³[. . .] all its shoots in [. . .]

Frag. 59, col. 1

¹[. . . they] walk ²[. . .] their assembly

Commentary

Line 2: "assembly" — עדה is one of the basic words designating the organization in the sectarian texts.

Frag. 65

¹[. . .] it is not like [. . .] ²[. . .] the earth and al[l . . .]

Frag. 68

¹[. . .] every generation [. . .] ²[. . .] the time and the assignment [. . .] ³[. . .] the assignments ⁴[. . .] ⁵[. . . y]ou, acquire understanding ⁶[. . .] be strengthened

Frag. 69, col. ii

¹[. . .] make you [re]joice ²[. . .] you shall get insight [. . .] with ³[. . .] Do they not walk in truth ⁴[all their waters?] With knowledge all their waves[. . . .] Now, foolish of heart, what is good that is not ⁵[created?] What is quiet for what does

not exist? What is justice for what is not established? What will the dead mourn for for al[l their da]ys? [6]You [. . .] were formed and to the pit forever is your return for you will awaken [. . .] your sin. [7]Its dark places will cry out for your trial and all that will be forever. Those who search for truth will awaken to your judgment. [Then] [8]all the foolish of heart will be destroyed and the sons of iniquity will not be found anymore. [All] who hold fast to evil will withe[r away. Then] [9]with your judgment the foundations of the heavens will shout and all the ho[sts of heaven] will thunder [. . .] love [. . .]

[10]You, chosen ones of truth and pursuers of [. . .] those who eagerly se[ek understanding] and those who are vigilant [11]concerning all knowledge. How do you say, "We have striven for understanding and we have been vigilant to pursue knowledge [. . .] with all [. . .] [12]He does not grow weary in all the years of eternity. Will he not take delight in truth forever and knowledge [? . . .] he will serve him and the so[ns] [13]of heaven whose inheritance is eternal life. Will they not truly say, "We have striven in the labor of truth and [we] have been vigilant [. . .] [14]in all ages. Will they not wa[lk] in light forever? G]lory and great honor you [. . .] [15]in the firmament [. . .] council of the gods. All [. . .]

You, son of [discernment . . .]

Notes

Line 1: "[. . .] make you [re]joice" — The reading in DJD 34:281 is rejected by Tigchelaar as not consistent with the traces of the remaining letters (*To Increase Learning*, 92).

Lines 4-5: The first word in each line, כול ("all") in line 4 and נוצר ("created") in line 5, is reconstructed on the basis of frag. 60, as proposed by Tigchelaar (*To Increase Learning*, 57-58, 91-92). In a note with regards to line 4, he suggests that rather than "[their waters]," משבריהם ("smash them") may more adequately fit the space left on the fragment.

Lines 4-8: These lines have a partial parallel in 4Q417 5.

Line 15: "council of the gods" — The presence of "in" just before these words, found in DJD 34:281-83, is not reflected on the original fragment according to Tigchelaar (*To Increase Learning*, 93).

Commentary

This column contains a vivid description of the anticipated universal judgment, also described in 4Q416 1 and already familiar from compositions such as *1 Enoch* 1–5. It provides clues concerning the fate of the righteous, "the chosen ones of truth." While fragmentary, their lot appears to be shared with the angels, "the sons of heaven whose inheritance is eternal life." See also 4Q416 1:10-12; 2iii:11-12; 4Q417 1i:17; 4Q418 55:8-11; 81+81a:4-5 (Goff, *Worldly and Heavenly Wisdom*, 206-14). For an extensive analysis of the role of the relationship of the addressees and the angels in creation, in life, and in the future see Wold (*Women, Men and Angels*, 124-82). This viewpoint can be found in more explicit form in other compositions from Qumran such as 1QH^a xix:6-17. The significance of the angelic realm is developed particularly in the MSS of the *Songs of the Sabbath Sacrifice*.[135]

This column also displays many literary similarities with frag. 55. See the discussion there for a description of them.

Lines 3, 14: "walk" — See 4Q416 2iii:9 and 4Q417 19:4.

Line 4: "waves" — While it is difficult to determine the precise meaning of the phrase here, its meaning in biblical and Qumranic usage is clear as referring to the waves of the sea (see DJD 34:284).

Lines 4-6: Menahem Kister has identified a parallel between these lines and the phrase in Matt 8:21-22//Luke 9:59-60: "Let the dead bury their own dead." He proposes some differences in translation based upon his understanding of this identification.[136]

Line 6: "your return" — The term תשובה is also the Hebrew term for "repentance."

Line 10: "chosen ones of truth" — Tigchelaar connects this with the "chosen righteous" in 4Q184 1:14; 4Q215a 1ii:3; 1QH^a x:15 (*To Increase Learning*, 215). He

---

135. Note also Louis Fletcher-Crispin, "Some Reflections on Angelomorphic Humanity Texts Among the Dead Sea Scrolls," *DSD* 7 (2000): 292-312; idem, *All the Glory of Adam: Liturgical Anthropology in the Dead Sea Scrolls* (STDJ 42; Leiden: Brill, 2002). Note the review of Carol Newsom in *DSD* 10 (2003): 431-35. For how this functions in *Instruction* see Macaskill, *Revealed Wisdom*, 72-114. For another analysis of this issue that overemphasizes the eschatological dimension see Émile Puech, "Les identités en présence dans les scènes du jugement dernier de 4QInstruction (4Q416 1 et 4Q418 69 ii)," in *Defining Identities: We, You, and the Other in the Dead Sea Scrolls: Proceedings of the Fifth Meeting of the IOQS in Groningen* (ed. F. García Martínez and M. Popović; STDJ 70; Leiden: Brill, 2008), 147-73.

136. Kister, "Divorce, Reproof, and Other Sayings," 198-99.

also lists 1QH[a] vi:26 among the passages for the "chosen righteous," but the Hebrew construction there is somewhat different, containing the Hebrew terms for both "righteousness" and "truth."

Line 15: "council" — The term סוד is common throughout the nonbiblical fragments of the Qumran texts referring particularly to the "council of God," "council of gods," and "council of men." In certain sectarian texts, particularly 1QS and the Cave 4 fragments of S and D, the related term יסוד היחד ("council of the community") is common with reference to the decision-making structure of the sect.

Frag. 70

[1][. . .] for [. . .] [2] [. . .] clouds and thick [darkness . . .] [3][. . .] they cease [. . .] [4][. . .] they seek [. . .]

Frag. 71

[2][. . .] life [3][. . .] in life and in you

Frag. 73

[1][. . .] every spirit of und[erstanding . . .] [2][. . .] upon all [. . .]

Frag. 74

[2][. . .] all that is fitting [. . .]

Commentary

Line 2: "that is fitting" — ראוי is a legal term used in texts such as 4QMMT to designate appropriate or approved activities; it is rather common in rabbinic literature.

Frag. 75

[1][. . .] be honored [. . .] [2][. . .] not [. . .]

Frag. 76

¹[. . .] upon every spirit [. . .] ²[. . .] men of righteousness not [. . .] ³[. . .] spirits of holiness [. . .]

Commentary

Line 2: "men of righteousness" — The word "holiness" was erased here and "righteousness" was substituted. The latter term is much more common in certain sectarian compositions and is considered to be indicative of particular viewpoints of the sect represented therein, for example, "sons of righteousness."[137] The phrase "men of holiness" occurs in 1QS v:13; viii:17, 23; ix:8.

Frag. 77

¹[. . .] sun [. . .] ²[. . .] mystery of existence and grasp the history of humankind and see that which is fit [. . .] ³[. . . assignment of] his [d]eed. Then you will understand the judgment of humankind and the weight [. . .] ⁴[utterance of his lips according to] his spirit. Grasp the mystery of existence concerning the weight of the times and the measure [. . .]

Notes

This fragment is composed of two pieces joined together. There is also a textual overlap with 4Q416 7.

Commentary

Lines 2, 4: "mystery of existence" — See the discussion of רז נהיה in the introduction to this chapter.

Frag. 78

¹[. . .] you will know the difference [. . .] ²[. . .] they were pursued [. . .] ³[. . .] for labor [. . .]

---

137. John Kampen, "'Righteousness' in Matthew and the Legal Texts from Qumran," in *Legal Texts and Legal Issues*, ed. Bernstein et al., 461-87.

Commentary

Line 1: "you will know the difference" — This is the normal construction for a phrase such as "know the difference between good and evil," found elsewhere in *Instruction*.

Frag. 79

²[. . .] your inner desire [. . .] ³[. . .] why [. . .]

Commentary

Line 2: "inner desire" — The term אוש is enigmatic and very particular to *Instruction*. See the discussion under "Key Terms" in the introduction to this chapter.

Frag. 81 + 81a

¹Open your lips, a spring to bless the holy ones. You as an eternal spring praise [. . . .] For he has separated you from all ²the spirit of flesh. You, keep separate from all that he hates and abstain from all of the abominations of the soul. For he made all things ³and he bestowed on every man his inheritance. He is your portion and your inheritance in the midst of the sons of men and over his inheritance he has made you ruler. You, ⁴with this give him glory when you keep yourself holy for him just as your name is among the most holy for all the world. Among all the godly beings ⁵ he has cast your lot and your very great glory and has set you up as a firstborn to him[. . . .] ⁶"My favor I will give to you." You, is not his favor for you? Walk with faith in him daily [. . .] ⁷your deeds. You, search his judgments from the hand of all who contend with you in all [. . .] ⁸love him and with loving-kindness (forever) and with mercy on all who keep his word. His zeal [. . .] ⁹you, he has unlocked insight for you and in his treasury he has made you ruler. A measure of truth he has appointed [. . .] ¹⁰they are with you. It is in your hand to turn away wrath from the men of favor and to appoint over [. . .] ¹¹with you. Before you take your inheritance from his hand, honor his holy ones and be[fore . . .] ¹²He opened a spring for all the holy ones and all who are called by his name are holy [. . .] ¹³with all times his splendor, his bough for an eternal planting[. . . .] ¹⁴world. In it all who inherit the earth will walk, for in the heav[ens . . .]

[15]You, man of discernment, if he has given you authority over craftsmanship and knowled[ge . . .] [16]inner desire for all humankind. From there you will attend to your sustenance [. . .] [17]gain greatly in understanding and from the hand of every sage grasp even more [. . .] [18]bring out from your need for all who seek delight. Then you will prepare [. . .] [19]you shall be filled and satisfied with abundant goodness. From your craftmanship [. . .] [20]for God has distributed [their] inheritance [among al]l [life] and given wisdom to all the wise of heart [. . .]

Notes

Lines 1-5: A parallel to this text is found in 4Q423 8. The text is considerably more complete in this copy. 4Q423 23 also may reflect these lines (Tigchelaar, *To Increase Learning*, 94-95).

Line 3: "made you ruler" — It is difficult to read the fragment at this point, but the second person singular reading is easier to make sense of than the other possibility of a third person plural (DJD 34:302). Note the textual comments of Tigchelaar (*To Increase Learning*, 95).

Line 8: "(forever)" — This word was erased in the text. It is a very infrequent biblical construction (DJD 34:306).

Line 12: "a spring" — This reconstruction is like line 1 rather than the "song" proposed in DJD 34:303.

Lines 12-13: "a spring for all" in line 12 and the latter half of "times" and the word "splendor" in line 13 are based on a small fragment that has been incorporated into this fragment on the later museum plates.[138]

Line 17: "gain greatly in understanding" — This unusual phrase is also found in 4Q415 11:12 and 4Q417 3:3.

Line 20: "[among]" — On the basis of the available space on the fragment, Tigchelaar proposes that the inclusion of the Hebrew preposition ‫ב‬ is impossible at this point (*To Increase Learning*, 96).

---

138. Tigchelaar labels it Frag. 81b (*To Increase Learning*, 96).

Commentary

Line 2: "spirit of flesh" — The spirit of flesh is associated with a sphere that is in opposition to the will of God. In 4Q416 1:10-13 those related to the spirit of flesh are contrasted with the "sons of his truth," also called the "sons of heaven." This passage supports the thesis that this was so from creation. The connection of the use of this phrase with similar perspectives in the writing of Paul is discussed in the introduction (p. 32).[139]

Line 3: "He is your portion and your inheritance in the midst of the sons of men" — Note Num 18:20, "I am your portion and your inheritance in the midst of the sons of Israel," where this refers to Aaron and the priesthood. Tigchelaar suggests this is evidence of the sacerdotal interests we find expressed in certain sections of this composition (*To Increase Learning*, 230-36). The man of discernment (מבין) addressed here is placed within the perspective of all humankind, but simultaneously is exhorted to be separated from the spirit of flesh, abominations, and everything that God hates. In other words there is a reconfiguration of the definition of the leadership of the people of God, hence of the people of God themselves. This line provides a glimpse into the manner in which traditional Israel with its leadership, its obligations, and its relationship to God is being redefined in this text.

Lines 4-5: "godly beings" — The "glory" of the אלים, presumably angelic figures, is described in greater detail in 4Q400-407. In this text it is the addressee of *Instruction* who is given this "elect" status. It does appear that this status among the "godly beings" is intended for a group, hence the importance of this text to undergird the sectarian ideology advanced in subsequent compositions.[140] For an extensive analysis of the role of the relationship of the addressees and the angels in creation, in life, and in the future, see Wold (*Women, Men and Angels*, 124-82). For commentary on the significance of these references to the angels, see 4Q418 69.

Line 12: "all who are called by his name are holy" — See commentary to 4Q417 13:2 above.

Line 13: "bough" — While the term פארת could refer to glory, it seems more likely in this case to designate branches, known from Isa 10:33 and Ezek 17:6;

139. Jörg Frey, "The Notion of Flesh in 4QInstruction and the Background of Pauline Usage," in *Sapiential, Liturgical and Poetical Texts*, ed. Falk et al., 197-226.
140. Goff, *Worldly and Heavenly Wisdom*, 265-77.

31:5, 6, 8, 12, 13. In 4Q433a (papHodayot-like Text B) 2:6 we read of the "bough for everlasting generations."

Line 13: "eternal planting" — This is a significant reference in other Qumran literature as well as in biblical materials. The most important biblical allusions to the "plant" are found in Isa 5:7; 60:21; 61:3. In the latter two references it is applied to the restored Israel of the future. This metaphor then appears in Second Temple literature. In *1 Enoch* it can refer either to the present righteous or the future restored people of God (10:16; 84:6; 93:5, 10). In *Jubilees* this is limited to Israel and also alludes to a possible association of the image with the immediate presence of God or angels (1:16; 16:26; 21:24; 36:6). This reference appears to be similar to the options in *Jubilees*. The sectarian literature picks up the image and applies it to the community itself, both present and future ideal (e.g., CD i:7; 1QS viii:5; xi:8; 1QH^a xiv:18; xvi:7, 10, 11). The metaphor is fixed enough to suggest some connection among the documents that employ it.[141]

Line 14: "walk" — See commentary to 4Q416 2iii:9 and 4Q417 19:4.

Lines 15, 19: "craftsmanship" — Literally "wisdom of hands," which also designates artisans in Sir 9:17. The phrase here probably means the mastery of a craft. See the discussion of חכמה among "Key Terms" in the introduction to this chapter.

Line 16: "inner desire" — See discussion of אוט under "Key Terms" in the introduction to this chapter.

Line 16: "humankind" — A literal translation of the Hebrew would be "walkers of man." The participle "those who walk" is used in phrases such as "those who walk in perfection" and "those who walk in the ways of evil." It would appear that the significance of the term "man" here is to designate the human condition.

Line 20: "for God has distributed [their] inheritance [among al]l [life]" — The sense of the sentence is that God has determined what their destiny is in the midst of all of life rather than that their particular fate has been divided up and distributed throughout all the world.

141. Patrick Tiller, "The 'Eternal Planting' in the Dead Sea Scrolls," *DSD* 4 (1997): 312-35.

Frag. 82

[1][. . .] will love as much [. . .]

Frag. 83

[1][. . .] you have known [. . .]

Frag. 84

[1][. . .] all [. . .] [2][. . .] not [. . .]

Frag. 85

[2][. . .] in truth [. . .]

Frag. 86

[1][. . .] for his fury, and as a father over [his] sons [. . .] [2] [. . .] the days allotted to it [. . .] [3][. . .] heavens [. . .] [4][. . .] your throne [. . .]

Notes

This fragment should probably be rejected as a fragment of 4Q418 (DJD 34:314; Tigchelaar, *To Increase Learning*, 96).

Line 2: "allotted to it" — Literally "days of its lot." The suffix here is third person feminine singular, so it could be "her" or "it."

Frag. 87

[2][. . .] deceit [. . .] [3][. . .] for wisdom [. . .] [4][. . .] in it [. . .] [5][. . .] from the house of [. . .] [6][. . .] poverty [. . .] [7][. . .] take on a pledge for a stranger [. . .] [8][. . .] your scar and a wound of [. . .] [9][. . .] and ask [. . .] [10][. . .] anger in all the ways of [. . .] [11][. . .] walk in truth [. . .] [12][. . .] contain and by weight [. . .] [13][. . .] your hand is extended [. . .] [14][. . . you shall not become impoverished [. . .] [15][. . .] If there is a dispute [. . .]

Notes

Line 3: "for wisdom" rather than "thy bread" (DJD 34:316).

Line 9: "and ask" — This translation is based on the observations of Tigchelaar (*To Increase Learning*, 96-97).

Commentary

Line 7: "take on a pledge for a stranger" — Since elsewhere the taking of loans is prohibited it seems strange if this text would have supported it. Perhaps it is stated in the negative in the portion of the text not preserved (Goff, *Worldly and Heavenly Wisdom*, 142). See 4Q418 88ii:3 below.

Line 8: "scar" — Hebrew נגע can refer to the marks of skin diseases such as leprosy.

Frag. 88, col. ii

¹you shall establish for a[ll . . .]your requirements [. . .] ²in your life and your peace for the numerous years [. . .] ³you, beware lest you shall pledge [. . .] ⁴injustice you shall judge. With the strength of your hand [. . .] ⁵he will close his hand to your poverty[. . . .] ⁶to the sole of your feet, for God seeks [. . .] ⁷in your hand for life. You are gathered in sorrow [. . .] ⁸and with truth your inheritance shall be full. You shall be [. . .]

Notes

There probably is no column i, as was hypothesized by the editors based on the possible evidence of one dot in the photographs (Tigchelaar, *To Increase Learning*, 97).

Commentary

Line 5: "he will close his hand to your poverty" — See 4Q417 2i:24 for this statement in a less fragmentary context. It is also found in 4Q418 7b:7.

Frag. 89

[1][. . .] by your hand [. . .] [2][. . .] in all things [your hand] is extended [. . .]

Frag. 90

[1][. . .] these things [. . .]

Frag. 91

[1][. . .] in your lives [. . .] [2][. . .] over all [. . .]

Frag. 92

[2][. . .] not [. . .]

Frag. 94

[2][. . .] all the m[en of . . .] [3][. . . re]quirement for [. . .]

Frag. 95

[1][. . .] p[o]wer of [. . .] [2][. . .] your council with the foundations of [. . .] [3][. . .] you shall not darken knowledge [. . .]

Commentary

Line 2: "your council" — This term appears elsewhere in *Instruction* only at 4Q415 6:3, where it is partially reconstructed. It is rather common in some sectarian texts such as 1QS (and 4QS MSS), 1QSa, and 1QSb, as well as in 1QpHab xii:4, where it most frequently appears in the phrase "council of the community" or "council of God."

Line 2: "foundations" — Elsewhere in *Instruction* found only at 4Q417 1i:9, 25. It is also found in 4Q299 38:2.

Line 3: "darken knowledge" — This strange phrase seems to be based on Job 38:2, "Who is this that darkens counsel by words without knowledge?" The עצה ("counsel") mentioned in the biblical verse is a different inflection of the word עצת ("council") in line 2.

Frag. 96

¹[. . .] do wondrous [. . .] ²[. . . se]arch all the[se things . . .] ³[. . .] you shall not stretch your hand against ⁴[. . .] in vain [. . .] ⁵[. . .] shall send [. . .]

Frag. 97

¹[. . . wi]thout oppressing [. . .] ²[. . .] your [po]verty, take from his hand [. . .] ³[. . .] it will not be found. He shall not return [. . .]

Frag. 100

¹[. . . re]joicing of [. . .]

Frag. 101, col. i

²[. . .] his deeds ³[. . .] your inner desire ⁴[. . . .] You

Commentary

Line 3: "inner desire" — See the discussion of אוט in the "Key Terms" in the introduction to this chapter.

Frag. 101, col. ii

²sin [. . .] ³you shall not be in his house for [. . .] ⁴he will spare his wealth. He shall be [. . .] ⁵[. . .] his flesh. He shall not act unfaithfully against his own flesh [. . .]

Commentary

Line 5: "flesh" — In this case it refers to kin.

Frag. 102a + b

¹[...] in the pit [...] ²[...] will and truth. The righteousness of all his deeds [...] ³[... You,] man of discernment in truth from the skill of all your craftsmanship [...] ⁴[...] you walk about and then he will seek your will, for all who inquire of it [...] ⁵[... from] the iniquity of abomination you shall be innocent, and with the joy of truth you will [...]

Notes

Line 2: "righteousness of all his deeds" — In DJD 34:327 there appears to be a space between these two words, but there is no extra space available on the plate (Tigchelaar, *To Increase Learning,* 99).

Commentary

Line 1: "pit" — This is also a metaphor for the destruction God brings in the end times, for example, "eternal destruction" in 4Q418 69ii:6 and 162:4. Note also 4Q184 i:5, 11; the "men of destruction" in 1QS ix:16, 22; and the "sons of destruction" in CD vi:15; xiii:14.

Line 3: "the skill of all your craftsmanship" — Literally "from the hand of all of the wisdom of your hands," this expression applies to the artisan as it does in 4Q418 81+81a:15, 19; 137:2, as well as in Sir 9:17. On wisdom see discussion of חכמה under "Key Terms" in the introduction to this chapter.

Line 4: "walk" — See 4Q416 2iii:9 and 4Q417 19:4.

Frag. 103, col. i

⁹[...] flesh [...]

Frag. 103, col. ii + 4Q418a 4

²[. . .] farmers until all [. . .] ³[. . .] bring into your baskets and your storehouses [. . .] of your land [. . .] ⁴will compare, in every season seek them. Do not be silent [. . .] Do not [. . .] ⁵for all of them they shall seek in their season. A man according to [his] will [. . .] and he will find paths of [. . .] ⁶like a spring of living water that fills [his] hidd[en de]sire [. . . In] your merchandise do not mix that [. . .] ⁷lest it will be of two kinds as with a mule and you will be as if you were wear[ing mixed material] of wool and flax, your labor will be as if plough[ing] ⁸with an ox and an a[s]s [to]geth[er]. Also your produce will [be for you as if] you planted two kinds, both seed and full fruit and the produ[ce] ⁹of the [vineyard] will be sanctifi[ed together. Al]so your wealth with your flesh [. . .] your life will be finished together, but in your life you will not find

Notes

Line 3: An untranslated word at the end of the preserved text could be either "all" (כול) or "for" (כי), as proposed in DJD 34:330. Either reading appears possible from photographs of the fragment.

Line 5: "they shall seek" — The emphatic "they shall surely seek" occurs in 4Q418a 4:3.

Commentary

Lines 6-9: This discussion of mixing of two kinds is based on Lev 19:19 and Deut 22:9-11, even though it follows directly neither text and the conclusion in line 9 is not found in a biblical text. The fragmentary nature of the last lines makes a full comprehension of the paragraph difficult. Concerns about "mixing" are found elsewhere in Qumran texts, most notably in 4Q396 1-2iv:5-11 and 11Q19 xxxv:10-15. Note the prohibition against "mixing" the wealth of the initiate with the property of the sect until a full examination in 1QS vi:17, 22; vii:24; viii:23; ix:8. The term כלאים ("two kinds") also appears in frag. 29 without context for interpretation.

Line 9: "[together]" — See the discussion in the introduction to 4Q525 under "Literary Questions."

Frag. 105

[1][. . .] you shall [no]t wear [. . .] [2][. . .] [3][. . . p]it [. . .]

Commentary

Line 3: "[. . . p]it" — On the evidence of the photographs, the Hebrew term
שחת here is a more likely reading of the fragment than שמחה ("joy"), as proposed by the editors (DJD 34:334; see Tigchelaar, *To Increase Learning,* 100).
This symbol of destruction and/or damnation appears elsewhere in the
Qumran wisdom texts in 4Q184 1:5(2x), 11; 4Q418 69ii:6; 102a+b:1 (note commentary there); 162:4; 177:2; 4Q525 15:7. It is common throughout the major sectarian texts from Qumran.

Frag. 106

[1][. . .] will [. . .] [2][. . .] why [. . .]

Frag. 107

[1][. . . they re]quest and then you will fi[nd . . .] [2][. . .] upwards [. . .] [3][. . .] for
your poverty [. . .] [4][. . .] inner desires your merchandise and your labor with
the requirements [. . .] [5][. . .] with all the shoots of the earth for all of [them] will
seek [. . .] [6][. . .] grass with the roots [. . .] [7][. . .] with [. . .]

Commentary

Line 3: "poverty" — Note that with the transposition of two letters in the word
מחסור ("poverty") we have מסחור ("merchandise"), found in line 4. Both terms
are common in *Instruction,* so it would be a reasonable error for a scribe to
transpose these letters in this and other instances throughout the text.

Line 4: "inner desires" — See the discussion of אוט in the "Key Terms" in the
introduction to this chapter. This plural reading is a scribal correction from an
original second person singular suffix ("your inner desire"). The latter is much
more common in *Instruction,* the primary composition in which this term appears.

Frag. 108

²[. . .] their labor [. . .]

Frag. 112

¹[. . .] righteousness [. . .]

Notes

Perhaps this fragment should be placed with 4Q418b (DJD 34:339; Tigchelaar, *To Increase Learning,* 101).

Frag. 113

¹[. . .] until the end of iniq[uity . . .] ²[. . .] the visitation of pe[ace . . .] ³[. . .] and (it) will cease [. . .]

Frag. 114

²[. . .] he established [. . .]

Notes

This fragment does not belong with the materials of 4Q418 (DJD 34:340; Tigchelaar, *To Increase Learning,* 340).

Frag. 116

¹[. . .] waters and by the sound of their voice [. . .] ²[. . .] if it will be silent [. . .]

Frag. 117

¹[. . .] all knowledge [. . .] ²[. . .] understand [. . .]

Commentary

Line 2: The fragmentary nature of the text does not permit us to determine whether this is a noun or verb form, or whether it might even be the preposition "between."

Frag. 118

[2][. . .] season and keep watch [. . .] [3][. . .] for all th[eir] festivals [. . .]

Commentary

Line 3: "festivals" — As noted in DJD 34:342, the term מעד rather than מועד is highly unusual in the orthography of the Qumran scrolls. However, it is employed as the standard spelling in 4Q329a.

Frag. 119

[1][. . . w]ork[s . . .] [2][. . .] the deep [. . .] [3][. . .] the deep was born [. . .] [4][. . .] depths of the sea [. . .]

Notes

Line 3: I have not included the preposition ב ("in"), as found in DJD 34:343, following the observations of Tigchelaar (*To Increase Learning*, 102). This appears to be confirmed by the photographs.

Frag. 120

[1][. . .] testimony [. . .] [2][. . .] say [. . .]

Notes

It is very difficult to determine the reading of line 1 due to its fragmentary nature.

Frag. 121

¹[. . .] righteous judgment you shall re[nder . . .] ²[. . .] service of wicked[ness . . .]

Frag. 122, col. i

¹[. . .] they shall be established ²[. . .] ruler ³[. . .] loves truth ⁴[. . .] if a man ⁵[. . .] understand your merchandise and not ⁶[. . . no]t will he compare with your labor or to what yet ⁷[. . .] your merchandise and thus you will be patient and not [. . .] ⁸[. . .] to keep watch [. . .]

Notes

It is possible that the few words of frag. 122ii should be joined with frag. 126ii. Note that discussion.

Line 7: "you will be patient and not" — These words are added on the basis of Tigchelaar's proposal (*To Increase Learning*, 102).

Frag. 123, col. i

¹[. . . understand]ings of ²[the flesh shall not lead you astray . . .]you [shall not] say [. . .] ³[. . .] with all wealth ⁴[. . .] and according to your statute

Notes

Lines 2-3: These lines seem to find a parallel in 4Q417 1ii:15-16. The textual connections are noted there. The reconstruction here follows the text of Tigchelaar (*To Increase Learning*, 103-4).

Commentary

Line 2: The negative construction here is a frequent introductory formula found in biblical sapiential texts and *Instruction* (DJD 34:348).

Frag. 123, col. ii

²for the entrance of years and the exit of epochs [. . .] ³all that exists in it, that which was and that which will be in it [. . .] ⁴its epoch that God uncovered the ear of those who understand through the mystery of existence [. . .] ⁵You, man of discernment, when you observe all these things [. . .] ⁶[. . .] weigh your deeds with the epochs [. . .] ⁷[. . .] appoints you, keep careful watch from [. . .] ⁸[. . . ju]dge iniquity [. . .]

Commentary

Line 3: On the temporal dimensions of the verb "to be" (היה) in *Instruction* and the "mystery of existence" see 4Q417 1i:3-5 and the introduction. The temporal construction that incorporates past, present, and future into an understanding of the epochs of time is remarkably similar.

Line 4: "God uncovered the ear of those who understand through the mystery of existence" — This phrase also appears in 1Q26 1:4; 4Q416 2iii:17-18; 4Q418 184:2; 190:2; 4Q423 5:1; the first part in 4Q299 8:6. The phrase "to uncover your ear" is found in Isa 22:14, with regard to revelation concerning the consequences of the iniquity of Israel. In Job 33:16 and 36:10 the revelation concerns מוסר ("instruction" or "discipline"). In Job 36:15 he "opens their ear" by oppression or affliction. The term אל can mean either "God" or the preposition "to." It is treated as a preposition in DJD 34:347. See the introduction for a discussion of the "mystery of existence."

Frag. 126, col. ii

¹[. . . n]ot shall one depart from their host [. . .] ²or [. . .] in truth from the hand of every inner desire of men [. . .] ³[for . . .] with an ephah of truth and a weight of righteousness God has measured all [. . .] ⁴he spread them out, with truth he placed them and for their will they will seek [. . .] ⁵all things will be hidden. Also they will not occur apart from his desire and from [his] wisd[om . . .] ⁶judgment to return vengeance to those who practice iniquity and the visitation of [. . .] ⁷to lock up the wicked, to raise up the head of the poor [. . .] ⁸with glory forever and eternal peace. To separate the spirit of life [. . .] ⁹all the sons of Eve and with power of God and the abundance of his glory with his goodness [. . .]

¹⁰And on his trustworthiness they will meditate all the day. Daily they will praise his name [. . .]

¹¹You, walk in truth with all who seek [. . .] ¹²by your hand his inner desire and from your basket he will seek what he wills. You, man [of discernment . . .] ¹³if he will not extend his hand to your poverty and the poverty of his inner desire [. . .] ¹⁴[. . .] his mouth and he will not set apart from his will for God [. . .] ¹⁵[. . .] your hand for profit and your livestock will increase [. . .] ¹⁶[. . .] forever according to what you shall inherit [. . .]

Notes

It is possible that the few words of frag. 122ii should be joined with frag. 126ii:2-4.

Line 6: "those who practice iniquity" — This is based on the reading פעלי און, proposed by Tigchelaar (*To Increase Learning*, 103) and supported by the photographs, rather than בעלי און ("masters of iniquity") (DJD 34:350, 352).

Line 14: "his mouth" — Tigchelaar reads [או]טהו ("his inner desire") at this point (*To Increase Learning*, 103). Only a few traces of the tips of the letters are available. Strugnell's earlier reading was apparently טהו (*PEUDSS* 2:116).

Line 16: "according to what you shall inherit" — Proposed by Tigchelaar and in the notes of the editors (DJD 34:352; Tigchelaar, *To Increase Learning*, 103).

Commentary

Lines 2, 12, 13: "inner desire" — See the discussion of אוט in the "Key Terms" in the introduction to this chapter.

Line 4: "for their will they will seek" — This appears to be based on Ps 111:2.

Lines 4-5: These lines highlight the pivotal role of wisdom in the act of creation, as developed also in 4Q417 1i:8-9. On חכמה, "wisdom," see discussion of "Key Terms" in the introduction to this chapter.

Line 8: "To separate the spirit of life" — Strugnell and Harrington suggest that this should be followed by "from the spirit of darkness" (DJD 34:352). This seems a likely interpretation of the use of the verb "separate" (להבדיל) in a number of Qumran texts. While rare in *Instruction* (4Q418 81+81a:1, 2), it is common in those texts that deal with legislative issues (11Q19 and 20), and especially communal legislation (1QS and 4Q255-264, CD and 4Q266-273, and 4Q265).

Line 9: "sons of Eve" — This is an unusual designation, not found in either biblical or Second Temple literature. In most Second Temple literature Eve is regarded as either the source of sin or of life. This phrase could also translated "sons of life," a phrase equally unattested in the comparable literature (DJD 34:354-55).

Line 11: "walk" — See 4Q416 2iii:9 and 4Q417 19:4.

Frag. 127

[1][. . .] your source, and your poverty you will not find and your soul grows faint from (want of) all good unto death [. . .] [2][. . .] all the day and your soul desires to enter into its gates and you will be buried and covered [. . .] [3][. . .] your body and you will be food for the teeth and heat for the flame in the face of dea[th . . .] [4][. . . see]kers of delight you oppressed in their path. Also you [. . .] [5][. . .] to you for God has created all the delights of the inner desire. He has measured them in truth [. . .] [6][. . .] with accurate scales he weighed their plan and in truth [. . .]

Commentary

Line 3: See Deut 32:24 for the allusions in this line. Presumably it is food for the teeth of beasts and heat for the flame of Sheol. Deuteronomy here describes in graphic terms the results when Israel forgets God.

Lines 4, 5: "delight" — For a discussion of חפץ see commentary to 4Q416 1:2 and 4Q416 2i:12.

Line 5: "inner desire" — For a discussion of יאוט see the "Key Terms" in the introduction to this chapter.

Line 6: "plan" — For a discussion of this term see commentary to 4Q415 9:6.

Frags. 128 + 129

[1]your peace [. . .] [2]in front of [. . .] [3]Also all your desires [. . .]

Frag. 130

¹the world will shine forth [. . .] ²the sick the reward [. . .] ³[. . .] vow [. . .]

Frag. 131

¹[. . .] with [. . .] ²[. . .] with [. . .] ³[. . .] they will seek for you [. . .] ⁴[. . .] not [. . .] ⁵[. . .] give you light [. . .]

Frag. 132

¹[. . .] all [. . .] ²[. . .] their host [. . .]

Frag. 133

²[. . .] farmers [. . .]

Frag. 135

²[. . .] make known in front of ³[. . .] men

Frag. 137

²[. . . cra]ftsmanship he will increase for you [. . .] ³[. . .] righteousness with your wage because for your labor [. . .] ⁴[. . .] length of your days will increase a great deal [. . .] ⁵[. . .] your recompense a day [. . .]

Commentary

Line 2: "[. . . cra]ftsmanship" — See discussion of חכמה ("wisdom") among "Key Terms" in the introduction to this chapter.

Frag. 138

²[. . .] portion in the inheritance of a father [. . .] ³[. . .] your [li]fe from faintness and with the delights [. . .] ⁴[. . .] your inner desire and all [. . .] your desires [. . .]

Notes

Line 3: "your [li]fe" — This reconstruction is based on the observations of Tigchelaar (*To Increase Learning*, 105-6).

Line 4: This line is reconstructed on the basis of the observations of Tigchelaar (*To Increase Learning*, 105-6).

Commentary

Line 4: "inner desire" — See the discussion of "Key Terms" in the introduction to this chapter for the discussion of Hebrew **אוט**.

Frag. 139

¹[. . .] you ²[. . .] with your craftsmanship ³[. . .] to all

Commentary

Line 2: "craftsmanship" — See discussion of **חכמה** ("wisdom") among "Key Terms" in the introduction to this chapter.

Frag. 140

²[. . .] those who remain [. . .] ³[. . .] you shall not take counsel [. . .] ⁴[. . .] you shall know a prince among princes [. . .]

Commentary

Line 3: "counsel" — The term **סוד** can also mean "council" and that is the more common meaning in Qumran texts. See commentary to 4Q415 6:1 above.

Line 4: "prince among princes" — For this phrase see 4Q417 2i:5. Also see commentary to 4Q416 2iii:11.

Frag. 143

²[. . .] righteousness [. . .]

Frag. 144

²[. . .] and then [. . .] ³[. . .] and not [. . .]

Frag. 145

²[. . .] he will say [. . .]

Frag. 146

²[. . .] you shall [no]t extort the wa[ges of the oppressed and the needy . . .]

Commentary

This line is probably based on Deut 24:14. The "oppressed" (עני) and the "needy" (אביון) are common throughout the Qumran scrolls, hence the plausibility of reconstructing the text of the entire biblical verse at this point. See commentary to 4Q417 2i:16.

Frag. 147

²[. . .] truth [. . .] ³[. . .] for furious anger [. . .] ⁴[. . . in unr]ighteousness you walk about and [. . .] ⁵[. . .] have understanding about [. . .] ⁶[. . .] have understanding [. . .] ⁷[. . .] ⁸[. . .] and if [. . .]

Commentary

Line 4: "walk" — See 4Q416 2iii:9 and 4Q417 19:4.

Frag. 148, col. i

²[. . .] you shall [no]t find ³[. . . a]ll your deeds ⁴[. . .] and then ⁵[. . .] how much ⁶[. . .] water ⁷[. . .] portion of the sea

Commentary

Line 7: "portion of the sea" — In Zeph 2:5-7 חבל ים designates the "seacoast" that becomes the portion of the "remnant of the house of Judah" when the Lord restores the fortunes of the humble (ענוי) of the land. The term "humble" is very close to the "oppressed" mentioned in the previous fragment and elsewhere plays a significant role in a number of Qumran texts.

Frag. 148, col. ii

²who dwell in it [. . .] ³all who despise [. . .]

⁴A man [. . .] are you [. . .] ⁵knowledge of your service and from there [. . .] ⁶understanding for the former things put [. . .] ⁷knowledge and with all measurement of man [. . .] ⁸your deeds and trust in the fruit of [. . .] ⁹forever [. . .]

Notes

Line 4: "A man [. . .] are you" — The editors propose that perhaps the word רוש ("poor") can be reconstructed in this lacuna, based on the visible dots on the fragment (DJD 34:374). This yields a translation such as "A man of poverty you are." Such a construction with regard to the designation of the poverty of the addressee is not found elsewhere in *Instruction*. Tigchelaar suggests that there is not adequate room at that point for this word (*To Increase Learning,* 107).

Line 5: "knowledge of your service" — These words are also found in a fragment from an American museum catalog identified and classified by Esther and Hanan Eshel as 4Q416 23. For details see the discussion of "Manuscripts" in the introduction to this chapter (p. 38, n. 7 above).

Commentary

Line 6: "former things" — The term קדמוניות or קדמניות is also found in *Mysteries* (1Q27 1i:3; 4Q300 3:3), where it is mentioned in conjunction with developing an understanding of the "epoch of eternity" and in parallel construction with the "mystery of existence," presumably with a similar meaning. In *MMT* (4Q397 14-21:12; 4Q398 14-17i:4), it appears between the reference to the canonical writings and the future fate of the wicked. In both cases future catastrophe

for those outside the will of God is rooted in an understanding of the prior history of God and humankind. It is also found in 4Q298 3-4ii:10 in a usage rather
similar to the one apparent in this text.

Line 7: "measurement" — The term ספורות appears only once in the HB
(Ps 71:15), where it has sometimes been interpreted as referring to scribal ability,
but could also mean "measurement" or "number" (so NRSV). This is the meaning it acquires in rabbinic texts.

Frag. 149

¹[. . .] and then [. . .] ²[. . .] princes [. . .] ³[. . .] and then [. . .] ⁴[. . .] you [will ta]ke
pleasure in the li[fe of . . .] ⁵[. . . f]irst ⁶[. . .] give insight [. . .] ⁷[. . .] walk [. . .]

Notes

Line 7: "walk" — There appears to be an extra Hebrew letter ה reconstructed at
the beginning of this word in the text (DJD 34:377). I assume that this is simply
an error and has no impact on the translation of the term or the fragment.

Commentary

Line 2: "princes" — See commentary to 4Q416 2iii:11.

Line 5: "[. . . f]irst" — The most likely reconstruction of this term is ראשית, a
term that appears 22 times in the fragments of *Instruction*. Lack of context does
not permit an adequate interpretation.

Line 7: "walk" — See commentary to 4Q416 2iii:9 and 4Q417 19:4.

Frag. 150

²[. . .] about [. . .] ³[. . .] the evil [. . .]

Frag. 152

¹[. . .] with [. . .]

Frag. 158

²because those who lie in wait for [. . .] ³Seek all the will of [. . .] ⁴one who is discerning in your deeds [. . .] ⁵[. . .] and kings will glorify you [. . .] ⁶[. . . abu]ndance of insight [. . .]

Notes

Line 5: At the beginning of the line the editors have read פניכה, "thy presence" (DJD 34:381), but allowed for the alternative reading ב[י]ניכה ("among you" or "between you"). Tigchelaar rejected the former (*To Increase Learning*, 107) and favored the latter. I do not find either reading convincing.

Frag. 159, col. i

²[. . .] they shall request ³[. . .] ⁴[. . .] ⁵[. . .] stretch forth

Col. ii

¹vengeance [. . .] ²its acting unfaithfully the disaster [. . .] ³with his righteousness and with the might of [his] stre[ngth . . .] ⁴support with the deed of righteou[sness . . .] ⁵your walking and to pov[erty . . .] ⁶and the measure of your glory [. . .] ⁷the plan of the world [. . .]

Commentary

Line 5: "walking" — See commentary to 4Q416 2iii:9 and 4Q417 19:4.

Line 7: "the plan of the world" — See commentary to 4Q415 9:6.

Frag. 160

¹their waves [. . .] ²quickly [. . .] ³about [. . .]

Frag. 162

²[. . .] for you have said [. . .] ³[. . . in]crease his inheritance [. . .] ⁴[. . .] destruction forever. There will be glor[y] for you [. . .] ⁵[. . .] it bustles [. . .]

Frag. 163

²[. . .] understanding [. . .]

Frag. 164

²[. . .] his [ang]els and among [. . .] ³[. . .] and kings [. . .]

Frag. 165

²[. . .] all the deeds [of . . .] ³[. . .] his insight, understanding [. . .]

Frags. 167a + b

See 4Q415 11 for translation and commentary.

Frag. 168

²[. . .] that which one strikes, a stumbling block [. . .] ³[. . . the l]onging [. . .] ⁴[. . .] you, man of discern[ment . . .]

Commentary

Line 2: This collection of terms could be based on Isa 8:14, where the Lord is to be regarded as holy and then is "a stone one strikes against, a rock one stumbles over."

Frags. 169 + 170

¹[. . .] inheritance [. . .] ²[. . .] in his visitation [. . .] and when he walks [. . .] ³[. . .] instruction and with lovi[ng-ki]ndness [. . .] ⁴[. . .] and with all [. . .] ⁵[. . .] he will keep watch over you [. . .]

Commentary

Line 2: "walks" — See commentary to 4Q416 2iii:9 and 4Q417 19:4.

Frag. 172

¹[. . .] mystery of existence [. . .] ²[. . .] of the spirit and the weighing of [. . .] ³[. . .] how they have determined in comm[on . . .] ⁴[. . .] in the perfection of way with the end [. . .] ⁵[. . .] according to the abundance of the inheritance of man in tru[th . . .] ⁶[. . .] to you with her young sheep [. . .] ⁷[. . .] her sons peace and when you walk [. . .] ⁸[. . .] from the beasts of the field and from the young birds [. . .] ⁹[. . .] consume in the field of another he will make restitution [. . .] ¹⁰[. . .] with your pasturing and with the pasturing of [. . .] ¹¹with all their pasturing lest a year [. . .] ¹²[. . .] return it lest you destroy [. . .] ¹³[. . .] by your [ha]nd is the judgment of the flock and by [your] t[ongue . . .] ¹⁴[. . .] by the sword they were [. . .]

Notes

Line 3: The reading איכה ("how") is proposed by Tigchelaar (*To Increase Learning*, 110), rather than עליכה ("concerning you") (DJD 34:393-94).

Lines 6-7: These are proposed as a possible parallel to 4Q415 5 (DJD 34:352; Tigchelaar, *To Increase Learning*, 33, 110).

Commentary

Line 3: On the terminology in this line see 4Q415 11:4-5 above.

Line 4: "perfection of way" — See commentary to 4Q417 1ii:5.

Line 7: "walk" — See commentary to 4Q416 2iii:9 and 4Q417 19:4.

Line 9: Concerning restitution see Exod 22:4.

Frag. 173

²[. . .] their [pas]turing [. . .] ³[. . .] ⁴[. . .] ⁵[. . .] and with the pasturing of [. . .] ⁶[. . .] punish them [. . .]

Frag. 174

¹[. . .] your voice [. . .] ²[. . . judg]ment sanctify [. . .] ³[. . .] they will make insightful [. . .]

Frag. 175

²[. . .] you will compare [. . .]

Notes

Line 2: Or "you will set," according to Tigchelaar (*To Increase Learning*, 111).

Frag. 176

¹[. . .] the land [. . .] ²[. . . a]ll who dwell in it and those who mourn for righteousness [. . .] ³[. . .] you, man of discernment, in the afflictions of distress do not [. . .]

Commentary

Line 2: "mourn for righteousness" is an unusual phrase. A similar sentiment can be found in Matt 5:4, "Blessed are those who mourn," when we note that righteousness is the object in both Matt 5:6 and 10. Future comfort for those who mourn in Zion is found in Isa 61:2-3, where God promises that they will be called "oaks of righteousness."

Line 3: "afflictions of distress" — These two obscure words (הוות מדהבה) are difficult to translate; they occur also in 1QH^a 11:25. The second term is found in Isa 14:4. See commentary to 4Q416 2ii:14.

Frag. 177

²[. . . the pi]t and the underworld that in the end do not [. . .] ³[. . .] and cover your reproach [. . .] ⁴[. . .] and receive understanding. Listen to [. . .] ⁵[. . .] you

are poor and princes [. . .] ⁶[. . .] all righ[teousness . . .] ⁷ᵃ[. . .] You, know the mysteries of [. . .] ⁷[. . .] be ver[y] careful [. . .] ⁸[. . .] your inner desire [. . .]

Notes

Line 7a: The words of this line are written above line 7 in small letters. I have here translated "mysteries of," following Tigchelaar (*To Increase Learning*, 111), rather than the editors, "his mysteries" (DJD 34:401).

Commentary

Line 5: "poor" — The Hebrew terms רוש (verb) and ריש (noun) are found throughout *Instruction*, but only appear elsewhere in the wisdom corpus from Qumran at 4Q525 15:1 in noun form and in other Qumran texts as verbs at 1QHᵃ x:36; xiii:16, 22; 4Q372 1:17. See the discussion of "Social Location" in the introduction to this chapter.

Line 5: "princes" — See commentary to 4Q416 2iii:11.

Line 8: "inner desire" — See the discussion of אוט in the "Key Terms" in the introduction to this chapter.

Frag. 178

²[. . . in] your house you will help [. . .] ³[. . .] you will find the house of your sojourn [. . .] ⁴[. . . co]ver your reproach [. . .]

Frag. 179

²[. . .] he commanded [. . .] ³[. . . mystery] of existence that [. . .]

Frag. 180

¹[. . .] that [. . .] ²[. . .] all life [. . .] ³[. . .] for wealth [. . .]

Frag. 181

¹[. . .] and the flock [. . .] ²[. . . when] you [w]alk, do not [. . .]

Commentary

Line 2: "[wa]lk" — See commentary to 4Q416 2iii:9 and 4Q417 19:4.

Frag. 182

¹[. . .] there [. . .] ²[. . .] and you [. . .] ³[. . .] not with the dee[ds of . . .]

Frag. 183a + b

²[. . .] leave a seminal emission [. . .]

Commentary

Line 2: This line can also refer to sexual intercourse. In either case, it is impossible to determine the intent of this fragmentary legislation, presumably based in the purity legislation of Leviticus.

Frag. 184

¹[. . . he spo]ke through Moses and [. . .] ²[. . . th]at he uncovered your ear to the mystery of existence on the day [. . .] ³[. . .] to you and lest you eat and be satisfied [. . .]

Notes

Line 1: "spoke" (דבר) — This is reconstructed as צוה ("commanded") by Tigchelaar, based on the parallel with 4Q423 11:2 (*To Increase Learning*, 112). Neither term is convincing, based on the remaining traces of the letter on the photograph.

Commentary

Line 2: "uncovered your ear to the mystery of existence" — This phrase also appears in: 1Q26 1:4; 4Q416 2iii:18; 4Q418 10a-b:1; 123ii:4; 184:2; 190:2-3; 4Q423 5:1-2; the first part in 4Q299 8:6. The phrase "to uncover your ear" is found in Isa 22:14, with regard to revelation concerning the consequences of the iniquity of Israel. In Job 33:16 and 36:10 the revelation concerns מוסר ("instruction" or "discipline"). In Job 36:15 he "opens their ear" by oppression or affliction. See the introduction for a discussion of the "mystery of existence."

Frag. 185a + b

¹[...] for those who descend [...] ²[...] the inheritance [...] ³[...] for the lambs [...] ⁴[...] you shall inherit glory [...] ⁵[... y]ou [...]

Notes

There is some uncertainty about the joining of these two fragments (DJD 34:409-10; Tigchelaar, *To Increase Learning*, 112-13). If separate, the word "glory" in line 4 would go with frag. b.

Frag. 186

¹[...] drink [...] ²[...] pure [...]

Frag. 187

²[...] and he considered [...]

Notes

Tigchelaar considers this reading, וחשב, doubtful (*To Increase Learning*, 113; cf. DJD 34:411).

Frag. 188 + <u>4Q423 9</u>

²[. . .] death, majesty [. . .] ³[. . . when] you enter to [your] resting pla[ce . . .] ⁴[. . .] ⁵[. . .] fathers for i[t] is desirable [. . .] ⁶[. . . de]eds of the <u>covenant they will not seek it</u> [. . .] ⁷[. . .] lest they will go astray in <u>matters of [holiness</u> . . .] ⁸[. . .] you [and <u>your sons</u> . . .]

Notes

Lines 5-8: These lines have a parallel in 4Q423 9, and that text is included here as noted.

Frag. 189

¹[. . . le]st he will judge [. . .] ²[. . .] he will not understand [. . .]

Frag. 190

²[. . .] uncover your [ea]rs to the mystery of ³[existence . . . what will] be in eternity

Commentary

Line 2: "uncover your [ea]rs to the mystery of [existence . . .]" — This phrase also appears in 1Q26 1:4; 4Q416 2iii:17-18; 4Q418 10a-b:1; 123ii:4; 184:2; 4Q423 5:1; the first part in 4Q299 8:6. The phrase "to uncover your ear" is found in Isa 22:14, with regard to revelation concerning the consequences of the iniquity of Israel. In Job 33:16 and 36:10 the revelation concerns מוסר ("instruction" or "discipline"). In Job 36:15 he "opens their ear" by oppression or affliction. See the introduction for a discussion of the "mystery of existence."

Frag. 191

²[. . .] his healing [. . .]

Frag. 192

²[. . .] power [. . .]

Frag. 193

¹[. . .] understanding [. . .]

Frag. 196

¹[. . .] walk [. . .] ²[. . .] all [. . .]

Commentary

Line 1: "walk" — See commentary to 4Q416 2iii:9 and 4Q417 19:4.

Frag. 197

²[. . .] his insight in all things and not [. . .] ³[. . .] and ta[ke the] commandments [. . .] ⁴[. . .] ways of [. . .]

Notes

Line 3: "ta[ke]" — This reading is questioned by Tigchelaar on review of the fragment (*To Increase Learning*, 114). To "take/grasp commandments" is an unusual construction in these texts.

Frag. 198

¹daily in all [. . .] ²his deeds and with [. . .] ³hope has perished [. . .]

Commentary

Line 3: A possible parallel for this elusive line can be found in 4Q365 6aii:4 (DJD 34:419).

Frag. 199

¹[. . .] he who enters into the community [. . .] ²[. . .] not will you yet increase [. . .] ³[. . .] that is not [. . .]

Notes

Note the discussion at 4Q417 2i:17-20 of the combination of this fragment with others to form a parallel to that text.

Commentary

Line 1: This line is very similar to the discussions of persons entering into the community or the covenant throughout the *Community Rule* or into the "new" covenant throughout the *Damascus Document*. In 1QS i:16-17 we read, "All who enter into the rule of the community will pass over into the covenant before God to do according to all he commanded." 1QS v:7-8 similarly reads, "All who enter into the council of the community will come into the covenant of God." While this line is not by itself evidence of a similar sectarian provenance for *Instruction*, it does suggest the manner in which concepts and terminology available in this unique composition were important to the authors of these sectarian texts. On the term "community" (יחד), see commentary to 4Q416 2iii:21.

Frag. 200

¹[. . .] grief and with bitterness [. . .] ²[. . . in order] that you will shine forth like [. . .] ³[. . .] you will not remember [. . .]

Frag. 201

¹[. . . mystery of] existence God made known the inheri[tance . . .] ²[. . .] to lock up all the sons of in[iquity . . .]

Notes

Line 1: The traces at the beginning of this line are hard to evaluate. I am not convinced that they correspond to a ל ("to" or "for"), as maintained by Tigchelaar, since their placement is incorrect (*To Increase Learning*, 114). Thus I consider this proposed reconstruction the most likely possibility.

Frag. 202

¹[. . .] take the birth ti[mes of . . .] ²[. . .] hear [. . .]

Commentary

Line 1: "birth ti[mes . . .]" — See commentary to 4Q417 2i:11.

Frag. 204

[1]your hand [. . .] [2]in the heart of [. . .] [3]for the des[ire . . .]

Frag. 205

[2][. . .] foolish of heart [. . .]

Frag. 206

[3][. . .] beast and bird for [4][. . .] and rule, dominion [5][. . .] and you have toiled

Notes

Line 4: It is very difficult to determine the best reconstruction at the beginning of this line (DJD 34:426-27; Tigchelaar, *To Increase Learning*, 115).

Frag. 207

[3]and to as[k . . .] [4]with scales [. . .] [5]he will seek [. . .]

Frag. 208

[1][. . . al]l tha[t . . .] [2][. . . k]now [. . .]

Notes

Note the utilization of this fragment as well as the scattered letters of frag. 209 in the reconstruction of 4Q416 1:9-16 (Tigchelaar, *To Increase Learning*, 67-69).

Line 2: Tigchelaar here reads a ר rather than a ד, thereby suggesting a reconstruction other than "[k]now" (*To Increase Learning*, 116).

Frag. 210

¹[. . .] only to [. . .] ²[. . .] with his might [. . .] ³[. . .] not [. . .]

Frag. 211

²[. . .] and when they go forth [. . .] ³[. . .] throughout their pregnancy, is it not [. . .] ⁴[. . .] unrighteousness for the end will come [. . .]

Notes

Line 4: From the reading of Tigchelaar, the verb "perish" has been deleted from consideration for this translation (*To Increase Learning*, 116).

Commentary

Line 3: "pregnancy" — This form of the verb is most unusual, but similar vocalization of the Hebrew term is found in 1QIsaᵃ 23:6 and 35:8, even though not in the infinitive form as here.

Frag. 212

¹[. . .] the kingdom will quake [. . .] ²[. . .] the day of its judgment [. . .]

Notes

Note the utilization of this fragment as well as frag. 213 in the reconstruction of 4Q416 1:9-16 (Tigchelaar, *To Increase Learning*, 66-69, 74-75).

Frag. 214

¹[. . .] truth [. . .] ²[. . .] righteous [judg]ment [. . .]

Frags. 217-218

Notes

Note the utilization of these fragments in the reconstruction of 4Q416 1:9-16 (Tigchelaar, *To Increase Learning,* 69, 74-75).

Frag. 219

²[. . .] in the mystery of the wonders [. . .]

Commentary

Line 2: This interesting phrase, not present in biblical materials, is also found in 4Q417 1i:2, 13 as well as in the *Community Rule,* the *Hodayot,* the *Songs of the Sabbath Sacrifice,* and other scattered instances.

Frag. 220

²[. . .] iniquity [. . .] ³[. . .] and folly [. . .]

Commentary

Line 3: "folly" — אולת is a particular concern in *Instruction* (4Q415 9:5; 4Q416 2ii:3; 4Q417 1i:7; 4Q418 243:2; 4Q423 5:7), in Proverbs, and is also found in 4Q525 2ii+3:2.

Frag. 221

²[. . .] and to advance understanding for all the foolish [. . .] ³[. . .] to increase instruction for those who have discernment [. . .] ⁴[. . .] and know his judgment and then you shall distinguish bet[ween . . .] ⁵[. . . and] you shall gain in understanding to know the good [. . .]

Notes

Line 2: At the beginning of this line I have deleted the word נביאים, "prophets," on the basis of Tigchelaar's observations (*To Increase Learning*, 117). But his proposed reading, נכאים, is no more convincing than that of DJD 34:435-36.

Frag. 222

¹[. . .] sons [. . .] you have spoken it [. . .] ²[. . .] listen to his spirit and the utterance of his lips do not [. . .] ³[. . .] to reprove those who transgress and to [. . .] ⁴[. . .] know [. . .] for [. . .]

Commentary

Line 3: "reprove" — For a discussion of the significance of "reproof" in Qumran texts, see commentary to 4Q417 2i:1-6 above.

Frag. 223

²[. . .] by his hand [. . .] ³[. . .] on the day and the interpretations [. . .]

Notes

Line 3: On the basis of the reading of Tigchelaar, the reading פתריה ("[their?] interpretations") is preferable to פתאיה ("[their?] foolish ones") (*To Increase Learning*, 117).

Frag. 224

¹[. . .] for [. . .] ²[. . .] all [. . .]

Notes

Note the utilization of this fragment in the reconstruction of 4Q416 1:9-16 (Tigchelaar, *To Increase Learning*, 69, 74-75).

Frag. 225

²[. . .] watch [. . .]

Frag. 227

¹[. . .] man of discernment, a foundation [. . .] ²[. . .] for his intention and you shall be [. . .] ³[. . .] the deep and the dwe[lling . . .] ⁴[. . . o]pen [. . .]

Commentary

Line 2: "intention" — See commentary to 4Q416 2iii:14 and 4Q417 1ii:12.

Frag. 228

²[. . .] he will place her in authority. If you have uttered [. . .] ³[. . .] but rather make a judgment [. . .]

Frag. 229

²[. . .] they will run from the time of [. . .] ³[. . .] to be silent in all [. . .]

Notes

The reconstruction of line 1 by Tigchelaar (*To Increase Learning,* 118-19) appears too hypothetical: "[the st]ars of lig[ht] and to determi[ne the desires of]."

Frag. 230

²[. . .] with [. . .] ³[. . .] until the end of [. . .]

Frag. 231

¹[. . .] measure of [. . .]

Frag. 234

¹[. . .] inheritance of hol[iness . . .]

Notes

Tigchelaar has proposed this fragment as a parallel to 4Q415 1ii-2i:6-7 (*To Increase Learning*, 31-32, 225-30). He rightly questions the reading "are chosen" in line 2 on the basis of what is visible in the fragment (*To Increase Learning*, 119), hence it is not included in the translation.

Frag. 235

²[. . . will] sprout [. . .]

Notes

Tigchelaar has proposed this fragment as a parallel to 4Q415 1ii-2i:8 (*To Increase Learning*, 31-32, 119, 225-30). His reconstruction is יפרח, "blossom," rather than יפרד, "divide," as found in DJD 34:445.

Frag. 236

¹[. . .] and be renewed [. . .] ²[. . .] whether a female [. . .] ³[. . .] your heart ho[ly . . .] ⁴[. . .] put her to the test [. . .]

Notes

Tigchelaar has proposed this fragment as a parallel to 4Q415 1ii-2i:9 and then the following lines added as subsequent text (*To Increase Learning*, 31-32, 225-30).

Commentary

Line 4: Whether the third person feminine in this line is the subject or the object is impossible to determine. If the former, then the translation would read, "she put to the test."

Frag. 237

¹[. . .] resting place [. . .] ²[. . .] soul and [. . .] ³[. . .] treasu[ry . . .]

Frag. 238

¹[. . .] sage [. . .] ²[. . .] and with the deed [. . .] ³[. . .] be discerning in what will be fo[rever . . .] ⁴[. . . d]ays everlasting [. . .] ⁵[. . .] day [. . .]

Frag. 239

¹[. . . re]quest [. . .] ²[. . . by your hand is the judg]ment of the flock [. . .] ³[. . . se]ek them [. . .]

Frag. 240

²[. . .] ³your poverty [. . .]

Notes

Line 2: As suggested by Tigchelaar, the photograph does not support the reading ובבינת, "and with understanding," as found in DJD 34:449-50 (*To Increase Learning*, 119-20). His proposal that we find here the term יבב ("lament") seems very unusual, however, since it is rare in the biblical text and not attested elsewhere in the Qumran evidence. "And when her daughter" would also be a possible translation of ובבתה, the extant text; however, the context for that translation is not clear. Hence I leave it untranslated.

Frag. 241

²[. . .] when doing wondrously [. . .]

Frag. 242

²[. . .] your anger [. . .]

Frag. 243

²[. . .] and much folly [. . .] ³[. . .] do not send forth an evil root from [. . .] ⁴[. . .] as in the ends of the fields [. . .] ⁵[. . .] and a blow that is pronounced [. . .]

Commentary

Line 2: "folly" — אולת is a particular concern in *Instruction* (4Q415 9:5; 4Q416 2ii:3; 4Q417 1i:7; 4Q418 220:3; 4Q423 5:7) and in Proverbs; the term also occurs in 4Q525 2ii+3:2.

Frag. 244

¹[. . .] in your service [. . .]

Frag. 245

²[. . .] truth [. . .]

Frag. 246

²[. . .] will multiply very m[uch . . .]

Frag. 247

¹[. . .] for its deeds [. . .]

Frag. 249

¹[. . .] time [. . .] ²[. . .] to you and not [. . .] ³[. . .] poor is he and ne[edy . . .]

Commentary

Line 3: "poor" — The Hebrew terms רוש (verb) and ריש (noun) are found throughout *Instruction*, but only appear elsewhere in the wisdom corpus from

Qumran at 4Q525 15:1 and in other Qumran texts at 1QH^a x:36; xiii:16, 22; 4Q372 1:17. See the discussion of "Social Location" in the introduction to this chapter.

Frag. 250

^{1}[. . .] in all [. . .] ^{2}[. . .] forever [. . .] ^{3}[. . .] in it [. . .]

Notes

It is not clear that this fragment belongs to 4Q418 (DJD 34:455).

Frag. 251

^{1}[. . . inheri]tance of man [. . .] ^{2}[. . .] and your walking [. . .] ^{3}[. . .] very much [. . .]

Frag. 252

^{1}[. . . br]ing in all [. . .] ^{2}[. . .] in return for wages [. . .]

Frag. 254

^{1}[. . .] to not [. . .]

Frag. 259

^{2}[. . . place] him in authority [. . .]

Frag. 260

^{2}[. . .] with your hand [. . .]

Frag. 261

^{2}[. . .] if [. . .]

Frag. 264

¹[. . . al]l the issue [of . . .]

Frag. 265

²[. . .] the world [. . .]

Frag. 268

¹[. . . al]l knowl[edge . . .]

Frag. 269

¹[. . .] all [. . .] ²[. . .] be hidden [. . .] ³[. . .] this [. . .]

Frag. 271

¹[. . .] if [. . .]

Frag. 273

¹[. . .] man of discernment [. . .]

Frag. 277

²[. . .] watch [. . .]

Frag. 278

²[. . .] he [. . .]

Frag. 284

¹[. . .] and recount [. . .]

Frag. 286

¹[. . .] every spirit [. . .] ²[. . .] ³[. . .] festival [. . .] ⁴[. . .] during [. . .]

Notes

The proposal of Elgvin that this fragment overlaps with 4Q416 1:1-3, hence also with 4Q418 1i, is discussed by the editors in DJD 34:468 and Tigchelaar (*To Increase Learning*, 65-66), but none of them seem to be absolutely convinced.

Frag. 290

²[. . .] lov[es . . .]

Frag. 291

²[. . .] you shall not [. . .]

Frag. 293

¹[. . .] for [. . .]

Frag. 295

¹[. . .] with them [. . .]

Frag. 297

¹[. . .] instruction [. . .] ²[. . .] will pervert [. . .]

Notes

Line 2: "will pervert" — The inclusion of יעוה is based on Tigchelaar's reading of the fragment (*To Increase Learning*, 123). It occurs most commonly in the *Hodayot* (1QHᵃ v:32; viii:18; ix:24; xi:22; xv:30; xix:15; 4Q427 2:1; 4Q428 9:2), in the Niphal form.

Frag. 299

²[. . .] not [. . .]

Frag. 301

¹[. . .] inclination [. . .]

Frag. 302

³[. . .] understanding [. . .]

Frag. 303

¹[. . .] listen [. . .] ²[. . .] you shall n[ot] err [. . .] ³[. . .] these [. . .] ⁴[. . .] those who are struck [. . .]

Notes

This fragment has also been published as 4Q468k in DJD 36:420-21. Tigchelaar considers it to be of a different hand than either 4Q418 or 4Q418 1-2 (*To Increase Learning*, 123).

Instruction\u1d49 (4Q418a)

The fragments of this manuscript are extremely difficult to read since the majority of them are preserved in four wads, each of which consists of four to eight layers. This makes the photographic record of the fragments much more important and more complicated to unpack and decipher.

Frag. 1

¹[. . .] and according to [. . .]

Frag. 2

¹[. . .] give them insight [. . .] ²[. . .] you do for [. . .] ³[. . .] for he [. . .]

Frag. 3

²[. . . wi]th all the eld[ers . . .] ³[. . . judgme]nt of Korah and [. . .]

Notes

Line 3: This reconstruction is based on similarities to 4Q423 5:1.

Frag. 4

¹[. . .] of your land [. . .] ²[. . . in every season seek th]em. Do not be silent [. . .] ³[. . .] all of them they shall surely seek [. . .] ⁴[. . . will] fin[d paths . . .]

Commentary

Strugnell and Harrington suggest overlap of this fragment with 4Q418 103:3-5 (DJD 34:480-81). See commentary there.

Frag. 6

²[. . .] to you [. . .] ³[. . .] they have declared [. . .] ⁴[. . .] above the heavens [. . .]

Notes

The reading of this fragment is based on the observations of Tigchelaar (*To Increase Learning*, 137).

Frag. 7

²[. . .] man of discernment are you [. . .] ³[. . . po]or are you and kings

Notes

Line 3: The reconstruction is based on a possible parallel with 4Q415 6:2 (Tigchelaar, *To Increase Learning*, 136).

Frag. 8

¹[. . .] to all [. . .] ²[. . .] they will give them understanding with faithfulness [. . .] ³[. . .] they have not sought them [. . .]

Notes

Line 2: "they will give them understanding" (יבינום) — It is very difficult to determine this reading, but מענים ("oppressors") proposed by Tigchelaar does not seem to fit the context of *Instruction* (*To Increase Learning*, 136).

Frag. 9

²for he who loves [. . .]

Notes

These same words are found in 4Q416 4:1 (Tigchelaar, *To Increase Learning*, 132).

Frag. 10

¹to you [. . .] ²there is [. . .] ³and all his zeal [. . .] ⁴Give understan[ding . . .]

Notes

Line 4: "Give understand[ing]" — Rather than [. . . ן]הב, this line could be re-constructed [. . . ט]הב ("consider") (Tigchelaar, *To Increase Learning*, 132).

Frag. 11 + 4Q417 1i:21-24

¹[. . . with the mystery of] ²existence [. . . <u>every vision</u>] ³<u>know and with [all</u> . . . <u>you shall be strengthened</u>] ⁴<u>daily. You shall not re[ach out for unrighteousness</u> . . . <u>for anyone who reaches it]</u> ⁵<u>will not be innocent. [In accordance with his in-</u> heritance in it, he shall be decl<u>ared guilty]</u>

Notes

For other parallel passages and commentary see 4Q417 1i above.

Frag. 12

¹[. . .] end [. . .] ²[. . .] base of truth [. . .] ³[. . .] return of all [. . .] ⁴[. . .] and he shall not serve [. . .]

Commentary

Line 2: "base of truth" — For a discussion of this phrase, see commentary at 4Q417 1i:8.

Frag. 13

¹[. . . wh]ich are not to[gether . . .]

Notes

This fragment is connected with 4Q415 11:4 by Tigchelaar (*To Increase Learning,* 136).

Commentary

Line 1: On "to[gether . . .]" or "com[munity . . .]" see commentary to 4Q416 2iii:21 and 4Q418 199:1 above.

Frag. 14

¹[. . .] your mighty deeds [. . .]

Frag. 15

²[. . .] that they will not be [. . .] ³[. . .] one for their measure and a[s . . .] ⁴[. . .] omer by omer, eph[ah by ephah . . .]

Notes

This fragment is connected with 4Q415 11:2-3 by Tigchelaar (*To Increase Learning*, 136).

Commentary

Line 4: "omer by omer, eph[ah by ephah . . .]" — See commentary to 4Q415 11:3 concerning this phrase.

Frag. 16 + 16b

²[. . .] with[out . . .] ³[. . . t]oil of your distress [. . .] to the place [. . .] ⁴[. . .] when he comes to [. . .] ⁵[. . .] your mighty deeds [. . .]

Notes

This reconstruction differs from DJD 34:487-90 and follows Tigchelaar (*To Increase Learning*, 134-36).

Commentary

Line 3: "distress" — See commentary to 4Q416 2ii:14.

Frag. 17

¹[. . .] lest [. . .] ²[. . .] your [sp]irit the master [. . .] ³[. . .] with the helper [. . .] ⁴[. . .] not [. . .]

Notes

This fragment is translated on the basis of Tigchelaar's study (*To Increase Learning*, 134).

Frag. 18

¹[. . .] his heart [. . .] ²[. . .] daughters of your companions [. . .] ³[. . .] tha[t . . .] ⁴[. . . give au]thority to you to wa[lk . . .]

Notes

Evidence that this fragment and the previous one contained instruction concerning matrimony is to be found in the parallels between line 4 and 4Q416 2iv:7. Tigchelaar proposes that this text can be reconstructed on the basis of 4Q416 2iv:3-7 (*To Increase Learning*, 133).

Commentary

Line 4: "to wa[lk . . .]" — See commentary to 4Q416 2iii:9 and 4Q417 19:4 above.

Frag. 19

¹[. . .] you shall trust [. . .] ²[. . . s]age and also [. . .] ³[. . . then you shall] be a father to him [. . .] ⁴[. . .] your [re]proach [. . .]

Notes

This fragment corresponds to 4Q416 2ii:14-16 and parallel texts. See commentary there.

Frag. 20

³[. . .] all things that were ma[de . . .]

Frag. 21

¹[. . .] visit [. . .] ²[. . .] wonder [. . .] ³[. . .] for [. . .]

Frag. 22

This fragment coincides with 4Q417 2i:12-16, which in turn overlaps with 4Q416 2i. See translation and commentary to 4Q417 2i:12-16, where all three texts are integrated.

Frag. 23

²[. . .] judg[es . . .]

Notes

This fragment may rather be part of 4Q418 and was labeled earlier as 4Q418 4 (DJD 34:494; Tigchelaar, *To Increase Learning*, 139).

Frag. 24

¹wh[at . . .] ²you shall awaken [. . .] ³tru[th . . .] ⁴and [all . . .]

Notes

Fragments 24 and 25 may not be part of this MS. The reconstruction of these terms is based on possible parallels with 4Q418 69ii:5-8 (DJD 34:494; Tigchelaar, *To Increase Learning*, 139).

Frag. 25

¹all [. . .] ²and pleasure [. . .] ³or [. . .]

Commentary

Line 2: "pleasure" — עדן is also the word for Eden, the "garden of paradise/pleasure."

Instruction[f]? (4Q418c)

¹[. . .] depths [. . .] ²[. . .] and who will [. . .] ³[. . .] its boundary [. . .] ⁴[. . .] shut [. . .] ⁵[. . . de]stroy a[l]l iniqu[ity . . .] ⁶[. . . so that] they [shall ob]ey, his deeds [. . .] ⁷[. . . to give] him insight [. . .] ⁸[. . . mystery] of existence for there is no end [. . .] ⁹[. . .] epoch of peace [. . .] ¹⁰[. . . t]op of Carmel [. . .]

Notes

This MS has only one fragment, originally classified as frag. 161 of 4Q418.

Line 5: "[de]stroy a[l]l iniqu[ity]" — On the basis of the photographs it is not possible to determine whether the proposed reading here, [א]בד כ[ו]ל עול, based on DJD 34:502, is more accurate than that of Tigchelaar (*To Increase Learning*, 124, 125), עד כ[ו]ל עולם ("? a[l]l forever").

Commentary

Line 6: "[. . . so that] they [shall ob]ey, his deeds" — Here "obey" is a translation of the verb שׁמע, which most commonly means to "hear" or "listen." This translation is based on 1QS v:23: "they shall be inscribed in the order, each man before his companion, according to his insight and his deeds, in order that each man obeys his companion."

Instruction[g] (4Q423)

Frag. 1

¹[. . .] and all the fruit of the produce and every pleasant tree, desirable for making wise. Is it not a pl[easant] garden ²[. . .] for making exceedingly wise? Over it he has given you authority to serve it and keep it. A garden of pasture ³[. . . the earth] will sprout thorns and thistles for you and its might it will not give to you [. . .] ⁴[. . .] when you act unfaithfully [. . .] ⁵[. . .] She gave birth and all the wombs of concep[tion . . .] ⁶[. . .] with all of your desires for it will sprout everything [for you . . .] ⁷[. . .] and with the planting [. . .]

Notes

While frags. 1 and 2 are joined by the editor (DJD 34:507-8), I treat them separately, following Tigchelaar's caution (*To Increase Learning*, 141).

Commentary

The text of these two fragments interprets the story of the garden of Eden, rooting ethical injunction in the story of creation. The ability to discern the difference between good and evil as well as to recognize the two ways open to humankind that begin to be developed in lines 5-9 are rooted in the creation account of the earlier lines. See my discussion in the introduction, pp. 32-33 above.

Line 1: "desirable for making wise" — Gen 3:6.

Line 2: "he has given you authority to serve it and keep it" — Gen 2:15.

Line 3: "[. . . the earth] will sprout thorns and thistles for you" — Gen 3:18.

Line 3: "its might it will not give to you" — Gen 4:12.

Line 7: "planting" — See commentary to 4Q418 81+81a:13.

Frag. 2, col. i

⁵every inner desire ⁶[. . .] daily not ⁷[. . . he despises] the evil and knows the good ⁸[. . . bet]ween his way and the way of ⁹[. . .] and bread

Commentary

Line 5: "inner desire" — For a discussion of אוש see the "Key Terms" in the introduction to this chapter.

Frag. 2, col. ii

⁹his strength [. . .] ¹⁰to [. . .]

Frag. 3 + *1Q26 2*

¹[... your] mig[ht will be exhaus]ted in vain [...] ²[... with the mystery of] existence and thus walk and <u>all your produce</u> shall increase [...] ³[... for the po]ssession of the land and according to his word every [womb] shall bear [...] ⁴[... and you shall enter before your God wi]th the firstborn <u>of your womb and the</u> firstborn of all [your cattle...] ⁵[... and you shall enter before yo]ur [God], saying, "I have sanctified all [the firstborn to God...]"

Commentary

Line 1: This citation of Lev 26:20 provides support for the relationship between disobedience of the statutes and commandments of God and the land not yielding its harvest, the theme of this text as well as frags. 4 and 5, and a logical development from frags. 1 and 2.

Frag. 3a

²[...] and in your kindness [...] ³[...] with the fruit of his womb [...]

Frag. 4 + *1Q26 1*

⁰¹[... <u>with the mystery of existence</u> ...] ⁰²[...] ⁰³[... <u>your produce</u> ...] ⁰⁴[... just as <u>he uncovered your ear to the mystery of existence</u> ...] ¹[... <u>to you.</u> Wa]tch [yo]urse[lf lest] you will glorify yourself more than him and [...] ²[in your service <u>and you will be cursed with a</u>]ll [your] produce [and] you will [be asham]ed <u>in all your deeds</u> with [...] ³ᵃ[... <u>for your lawsuit and by</u>] his [hand] visit [judgment ... <u>and he says to him, "I am</u> your portion] ³[and your inheritance in the midst of humankind. ... <u>I will make</u>] you [great] in the sig[ht of all ... <u>and all</u> ...]

Notes

Line 2: "[in your service]" — This phrase was identified from 4Q418 244:2 by Tigchelaar (*To Increase Learning*, 120).

Line 3a: While this line is added by the scribe between the lines of frag. 4, they are part of the normal text structure in 1Q26 1:7.

Commentary

Lines 3a-3: The quotation of Num 18:20 here is the basis for the reconstruction.

Frag. 5

¹ª[. . .] Watch yourself lest you return to Levi the prie[st] ¹[. . .] the judgment of Korah and he uncovered your ear ²[to the mystery of existence . . . every h]ead of [your] fathers [. . .] and the prince of your people ³[. . .] he divided the inheritance of all who have authority and every deed was created by his hand and the reward for ⁴[their deeds he knew. He will judg]e all of them with truth, he will visit fathers and sons, [proselyt]es with all the native-born, he will speak ⁵[. . . if you are a m]an of the earth, observe the festivals of the summer, gather your produce in its time and the cycle of ⁶[the harvest for its festival. Gain] in understanding of all your produce and in your service become insight[ful concerning knowledge of] good and evil. ⁷[. . . a m]an of insight with a master of folly [. . .] Thus a man ⁸[of insight . . .] all [. . .] he shall say [. . . with the abu]ndance of his insight [. . .] ⁹[. . . mystery of] existence in every [wa]y of his that is vain [. . .] to not [. . .] ¹⁰[. . .] among you and even [. . .]

Notes

Line 1: The reference to the judgment of Korah is also found in 4Q418a 3:3.

Commentary

Line 1a: "lest you return to Levi the prie[st]" — This elusive reference, added by a later scribal hand, requires more adequate context for interpretation. The story of Korah in the next line could continue some theme about the criteria for judging the priesthood. (For further information see Michael E. Stone, "Levi," *EDSS* 1:485-86; and Robert Kugler, "Priests," *EDSS* 2:688-93.)

Line 1: "Korah" — The judgment of Korah and his company in Numbers 16 here provides a basis for making judgment upon leading figures. Korah is also referred to in 4Q418a 3:3. While the destruction of Korah and his company would have stirred the imagination of an author who envisioned eternal destruction for those who were of the spirit of flesh, there is no reason to regard it as a reference to some significant division in the sectarian history related to Qumran, as proposed by James M. Scott.[142]

Lines 1-2: "uncovered your ear [to the mystery of existence . . .]" — This phrase also appears in 1Q26 1:4; 4Q416 2iii:17-18; 4Q418 10a-b:1; 123ii:4; 184:2; 190:2; the first part in 4Q299 8:6. The phrase "uncover the ear" is found in Isa 22:14, with regard to revelation concerning the consequences of the iniquity of Israel. In Job 33:16 and 36:10 the revelation concerns מוסר ("instruction" or "discipline"). In Job 36:15 he "opens their ear" by oppression or affliction. See the introduction for a discussion of the "mystery of existence."

Line 2: "prince" — See commentary to 4Q416 2iii:11.

Lines 5-6: The relationship of the "[m]an of the earth," that is, farmer, to the preceding statements about those in authority and the subsequent development of the theme of knowledge and insight with regard to good and evil is not clear. It does appear that the use of the term "festival" (מועד) in these lines is a reference to the sacrificial calendar as it relates to the agricultural cycle. This is developed most extensively in 11Q19 xiii–xxix.

Line 7: "folly" — אולת is a particular concern in *Instruction* (4Q415 9:5; 4Q416 2ii:3; 4Q417 1i:7; 4Q418 220:3; 243:2) and in Proverbs; the term also occurs in 4Q525 2ii+3:2.

Frag. 5a

¹[if a m]an of the earth you are [. . .]

Frag. 6

²[. . .] he has not given [. . .] ³[. . .] your heart. And what indeed all [. . .] ⁴[. . .] God judges righteousness for all [. . .] ⁵[. . .] wealth [. . .]

---

142. Scott, "Korah and Qumran," in *Bible at Qumran,* ed. Flint, 182-202.

Frag. 7

¹[. . .] for ²[. . .] your fury ³[. . .] according to the mercies of the father ⁴[. . .] a[ll] his [de]eds and his mercies ⁵[. . .] commanded you [. . .] to not ⁶[. . .] on the same day. Did he not uncover ⁷[your ears to the mystery of existence . . .] to [make] your heart understand

Frag. 8

A parallel copy with more complete text is found at 4Q418 81:1-5. Translation and commentary are to be found there.

Frag. 9

A parallel copy of this text is found at 4Q418 188:5-8 and the text is translated there.

Frag. 10

¹[. . .] your hands in al[l . . .]

Frag. 11

²[. . . just as he comman]ded by the hand of Mos[es . . .] ³[. . . that he un]co[vered your ear to the mystery of existence on the day . . .]

Notes

The reconstruction is based on parallels with 4Q418 184:1-2 (Tigchelaar, *To Increase Learning*, 144).

Frag. 12

¹[. . .] statut[es . . .] poverty [. . .] ²[. . .] his [in]heritance and afterward you will stretch forth [your hand . . .] ³[. . .] in the day[s of] your pr[oduc]e [. . .]

Commentary

Line 3: Presumably speaking of the harvest noted in frag. 5 above.

Frag. 13

[4][. . . Go]d [gave] by the hand of man [. . .]

Frag. 14

[2][. . .] those who take [. . .]

Frag. 15

[2][. . .] all [. . .] [3][. . . when] they are [. . .]

Frag. 16

[2][. . .] abundance [. . .]

Frag. 17

[2][. . .] in vain [. . .]

Frag. 20

[1][. . .] the heavens [. . .] [2][. . .] according to [. . .]

Frag. 21

[1][. . .] you [. . .]

Frag. 22

[2][. . .] cleverness and wealth [. . .]

Frag. 23

¹[. . .] the man [. . .] ²[. . .] ³[. . .] for al[l . . .]

Notes

This fragment may overlap with 4Q418 81+81a:3-5 (Tigchelaar, *To Increase Learning*, 94-95). See commentary there.

Instruction (1Q26)

Frag. 1

A parallel text is found in 4Q423 4. Translation and commentary can be found there.

Frag. 2

A parallel text is found in 4Q423 3. Translation and commentary can be found there.

Frag. 3

²[. . .] for you are to him a fi[rstborn] son [. . .]

Frag. 4

²[. . .] one [. . .]

Unidentified Text (XQ7)

¹[. . . you shall not] abandon [it] lest [. . .] ²[. . . be]cause he will glorify you [. . .] ³[. . .] for your companions and all [. . .] ⁴[. . .] with the glory [. . .] ⁵[. . .] when he will raise [. . .] ⁶[. . . in]sightful [. . .]

Notes

While this fragment was published as an "unidentified text" in DJD 36, Émile Puech and Annette Steudel have now identified it as belonging to 4Q417 or 418.[143] This translation takes into account their reconstruction of the text.

Line 5: This line is based on the observations of Tigchelaar (*To Increase Learning*, 125). He points to 4Q416 2iii:11.

---

143. Puech and Steudel, "Un nouveau fragment du manuscrit *4QInstruction* (*XQ7* = *4Q417* ou *418*)," *RevQ* 19 (2000): 623-27.

Mysteries (1Q27, 4Q299-300, 301?)

Introduction

Content

All of the available evidence suggests that the fragmentary material of 4Q299 1 + 1Q27 1 + 1Q300 3 reflects the beginning of the composition. If this is the case then the integration of wisdom and eschatology is integral to the composition. The name comes from the repeated references to the רזים ("mysteries"), most commonly to the "mystery of existence" also encountered throughout *Instruction* (see the introduction there), but found in other formulations here as well. In *Mysteries* wisdom is integral to salvation. Understanding the mystery of existence is the core of wisdom, and a failure to grasp this mystery has been characteristic of persons in the past. This mystery is anchored in creation. The failure to grasp it results in an inability to comprehend the inevitable predetermined course of world history, hence the inability of persons to save themselves from eternal nonexistence. Righteousness will come to the fore in this predetermined schema as the offspring of unrighteousness are shut up and wickedness is vanquished forever. In this future era knowledge will fill the world and folly will be eliminated. There is a marked division in this composition between those who do good and those who do evil that parallels the eternal fate of those who comprehend the mysteries of existence and those who do not. This division is characteristic of a dualism that dominates the entire composition. The contrast between darkness and light is also used to express this dualism. As in apocalyptic traditions, this wisdom is sealed and only available to the elect or righteous, that portion of humankind which God permits to see and understand it. In this composition such dualism is related to the fate of world history, to the place of righteousness among the nations, to the future of Israel, to the responsibilities of kings, and to the care of the needy. Wisdom is also character-ized as a vision within this work, pointing to its revelatory nature. While frag-mentary enough to prohibit a comprehensive understanding of all its content, there is evidence that the original composition also dealt with matters of the priesthood and temple service. Evidence concerning stances on certain halakic issues such as swearing of oaths and vengeance or reproof is also present.

Manuscripts

Four manuscripts were classified as copies of this composition by J. T. Milik: 1Q27, 4Q299, 4Q300, and 4Q301. The text of 1Q27 is found in DJD 1, the re-mainder in DJD 20. The relationship of 4Q301 to the other texts is discussed be-low. 4Q299 is the most significant in terms of quantity of preserved material and number of fragments. F. M. Cross classified the script as a developed Herodian semiformal hand, hence dated to 20-50 C.E. (DJD 39:428). While more limited in quantity, 4Q300 permits the fuller reconstruction of some sig-nificant material. This script has been classified as late Herodian formal bookhand, hence dated as late as 30-68 C.E. (DJD 39:431). 4Q301 also is classi-fied as a late Herodian formal bookhand. Some features of Qumran orthogra-phy point to the copying by a scribe using characteristic Qumran features sometimes considered sectarian. 1Q27 was not given a paleographic date in the publication. It could be classified earlier than the other copies, even though not remarkably so. Torleif Elgvin also classifies it as late Herodian.[1] On the whole, the manuscripts appear to be later than those represented in the *Instruction* col-lection.

The Status of 4Q301

This text was classified as 4QMysteries[c] by Milik, even though no definite tex-tual overlap with any of the other copies of *Mysteries* is in evidence. Although Lawrence Schiffman regards the *Mysteries* texts as similar in genre and content to *Instruction,* those similarities are not found in 4Q301. When combined with the lack of textual overlap, Schiffman argues that it is "extremely unlikely" that this text is a witness to the same composition (DJD 20:113). He finds it to have more connections with the *Hekalot* literature. On the other hand, Armin Lange argues for it as a copy of *Mysteries,* and A. Klostergaard Petersen employs the

---

1. Elgvin, "Priestly Sages?" 69-70.

copy in his discussion.[2] Erik Larson, who worked with Schiffman on these texts, also favors Milik's identification (*EDSS* 1:587). The fragmentary nature of the text prohibits a definitive answer to this question. It is important to note, however, that the distinctive similarities with *Hekalot* literature are confined to frags. 2 and 3. Eibert Tigchelaar provides a valuable reading of the text, pointing out that the terminological correspondences between the texts are neither incidental nor arbitrary; hence it can be regarded as a manuscript of *Mysteries*, or at least a different version of that composition.[3]

Further complications concerning the identity of 4Q301 arise from some unusual notations present in the top left-hand corner of frag. 3b. Emanuel Tov has proposed that these marks are from the Cryptic A alphabet and constitute part of a physiognomic text concerning horoscopes and divination, such as found in 4Q186.[4] This is refuted by Lange, who suggests that this is a hymn concerning God's grace and wrath in an eschatological context, related to the heavenly realms.[5] Evidence of eschatological conflict in the heavenly realm can also be found in the *War Scroll*. Schiffman points out that descriptions of heavenly praise are also found in other Qumran compositions such as the *Songs of the Sabbath Sacrifice* (DJD 20:117-18). The arguments for interpreting the unique aspects of this column within the context of *Mysteries* appear most compelling.

Historical Context

The literary questions concerning the relationship of this composition to *Instruction* have been addressed above.[6] The ties between those two documents and connections with other compositions point to this work as an integral part of a wisdom corpus at Qumran that is characterized by the integration of wisdom with eschatology.

2. Lange, "Die Weisheitstexte aus Qumran: Eine Einleitung," in *Wisdom Texts from Qumran*, ed. Hempel et al., 12 n. 64; Petersen, "Wisdom as Cognition," 415 n. 25.

3. Tigchelaar, "Your Wisdom and Your Folly," 70-73.

4. Emanuel Tov, "Letters of the Cryptic A Script and Paleo-Hebrew Letters Used as Scribal Marks in Some Qumran Scrolls," *DSD* 2 (1995): 334; idem, "Scribal Markings in the Texts from the Judean Desert," in *Current Research and Technological Developments on the Dead Sea Scrolls: Conference on the Texts from the Judean Desert, Jerusalem, 30 April 1995* (ed. Donald W. Parry and Stephen D. Ricks; STDJ 20; Leiden: Brill, 1996), 60-61; idem, *Scribal Practices and Approaches Reflected in the Texts from the Judean Desert* (STDJ 541; Leiden: Brill, 2004), 203-6.

5. Lange, "Physiognomie oder Gotteslob?"

6. See also John Strugnell, "The Smaller Hebrew Wisdom Texts Found at Qumran: Variations, Resemblances, and Lines of Development," in *Wisdom Texts from Qumran*, ed. Hempel et al., 47-49.

There is evidence within the very first column of a great division between those who know and those who do not know, hence defining the social context for the composition. Since certain unspecified segments of Israel did not know the difference between good and evil, between falsehood and truth, they did not understand the mystery of transgression, that is, the mystery of existence. This leaves them without knowledge, and because they do not know what is ahead, they are unable to save their lives. So in that future, when wickedness is revealed in the presence of the righteous and righteousness will be revealed like the sun within the predetermined order of the world, all those who cling to the mysteries of transgression will no longer be. The determinism attached to this division within the created order suggests that a marked dualism characterizes the conceptual framework of the composition. I find this dualism to be more marked than that of *Instruction*, suggesting that its composition is closer to an actual division within the religious institutions and communities of Israel. Petersen describes the manner in which *Mysteries* develops and advocates a strategy of polarization that strengthens the identity of an in-group. It expropriates the tradition of the parent body and adopts its marks of identity, claiming that it is either obsolescent or its validity has come to an end.[7] John Collins proposes that the extent to which the work appeals to special revelation makes it the product of a sectarian milieu.[8] The paleographic evidence supports the hypothesis of a later date of composition than *Instruction*.

Lange notes the absence of "Essene" vocabulary and theology in *Mysteries*. Combining this observation with evidence of interest in temple matters, he proposes a date of composition at the end of the third or the beginning of the second century B.C.E.[9] For Lange, the dualism and eschatology of *Mysteries* predates the "Treatise on the Two Spirits" (1QS iii:13–iv:26), leaving a date of composition prior to the mid-second century B.C.E.[10] He notes in the vocabulary of all three compositions certain terms with similar meanings: "intention" (מחשבה), "history" (תולדות), and "inheritance" (נחל or נחלה).[11] All three compositions are characterized by a particular combination of Torah, wisdom, and eschatology, but the dualism becomes more central and pronounced as one advances chronologically through the compositions. While Elgvin sees *Instruction* and *Mysteries* as being attached to two different tradi-

---

7. Petersen, "Wisdom as Cognition," 414-20.

8. Collins, *Jewish Wisdom*, 127-28.

9. Lange, "Weisheits Texte aus Qumran," 23-24.

10. Armin Lange, "In Diskussion mit dem Tempel: Zur Auseinandersetzung zwischen Kohelet und weisheitlichen Kreisen am Jerusalemer Tempel," in *Qohelet in the Context of Wisdom* (ed. A. Schoors; BETL 136; Leuven: Leuven University Press/Peeters, 1998), 127-34; idem, "Weisheits Texte aus Qumran," 13.

11. Lange, "Weisheits Texte aus Qumran," 25-26.

tions, he does hold out for the possibility that the former composition was available when *Mysteries* was penned.[12] These perspectives also relate to the issue of the addressee.

Menahem Kister has advanced the interesting proposal that this composition is addressed to the diviners (חרטמים) found in 4Q300 1aii-b:1.[13] While he has rightly discerned that the contest is between two types of wisdom, it is not convincing to argue that it is between the diviners and the proponent(s) of this composition. The extant text mentions the diviners only once, and immediately after that reference the construction changes to the second person plural. While the diviners are clearly identified as the opponents of wisdom, they are not the second person plural addressees of the composition. Tigchelaar analyzes the second person plural texts in an attempt to identify the addressees. He also considers the problem of the foreign magicians, but concludes that the text originates in the circles of the priestly sages, who are sometimes addressed in the second person plural.[14] Elgvin questions whether the level of interest in priestly matters is sufficient to warrant the designation "priestly sages."[15] Lange also highlights the cultic interests identified in *Mysteries*.[16] At this point, however, the caution of Tigchelaar is worthy of note: "A sharp distinction between sages and priests is not warranted."[17] Within the second century B.C.E. it does appear that issues relating to the temple and cultic service were such an integral part of Torah and piety that it is almost impossible to determine whether authors or addressees were priests unless it is explicitly stated. The temple was an integral part of religious (hence Jewish) life.

Literary Questions

The composition most similar to *Mysteries* in content and structure is *Instruction*. Key terms and concepts such as "mystery (רז), mystery of existence" (רז נהיה), "intention" (מחשבה), and "wisdom" (חוכמה) are central to both compositions. The extensive use of "understanding" (בינה) with cognates "be discerning" (התבונן) and "man of discernment" (מבין) as well as the verb "to know" (ידע) and its cognates also characterize the two compositions. Both works share the key phrase אל הדעות ("the God of knowledge"), considered significant in the sectar-

12. Elgvin, "Priestly Sages?" 73, 83-84, 86.
13. Kister, "Wisdom Literature," 25-28.
14. Tigchelaar, "Your Wisdom and Your Folly," 73-78.
15. Elgvin, "Priestly Sages?" 60-77.
16. Lange, "In Diskussion mit dem Tempel," 133-34.
17. Tigchelaar, "Your Wisdom and Your Folly," 82.

ian literature of the Qumran corpus. Concerning this appellation note the commentary to 4Q417 1ii:8 above as well as the discussion of "intention" (מחשבה) among the "Key Terms" in the introduction to *Instruction*. "Mystery of existence" is also one of the key terms discussed there. The similarities to *Instruction* and the extensive use of terminology from the semantic domain of wisdom within these fragments support the classification of these texts among the wisdom compositions from the Qumran corpus.[18]

The reference to the diviners in 4Q300 1aii-b + 4Q299 3c points to similarities with the book of Daniel (Dan 1:20; 2:2, 27; 4:7, 9; 5:11). As in Daniel, the wisdom of the diviners is inferior and even invalid. Here it results in stupidity, since the vision is sealed and inaccessible to them. They have not considered the testimonies of the heavens nor have they paid attention to the eternal mysteries or to the root of wisdom. They have not pondered with understanding. We also note, "sealed from you is the seal of the vision . . . If you would open the vision" (4Q300 1aii-b:2-3; 4Q299 3c:2-3). Eternal mysteries and hidden wisdom are all sealed in that vision. Daniel is the master of wisdom, including visions and dreams (1:17). He interprets visions throughout the biblical book. In the last lengthy apocalypse he is given to understand what will happen to his people at the end of days, for "there is yet a vision for the days" (10:14). In 11:14 we find an abortive effort to fulfill the vision. Then at the conclusion of the work Daniel is instructed to go away, "for the words are to remain secret and sealed until the time of the end" (12:9). The relationship of wisdom and knowledge to the discernment of the times specified by the Creator is integral to *Mysteries,* as it is to Daniel.

Tigchelaar has also pointed to the presence of a ריב pattern, a "disputation form," in *Mysteries.*[19] He points to the description of this pattern in George Nickelsburg's commentary on *1 Enoch:* "A number of Israelite texts contrast nature's steadfast obedience to God's command with humanity's divergence from the divine statutes."[20] One way of demonstrating the manner in which humanity has strayed is to highlight the constancy of nature. There is an order to the structure of creation, evident within it, that is violated by human society. This leaves human society as the deviant portion of creation in a dispute with its Creator. When the Creator ultimately wins and harmony is restored, only that portion of human society that has recognized this reality will be a participant in this restoration, a "new creation."

---

18. On this question see Matthew J. Goff, *The Worldly and Heavenly Wisdom of 4QInstruction* (STDJ 50; Leiden: Brill, 2003), 169 n. 4.

19. Tigchelaar, "Your Wisdom and Your Folly," 80-81.

20. George W. E. Nickelsburg, *1 Enoch 1: A Commentary on the Book of 1 Enoch, Chapters 1–36; 81–108* (Hermeneia; Minneapolis: Fortress, 2001), 152-54.

Bibliography

Note also the bibliography in the introduction to this volume.

Elgvin, Torleif. "Priestly Sages? The Milieus of Origin of *4QMysteries* and *4QIn-struction*." In *Sapiential Perspectives*, ed. Collins et al., 67-87.

Kister, Menahem. "Wisdom Literature and Its Relation to Other Genres: From Ben Sira to *Mysteries*." In *Sapiential Perspectives*, ed. Collins et al., 13-47.

Lange, Armin. "Physiognomie oder Gotteslob? 4Q301 3." *DSD* 4 (1997): 282-96.

Petersen, A. Klostergaard. "Wisdom as Cognition: Creating the Others in the Book of Mysteries and 1 Cor 1-2." In *Wisdom Texts from Qumran*, ed. Hempel et al., 405-32.

Schiffman, Lawrence. "299-301. 4QMysteries[a-b, c?]." DJD 20:31-123.

Tigchelaar, Eibert J. C. "Your Wisdom and Your Folly: The Case of 1-4QMysteries." In *Wisdom and Apocalypticism*, ed. García Martínez, 69-88.

Mysteries[a] (4Q299)

Frag. 1 + 1Q27 1i + 4Q300 3

[01][. . . all . . .] [02][. . . in order that they would know (the difference) between good and evil, between falsehood and truth . . .] [03][and that they might understand the mysteries of transgression . . . all their wisdom, they do not know the mystery of existence. Concerning the former things they do not] [04][possess understanding so they do not know what will come upon them and they do not save their lives from the mystery of existence.] [05][This is for you the sign that it will occur, when the birth times of unrighteousness are shut up and wickedness is revealed in the presence of righteousness] [06][just as darkness is revealed by light. Just as smoke vanishes and is no more, so wickedness will vanish forever] [07][and righteousness will be revealed like the sun, the plan of the world. All who hold on to the mysteries of transgression will no longer be.] [08][Knowledge will fill the world and there is no folly any longer. That which is to come is determined, the prediction is true.] [1][From this it will be known to you that it cannot be turned back. Don't all the natio]ns hate injustice? [2][But by the hand of all of them it walks about. Does one not hear] truth [from all the peoples?] Is there a language or a tongue [3][that sustains it? Which nation takes pleasure in being oppressed by one stronger than it?] Which nation has not stolen [4][wealth of another . . .] placement of birth times is inscribed [5][. . .] men of intention for

all ⁶[. . .] to be put to the test, the words ⁷[. . .] their [con]sequences ⁸[. . .] and for a[ll]

Notes

The first lines (01-08) of this fragment are reconstructed on the basis of 1Q27 and 4Q300. Hence line 1 represents the first line in this column that is visible on frag. 1 of 4Q299.

Line 02: "[in order that they would know (the difference) between good]" — This line is reconstructed from 4Q300 3:2, which contains the words translated in this note in the fragment. The remainder is reconstructed from this base.

Line 03: "[all their wisdom]" — From 4Q300 3:3 (incorrectly marked in DJD 20:35).

Line 07: "[mysteries of transgression]" — While the original publication of 1Q27 suggests the reading "marvelous mysteries" (רזי פלא; DJD 1:103, 105), Schiffman in his reconstructed text related to the publication of 4Q299 suggests that Belial "or some synonym" is more appropriate (DJD 20:37). It is almost impossible to determine the reading for this term on the basis of the photographs of 1Q27. It is more likely that the reconstruction should follow the parallel construction in 1Q27 1ii:2, "mysteries of transgression" (here 4Q299 1:03 above), also found in 1QHᵃ xiii:38; xxiv:9.

Commentary

Line 05: "[This is for you the sign]" — See 4Q387 2iii:5 and 4Q389 8ii:5 for this phrase. This picks up a common biblical phrase indicating that the Lord will do as promised or as indicated (Exod 3:12; 1 Sam 2:34; 2 Kgs 19:29; 20:9; Isa 37:30; 38:7). In the NT, particularly in the Gospels, the debates over and requests for a "sign" are also rooted in this prophetic tradition.

Line 07: "[the plan of the world]" — See commentary to 4Q415 9:6.

Line 08: "[Knowledge]" (דעה) — "The God of knowledge" (אל הדעות; 35:1 [partially reconstructed]; 73:3) is an appellation used for God that is not found in the HB, but that is identified as well in *Instruction* (4Q417 1ii:8; 4Q418 43-45i:6; 55:5) and opens the "Treatise on the Two Spirits" (1QS iii:15). Note the discussion under the "Literary Questions" in the introduction to *Instruction*. The term "knowledge" is common in the sectarian texts of S, D, and H, while the term "wisdom" is largely absent.

Line 08: "[That which is to come is determined]" — This line adopts the language of Deut 13:14 and 17:4 employed in determining the certitude of whether an Israelite town or individual Israelites were worshiping other gods. If the truth of the matter (here translated "that which is to come") was determined, death was the required penalty.

Line 3: 1Q27 1i:10-12 has additional and different text that begins with the question, "which nation," here in line 3: "Which nation takes pleasure in being oppressed by one stronger than it? Who desires that his wealth be stolen by an evil man? Which nation has not extorted an ephah from its neighbor, a people that has not stolen the wealth of another?" This additional text would appear to place an even greater emphasis on the recognition of the corruption of imperial and other political powers than our version in 4Q299.

Line 4: "placement of birth times is inscribed" — There are two enigmatic terms in this phrase. "Birth times" (מולדים) is not known in Biblical Hebrew but it does appear four times in the *Mysteries* texts and seven times in *Instruction*. Note that it is found in 1Q27 1i:5, hence in line 05 reconstructed earlier in this column. It appears to be related to some comprehension of God's plan for the world, hence some understanding of the world's "origins" as well as the predetermined place and fate of individuals within it. Lawrence Schiffman in his treatment of the term proposes that the term בית מולדים ("house of birth times") refers "to the time of birth which is seen to affect the future and nature of the individual" (DJD 20:37). He finds such a use in *Tg. Onq.* to Gen 40:20 and in the use of this same term to designate the onset (or "birth") of the new moon in rabbinic literature (see Jastrow, 742). Matthew Morgenstern provides further evidence for this interpretation, which is rooted in the use of ancient horoscopes.[21] The term is used in 4Q186 1ii:8 and 2i:8. Both Tigchelaar and Matthew Goff support this translation.[22] Note also the "Comments" to 4Q416 2iii:9 in DJD 34:117. See commentary to 4Q417 2i:11 above for further discussion.

"Is inscribed" (נשטרה) does not appear as a verb in Biblical Hebrew but is related to an Akkadian term meaning "to write" or "to inscribe" (see *HALOT* s.v.

---

21. Matthew Morgenstern, "The Meaning of בית מולדים in the Qumran Wisdom Texts," *JJS* 51 (2000): 141-44.

22. Tigchelaar, "Your Wisdom and Your Folly," 87; Goff, *Worldly and Heavenly Wisdom*, 195-96.

שׁטר). The term describing "officers" or "officials" (שׁוטרים) in Biblical Hebrew is a cognate of this verb. We do find this term used in 1QSa and the *War Scroll*. Much more common in the Qumran texts is the verb חקק ("inscribe, decree").

Line 5: "men of intention" — See commentary to 4Q416 2iii:14 and 4Q417 1ii:12. Presumably "men of intention" are those who have some understanding of the "intent" of God in creation and the significance of that insight for some comprehension of world history.

Line 7: "[con]sequences" — This term (תוצאותם) also occurs in 4Q417 1ii:13, a column with a number of similarities to this column.

Frag. 2 + 1Q27 1ii

01[... to him plans are like ...] 02[... what is better ...] 03[... except the one who does good and the one who does evil, if ...] 1[...] he will not be good [for any-thing, thus all the good of his riches ...] 2[...] he shall be exiled without we[alth and be sold without a price for ...] 3[... be eq]ual to it. What[... except every ...] 4[...] 5[... value and it will not be worth an(y pr)ice ...] 6[... for all the na-tions ...] 7[... the Lord knows all ...]

Commentary

Line 01: "[plans]" — חשבונות probably refers to the design of God for cre-ation and human history. This term also can be translated as "reckoning," since it includes calendrical and terrestrial observations and calculations.

Line 1: The term ממון ("mammon") appears to come from the biblical המון, which also means a crowd or multitude, but in Late Biblical Hebrew refers to abundance, hence "[riches]."

Line 2: This line suggests Jer 15:13-14, where God gives Israel's wealth as booty and Israel goes into exile as the result of its sin (see also Deut 28:68). Presum-ably this points to the major theme of the column, even though the subject of these actions is not specified in the extant portion.

Frag. 3a, col. i

4[...] he 5[...] what

Frag. 3a, col. ii-b + 4Q300 5

⁰¹[intention, understanding . . .] ⁰²[judgment for the sake of wealth . . .] ¹[. . . needy] ²what is called [. . . his] deed[s . . .] ³and every deed of the righteous is un[clean . . . What] is a pers[on] called [. . .] ⁴wise and righteous for it is not for a person [. . .] and no[t . . . wisdom is hidden, for] ⁵if the wisdom of evil cunning or the in[tention of the evil inclination . . .] ⁶a deed that he will not do anymore except [. . .] ⁷command of his Maker. What is it that a m[an] shall do [. . .] ⁸rebel against the command of his Maker, his name shall be obliterated from the mouth of all [. . .]

⁹Listen, adherents of [. . .] ¹⁰forever. The purposes of every deed and the inte[ntions . . .] ¹¹every mystery. He establishes every intention, makes all [of what will be . . .] ¹²H[e is from bef]ore eternity, the Lord is his name, and for[ever . . .] ¹³[. . . in]tention of the placement of birth times he opened befor[e them . . .] ¹⁴[. . .] they repented for he tested our heart and he gave us an inheritance [. . .] ¹⁵[. . .] every mystery and the pangs of every deed. What [. . .] ¹⁶[. . .] peoples th[at] he created them and [their] deed[s . . .]

Commentary

Line 01:   "[intention]" — See commentary to 4Q416 2iii:14 and 4Q417 1ii:12.

Line 1:   "[needy]" (אביון) — See commentary to 4Q417 2i:16.

Line 5:   "in[tention of the evil inclination . . .]" — While Schiffman reconstructs this phrase "de[vices of Belial]," the latter term is not attested in the extant fragments of either *Mysteries* or *Instruction*. The reconstruction proposed here is attested in 4Q417 1ii:12 (see commentary there). See also commentary to 4Q416 2iii:14.

Line 12:   "the Lord is his name" — The use of the Hebrew third person singular pronoun for the tetragrammaton is attested in CD ix:5 in a quote from Nah 1:2 and in 1QS viii:13.[23]

Line 13:   "placement of birth times" — See commentary to 4Q299 1:4 and 4Q417 2i:11 above.

23. See Lawrence H. Schiffman, *Sectarian Law in the Dead Sea Scrolls* (BJS 33; Chico, Calif.: Scholars Press, 1983), 100-101 n. 16, 136.

Line 14: "tested our heart" — For this expression see Jer 11:20; 12:3; 17:10; Ps 17:3; 26:2 Prov 17:3. Since the most likely translation of this line is with a first person plural accusative, it is possible that this is also the case for the subject of the verb "call" in lines 2-3, that is, "we are called" rather than the present translation as a Niphal perfect ("what is called").

Line 15: "pangs of every deed" — This strange phrase, appearing here in a fragmentary context, appears to continue the theme of the foreknowledge of God as wisdom, active in the work of creation; thereby all the deeds of humankind have their origin in the birth pangs of creation.

Frag. 3c + 4Q300 1a ii-b

01[. . . the diviners who teach transgression speak the parable and relate the riddle before it is discussed. Then you will know whether you have considered] 02[and the testimonies of the heavens . . . your stupidity for sealed from you is the seal of the vision. You have not paid attention to the eternal mysteries and with understanding you have not pondered.] 03[Then you will say to . . . because you have not paid attention to the root of wisdom. If you would open the vision] 1[. . .] 2[. . .] be concealed from you 3[. . .] all your wisdom for yours is the parable [. . .] Listen, for what 4[is wisdom that is hidden . . .] there 5[. . . still you will not be . . .] eternal mysteries 6[. . . vision . . .] His deeds [. . .]

Notes

4Q300 1b was proposed by Milik as a group of subfragments that represented the left side of 4Q300 1aii. For the transcription of the separate fragments see DJD 20:100-103.

Line 3: "Listen" — In 4Q300 1b:4 the text appears to read שמו ("his name"), rather than שמעו.

Commentary

Note that both this fragment and the previous one have plural addressees. While 4Q299 3aii-b has a first person plural addressee, this column is written in the second person plural. The personal nature of wisdom literature tends to prefer the singular.

Line 01: "[diviners]" — See discussion under "Historical Context" in the introduction. This reference points to similarities with the book of Daniel (Dan 1:20; 2:2, 27; 4:7, 9; 5:11). As in Daniel, the wisdom of the diviners is inferior and even invalid. Here it results in stupidity since the vision is sealed and inaccessible to them. They have not considered the testimonies of the heavens nor have they paid attention to the eternal mysteries or to the root of wisdom. They have not pondered with understanding.

Line 01: "[discussed]" — The rare Niphal use of the verb דבר ("to speak") is employed in Mal 3:16 with reference to those who fear the Lord who are then recorded in the book of remembrance.

Line 02: "[testimonies]" — This rare biblical term appears throughout the sectarian compositions among the Qumran scrolls in contexts where it suggests the connection between the structure of creation and the lot of humankind. These "testimonies" bear witness to God's plan for creation and are sometimes so literal that they refer to the calculations of the calendar.

Frag. 4

¹[. . . so as] not to [. . .] ²[. . .] ³[. . .] land and like it [. . .] ⁴[. . . he] knew and the for[mer things] were reckoned [. . .] ⁵[. . .] it is not for peace [. . .]

Commentary

Line 4: "for[mer things]" — The רישונים are important in certain sectarian texts, namely the *Community Rule,* the *Damascus Document,* and the *War Scroll.* In these texts the "former things" frequently designate either events of the past in Israelite history or some earlier stage in the sectarian experience. In *Jub.* 1:26 "the first and the last" seems to designate the biblical account and the new revelation, respectively. In 1QS ix:10 we read, "They shall be judged by the former rulings in which the men of the commune walked." In CD xx:8-9 both "the first and the last set idols upon their hearts and walked in the stubbornness of their hearts." The terms point to a periodization of Israelite history and the manner in which there is hidden or new knowledge that is available to the present generation.

Frag. 5

[1][. . . ligh]ts of the stars for a m[emo]rial of [his] name [. . .] [2][. . . mi]ght of the mysteries of light and the ways of darkn[ess . . .] [3][. . .] seasons of heat with pe-riod[s of . . .] [4][. . . coming of the day] and the going out of the night [. . .] [5][. . .] placement of birth times [. . .]

Commentary

Line 1: "m[emo]rial of [his] name" — Perhaps a reference to Mal 3:16.

Line 2: Light and darkness is one of the basic contrasts in the sectarian com-positions of the scrolls, using the contrasting images to convey its understand-ing of the cosmic order and its dualistic teachings (see Jean Duhaime, "Dual-ism," *EDSS* 1:215-20; idem, "Light and Darkness," *EDSS* 1:495-96, for a summary of texts and viewpoint).

Line 3: "heat" — The link between seasons of hot and cold with the cosmic structure of the universe can be seen in the fragments of *Jubilees*, 4Q216 v:8 (*Jub.* 2:2).

Line 4: While this reconstruction is conjectural, the reverse order of the same phrase can be found in 1QH[a] xx:10, in the context of a description of the struc-ture of the universe. In an interesting variation of the phrase, the author in 1QS x:10 uses this imagery to describe the entry of the adherent into the covenant of God, thereby connecting membership in the sect with the cosmic structure of the universe and its earthly manifestations.

Line 5: "placement of birth times" — See commentary to 4Q299 1:4 and 4Q417 2i:11 above.

Frag. 6, col. i

[1][. . .] water [2][. . .] [3][. . .] their service they shall strengthen [4][. . . lightn]ing he makes forever, rain [5][. . . wat]er and with the measure they shall drink [6][. . .] he shall say to them. They shall give [7][. . .] with his might he created [8][. . .] its [mo]untains all [9][. . .] all of its offspring [10][. . .] spread from its center [11][. . .] time by time [12][. . .] to give water to all [13][. . .] for their structure is of dust [14][. . .] all

their reservoirs and the chamber ¹⁵[...] He gave dominion to strengthen ¹⁶[...]
all strength ¹⁷[...] and strengthens all ¹⁸[...] labor of a man ¹⁹[...] his [la]bor

Frag. 6, col. ii

¹[no]t [...] ²and concerning you the living [...] ³foolish who conceal [...]
⁴hidden from all the adherent[s of...] ⁵What is a father to sons rather than a
man [...] ⁶except the land to honor [...] ⁷from it, except the spirit [...]
⁸peoples. What is it that [...] ⁹that is not [...] ¹⁰darkn[ess] and li[ght...] ¹¹thus
it will be [...] ¹²heart of his companion and he lies in wait [...] ¹³from a foolish
man much property [...] ¹⁴according to the yield. What [...] ¹⁵its abundance or
the end of [...] ¹⁶one plan and not will he be sa[tisfied...] ¹⁷judgment, thus it
will come down [...] ¹⁸if he threshed he will increase [...] ¹⁹he [...]

Commentary

Line 10:   "darkn[ess] and lig[ht...]" — See commentary to 4Q299 5:2 above.

Line 13:   "much property" — For the translation of repeated nouns see *IBHS*
§7.2.3.

Line 16:   "one plan" — On תכון see commentary to 4Q415 9:6.

Frag. 7 + *4Q300 6:4-5 and 7:2*

¹[...] he [...] ²[...] near to [...] ³[what is furth]er from a person than an ac[t
...] ⁴in front of a man and he is far from [... and there is no bitterness] ⁵before
him greater than the one who bears a grudge [to tak]e ven[gea]nce without
judg[ment...] ⁶wh[o tres]passed and did [...]

Notes

4Q300 6:4-5 and 7:2 seem to contain parallels to the lines indicated, but it is not
clear that they are overlapping copies of the same text.

Commentary

Line 4:   "[bitterness]" — This is the Hebrew term for wormwood, hence also used to designate "bitterness." The basis for the translation of the term as "poison" is not clear (DJD 20:49, 103-4). In 1QH^a xii:15//4Q430 2 we read "a root that produces poison and bitterness is in their intention," but the term for "poison" there is רוש. "Bitterness" is also found in 4Q265 c:3; 4Q300 2i:5; 6:5; 7:2.

Line 5:   "the one who bears a grudge [to ta]ke ven[gea]nce without judg[ment]" — On the laws of reproof see CD vii:2-3; ix:2-8; xiv:22; 4Q417 2i:1-6 (see commentary there).

Frag. 8

^{1}[. . .] he established [. . .] ^{2}[. . .] he apportioned their insight [. . .] ^{3}[. . .] he [. . .] ^{4}[. . .] ^{5}[. . .] how can a ma[n] understand who did not know and had not heard [. . .] ^{6}[. . .] understanding the inclination of o[ur] heart with abundant insight he uncovered our ear and we he[ard . . .] ^{7}[. . .] inclination of understanding for all who pursue knowledge [. . .] ^{8}[. . .] all insight forever. He will not change [. . .] ^{9}[. . .] he shut up behind the waters so that n[ot . . .] ^{10}[. . .] heavens above to the heavens [. . .]

Commentary

Line 5:   "how can a ma[n] understand who did not know and had not heard" — This phrase points to Isa 40:21 and 28, related to the difficulties human beings have in understanding the purposes of God in creation. Note also Ps 78:2.

Line 6:   "with abundant insight he uncovered our ear" — For Collins this appeal to "special revelation" suggests a sectarian milieu for this composition. He also notes that in 4Q300 1aii-b:1-5 knowledge is sealed in a "vision."[24] It is much more likely that the relationship described here between revelation and wisdom is the same as in *Instruction*. In that case, the phrase "uncovered our ear" is used six times in the phrase "uncovered your ear to the mystery of existence" (1Q26 1:4; 4Q416 2iii:17-18; 4Q418 10a-b:1; 123ii:4; 184:2; 190:2; 4Q423 5:1).[25]

24. *Jewish Wisdom,* 128. This connection is critiqued by Charlotte Hempel, "The Qumran Sapiential Texts and the Rule Books," in *Wisdom Texts from Qumran,* ed. Hempel et al., 279.

25. On this connection see Michael A. Knibb, "The Book of Enoch in the Light of the Qumran Wisdom Literature," in *Wisdom and Apocalypticism,* ed. García Martínez, 202.

Frag. 9

²[. . .] princes to me, the shining of the land to [. . .] ³[. . . ki]ng is glorified and the splendor of his kingdom fills [. . .] ⁴[. . .] with all the ho[st . . .] ⁵[. . .] longsu[ffering . . .]

Commentary

Line 3: "glorified" — The Niphal form of the verb כבד ("be honored") is much more common in the Qumran texts than in the HB, particularly prominent throughout 4Q301 as well as the texts of the *Songs of the Sabbath Sacrifice* and of *Instruction,* appearing also in the MSS of the *War Scroll* and the *Hodayot.* On "glory" see commentary to 4Q417 2i:11.

Frag. 10

¹[. . .] king [. . .] ²[. . .] and mi[gh]ty men will strengthen the p[ost . . .] ³[. . . ra]ise Israe[l] over all the nations [. . .] ⁴[. . .] to form and to consider [. . .] ⁵[. . .] and judges for all the pe[oples . . .] ⁶[. . .] according to all their number [. . .] ⁷[. . .] and judge between the need[y . . .] ⁸[. . .] to measure out all the labor [. . .] ⁹[. . .] all their dominion [. . .] ¹⁰[. . .] daily [. . .] ¹¹[. . . their] inten[tions . . .]

Commentary

Line 2: "mi[gh]ty men" — The reference is to leading citizens as well as to an elite military force.[26]

Line 11: "inten[tions . . .]" — See commentary to 4Q416 2iii:14 and 4Q417 1ii:12.

Frag. 12

²[. . .] all from [. . .]

---

26. See John Kampen, *The Hasideans and the Origin of Pharisaism: A Study in 1 and 2 Maccabees* (SBLSCS 24; Atlanta: Scholars Press, 1988), 95-107.

Frag. 13a-b

¹[. . .] profane, between the im[pure . . .] ²[. . .] gave you dominion [. . . I]srael and you [. . .] ³[. . .] walked in [. . .]

Commentary

Line 1: "profane, between the im[pure . . .]" — Note the likely restoration proposed by Schiffman, "between the holy and the profane, between the impure and the pure" (DJD 20:54). See Lev 10:10; CD vi:18; xii:20.

Frag. 14

²[. . .] spring rain for [. . .] ³[. . .] and with the counsel of [. . .]

Frag. 15

²[. . .] he shall not touch [. . . st]reng[thened] al[l . . .] ³[. . .] he will strengthen [. . .] to listen to [. . .]

Frag. 16

¹[. . .] he made [. . .] ²[. . .] your spirit [. . .]

Frag. 17

¹[. . .] he made [. . .] ²[. . .] from wisdom [. . .]

Frag. 18

¹[. . .] he shall recompense the transgression [. . .] ²[. . .] and on the day [. . .] ³[. . .] from turning aside [. . .]

Frag. 19

¹[. . .] rule [. . .]

Frag. 20

¹[. . .] their plan except [. . .] ²[. . .] weight, for the plan [. . .] ³[. . .] together, an abundance of them [. . .]

Commentary

Line 1: "their plan" — On this term, also found in line 2, see commentary to 4Q415 9:6.

Line 3: "together" — See discussion in the introduction to *Beatitudes* (4Q525) under "Literary Questions."

Frag. 21

²[. . .] their waves by the hand of [. . .] ³[. . .] not all power [. . .] ⁴[. . .] treasury of all [. . .]

Commentary

Line 2: "waves" — While difficult to determine the context for its usage here, its meaning with reference to the sea is unambiguous in biblical and Qumran usage (e.g., see DJD 34:283-84 on 4Q418 69ii:4). While also difficult to determine the full meaning and context, 4Q418 69ii:4 places this reference to the sea in a wisdom context ("With knowledge all their waves . . ."), though in a column that concentrates on eschatological judgment.

Line 4: "treasury" — This term is frequently linked with wisdom and knowledge in other Qumran texts: 4Q286 1a-bii:7; 4Q298 3-4i:9; 4Q418 81+81a:9.

Frag. 22

¹[. . .] from the mouth of [. . .]

Frag. 23

²[. . .] he [. . .] ³[. . .] might [. . .] ⁴[. . .] person [. . .] ⁵[. . .] its length [. . .]

Frag. 24

²[. . .] it is [. . .] ³[. . . w]hich [. . .]

Frag. 25

³[. . .] not [. . .]

Frag. 26

¹[. . . ru]les [. . .] ²[. . .] and it is counted [. . .] ³[. . .] not [. . .]

Frag. 27

²[. . .] upon [. . .] ³[. . .] what [. . .] ⁴[. . .] stone [. . .]

Frag. 28

¹[. . .] those who are born [. . .] ²[. . .] they were astounded, thus those who are b[orn . . .]

Frag. 29

³[. . .] all life and with the measure [. . .] ⁴[. . .] he will swear [. . .]

Commentary

Line 4: "he will swear" — This could also mean "he will satisfy," but since swearing or taking an oath is an important subject in the MSS of both the *Community Rule* and the *Damascus Document*, I prefer this translation.

Frag. 30

²[. . .] when he completes [. . .] ³[. . . da]rkness. In darkness [. . .] ⁴[. . .] instruction not [. . .] ⁵[. . .] he increased [. . .]

Frag. 31

²[. . .] with all [. . .] ³[. . .] still [. . .] ⁴[. . .] by your hand [. . .]

Frag. 32

²[. . . they stu]mbled, what is the command[ment . . .] ³[. . . he st]rengthens and the generations of [. . .] ⁴[. . .] weight [. . .]

Frag. 33

²[. . .] his [inc]lination [. . .] ³[. . .] and if he will bear [. . .] ⁴[. . .] what is might without [. . .]

Frag. 34

¹[. . .] what he will establish [. . .] ²[. . .] if [they] will tur[n . . .] ³[. . .] man of discernment [. . .]

Commentary

Line 3: "man of discernment" — See the discussion of מבין under "Key Terms" in the introduction to *Instruction*.

Frag. 35

¹[. . . Go]d of knowledge [. . .] ²[. . .] through the angel[s . . .]

Commentary

Line 1: "[. . . Go]d of knowledge" — On the significance of this phrase see commentary to 4Q417 1i:8.

Frag. 36

¹[. . .] for all [. . .] ²[. . .] he will be [. . .]

Frag. 37

¹[. . .] every deed [. . .] ²[. . .] he opened [. . .]

Frag. 38

¹[. . .] before [. . .] ²[. . .] and the foundation[s of . . .]

Frag. 39

¹[. . .] children of Is[rael . . .] ²[. . .] for their plan [. . .]

Commentary

Line 2: "for their plan" — See commentary to 4Q415 9:6.

Frag. 42

²[. . .] except [. . .] ³[. . .] not [. . .] ⁴[. . .] the wisdom [. . .]

Frag. 43

²[. . .] adherents of the sec[rets of . . .] ³[. . .] be disc[erning . . .]

Commentary

Line 2: "adherents" — Literally "those who hold fast to," found throughout the *Mysteries* texts, 1Q27 1i:7; 4Q299 3aii-b:9; 6ii:4; 4Q300 8:5. Note also commentary to 4Q525 2ii+3:1.

Line 3: "be disc[erning . . .]" — This verb related to the noun בינה ("understanding") is evidence of the wisdom tradition that continues through this composition.

Frag. 44

²[. . .] deed[s . . .] ³[. . .] and now [. . .]

Frag. 45

¹[. . .] their heart [. . .] ²[. . .] they say [. . .] ³[. . . st]rength [. . .]

Frag. 46

²[. . .] discern [. . .] ³[. . .] he [. . .]

Frag. 47

²[. . .] and to bless [. . .]

Frag. 48

¹[. . . al]l who transg[ress . . .] ²[. . .] all [. . .]

Frag. 51

¹[. . .] angel[s . . .]

Commentary

This term could mean either angels or messengers. The former meaning is much more common throughout the scrolls as well as in this composition.

Frag. 52

³man [. . .] ⁴firstborn [. . .]

Commentary

Line 4: "firstborn" — This could also be translated as "in the furnace," which is also attested in a variety of compositions among the Qumran scrolls, referring to being tested by suffering: CD xx:3; 1QH^a xiii:18.

Frag. 53

¹[. . .] abominations [. . .] ²[. . .] in his holiness [. . .] ³[. . .] with you [. . .] ⁴[. . .] and there is not for the festiv[al . . .] ⁵[. . .] judgment for righteous is [. . .] ⁶[. . .] his [st]rength and strengthen [. . .] ⁷[. . .] to God to exact vengeance [. . .] ⁸[. . .] a dispute against the strong [. . .] ⁹[. . . Go]d and in the heavens is his dwelling [. . .] ¹⁰[. . .] ¹¹[. . .] I will announce [. . .] ¹²[. . .] with the king [. . .]

Commentary

Line 1: "abominations" — While it is difficult to determine the major topic of this column, this reference coupled with the term "festival" points to the conceptual world developed in the *Temple Scroll* and related texts where violations of the purity system constitute abominations (11Q19 xlviii:6; lii:4, 5; lv:6, 20; lx:17, 19, 20; lxii:16; lxvi:14, 17). It is also used to describe those men of injustice who oppose the covenant of God (1QS iv:10, 17, 21).

Line 4: "there is not for the festiv[al . . .]" — The Hebrew term שם can be translated either "there" or "name." The construction here makes the former more likely (see 1Q27 1i:7 or 4Q410 1:5).

Line 7: "to exact vengeance" — This is an important theme in a number of compositions among the Qumran scrolls. In the wisdom texts the most extensive reference to the legislation of Lev 19:17-18 is found in 4Q417 2i:1-6 (see commentary to that text). This may rather be a reference to those involved in the "abominations" identified earlier in line 1 above (e.g., 1QS v:12). There is limited evidence to support the hypothesis that the topic of this column is "the coming judgement in which God will avenge the violation of His law" (DJD 20:73).

Frag. 54

²[. . .] oppressed and robbed by [. . .] ³[. . .] for loving-kindness [. . .] ⁴[. . .] in all [. . .]

Commentary

Line 3:   "loving-kindness" — This phrase, found in Mic 6:8, is found in a variety of Qumran scrolls: CD xiii:18; 1QS ii:24; v:4, 25; viii:2; x:26 and other MSS of the *Community Rule;* 4Q418 169+170:3; 4Q437 4:4//4Q438 4aii,b-dii:4; 4Q502 14:5.

Frag. 55

¹[. . .] holy [. . .] ²[. . . the] righteous [judgm]ents [. . .] ³[. . .] for [. . .] ⁴[. . .] which they chose [. . .] ⁵[. . . serv]ice of his holiness and to make atonement for [. . .] ⁶[. . .] upon them [. . .]

Commentary

Line 5:   "[. . . serv]ice of his holiness" — This phrase, also found in 83:5, is not common in either biblical or Qumranic texts, but usually refers to some kind of temple service, "the service of the holy" (see Exod 36:1, 3; Num 7:9).

Frag. 56

²[. . .] their judge in the judgments [. . .] ³[. . . they] shall strengthen the hand of [. . .]

Frag. 57

³[. . .] that he will do [. . .] ⁴[. . .] which [. . .]

Frag. 58

²[. . .] he restored [. . .]

Commentary

Line 2:   "restored" — This term can also mean to turn around or turn back, but the surrounding fragments suggest a judicial context.

Frag. 59

¹he will consecrate [. . .] ²in judgment he will accuse [. . .] ³with all who transgress his utterance [. . .] ⁴those who support evil [. . .] ⁵[. . .] those who do [. . .] ⁶[. . .] ⁷[. . .] and let us bring an accusation [. . .]

Commentary

Line 3: "transgress his utterance" — Literally "transgress his mouth." The commandments came from the mouth of God.

Frag. 60

²[. . .] favor and appoint [. . .] ³[. . .] valued possession from all [the nations . . .] ⁴[. . .] and all the kings of the nati[ons . . .]

Commentary

Line 3: "valued possession from all [the nations . . .]" — In the Pentateuch this expression refers to Israel (see Exod 19:5; Deut 7:6; 14:2; 26:18).

Line 4: "kings of the nati[ons . . .]" — In Eccl 2:8 the author claims that he has gathered the "valued possession of kings and states."

Frag. 61

²[. . .] with the statutes [. . .]

Frag. 62

²[. . .] and a dispute [. . .] ³[. . .] And now [. . .] ⁴[. . .] your enemies will not be able [. . .] ⁵[. . .] for their courtya[rd]s to [. . .]

Commentary

Line 3: "And now" — This phrase begins a new literary unit in both biblical and Qumranic texts, most notably the introductory sections of the *Damascus Document* (CD i:1; ii:2, 14).

Frag. 63

¹[. . .] Listen [. . .] ²[. . .] ³[. . .] he will make him turn to the left [. . .] ⁴[. . .] his glory [. . .]

Commentary

Line 3: "make him turn to the left" — This line suggests Isa 30:21 in which the way is enjoined and adherents are given a warning that will keep them from departing to the right or the left. In Isa 30:20 the מורה ("teacher") is promised, the same word as in the title "teacher of righteousness" in the Qumran texts.

Line 4: "glory" — The term כבוד can be translated as either "honor" or "glory." In this context so closely related to apocalyptic imagery, it seems that "glory" is more likely. See commentary to 4Q417 2i:11.

Frag. 64

¹[. . .] the heavens [. . .] ²[. . .] hol[y . . .] ³[. . .] vanity [. . .]

Frag. 65

²[. . .] devastation is [. . .] ³[. . . po]verty and for the price [. . .] ⁴[. . .] he shuts the eye [. . .] ⁵[. . .] for his body [. . .]

Notes

Line 2: "devastation" — It is hard to determine whether the middle letter of this Hebrew term is a *waw* or a *yod*. On the basis of context I have selected the former. Schiffman leaves it untranslated in DJD 20:80, but chooses to translate it as "song" in the revision for *DSSR* 4:223. He is then reading it as שיר rather than שיד, while leaving the Hebrew text as originally constructed. Such a reading is doubtful in a wisdom context, even though the fragmentary state does not permit definitive answers.

Frag. 66

¹[. . .] and tongue[s . . .] ²[. . .] families [. . .] ³[. . .] Israe[l . . .] ⁴[. . .] they will give [. . .]

Frag. 67

²[. . .] all the families [. . .] ³[. . .] with him, from the priest [. . .] ⁴[. . .] all [. . .]

Frag. 68

¹[. . . Is]rael and the people [. . .] ²[. . .] for the children of Israel [. . .] ³[. . .] his [se]rvice [. . .] ⁴[. . .] knew [. . .]

Frag. 69

¹[. . . o]ne in the year [. . .] ²[. . . Ur]im and Thummim [. . .] ³[. . .] every human being [. . .]

Commentary

Line 2: "[. . . Ur]im and Thummim" — These were instruments of divination in the temple (Exod 28:30; Lev 8:8).

Frag. 70

¹[. . .] statute [. . .] ²[. . .] you did not know [. . .] ³[. . .] the profane, and yo[u . . .] ⁴[. . .] with guilt [. . .]

Commentary

Line 3: "the profane" — The construction suggests the line "between the sacred and the profane" (see Lev. 10:10; CD vi:18; xii:20 as well as frag. 13a-b:1 above).

Frag. 71

¹those who have turned from transgres[sion . . .] ²scorched you [. . .] ³you disdained [. . .] ⁴and he will cleanse [. . .]

Commentary

Line 1: "those who have turned from transgress[sion . . .]" (שבי פשע) — This Hebrew verb can also be translated as "repent" in appropriate contexts, and the same root is employed in the term *teshuvah* ("repentance"), a significant term in rabbinic literature. This phrase is well known to scholars of Qumran from the references in CD ii:5 (//4Q266 Dᵃ 2ii:5) and xx:17, as well as other sectarian texts. In CD it designates the members of the covenant "who live according to the commandments of those who enter the new covenant in the land of Damascus" (vi:19). They are also referred to as the "penitents of Israel" (שבי ישראל) in CD iv:2 and vi:5//4Q267ᵇ 2:11. This very concrete sociological meaning for the phrase also finds expression in more theological contexts related to those attempting to grow in the sectarian way of life: 1QS x:20//4Q260 Sᶠ iv:10; 1QHᵃ vi:35; x:11; xiv:9; 4Q400 1ii:16 (not necessarily sectarian); 4Q512 70-71:2 (very fragmentary context). In CD viii:16//xix:29 this same phrase is used to designate those who turned away from the "way of the people."

Frag. 72

¹[. . . He] is holy, he [. . .] ²[. . .] mighty men of righteousness ³[. . .] they knew that [. . .] ⁴[. . .] concerning [. . .]

Commentary

Line 2: "mighty men" — For this translation see commentary to 10:2 above.

Frag. 73

²[. . .] and there is not [. . .] ³[. . .] the God of knowl[edge . . .]

Commentary

Line 3: "the God of knowl[edge . . .]" — On the significance of this phrase see commentary to 4Q417 1i:8.

Frag. 74

²[. . .] Moses a face. Stones of [. . .] ³[. . .] for a remembrance of the holy ones upon [. . .]

Commentary

The words suggest a context for Moses' reception of the stone tablets as stated in Exod 24:12 and 34:1-28.

Frag. 75

¹[. . .] blue [. . .] ²[. . .] glory to open [. . .]

Commentary

Line 2: "glory" — The term כבוד can be translated as either "honor" or "glory." In this context so closely related to apocalyptic imagery, it seems that "glory" is the more likely meaning, referring to the "glory" of God rather than the "honor" given to humans. The "glory" of the Lord is present to Moses during the receiving of the tablets of stone, as proposed for the previous fragment (see Exod 24:16 and 34:29-35). See commentary to 4Q417 2i:11.

Frag. 76

²[. . .] from his mouth to op[en . . .] ³all the fathers of the congregation [. . .] ⁴[. . .] between a man [. . .]

Commentary

Line 3: "fathers of the congregation" — In the Hebrew Scriptures this phrase appears only at Num 31:26. Its use in some key Qumran texts is noteworthy:

1QSa i:16, 24; ii:16; 1QM ii:1, 3, 7; iii:4. While usage in the *War Scroll* appears to imitate the clan or household structure implied in the biblical text, the uses in the *Rule of the Congregation* refer to a role in the communal hierarchy of the sectarian organization (cf. 1QS v:1, 20). Its possible reconstruction in 4Q375 1ii:8-9 would be similar in usage to 1QSa.

Frag. 77

¹[. . .] a man [. . .] ²[. . .] everything in your hands [. . .] ³[. . .] and he [. . .]

Frag. 78

¹[. . .] its statutes [. . .] ²[. . .] its boundaries [. . .]

Commentary

Line 2: "boundaries" — The association of boundaries and the law of God is of particular importance in the *Damascus Document* (i:16; v:20; xix:16; xx:25).

Frag. 79

²[. . .] upright [. . .] ³[. . .] way of life [. . .] ⁴[. . .] his will [. . .] ⁵[. . .] land of his splendor and he [. . .] ⁶[. . .] in their tents and Aaron [. . .] ⁷[. . . pl]easing [fragrance] for a memorial [. . .] ⁸[. . .] all the people [. . .] ⁹[. . .] to b[e . . .]

Commentary

This fragment may be related to frags. 74-76 on the basis of its legal context.

Frag. 80

¹[. . .] he called [. . .] ²[. . .] and now [. . .] ³[. . . ju]dgments of righteousness [. . .]

Frag. 81

¹[. . .] the land to [. . .] ²[. . .] he shall judge [. . .]

Frag. 82

²[. . .] he shall place [. . .] ³[. . .] Israel [. . .] ⁴[. . .] day [. . .]

Frag. 83

²[. . .] before [. . .] ³[. . .] ⁴[. . .] covenant [. . .] ⁵[. . . ser]vice of the hol[y . . .]

Frag. 85

⁴[. . .] for you [. . .]

Frag. 86

³[. . .] he [. . .]

Frag. 87

²[. . . serv]ice with the bread [. . .]

Frag. 88

¹[. . . se]rvice of [. . .] ²[. . .] his holiness [. . .]

Frag. 89

²[. . .] days [. . .]

Frag. 97

¹[. . .] those who dwell in [. . .]

Frag. 99

¹[. . .] for all [. . .] ²[. . .] he did [. . .]

Frag. 101

²[. . .] not in [. . .]

Frag. 102

¹[. . . n]ot [. . .]

Frag. 106

²[. . .] Abra[ham . . .]

Mysteries^b (4Q300)

Frag. 1a, col. i

¹[. . .] see ²[. . .] ³[. . .] deeds of the land ⁴[. . . wo]rk of anger and the service of

Frag. 1a, col. ii

See 4Q299 3c above.

Frag. 1b

See 4Q299 3c above.

Frag. 2, col. i

⁵[. . .] bitterness

Commentary

Line 5:   The term לענה is the name of a plant usually translated as "worm-wood." See commentary to 4Q299 7:4 above. I do not see why it should be

223

translated "poison" in the references in this text (4Q300 6:5; 7:2; contra Schiffman, DJD 20:104).

Frag. 2, col. ii

¹[...] days [...] ²falsehood. What is fear [...?] ³he shall abandon the jealousy of strife [...] ⁴his transgression which he committed [...] ⁵evil except for him beloved [...]

Frag. 3

See 4Q299 1 above.

Frag. 4

²[...] he will recompense [...] ³[...] and he [...] ⁴[...] to place for go[od...]

Frag. 5

See 4Q299 3aii-b above.

Frag. 6

¹[...] they [shall] know va[nity...] ²[...] a man and what is the d[eed...] ³[...] with those who know [...] ⁴[...] and it is fa[r...] ⁵[... and there is no] worse bitterness against him [...] ⁶[...] how unfathomable it is for a m[an...]

Notes

Lines 4-5 have parallels in 4Q299 7:4-5 and 4Q300 7:2.

Commentary

Line 1: "va[nity...]" — I prefer this reconstruction (ההבל) to "difference" or "distinction" (ההבדל) in DJD 20:108. It more adequately fits the thematic context of these columns. See 1QS v:19; 4Q184 1:1; 4Q258 i:10; 4Q299 64:3.

Line 5: "bitterness" — See commentary to 4Q299 7:4 and 4Q300 2i:5 above.

Line 6: "unfathomable" — While the term עמוק means "deep" in Biblical Hebrew, there are a number of references scattered throughout Qumran texts to "hearing deep things" (1QM x:11; 4Q266 2i:5; 4Q463 1:4), hence this translation.

Frag. 7

¹[. . . what is worse for a man than] evil and what is more lofty for a man than righteousness [. . .] ²[. . .] and there is no worse bitterness against him than the one who takes vengeance by bearing a grudge without judgment [. . .] ³[. . .] judgment of his life fo[r] he is righteous in all [his ways . . .] ⁴[. . . what is a worse] evil than hating [. . .]

Notes

Line 2: Note parallels to this line in 4Q299 7:4-5 and 4Q300 6:5.

Commentary

Line 2: On the laws of reproof see CD vii:2-3; ix:2-8; xiv:22 and 4Q417 2i:1-6 (see commentary there).

Frag. 8

¹[. . . v]ision of our days [. . .] ²[. . .] what is before and what is aft[er . . .] ³[. . .] we open [. . .] ⁴ᵃ[. . .] and we shall make known [. . .] ⁴[. . .] for those who walk with foolishness in all [. . .] ⁵[. . .] to you who hold fast to the mysteries [. . .] ⁶[. . .] you will know whether you have understanding and whether [. . .] ⁷[. . .] and it was not. What is the mystery [. . .] ⁸[. . .] for a man and he [. . .]

Frag. 9

¹[. . .] testimonies they did not grasp it [. . .] ²[. . .] for on it is the day of the dispute [. . .] ³[. . .] it is from eternity and fo[rever . . .]

Notes

Line 1: "testimonies" — The remnants of the first letter on the photograph do not suggest the term סודות ("secrets") as proposed by Schiffman (DJD 20:110), but rather תעודות.

Frag. 10

¹[. . .] for a man [. . .] ²[. . . ju]dgment. What is evil for a man [. . .] ³[. . .] he shall not take [. . .]

Frag. 11

¹[. . .] righteousness [. . .] ²[. . .] and in his hand is the judgment of all of them. Righteous[ness . . .]

Frag. 12

¹[. . . sw]eet, what [. . .]

Commentary

This very fragmentary line probably parallels 4Q416 2iii:15 and 4Q418 9+9a-c:16: "then you will know what is bitter to a man and what is sweet to a fellow."

Frag. 13

¹[. . .] the day [. . .]

Mysteries (1Q27)

Frag. 1, col. i

See 4Q299 1 above.

Frag. 1, col. ii

See 4Q299 2 above.

Frag. 2

¹[. . .] he uncovered the heart [. . .] ²[. . .] to the end of all that [. . .]

Notes

From frags. 2-13 the photographs are very difficult to read, so this translation rests on the transcription of J. T. Milik and R. de Vaux (DJD 1:106-7).

Frag. 3

¹[. . .] from all of them [. . .] ²[. . .] to him for the priests [. . .] ³[. . .] that all [. . .]

Frag. 4

¹[. . .] might, he ceased [. . .]

Frag. 5

²[. . .] from the law [. . .]

Frag. 6

²[. . .] of them, he will make atonement for his inadvertent sin [. . .] ³[. . .] forever before him to make atonement for [. . .] ⁴[. . .] days [. . .]

Commentary

Line 2:   "make atonement for his inadvertent sin" — The sacrifice for an inadvertent sin is spelled out in Lev 5:17-19.

Frags. 9-10

¹the day [. . .] ²except [. . .] what is he [. . .] ³kings of pe[oples] listen [. . .] with it and they are like [. . .] ⁴with all the judges of [. . .] him and [. . .]

Frag. 12

²Is there an order [. . .] ³for [al]l [. . .]

Commentary

Line 2: "order" — The term ערך can refer to the ordering of some item like the two "rows" of the bread of the presence as well as to valuation.

Frag. 13

²[. . .] bring for the dead [. . .] ³[. . .] mysteries of the deep and the search [. . .] ⁴[. . .] night [. . .]

Mysteriesᶜ (4Q301)

A review of the debate concerning whether this is to be regarded as a copy of *Mysteries* is in the introduction to this text under "Manuscripts" above.

Frag. 1

¹[I] will pour out my spirit, and according to your kinds I will apportion my words to you [. . .] ²[pa]rable and riddle. Those who search the roots of understanding with those who hold fast to the [wondrous] myst[eries . . .] ³those who walk in foolishness and the men of intention for all the service of their deeds [. . .] ⁴neck [. . .] he[ad . . . Al]l of [the] tumult of the people with [. . .]

Commentary

Line 1 is based on Prov 1:23. Note that in Prov 1:22-33 both the "foolish" and the "scoffers" receive mention. The former term, פתי, is significant with its appearances in "sectarian" texts such CD xiii:6; xiv:2; xv:15 (and the Cave 4 MSS of D); 1QSa i:19; 1QpHab xii:4; 1Q14 7:3; 8-10:5; 20-21:1. It also appears in *Instruction* (4Q418 221:2; 223:3). The "scoffers" also are important as the opponents of the sect in CD i:14 (singular) and (in the plural) in CD xx:11; 4Q162 ii:6, 10; 4Q525 23:8.

Of particular interest in this text is the consequence of ignoring God's counsel and reproof. In this case the word for "counsel" (עצה) is also the term employed for "council," most notably in the *Community Rule*, *Pesher Habakkuk*, and the *Hodayot* texts, all regarded as "sectarian" compositions, as well as other texts in the Qumran corpus. "Reproof" also was of particular interest to the sectarians (see commentary to 4Q417 2i:1-6 above).

Line 1: "according to your kinds I will apportion my words to you" — This clause appears to reflect this author's understanding of the phrase "I will make known my words to you" in Prov 1:23. As hinted at in this passage, there is some apportionment according to specified categories not detailed in the fragments of this text. Note 1QS iii:14: "The sage is to give understanding and to teach all of the sons of light in the history of all of humankind for *all the kinds of* their spirit." This specification is found in the *Temple Scroll* (11Q19 xlviii:1, 3, 4; l:20), the Hebrew fragments of *Jubilees* (4Q216 vi:14; vii:4, 9, 15), *Reworked Pentateuch* (4Q365 15a-b:5; 4Q366 5:1, 2, 3), and *ApocJerB* (4Q384 8:3). This author seems to understand the injunctions of Proverbs in a more legal context. Tigchelaar goes on to propose that the term מין, here translated "kinds," may point to the rabbinic usage of this term to mean "sectarian."[27]

Line 3: "foolishness" — See the discussion of "foolish" in the commentary to line 1 above.

Frag. 2a-b

¹judgments of the fool and the inheritance of the wise [. . .] What is the riddle for you who se[ar]ch the ro[ot]s of understanding? ²[. . .] how honored of heart. It is from a parab[le . . .] parable. How majestic it is for you! It is to rul[e . . .] prince ³rules [. . .] without strength. He will rule over him with a whip without hire. Who will sa[y] ⁴[. . .] Who among you seeks the presence of light and the lum[inaries] ⁵[. . .] image of a male that was not [. . .] ⁶[. . .] with the angels of [. . .] ⁷[. . . pr]aising [. . .]

27. Tigchelaar, "Your Wisdom and Your Folly," 70.

Notes

Whether 2a and 2b constitute the same fragment is difficult to determine. They were arranged as such by Milik, but Schiffman treats them separately (DJD 20:115-16). They are so closely related in content that Milik's hypothesis appears reasonable.

Commentary

Line 2: "honored" — See commentary to frag. 3a-b:4-6 below.

Line 5: "image of a male" — Schiffman (DJD 20:117) points to this phrase in Deut 4:16, where it refers to the prohibition of idolatrous images.

Frag. 3a-b

[4][. . .] honored is h[e] with his lo[ng]-suffering and [gre]at is he with his ample anger. [G]lo[rious is . . .] [5][. . .] he with the abundance of his mercy and fearful is he with the plan of his anger. Honored is [. . .] [6][. . .] and because they rule over the earth. Honored is God by the people of his holiness and glorified is [. . .] [7][. . . for] his chosen ones. Glorified [is he by the exaltation of] his [hol]iness, great is he by the blessings of [. . .] [8][. . .] their splendor [. . .] with the comple[tion of] the evil epoch and to do [. . .]

Notes

A similar problem to frag. 2a-b can be identified in the relationship of 3a to 3b. Here Schiffman favors Milik's restoration (DJD 20:117).

Commentary

As pointed out by Schiffman (DJD 20:117-18), this fragment is related to the perspectives developed in *Hekhalot* literature. Within that literature we find the attributes of God presented in repeatedly glorified terms that have their basis in descriptions of ascent to and through the heavens.[28]

28. The basic reference for this material is Gershom G. Scholem, *Major Trends in Jewish Mysticism* (3d ed. 1941; repr. New York: Schocken, 1967), 44-79.

Lines 4-6: "honored" — The Niphal form of the verb כבד ("be honored" or "glorified") is much more common in the Qumran texts than in the Hebrew Bible, particularly prominent throughout 4Q301 as well as the texts of the *Songs of the Sabbath Sacrifice* and of *Instruction*, appearing as well in the MSS of the War Scroll and the *Hodayot*. On "glory" see commentary to 4Q417 2i:11. The Hebrew term נהדר in lines 4 and 6 is translated as "glorified" in this particular passage to distinguish it from נכבד.

Frag. 4

²[. . .] every spirit of his understanding. [They] do not know [. . .] ³[. . .] time with all his glory. What are the ashes [. . .] ⁴[. . .] it is glorious splendor [. . .]

Notes

Line 3: "glory" — See commentary to 4Q417 2i:11.

Line 3: "ashes" — This line has frequently been reconstructed as "dust [and ashes]," but that phrase always begins with עפר ("dust") in the HB (Gen 18:27; Job 30:19; 42:6), rather than אפר, the term present in this fragment (DJD 20:119).

Frag. 5

²[. . .] temple of his kingdom [. . .] ³[. . . wh]at is flesh that [. . .] ⁴[. . .] great [li]ght and honor[ed is . . .] ⁵[. . .] light and his light [. . .]

Commentary

Line 4: "honor[ed]" — See commentary to frag. 3a-b:4-6 above.

Frag. 6

¹[. . . fo]r he does not have [. . .] ²[. . .] his we[a]lth and the step of [his] glo[ry . . .] ³[. . .] he to them, he [. . .] ⁴[. . .] is it not [. . .]

Commentary

Line 2: "glo[ry . . .]" — See commentary to 4Q417 2i:11.

Frag. 7

²[. . .] until it is fill[ed . . .] ³[. . . ev]il of his heart [. . .] ⁴[. . .] not [. . .]

Frag. 9

²[. . .] spirit [. . .] ³[. . . honor]ed is he [. . .]

Commentary

Line 3: "[. . . honor]ed" — See commentary to Frag. 3a-b:4-6 above.

Frag. 10

²[. . .] between [. . .] ³[. . .] intent[ion . . .]

Commentary

Line 3: "intent[ion] — A common term in *Mysteries* and *Instruction*. See commentary to 4Q416 2iii:14 and 4Q417 1ii:12.

The Evil Seductress (4Q184)

Introduction

Content

Originally entitled "Wiles of the Wicked Woman" in a provisional publication by John Allegro, a name he did not repeat in the "official" DJD version, this unfortunate title has remained attached to this text and continues to be repeated in successive versions and translations. A welcome corrective was proposed by Geza Vermes, "The Seductress." My choice of title is explained below under "Literary Questions." This highly suggestive composition, the major fragment of which is in a poetic format, describes in rather graphic terms the temptress herself as well as the variety of methods and the allure that will lead a person astray from the "way" of a life of wisdom. In stark detail her connection with perversity and wickedness is developed in the context of her connection with the "depths" and with darkness. This portrayal includes various parts of her body as well as her attire. As we move toward a description of her abode and its furnishings, more correlations are made with the theme of destruction. Her abode is in the midst of an eternal mass of fire. She is the source of perversity and has dominion, hence the realm of evil is her creation and under her control. The focus of this section concludes with a shift to those who associate with her. Resident in Sheol, her paths are the way to death and destruction.

Her allure is powerful as she temptingly displays herself in the public square but also lurks in "mysterious" places. "Incessant fornication" is her obsession as she is constantly engaged in perverting and leading astray upright and righteous men. The fragment ends with that description, leaving the present-day reader to wonder whether there was a further portrayal of the lot of the upright caught in the realm of evil.

Subsequent fragments demonstrate evidence of connection with the terminology of this first fragment but are not substantial enough to add to the portrayal.

Manuscripts

There is only one manuscript of this composition. While the edition by John Allegro in DJD 5 includes six fragments (see plate 28), only five are available on the Rockefeller Museum plates PAM 42.621 and 43.432 (there are more plates of frag. 1). Fragment 2 is in the Oriental Institute Museum Collection (47799). Use of the DJD edition must be coupled with the notes of John Strugnell.[1] My translation assumes the DJD text and notes where the reconstruction of Strugnell has been employed in the creation of the Hebrew text that underlies it. Strugnell labels the script "rustic semiformal,"[2] thereby correctly making it relatively early in the paleographic development reflected in the majority of the compositions found in the Qumran library, dating ca. 30 B.C.E.-20 C.E. A new DJD edition of this volume is underway.

Historical Context

The graphic description of the seductress, her activities, and her surroundings as well as of the drastic consequences for affiliating with her has led many scholars to assume that this composition is an allegory. Proposals have included the possibility that Rome is a polemical target, that there is an "ideologically hostile group" within Judaism at which it is aimed, and even suggestions as specific as Simon Maccabee.[3] A possible identification with the "Man (or Preacher) of Lies," an opponent of the Qumran group as described in the *Damascus Document,* has also been an attempt to explain the specificity and force of the composition.[4] It is not clear, however, that it is necessary to posit a specific allegorical opponent to understand the intensity of this composition. In

1. Strugnell, "Notes en marge du Volume V des *Discoveries in the Judaean Desert of Jordan," RevQ* 7 (1970): 163-276, esp. 263-68. While arriving too late to be incorporated into this volume, see now also Eibert Tigchelaar, "Constructing, Deconstructing, and Reconstructing Fragmentary Manuscripts: Illustrated by a Study of 4Q184 (4QWiles of the Wicked Woman)," in *Rediscovering the Dead Sea Scrolls: An Assessment of Old and New Approaches and Methods* (ed. Maxine L. Grossman; Grand Rapids: Eerdmans, 2010), 26-47.

2. Ibid., 263.

3. See the summary of Moore, "Personification," 505-7.

4. J. Maier, "Wiles of the Wicked Woman," *EDSS* 2:976.

this translation and commentary I presume that this work is not so specifically directed to an opponent. Its objective could be some kind of group or ideological cohesion within a context of perceived diverse or disparate threats.

It is also highly unlikely that this is a composition by a member of the Qumran sect or at least intended to reflect that viewpoint. The available fragments reflect none of the specific legal and ritual concerns identified in those texts nor does it bear any of the marks of that social structure.[5] There is no evidence of any of the figures that advocate wisdom in those texts such as a teacher of righteousness, a "sage," or even a priest. Noted in the commentary are terms found in the book of Proverbs but not used in the sectarian literature from Qumran. There is evidence of the significance of the struggle in which humankind is engaged, that is, it is set in a cosmological framework with the fate of the created order at stake, a viewpoint familiar from other apocalyptic literature such as *1 Enoch*. The manner in which sectarian authors of Qumran literature would have been at home with its imagery is apparent. This leads to the proposition that it is part of the wisdom corpus of material identified with Qumran, but not a sectarian composition. This most likely places it in that category of literature designated as pre-Qumranic. This conclusion suggests a date of composition in the latter portion of the third or during the second century B.C.E.[6]

Literary Questions

Scholars working on this composition have tended to designate it a poem and even developed its poetic structure.[7] The arguments for doing this are quite compelling and we probably have no other manner in which to approach the literature. Other fragments of the work do suggest a note of caution, however. Does frag. 1 embody a specific poetic piece within a larger prose composition or does that fragment represent the nature of the whole? The available fragments do not permit an answer to that question nor do they provide enough material to develop a further understanding of the work's content.

While the imagery of the poem as a whole develops concepts and even a framework familiar from Second Temple apocalyptic literature, its inspiration rests on the portrayal of the adulteress in Proverbs 7, also sometimes referred to as

5. See John Strugnell, "The Smaller Wisdom Texts Found at Qumran: Variations, Resemblances, and Lines of Development," in *Wisdom Texts from Qumran*, ed. Hempel et al., 40.

6. This proposal places it in the earlier portion of the range of dates proposed by many of its interpreters: Lange, "Die Weisheits Texte aus Qumran: Eine Einleitung," in *Wisdom Texts from Qumran*, ed. Hempel et al., 10; Goff, *Discerning Wisdom*, 106.

7. E.g., Moore, "Personification."

the "strange woman" in 2:16-19; 5:1-14; 6:23-26; 9:13-18. She is described as an adulteress in 2:16 and 7:18-20. In the NRSV the נכריה (literally "foreign woman") is translated as "adulteress" in 2:16; 5:20; 6:24; 7:5. References to the אשה זונה ("prostitute") occur only in 6:26 and 7:10.[8] However, her personification in 4Q184 heightens her seductive powers. The central theme of this poem is found in line 8: "She is the origin of all of the ways of perversity."[9] She is both harlot and seductress in the available fragments of this poem. There is no evidence of her as an adulteress, but she does seduce men into adultery, "to turn aside their footsteps from the ways of righteousness" (1:16). Noteworthy is the attribution, "Nothing can make her de[sist] from incessant f[ornicat]ion" (1:12-13). "Fornication" is a very significant term in other Qumran texts, including primarily the sexual sins of adultery, incest, and other deviant behavior that violated the laws of the sect, as well as divorce (see commentary to 1:12-13 below). The personified "iniquity" in *1 En.* 42:3 suggests a similar image juxtaposing its acceptance with the rejection of wisdom, in this case presumably related to the revelation of apocalyptic mysteries.

There is some evidence to suggest that the "Treatise on the Two Spirits" (1QS iii:13–iv:26) is particularly reliant on 4Q184.[10] Connections with this text can also be found in the commentary. Whether the linkages are specific enough to suggest a literary dependence could be a matter of debate, but the close connections between the texts suggest a substantial overlap in the thought worlds of the authors of the two documents.

The conflicts developed in the text receive an insightful feminist analysis from Melissa Aubin.[11] In this analysis the symbol of the heretical woman is employed to mediate conflicts between men, orthodox and heterodox as understood by the writer. This female figure is fashioned to resist everything of value in the orthodoxy of the author. Aubin demonstrates the manner in which this figure becomes a vehicle for promoting the values of the author. Thus the feminine figure is neither a real woman nor a symbol for a particular viewpoint or social outlook opposed to that of the author.

---

8. Note the study by Matthew Goff comparing this poem with the MT and LXX versions of Proverbs: "Hellish Females: The Strange Woman of LXX Proverbs and 4Q184 (Wiles of the Wicked Woman)," *JSJ* 39 (2008): 20-45. It is not clear to me that the move to a metaphorical figure, as opposed to a literal warning against the problem of adultery, lowers the seductive nature of the argument in the text. Metaphor in this case may not be dealing with abstract ideas, but rather concrete affiliation with the groups that espouse those ideas. In that case members can also be seduced into breaking allegiance with the group, or joining another group, both potentially seductive possibilities.

9. Moore, "Personification," 509.

10. Note Moore, "Personification," 506-7; Crawford, "Lady," 361-62.

11. Aubin, "She is the beginning." See also Goff, *Discerning Wisdom*, 104-21.

Bibliography

Note also the bibliography in the introduction to this volume.

Allegro, John M. "184." DJD 5:82-85, plate 28.

Aubin, Melissa. "'She is the beginning of all the ways of perversity': Femininity and Metaphor in 4Q184." *Women in Judaism* 2, no. 2 (2001): 1-23.

Baumgarten, Joseph M. "On the Nature of the Seductress in 4Q184." *RevQ* 15 (1991): 133-43.

Broshi, Magen. "Beware of the Wiles of the Wicked Woman: Dead Sea Scroll Fragment Reflects Essene Fear of and Contempt for Women." *BAR* 9, no. 4 (1983): 54-56.

Carmignac, Jean. "Poème allégorique sur la secte rivale." *RevQ* 5 (1964-66): 361-74.

Crawford, Sidnie White. "Lady Wisdom and Dame Folly at Qumran." *DSD* 5 (1998): 355-66. Reprinted in *Wisdom and Psalms*. Ed. Athalya Brenner and Carole R. Fontaine, 205-17. FCB 2/2. Sheffield: Sheffield Academic Press, 1998.

Gazov-Ginzberg, A. M. "Double Meaning in a Qumran Work ('The Wiles of the Wicked Woman')." *RevQ* 6 (1967-68): 279-85.

Goff, Matthew. *Discerning Wisdom,* 104-21.

Harding, James E. "The Wordplay between the Roots כשל and שכל in the Literature of the Yahad." *RevQ* 19 (1999): 69-82.

Hoenig, S. B. "Another Satirical Qumran Fragment." *JQR* 55 (1965): 256-59.

Jones, Scott C. "Wisdom's Pedagogy: A Comparison of Proverbs VII and 4Q184." *VT* 53 (2003): 65-80.

Licht, Jacob. "(4Q184 של כתביה בשרידי שנמצא שיר הזרה: האשה של רעתה כת מדבר יהודה" ("Wiles of the Wicked Woman"). In *Bible and Jewish History: Studies in Bible and Jewish History Dedicated to the Memory of Jacob Liver.* Ed. Benjamin Uffenheimer, 289-96. Tel-Aviv: Tel Aviv University, Faculty of the Humanities, 1971.

Maier, Johann. "Wiles of the Wicked Woman." *EDSS* 2:976.

Moore, Rick D. "Personification of the Seduction of Evil: 'The Wiles of the Wicked Woman.'" *RevQ* 10 (1981): 505-19.

Strugnell, John. "Notes en marge du Volume V des *Discoveries in the Judaean Desert of Jordan.*" *RevQ* 7 (1970): 163-276, esp. 263-68.

Wright, Benjamin G., III. "Wisdom and Women at Qumran." *DSD* 11 (2004): 240-61.

Zur, Yiphtah. "Parallels Between Acts of Thomas 6-7 and 4Q184." *RevQ* 16 (1993): 103-7.

Frag. 1

[1][from] her [mouth] she brings forth vanity and [. . . .] Errors she seeks constantly [. . . to] sharpen [her words . . .] [2]and mockingly she flat[te]rs, to deride altogether with l[ips] of perversity. Her heart prepares snares and her inner being tr[aps. Her lips] [3]are defiled with perversity, her hands grasp the depth, her feet sink down to do wickedness and to walk in guilty acts of [transgression]. [4]Foundations of darkness and a multitude of transgressions are under her skirts [. . .] depths of night and her garments [. . .] [5]Her coverings are the darkness of twilight. Her adornments are marks of destruction, her beds couches of destruction [. . .] [6]depths of the pit. Her lodgings are beds of darkness and in the middle of the nigh[t] is her [dom]inion. On foundations of darkness [7]she pitches a tent for rest and dwells in tents of silence in the midst of an eternal mass of fire. Her inheritance is not in the midst of all those [8]who shine brightly.

She is the origin of all of the ways of perversity. Woe comes to all who possess her, she brings devastation to all [9]who grasp hold of her, for her ways are ways of death and her paths are pathways of sin. Her tracks lead astray [10]to perversity and her roadway[s] are guilty acts of transgression. Her gates are gates of death. When entering her house she steps into Sheo[l]. [11]A[l]l who [enter it will not] return and all who possess her descend to destruction.

S[h]e lies in wait in secret places, [12]all [. . . .] In the open squares of the city she adorns herself and in the gates of the towns she stations herself. Nothing can make her de[sist] from [13]incessant f[ornicat]ion. Her eyes gaze intently here and there and she raises her eyelids in reckless abandon to seek [out a] righteous [14]ma[n] and overtake him, a [po]werful man and make him fall, to turn the upright aside from the way, the chosen righteous [15]from keeping the commandment; those of firm re[so]lve to bring down with reckless abandon, to make those who walk upright pervert the pre[cept], to make the meek [16]rebel against God, to turn aside their footsteps from the ways of righteousness, to place inso[le]nce in their [hear]ts, so that they do not walk [17]in the tracks of uprightness, to make men attain the ways of the pit and to seduce with flattery [all] mankind.

Notes

Line 1:   "[from] her [mouth]" — Cf. Moore ("Personification," 510), who acknowledges that Strugnell's reconstruction ("Notes," 266), adopted here, might be correct. See commentary below.

Line 2:   On the basis of the observations of Strugnell ("Notes," 264), I have re-constructed the Hebrew text of the second half of this line as follows: לבה יכין פחין וכליותיה מק[שות שפתיה] ("Her heart prepares snares and her in-ner being tr[aps. Her lips]").

Line 2:   "[Her lips]" — This reconstruction is based on the reference earlier in this line to the verbal actions of flattery and derision. Since the most common item to be defiled in the biblical materials is the person as a whole (נפש), there is no parallel there to help us determine the most appropriate body part to be mentioned here. This reconstruction still fits the proposed hypothesis that these references start at the top of the body and go down while rejecting the possibility of a reference to the "fingers" on the basis of lack of evidence (Moore, "Personification," 512).

Line 3:   See Strugnell ("Notes," 264-65). Due to the presence of the same phrase in line 10, I retain the original reconstruction proposed by Allegro.

Line 6:   "in the middle of the nigh[t]" — Contra Strugnell ("Notes," 265), who says the first *yod* of ובאישני is a doubtful transcription, but it is clearly visible on the plate. I see no reason to question the use of the term אישון, since it fits both context and orthography. For the usage of this meaning of the term, see Prov 7:2. One form of the plural cited in Jastrow is אִשּׁוּנֵי (p. 60), which here is attested in the defective form, not uncommon in Qumran orthography (*HDSS* 18). It is also found in frag. 3, line 5.

Lines 12-13:   "from incessant f[ornicat]ion" — The letters here are not very clear on the plate. See also commentary on this phrase.

Line 15:   "those of firm re[so]lve" (סומכי י[צ]ר) — The tear in the fragment prohibits definitive identification. I would prefer to reconstruct "righteousness" at this point based on other material in this fragment and Ps 37:17, a well-attested psalm in Qumran texts, but the remaining traces of the letters do not permit such a hypothesis.

While I accept the reconstruction on paleographic grounds, it is important to note that the Qumran parallels reverse the two terms and leave them in the sin-gular, reading יצר סמוך: 1QS iv:5; viii:3; 1QH^a ix:37; x:11, 38; 4Q257 3ai,3bv:2; 4Q259 2ai,2b-dii:11; 4Q428 3:5; 4Q437 4:2 (reconstructed); 4Q438 4a,b,c,dii:2.

Line 15:   "to bring down" (הביל, from the root נבל) — This term is not found in the Hiphil form in Biblical Hebrew (*HALOT* s.v. נבל), nor in classical rabbinic texts (Jastrow, 869). Qimron notes that a number of verbs are used in the Hiphil in the Qumran texts rather than in the Qal form (*HDSS* §310.16).

Line 17: "mankind" — I intentionally have given בני איש a male translation. This is justified on the basis of the imagery of seduction found there.

Commentary

Line 1: "[mouth]" — The term for "mouth" is based on Prov 5:3 (also 8:7 and 24:13 as well as a number of references in Job).

Line 1: "she seeks" — Note Prov 7:15 for שחר with regard to the seductress, also found in Prov 1:28; 8:17; 11:27; 13:24.

Line 1: "[. . . to] sharpen [her words . . .]" — While here attributed to the seductress, a similar idea in the form of a pious prayer, hence in a positive sense, is found in the fragmentary text, 4Q440a 1:5: "My words you sharpened like a sword." The previous line in that fragment refers to "my lips and my tongue." In Ps 64:3 evil men are accused of sharpening their tongues like swords. The petitioner asks for deliverance in Ps 57:4, because "I lie down among man-eating lions, whose teeth are spears and arrows, whose tongue is a sharp sword" (JPS v. 5); and in Ps 140:3 the evil men, the lawless, "sharpen their tongues like serpents; spiders' poison is on their lips" (JPS v. 4). Note Prov 25:18: "Like a club, a sword, a sharpened arrow, is a man who testifies falsely against his fellow."

Line 2: "flat[te]rs" — The verb "smooth" (חלק) refers to "flattery" and is found also in line 17 of this column. This Hebrew term also appears in Prov 6:24; 7:5, 21 (note Prov 2:16 as well). The ability of the seductress to use her mouth to flatter in a mocking manner as well as to seduce is based on the use of the biblical figure in Proverbs 5–7 (see also Moore, "Personification," 511).

This particular attribute of the seductress is of greater significance in Qumran literature since it forms part of the sobriquet "seekers of smooth things," a reference to some opponents of the group described in the sectarian texts (see Albert I. Baumgarten, "Seekers after Smooth Things," *EDSS* 2:857-59). The majority of the references are found in 4Q169 to designate an organized group related to government that is in collusion with the gentiles and leads officials as well as ordinary people astray through a false or fraudulent interpretation of Scripture, that is, taking the "easy" or "smooth" path (see Isa 30:10) rather than the difficult but perfect way. References to this group also appear in other pesher compositions and in the *Hodayot* with a slight variant found in CD i:18.

Line 2: "to deride" — This Hebrew root (לִיץ or לוּץ) becomes important in compositions describing the life and thought of the sectarians associated with Qumran. "The men of derision" (אַנְשֵׁי הַלָּצוֹן) are cited in 4Q162 ii:6, 10; 4Q525 23:8. From Jerusalem, they have despised the law of the Lord and discarded the word of the Lord. CD i:14 mentions "the man of derision" who "spouted to Israel from the waters of lying." Most see this title as a synonym for "the man of the lie" and "the spouter of the lie," cited in *Pesher Habakkuk* and the *Damascus Document* (see Timothy H. Lim, "Liar," *EDSS* 1:493-94). Both "flatter" and this term point to labels applied to the opponents of the sectarians.[12]

Line 2: "altogether" — This translation follows Moore ("Personification," 511-12). Here García Martínez and Tigchelaar (*DSSSE* 1:377) and Crawford ("Lady," 360) translate יחד as "community." It is not clear that this is a noun in the text and evidence in the rest of the document to a sectarian provenance is absent. Van der Woude's translation, "thoroughly," seems to capture the comprehensive nature of the act of derision implied in the use of this adverb. Its use as both adverb and verb (sometimes וחד) can be found in other wisdom texts from Qumran, especially *Instruction*: 4Q415 9:7; 11:4; 4Q416 2iii:21; 2iv:5; 4Q417 2i:6(?); 4Q418 103ii:8, 9; 167a+b:5, 6; 172:3; 199:1 (very fragmentary but probably a noun). For comments see DJD 34:25, 56, 395. Note also 4Q299 20:3; 4Q525 2ii+3:8; 14ii:9, 15, 16, 27; 22:3.

Line 2: "with l[ips] of perversity." — The lips of the seductress also are mentioned in Prov 5:3 and 7:21. Five references to "perversity" are evident in the fragments of this composition (also 1:3, 8, 10; 3:4). This is a defining term in some sectarian compositions, with fourteen references in 1QS alone. When the "Treatise on the Two Spirits" (1QS iii:13–iv:26) outlines its ideology, we see that humankind was created with two spirits, "the spirit of truth and the spirit of perversity" (1QS iii:19). "The men of the community" are to be separated from "the council of the men of perversity" (1QS v:1-2).

Line 2: "Her heart prepares snares and her inner being tr[aps]." — The seductress is the one who with her mouth and smooth words prepares a snare for the unwitting in Prov 7:23. See also the commentary to 4Q185 1-2ii:5. The avoidance

12. They appear in parallelism or close proximity in 1QHᵃ x:13-15, 31-32; xii:7-10 (Moore, "Personification," 511).

of traps is a common theme throughout that biblical book (13:14; 14:27; 18:7; 20:25; 22:25; 29:6, 25). Note particularly the terminology in 12:13: "Perversity of the lips is a trap for an evil man."

Line 3: This line includes a fascinating collage of images from Proverbs. First of all note "the depth." The precise meaning of this word is unclear, but is probably related to the verb "to sink" in Prov 2:18, even though the specific meaning of "pit" is attested for שׁוחה (see *HALOT* s.v. שׁוּחה) and שׁיחה (see *HALOT* s.v. שׁיחה). Then note the terminology utilized in our text from Prov 5:5, where it says of the seductress that "her feet sink down to death and her steps grasp Sheol," imagery appearing in Prov 7:27 and later in our composition.

Lines 4-6: The imagery of darkness in these lines is a compelling literary device. They apparently take their inspiration from Prov 7:9-10: "In the twilight, in the middle of the night, and in the darkness, behold, a woman dressed as a harlot meets him." All of these same terms are used to build the picture in these lines. However, one additional term also makes its appearance in both lines 4 and 6, חושׁך, the most common Hebrew word used to designate "darkness." It is this term which is so common in some of the sectarian scrolls, particularly the title "children of darkness" and the "ways of darkness" in 1QS, as well as the additional phrase "lot of darkness" in 1QM.

A second type of imagery demonstrates the use of Proverbs 7. In Prov 7:16-17 her furnishings are described. "Her bed" in line 5 and the "beds of darkness" in line 6 utilize the terminology from Proverbs. Even more indicative of the close relationship is the unusual verb in this context, "she pitches a tent" in line 7 and the noun "aloes" in Prov 7:17, explained upon the basis of the use of the term with the identical consonants in its root.

Line 5: "Her adornments are marks of destruction, her beds couches of destruction" — The word "destruction" is also found in line 11: "All who possess her descend to destruction." The clear message is that any liaison with the seductress leads to destruction. Such imagery would have been very welcome to the author(s) of 1QS, who describes the "men of destruction" as one of the bodies who are not to be confronted nor grappled with until the "day of revenge" (ix:16, 22; x:19), presumably because then human effort would not be required to deal with them. The "sons of destruction" in CD vi:15 and xiii:14, who must avoid the "traps of destruction" in CD xiv:2, are presumably the same group. The term is also found in 1QH[a] and other MSS of that composition *(Hodayot)* as well as other MSS of the *Community Rule* and the *Damascus Document*. Interestingly the term reappears in other Qumran wisdom texts as well, most notably 4Q 418 69ii:6; 102a,b:1; 162:4; 177:2; 4Q525 5:7 as well as quite extensively in the fragments of 4Q286 and 4Q287.

Line 6: "her [dom]inion" — Contra Strugnell ("Notes," 265). This term ממשלות in plural form is found in the HB only in Ps 136:9, which could well provide the background for its use in this composition at this point. The idea that there is a realm that is ruled by evil is captured in the phrase "dominion of perversity" in 1QS iv:19. Within the "Treatise on the Two Spirits" (1QS iii:13–iv:26) we see that the "sons of perversity 'are ruled by' the angel of darkness." References to the "dominion of Belial" elsewhere in 1QS (i:18, 23; ii:19) develop this same picture. The "dominion" of the seductress would have been imagery quite intelligible to the author(s) of this sectarian composition.

Line 7: "silence" (דומה) — Note that while the usual translation of this term is "silence" (e.g., *DSSANT* 273), in this context it only makes sense if one understands that this can also mean lack of speech and motion, even to the point of death (BDB s.v. דמם; and *HALOT* s.v. דומה and דומם).In rabbinic literature this is the name of "the guardian angel of the deceased" (Jastrow, 286; see *b. Ber.* 18b; *b. Ḥag.* 5a; *b. Šabb.* 152b).

Line 7: "eternal mass of fire" — מוקדי עולם also occurs in Isa 33:14. The final lot of the wicked in fiery judgment is commonplace within Qumran literature (1QpHab x:5, 13; 1QH[a] xiv:20-22; CD ii:5; 1QS iv:13; etc.; see Moore, "Personification," 514). The concept is usually described using the term אש ("fire"), however, rather than the much rarer expression found in our text.

Lines 7-8: "those who shine brightly" — They shine presumably because they are in the company of angels and/or in the presence of the Divine. While it is possible to surmise a connection between "those who shine brightly" here and the "sons of light" of the *Community Rule* and the *War Scroll*, the direct literary relationship is not as clear as the case regarding darkness discussed above.

Line 8: The division between paragraphs here follows Moore ("Personification," 508-9), who regards this line as the center of the poem.

Line 8: "origin" — The term literally means "first" but designates "what comes first, beginning" in the HB (*HALOT* s.v. ראשית). Here the author is apparently making the claim that this is the explanation for the origin of the presence of perversity among humankind. This is an important term for sectarian history as it is outlined in CD i:4, 16; iii:10; iv:8, 9; vi:2; vii:21 (xix:11); viii:17 (xix:29);

xx:8, 31; 1QS ix:10. It is easy to understand how the author of 1QS iii:13–iv:26 would have seen in this poem a description of the origins of the "children of perversity" who walk in the "ways of darkness" (1QS iii:21). They are ruled by the "hand of the angel of darkness" (see commentary on line 6 above).

John Collins notes the parallel with the misogynistic claim of Sir 25:24, "From a woman sin had its beginning, and because of her we all die." However, he also notes that 4Q184 does not make the connection with Eve, or address directly the question of the origin of sin.[13] On this text see also Aubin, "She is the beginning."

While the term "woe" is often the first word of a literary unit, there is no evidence here of the poem being composed in a "woe" format as a whole.

Line 9: "her paths are pathways of sin" — In Prov 2:19 and 5:6 the phrase is "paths of life," an allusion to the contrast with death in these lines.

Lines 9-10: "her ways are ways of death. . . . Her gates are gates of death" — The biblical description of the seductress provides the basis for this vivid statement on the consequences of yielding to her entreaties (Prov 5:5; 7:27). In Prov 8:35-36 we see as a summary conclusion of these chapters that those who find wisdom find life and those who hate wisdom love death. This is the type of stark wisdom that is important for supporting an ideology that undergirds a sectarian movement.

Line 10: "When entering her house she steps into Sheo[l]" — See Prov 7:27. The verb "steps" is also found in Prov 7:8, where it designates the action of the man coming to visit the seductress. A warning against "entering her house" is encountered in Prov 5:8. Rather than emphasizing the dangers of a visit to the seductress, our text appears to utilize the imagery to suggest that she resides in Sheol. This is the place of death, hence to follow her is to enter into the place of death.

Lines 11-12: "lies in wait in secret places . . . open squares" — The brazen public positioning of the seductress on the street and in the square coupled with the "lying in wait" seems inspired by Prov 7:12. The additional element in our text is the reference to the "secret places." The only other use of this term in the nonbiblical Qumran scrolls appears to be in 4Q424 1:4. This relationship between secret and public is characteristic of much of apocalyptic literature from the Second Temple period. Lawrence Schiffman attempts to capture this dynamic in his analysis of

13. Collins, *Seers*, 372; idem, *Jewish Wisdom*, 67.

the *nistarot* and the *nigleh* in CD.[14] In the Qumran wisdom literature this dynamic is best represented rather in the use of the term "mystery." This term forms the basis for the composition entitled *Mysteries* and is also ubiquitous in *Instruction*. Note the discussion of those texts in this volume.

Lines 12-13: "from incessant f[ornicat]ion." — Fornication (זנות) is an important topic in a number of the sectarian Qumran texts. In CD iv:17 it is the first of the three nets of Belial, which are portrayed as three kinds of righteousness and in which people become ensnared. Included are bigamy, divorce, and incest. These include some of the most important issues by which the new covenant in the land of Damascus defines itself. The term is also present in 4Q397 *(Miqsat Ma'aseh ha-Torah*[d], abbreviated MMT[d]; also called *Halakhic Letter*[d]*)*, another crucial document for understanding the self-definition of the sect: "And concerning fornication that is done among the people . . ." (6-13:12). Included among the list of issues is the matter of "the mixing of diverse kinds," made up of mating cattle of two kinds, wearing clothes of two kinds of material, and sowing with two kinds of seeds. In 4QMMT this is also applied to intercourse between priests and "the people," who in so doing "defile the seed." In my study of this term I concluded that "זנות is one of a few major terms employed for the purpose of defining activities contrary to the sectarian lifestyle elaborated in the various compositions, most frequently referring to issues of marriage and sexual relations, herein (i.e., CD) mentioned in conjunction with a category of prohibited marriages."[15]

Lines 13-14: James Harding has proposed an intentional wordplay between "gaze intently" in line 13 and "make him fall" in line 14.[16] The first verb is from the same root as שכל ("insight"), one of the synonyms for "wisdom." The second term is familiar to readers of the NT from the Greek word σκανδαλίζω ("cause to be caught" or "fall," i.e., cause to sin, stumble), found in texts such as Matt 5:29-30; 13:21, 57. Obviously the wordplay rests on the reversal of the first

---

14. Lawrence H. Schiffman, *The Halakhah at Qumran* (SJLA 16; Leiden: Brill, 1975), 22-32.

15. John Kampen, "The Matthean Divorce Texts Reexamined," in *New Qumran Texts and Studies: Proceedings of the First Meeting of the International Organization for Qumran Studies, Paris 1992* (ed. George J. Brooke; STDJ 15; Leiden: Brill, 1994), 161. See also Robert Kugler, "Halakic Interpretive Strategies at Qumran: A Case Study," in *Legal Texts and Legal Issues: Proceedings of the Second Meeting of the International Organization for Qumran Studies, Published in Honour of Joseph M. Baumgarten* (ed. Moshe J. Bernstein, Florentino García Martínez, and John I. Kampen; STDJ 23; Leiden: Brill, 1997), 133-47.

16. "Wordplay," 70, 78.

and second letters of the root in these two cases. Harding provides numerous examples of an implicit opposition between these two terms in a variety of Qumran texts, and these are insightful for our comprehension of specific texts, as in this case. Less convincing is the argument that these two terms represent Qumran dualism in the same manner as terms such as "sons of light" and "sons of darkness."

Line 14: "the chosen righteous" — This phrase is found elsewhere in the Qumran literature only in 4Q215a 1iii:3 and 1QHᵃ x:15. Each of the two terms, however, is prominently scattered throughout Qumran literature. Of particular significance in this corpus is the use of the term "righteousness."[17] Tigchelaar connects this with the "truly chosen ones" (בחירי אמת, literally "chosen ones of truth") of 4Q418 69ii:10.[18] He also lists 1QHᵃ vi:26 among the passages for the "chosen righteous" but the Hebrew construction there is somewhat different, containing the Hebrew terms for both "righteousness" and "truth."

Line 15: "from keeping the commandment" — While this is not the most common verb for conveying this idea in biblical literature, 19 of the 61 uses of the term in the biblical materials are from the book of Proverbs. Included is the injunction in 5:2, that "your lips may guard knowledge," before the text commences with the speech of the seductress in the next verse. Prov 2:8 and 11 use this verb in their injunctions prior to the description of the seductress in that chapter.

Line 15: "to make those who walk upright pervert the pre[cept]" — The verb שנה ("change, pervert") is not attested in Biblical Hebrew in the Hiphil form and barely receives mention in Jastrow (p. 1605), but note Qimron's comments on words that may have been borrowed from Aramaic (HDSS §600). The other term that carries a related but slightly stronger meaning in the biblical and rabbinic legal materials is הפך, which comes closer to "breaking" or "violating" the law. The latter term is also more common in the Qumran materials. Important for our purposes is to note that שנה is used more often than הפך in the book of Proverbs.

17. On this term at Qumran see Benno Przybylski, *Righteousenss in Matthew and His World of Thought* (SNTSMS 41; Cambridge: Cambridge University Press, 1980), 13-38; Joseph M. Baumgarten, "The Heavenly Tribunal and the Personification of *Sedeq* in Jewish Apocalyptic," ANRW 2:219-39; John Kampen, "Righteousness in Matthew and the Legal Texts from Qumran," in *Legal Texts and Legal Issues,* ed. Bernstein et al., 461-87.

18. Eibert J. C. Tigchelaar, *To Increase Learning for the Understanding Ones: Reading and Reconstructing the Fragmentary Early Jewish Sapiential Text 4QInstruction* (STDJ 44; Leiden: Brill, 2001), 215.

Line 15: "the meek" — While this is a well-known biblical word, it becomes one of the important terms for self-designation in the sectarian literature.

Frag. 2

¹[. . .] your life [. . .] ²[. . .] and with the la[w . . .] ³[. . .] heart, and heart [. . .] depend upon him [. . .] ⁴[. . .] a contrite heart seek his favor [. . .] ⁵[. . .] and haughty eyes, an uncircumcised heart [. . .] ⁶[. . .] haughty of heart and also the anger of [. . .]

Notes

Line 5: "haughty eyes, an uncircumcised heart" — See Prov 21:4. Verses 2 and 3 of this chapter are very compatible with the theme of this composition as expressed in col. i.

Line 6: "and also the anger of" — This is a difficult line to translate. The proposal of Strugnell ("Notes," 268), on the basis of other usages of the phrase in Qumran materials, that it should read אף אף ז (which must be a misprint for אף זעף, "furious anger"), cannot be accepted because the plate clearly has an *aleph* rather than an *ayin*. On the basis of the photo, the original reading is accurate. While it is more common to translate this form of אף as "anger," it can also mean "face" or "countenance."

Frag. 3

¹[. . .] you will deliver [. . .] ²[. . .] daily purify for him [your] ha[nds . . .] ³[. . . st]retch out to him your hands in pra[yer . . .] ⁴[. . . He will re]move perversity from you [. . .] ⁵[. . .] in the midst of reckless abandon [. . .]

Notes

Line 2: "[your] ha[nds . . .]" — For the reconstruction see Strugnell ("Notes," 268). It is very hard to determine from the fragmentary context where there is a sentence break in the middle of the preserved remnants of this line.

Line 4:   "[. . . He will re]move perversity from you" — Strugnell ("Notes," 268) reads the first letter of the second word as either a *mem* or *samek*. I opt for the latter since it permits a more plausible reconstruction. Note 4Q177 1-4:2 and Deut 7:15.

Line 5:   "midst" — For this usage of the Hebrew term אִישׁוֹן see Prov 7:2.

Commentary

Line 2:   This line may be based upon Eliphaz's response to Job in Job 22:30: those who are not innocent will be delivered by the purity of Job's hands.[19] This is a response to the earlier lament of Job in which he expresses the futility of the possibility of God's response, even if he were to purify his hands with lye (9:30). This possibility could also include the verb "deliver" in line 1, even though the root here is חלץ, while the author of Job uses מלט.

Line 3:   "[. . . st]retch out to him your hands" — This repeats the action of Moses in Exod 9:33 when the Lord stops the rain, the thunder, and the hail.

Frag. 4

²[. . .] depths [. . .] ³[. . .] like water [. . .] ⁴[. . .] son of man and his spirit [. . .]
⁵[. . .] not with the guilt of treach[ery . . .]

Notes

Line 2:   "depths" — See 1:6 above.

Line 3:   Strugnell ("Notes," 268) demonstrates that the word "will be filled" is from a different fragment, so I have not included it.

Line 4:   "son" — Strugnell ("Notes," 268) proposes that בן is a defective spelling for the preposition בין, "between." The term "son of man" is common enough in these compositions that I see no need to consider such a proposal.

19. On this controversial verse see Marvin H. Pope, *Job: Introduction, Translation, and Notes* (AB 15; Garden City, N.Y.: Doubleday, 1965), 152-53; Robert Gordis, *The Book of Job: Commentary, New Translation, and Special Studies* (New York: Jewish Theological Seminary, 1978), 252.

Frag. 5

²[. . . her inn]er being abo[ve . . .] ³[. . .] you shall not opp[ress . . .] ⁴[. . .] from the ear he will te[st . . .] ⁵[. . . judg]ment and precept [. . .]

Notes

Line 2: "[inn]er being" — See Strugnell ("Notes," 268).

Line 4: "he will te[st . . .]" — See Strugnell ("Notes," 268).

Frag. 6

¹[. . .] in [its] open squares [. . .] ²[. . .] you shall not enter into [. . .]

Commentary

Line 1: "open squares" — See commentary to 1:12 above.

Line 2: "you shall not enter into" — Whether this line has anything to do with entering the house of the seductress is impossible to determine.

Wisdom Composition (4Q185)

Introduction

Content

The official DJD listing dubs this fragment a "sapiential work" (*EDSS* 2:1020).[1] This composition is one of the few wisdom texts from the Qumran corpus that was published and brought to the attention of the academic community prior to 1991. While the term חכמה ("wisdom") never appears in the remaining fragments, the frequent use of the third feminine singular suffix (note the discussion of its referent below) suggests its centrality in at least the preserved portion of the original composition. This section is an admonition enjoining the addressees with the importance of heeding wisdom. The major concern of this text is that persons not only learn but also heed wisdom. Toward that end, the text lists both the benefits derived from following that path or road and warnings about the consequences of not doing so. In the fragments this theme begins with a mention of the wrath of God along with the presentation of the role of the angels in judgment, thereby establishing an eschatological, perhaps apocalyptic, context for the composition. This is followed by a statement of woe, addressed to the "sons of men" and based on Isa 40:6-8, in which the fate of humankind that does not heed wisdom is compared to dried-up grass and a withered flower.

With 1-2i:13 we begin literary units that are introduced with phrases familiar from biblical wisdom literature such as "listen to me," "pay attention,"

---

1. The opportunity to discuss this text with Hermann Lichtenberger while both of us were resident in Jerusalem and working on this text in the fall of 2000 was very beneficial for my treatment of it.

and "blessed are . . ." (the beatitude form). The first unit establishes the connection between wisdom and the saving activity of God. It is not clear to me that the author made this connection due to the belief that "Israel's current experience was characterized by affliction and oppression as once had been its lot in Egypt."[2] It may rather have more to do with building the rhetorical case for the connection between wisdom and Torah (see commentary to 1-2ii:2 below). This proposal is supported by the presence of terms such as "way of life" and "highway" in 1-2ii:2, a theme picked up in the next section with the inclusion of "pathway." In 1-2ii:3-8 "my sons" are warned about the consequences of not following the "way." The fragmentary remains permit only glimpses of the stated benefits of the value of being "in his house" and within "his will and knowledge." The text seems to find more specific focus as it moves from the "sons of men" in 1-2i:9 to "my people" in 1-2i:13 to "my sons" in 1-2ii:3.

These admonitions are followed by two beatitudes (the technical term is "macarism"). The first macarism is interesting in that it seems to make a distinction between those to whom wisdom has been given and those who have not received her. A more careful reading of the text, however, does not suggest that there are predestined persons who receive her, but rather points to those who take pride in saying that they have not received her. This group of persons appears to be the concern so far as we can establish it in a fragmentary text. The rewards for those who have received it are enumerated. The second macarism, on the basis of the available material, changes the focus solely to those who have received wisdom and is concerned with their attitude regarding wisdom. The final column available appears to return to a topic alluded to in 1-2ii:4-6, the temple and purity concerns. The remaining fragments do not extend our understanding of the content of the original composition in any significant manner.

Manuscript

The remaining fragments of this composition all appear to be from one manuscript. Fragments 1-2 contain portions of three columns, whose content is supplemented by frags. 3 and 7. The particular context for each of the small remaining fragments is very difficult to determine. The script is considered to be of the "formal" type, dating from the mid- or late first century B.C.E., thereby establishing the terminus ad quem for its date of composition (75-25 B.C.E.).[3] This

---

2. Verseput, "Wisdom," 700.

3. Brian Webster, "Chronological Index of the Texts from the Judaean Desert," DJD 39:398.

text was published by John Allegro (DJD 5:85-87), but needs to be accompanied by the notes of John Strugnell.[4]

Historical Setting

Certain features of this work differentiate it from biblical wisdom texts. The presence of angels in this composition is such an item. This element represents one portion of an ideological tenor that establishes eschatology as a horizon for ethical activity in a wisdom composition. Here the angels have the focal role in a judgment accompanied by fire (1-2i:7-9). Parallel roles for angels can be seen in apocalyptic Jewish texts from the Second Temple era such as Daniel and *1 Enoch* 91–105 in addition to Qumran texts from a wide variety of literary genres such as CD ii:5-6, 1QS iv:11-13, and 1QM.[5] Wisdom texts bearing references to angels include 4Q299, 4Q301, and 4Q418. References to "his wrath," "no one has the strength to stand before her," the comparison with the dry grass and the flower blown away leaving "no place to stand" hence "perishing," and the ardent admonitions that include the dire consequences of not accepting wisdom all point to an eschatological context for wisdom. The integration of wisdom with accounts of salvation history and the giving of the law in this document is also a postbiblical development in Jewish wisdom literature (see commentary to 1-2i:13-ii:3) that fits well with the eschatological setting. There is enough evidence in the fragments to suggest the composition anticipated judgment as a consequence of not accepting wisdom. There is no evidence, however, to suggest that this judgment was understood in a sectarian context. There are no hints of a dualistic universe nor are there any known vocabulary items that suggest sectarian social structures in these fragments. There are good reasons for understanding why Jewish sectarians would have liked the text, but no suggestions of sectarian authorship.[6] It is thus possible to consider a late-third or early-second-century B.C.E. date of composition.

Literary Questions

The term "wisdom" (חכמה) never appears in these fragments. The use of the third feminine singular pronoun suggests its presence at least as referent and

---

4. Strugnell, "Notes," 269-74.

5. Tobin, "4Q185," 150-51.

6. See Lichtenberger, "Mahnrede," 161-62; idem, "Weisheitstext," 129; van der Woude, "Wisdom at Qumran," 248; Tobin, "4Q185," 152.

most likely in actuality in the full composition. As argued throughout the commentary, the work does offer evidence for the equation of wisdom with Torah, as found in Sirach 24 and Bar 3:9–4:4.[7] From the rhetorical structure of the fragments, however, it would appear that this is a case that the author felt compelled to make, rather than to accept as an assumption underlying the work.

In the HB, wisdom as a personified female figure is attested in Prov 1:20-33; 8:1–9:6; and 9:10-12. While Job 28:12-28 also is frequently included in such a list, wisdom is not a personified figure in this passage, nor are any feminine characteristics associated with it.[8] The use of the definite article with the term in this passage suggests its abstract nature.[9] Lady Wisdom is also personified in Sirach 24 and Bar 3:9–4:4, the two passages just listed as equating wisdom with Torah. In these passages she is a divine being who either is commanded by the Creator to dwell with Jacob (Sir 24:1-12) or is given by the Creator as a gift to him (Bar 3:29-37). In both sections it is wisdom as Torah that takes up residence with Jacob. The significant feature of wisdom's role in creation is attested in Prov 8:22-31, Job 28:25-27, and Sir 1:1-10. Wisdom's manifestation in human beings is the "fear of the Lord."[10] While developed most extensively in Sir 1:11-20, it is already present in Job 28:28 and Prov 9:10-12 and also found in Sir 15:1 in the context of the poetic description of Lady Wisdom in 14:20–15:10. Sir 51:13-22 also bears limited evidence of some personification. An original acrostic version of this poem in Hebrew is found in 11Q5 (Ps[a]). Also found in 11Q5 is Psalm 154, another piece with limited evidence of the personification of wisdom. Of less significance for the description of Lady Wisdom in our text is the reference in Wis 7:7–9:18. Her presence at creation is also described here (7:22b–8:1) and she is sought as a bride (8:2-16). Due to her purity she pervades and penetrates all things (7:24). She is "a spotless mirror of the working of God, and an image of his goodness. . . . She passes into holy souls and makes them friends of God, and prophets" (7:26-27).

The closest literary parallels in a nonbiblical text are between 1-2i:13-ii:3 and 4Q370 ii:5-9.[11] While these are by no means copies of the same work and there are no traces of overlap between the two compositions prior or subsequent to this section, the similarities between these two sections are noteworthy. The transient nature of human existence is described in 4Q185 1-2i:9-13 and 4Q370 ii:5-6, both accounts bearing similarities to Ps 103:15-17. In both works the next section refers to the strength (גבורה) of the Lord, to the mighty acts (נפלאות) of deliverance,

---

7. Crawford, "Lady," 363; Verseput, "Wisdom," 699.

8. Crawford, "Lady," 357.

9. Contra Hadley, "Wisdom," 240.

10. Crawford, "Lady," 357.

11. Tobin, "4Q185," 149; C. Newsom, "370: 4QAdmonition Based on the Flood," DJD 19:89-90; see also idem, "4Q370: An Admonition Based on the Flood," *RevQ* 13 (1988): 23-43.

and to the consequent requirement for "fear of him" (פחדו). While there is a strong case for some mutual relationship between these two texts, the question of priority is not as clear. Since 4Q370 is also dated to the late Hasmonean period, 75-50 B.C.E.,[12] both texts fall in the same place in the pattern of historical development sketched above (see "Historical Setting"). While one usually assumes the more succinct text is the older version, the corresponding pattern of citation of other texts in 4Q370 suggests its usage of 4Q185.[13] Evidence of a personified wisdom more closely related to apocalyptic mysteries is to be found in *1 Enoch* 42.

Bibliography

Note also the bibliography in the introduction to this volume.

Allegro, John M. "185." DJD 5:85-87, plates 29-30.

Crawford, Sidnie White. "Lady Wisdom and Dame Folly at Qumran." *DSD* 5 (1998): 355-66. Reprinted in *Wisdom and Psalms*. Ed. Athalya Brenner and Carole R. Fontaine, 205-17. FCB 2/2. Sheffield: Sheffield Academic Press, 1998.

Hadley, Judith. "Wisdom and the Goddess." In *Wisdom in Ancient Israel: Essays in Honour of J. A. Emerton*. Ed. John Day, Robert P. Gordon, and H. G. M. Williamson, 234-43. Cambridge: Cambridge University Press, 1995.

Lichtenberger, Hermann. "Eine weisheitliche Mahnrede in den Qumranfunden (4Q185)." In *Qumrân: Sa piété, sa théologie et son milieu*. Ed. M. Delcor, 151-62. BETL 46. Paris-Gembloux: Duculot; Leuven: Leuven University Press, 1978.

―――. "Die Weisheitstext 4Q185: Eine Neue Edition." In *Wisdom Texts from Qumran*, ed. Hempel et al., 127-50.

Strugnell, John. "Notes en marge du Volume V des *Discoveries in the Judaean Desert of Jordan.*" *RevQ* 7 (1970): 269-73.

Tobin, Thomas H., S.J. "4Q185 and Jewish Wisdom Literature." In *Of Scribes and Scrolls: Studies on the Hebrew Bible, Intertestamental Judaism, and Christian Origins, Presented to John Strugnell on the Occasion of His Sixtieth Birthday*. Ed. Harold W. Attridge, John J. Collins, and Thomas J. Tobin, 145-52. Lanham, Md.: University Press of America, 1990.

Verseput, Donald J. "Wisdom, 4Q185, and the Epistle of James." *JBL* 117 (1998): 691-707.

Wright, Benjamin G., III. "Wisdom and Women at Qumran." *DSD* 11 (2004): 240-61.

12. Webster, "Chronological Index," DJD 39:396.
13. Newsom, DJD 19:89-90.

Text

Frags. 1-2, col. i

[3][...] [4][...] pure and holy [...] [5][...] and according to his wrath [...] [6][...] and up to ten times [...] [7][...] No one has the strength to stand before her, and no one hope [8]before [his fierce] indignation [...] Who will endure to stand before his angels for with flaming [9]fire the[y] will judge [...] of his spirits.

You, sons of men, the human being [is nothing,] for look, [10]like gree[n g]rass it springs up from its soil and blossoms; like a flower is his faithfulness. When his wind blow[s] [11]its cut grass dries up, and the wind bears away its flower until there is no [p]lace to stan[d, for it will p]erish [12]and not be found, because of the wind [....] They will seek him and not find him; there is no hope. [13]And he, as a shadow are his days on the ear[th].

Now listen carefully, my people, and gain insight [14]from me. You who are naive, gain wisdom from the [st]rength of our Lord, remember the wonders he did [15]in Egypt and his signs in [the land of Ham], and may your heart tremble for fear of him.

Notes

Line 3:   This is the first partially preserved line in this column, containing only the letters כי, but it is the third line of the original copy, evident by comparison with cols. ii and iii.

Line 5:   "according to his wrath" (וכחמתו) — As Strugnell says, the reading is almost certain ("Notes," 269).

Line 8:   "before [his fierce] indignation" (לזעם [אפו]) — See Strugnell ("Notes," 269) and Lichtenberger ("Weisheitstext," 130, 132-33), though I do not accept all of Lichtenberger's reconstruction at this point; cf. Nah 1:6 and Lam 2:6.

Lines 8-9:   "with ... fire" (באש) — This is preferable to "like ... fire" (כאש); see Strugnell ("Notes," 269). Note also 4Q433a 3:5 for the phrase "with flaming fire" (באש להבה) in a context of judgment.

Line 9:   "[is nothing]" ([הוא פס]א) — Contra Skehan and Strugnell ("Notes,"
269, 272), who read [לכם וי]א אדם בני, "sons of man, w[oe to you]." See comments of Lichtenberger, who prefers [כח ין]א ("kraftlos," i.e., "without
strength"; "Weisheitstext," 133). The proposed translation is closer to the portrayal of the human in the *Hodayot*. See commentary below.

Lines 11-12:   "and the wind bears away his flower until there is no [p]lace to
stan[d, for it will p]erish and not be found, because of the wind" — See
Strugnell ("Notes," 270 and 272 n. 21) for the proposed reading by Skehan,
which, with the exception of the last two words, I have adopted: תשא וציצו
רוח כי ימצא ולא יא]בד כיא לעמ]וד מ]קום אין עד רוח.

Line 14:   "You who are naive, gain wisdom from the [st]rength of our Lord, remember the wonders" (נפלאות וזכרו אלהינו בורת ג]מן וחכמו פתאים) — See
Strugnell ("Notes," 270).

Line 15:   "in [the land of Ham] and . . . tremble" (ערץ חם] ב]ארץ) — See
Strugnell ("Notes," 270).

Commentary

Lines 3-9:   Based on our knowledge of the genre in the biblical literature, this
paragraph is not the introduction we would expect to find for a wisdom composition, identified as such on the basis of its subsequent structure and content.
While it does not appear to be the introduction to the entire composition, it
does set the context for its remaining fragments. The third feminine singular
suffix presumably designating wisdom, "before her," is already found in line 7.

The context established by this paragraph for these fragments is eschatological, perhaps even apocalyptic, even though the limited material available
does not permit a judgment on the latter question. In an allusion to Dan 11:15
the phrase "has no strength to stand," also found in Ezra 10:13, suggests an eschatological setting. Daniel is describing the power of the invincible forces of
the king of the north that have just crushed any hope of a successful rebellion
on the part of the "men of violence among your own people." Those Jews who
are wise, the *maskilim*, will wait for God's intervention (Dan 11:34-35) and then
"shine like the brightness of the firmament" (Dan 12:3). These phrases may also
be tied together through allusions to Nah 1:6, another eschatological referent. It
is impossible to determine whether the object is God or wisdom due to the
text's fragmentary nature. In line 8 the reference is to Mal 3:2, "Who will endure

the day of his coming?" which in our text reads, "who will endure to stand before his angels?" For "with flaming fire they will judge . . . of his spirits." Note
that in Mal 3:2-3 God is "like a refiner's fire . . . who sits . . . and purifies the sons
of Levi." We have already seen the word "pure" in line 4. These lines provide the
eschatological context for the wisdom statements that follow. Concerning an
eschatological context for a wisdom composition see also the introduction to
Instruction.

Line 4:   "pure and holy" — טהור ("pure") is common in biblical, rabbinic, and
Qumran legal and narrative literature but not usually found in wisdom compositions. The root טהר is found only 4 times in the book of Proverbs, with approximately 206 appearances throughout the HB. It occurs in 4Q418 186:2 and
in 4Q525 2+3ii:1 among the Qumran wisdom texts. The word קדוש ("holy") is
present in a greater diversity of genres but also uncommon in wisdom literature. The root קדש makes only 3 appearances in Proverbs, but 860 in the HB. It
occurs in 4Q299 64:2 and 72:1, also in 4Q418 48:2 and 81+81a:4.

Line 6:   "ten times" — The fragmentary context does not permit us to determine for certain whether "ten times" is based on "these ten times" of Num
14:22, referring to the disobedience of Israel in the wilderness, and Job 19:3, a
possible allusion to the pentateuchal passage.

Line 8:   "angels" — Mention of the "angels" distinguishes this wisdom composition from its biblical predecessors. The reference to "messenger" in Sir 43:26 is
much closer to the classic Hebrew meaning of the term than to intermediary
heavenly figures. In the HB the question more frequently is: "Who will stand
before you, with the force of your anger?" (Ps 76:7); or "Who will endure the
day of his coming?" (Mal 3:2). In other words, the angels (messengers of God)
are here acting as intermediary figures with a role in the act of judgment.

Line 9:   "the[y] will judge [. . .] of his spirits" — I am not convinced by the argument of Verseput ("Wisdom," 697 n. 20) to make the "spirits" the subject of a
Niphal form of the verb "to judge." This confuses the symbolic system in which
the angelic figures are agents of the Divine while the "spirits" are more closely
related to the cosmic dimensions of humanity. In some Qumran texts, however,
these two appear to merge (see Michael Mach, "Angels," *EDSS* 1:25).

Lines 9-13:   The influence of Isa 40:6-8 is apparent. While the literary heading
of the section is in the second person plural, a characteristic continued in lines
13-15, the author here employs the third person singular of the biblical text. We

might recall that Isa 40:6 is only three verses after 40:3, an important reference in various Qumran texts that fits the eschatological orientation of this introductory piece.[14] While this section reflects a clear dependence on Isa 40:6-8, with an allusion to Isa 51:12 (Verseput, "Wisdom," 697), similar imagery also occurs in Pss 90:5-6, 92:5-9, and especially 103:15-17. Note also Job 14:1-2; Pss 102:11; 144:3-4.[15]

This reconstruction proposed by Lichtenberger ("Weisheitstext," 133) undergirds the connection with 1QH[a] noted in the commentary to line 12 below. The low estate of the human being is a common theme in that composition, and the term "nothing" (אפס) occurs in 1QH[a] x:35; xi:31, 37; xiv:20; xx:13; xxi:30.[16] See my further comment to line 13 below. The Strugnell-Skehan reconstruction makes it a woe saying, "w[oe to you]" (א[וי לכם]), a most unusual expression of that literary form since the term "woe" in this case would be preceded by "You, sons of men" (ואתם בני אדם). Common usage in the HB as well as in the NT has the term "woe" appearing first in the clause.

Line 12: "there is no hope" — In contrast to the statements in 1QH[a] (xi:21; xiv:9; xvii:14; xxii:11, 18, 37), where the total reliance of the lowly mortal on God provides hope, this paragraph concludes with the description of the human condition. The solution comes in the following paragraph. The repetition of the terms "stand" and "hope" in the negative at the end of this section in lines 11-12 points back to these same terms at the conclusion of the previous paragraph in lines 7-8. The lack of hope is to be understood in an eschatological context.

Line 13: "Now listen carefully" — The introduction to this section uses a familiar address from biblical wisdom literature, ועתה שמעו נא (e.g., Prov 5:7; 7:24; 8:32), and in col. ii, lines 8 and 13, couples it with the beatitude form אשרי ("blessed is . . .") as in Prov 8:32. Here in line 13 the addressee is "my people" rather than the "sons" of the Proverbs texts. In the progression of this text the important change is from the "sons of men" in line 9 to "my people" in line 13.

---

14. S. Talmon, "The 'Desert Motif' in the Bible and in Qumran Literature," in *Biblical Motifs* (ed. A. Altmann; Texts and Studies 3; Cambridge: Harvard University Press, 1966), 31-63; George J. Brooke, "Isaiah 40:3 and the Wilderness Community," in *New Qumran Texts and Studies: Proceedings of the First Meeting of the International Organization of Qumran Studies, Paris 1992* (ed. Brooke; STDJ 15; Leiden: Brill, 1994), 117-32.

15. Tobin, "4Q185," 146.

16. On the manner in which the rhetoric of the *Hodayot* creates a human being willing to accept the constraints of the sectarian lifestyle, see the treatment by Carol A. Newsom, *The Self as Symbolic Space: Constructing Identity and Community at Qumran* (STDJ 52; Leiden: Brill, 2004), 191-345.

The general statement about the lot of humankind in lines 9-13 is now followed by an admonition addressed to God's chosen people, followed by a more focused address to "my sons," presumably those who have chosen God, beginning in ii:3. This form of address also introduces literary sections in CD i:1; ii:2, 14, suggesting a certain literary similarity to i:9, 13, and ii:3 in this composition.[17]

Lines i:13–ii:3:   In this section wisdom is rooted in the events of the exodus, the saving activity of God. This theme is more prominent here than in the closely related text of 4Q370 ii:5-9 (see "Literary Questions" in the introduction to this chapter). This is where God acted on behalf of "my people," hence the title for this section, perhaps meant to evoke Ps 78:1-8. True to the Exodus account of the deliverance, this act of salvation included the giving of the Torah on Mount Sinai, a "way to life." Deuteronomy 6 represents the classic statement of this connection, including its repeated emphasis on its significance for "your sons" in v. 7 and elsewhere. The mention of "your children after you" is already found in the introductory section to the Ten Commandments in Deut 4:40, repeated in 12:25 and 28. Our author is presenting the case for wisdom as Torah, particularly as Torah is understood in the book of Deuteronomy and the subsequent biblical traditions built on that viewpoint.[18] The idea of Torah as the way of life is expressed in a wisdom context in Prov 6:23 (on the significance of "way" in wisdom see Roland E. Murphy, "Wisdom in the OT," *ABD* 6:925). In this case the *lamed* signifying the preposition "to" in 4Q185 1-2ii:2, "way to life," is not found in the biblical text. Nor is it present in the other two places where the phrase "way of life" is found in the Qumran texts.

A sectarian text making ample use of wisdom vocabulary, 4Q270 (D^e) 2ii:19-20, also includes this phrase, though in the plural: "And now hearken to me, all who know righteousness [and put (?)] the la[w of God in your hearts, that I may reveal] to you the *ways of life* and open [before your eyes] the paths of destruction."[19] While fragmentary, we see preserved in the formula of the introduction, already identified in CD i-ii in the previous paragraph, references that include "Torah" and "ways of life" in a context that connects it with knowledge of eschatological matters. Also significant is its appearance in 4Q439 1i+2:1-2 "to

17. For the development of this theme in Jewish literature of the Second Temple period see Benjamin G. Wright III, "From Generation to Generation: The Sage as Father in Early Jewish Literature," in *Biblical Traditions in Transmission,* ed. Hempel and Lieu, 309-32.

18. See also George J. Brooke, "Biblical Interpretation in the Wisdom Texts from Qumran," in *Wisdom Texts from Qumran,* ed. Hempel et al., 211-12. He speaks of it as parenetic literature without the explicit connection with Torah.

19. DJD 18:145 (reconstruction is according to the text of Joseph Baumgarten and J. T. Milik).

establish the way of life." In this case it is designated for "the righ[teous of] my people . . . [to make pass ov]er into the covenant the men of my council." The presence of the term "instruction" (מוסר) in line 4 of 4Q439 suggests the possibility that this is a sectarian wisdom text, but its fragmentary nature permits no decisive conclusion. In 4Q299 79:3 it is found in a very fragmentary context, which makes it hard to identify; it is possibly misplaced (L. Schiffman, DJD 20:87-88).

Line 14: The "naive" (פתאים) are most commonly referred to as the "simple" in biblical translations. In this text and elsewhere in both Qumran and biblical sources, however, these are persons that are quite capable of learning but have not had available, or availed themselves of, the occasions for learning and/or life experiences that would permit them to grow in knowledge and understanding. They are addressed frequently in Proverbs (1:22, 32; 8:5; 9:6; 14:18) as well as in Pss 19:7; 116:6; 119:130.[20] In 1QpHab 12:4 the "naive" or "simple" of Judah are synonymous with the "poor," a term frequently used as a synonym for the members of the community in the sectarian scrolls. References to the "naive," used in both positive and negative senses, are scattered throughout Qumran literature: 4Q169 3-4iii:5, 7; CD xiii:6; xv:15; 4Q267 9v:5; 4Q381 1:2; 4Q418 221:2; 223:3; 4Q439 1i+2:7.

Line 14: "[st]rength" — Strugnell ("Notes," 270) and Tobin ("4Q185," 150) point to the term גבורה as really meaning "mighty wisdom" in this context, a usage found in Qumran texts (1QS iv:3; 1QH^a xx:16) but not in biblical texts (it is included in the list of the attributes of wisdom in Prov 8:14). The association of "wisdom" with "strength" is the major point of this paragraph: the adherent is to "gain wisdom from the strength of our Lord" by remembering "the wonders he did in Egypt and his signs in [the land of Ham]." This association is important for understanding "wisdom" and its cognates in a number of Qumran texts. However, only in 1QS iv:3 is the translation "mighty wisdom" appropriate, since here the Hebrew terms are in a construct relationship (see IBHS §9.5.3).

Lines 14-15: The wording of these two lines draws on Pss 105:5, 27; 106:21-22.

Line 15: [the land of Ham] — This is synonymous with Egypt (see also Gen 10:6).

20. Tobin, "4Q185," 146.

Frags. 1-2, col. ii

¹and do his wi[ll . . . y]ourselves according to his wonderful acts of mercy. Search out for yourselves the way ²to life and a highway [. . .] for a remnant for your sons after you. Why do you give ³your[selves] to vanity [. . . ju]dgment?

Listen to me, my sons, and do not defy the words of Yahweh. ⁴Do not step [. . . J]acob, a pathway he inscribed for Isaac. Is not one day better ⁵[in his ho]use when doi[ng . . .] fear of him and not be led astray by terror and by the snare of the fowler ⁶[. . .] and to be separated from his angels, for there is no darkness ⁷nor gloom [. . . .] It is [. . .] his [w]ill and his knowledge. And you, ⁸what are you [gaining] in un[de]rstandin[g? . . . from] his presence disaster goes out to all people.

Blessed is the man to whom she has been given, ⁹for thus, [. . . those who k]now and do not let the wicked boast, saying, "It has not been given ¹⁰to me nor [. . .] to Israel." From a meas[ure of good]ness he will measure it out and all his people redeem ¹¹and kill those who hate [his w]isd[om . . .] dest[roy. . . . and] he will say, "He who glorifies her will find her." See[k her] ¹²and find her, hold her fast and claim her as an inheritance. With her is [length of d]ays, fatness of bone and joy of heart [. . . .] ¹³His faithfulness is eternal and the salvation [. . . .]

Blessed is the man who observes her and does not utter slander concerning [her;] with a spir[it] ¹⁴of treachery he does not seek her and with flattery he does not hold her fast. Just as she was given to his fathers so he will inherit her and [hold] her [fast] ¹⁵with all the power of his strength and with all his [mig]ht that is immeasurable. He shall give her as an inheritance to his offspring and his knowledge to her people in abundance . . .

Notes

Line 1:   "his wi[ll . . .]" — See Strugnell ("Notes," 270).

Line 1:   I do not find a basis for the reconstruction of "renew" (חדש) in this lacuna, contra *DSSANT* 274.

Line 1:   "[y]ourselves" — Here and in line 3 I translate נפש (usually translated "soul") as a reflexive in the plural since the suffix and the remainder of the sentence are plural.

261

Line 2: ומסלה ("and a highway") — See Strugnell ("Notes," 270).

Line 3: "your[selves] to vanity" — See Strugnell ("Notes," 270).

Line 3: "Listen to me, my sons, and do not defy the words of Yahweh" — See Strugnell ("Notes," 270), who points to Ps 105:28 for the end of the line.

Lines 4-5: "Is not one day better [in his ho]use when do[ing . . .]" — See Strugnell ("Notes," 271) and Ps 84:10.

Line 5: "be led astray" (לעתת) — The meaning of this word is unclear (see Strugnell, "Notes," 271, for a tentative proposal meaning "afflict"). It seems that a more productive proposal could be advanced on the basis of the root עות, which can mean "bend" or "falsify" (*HALOT* s.v. עות) and "pervert" or "corrupt" (Jastrow, 1059). This range of meaning is supported by Syriac usage, where ʿat, based on the root ʿanat, means "commit fraud, defraud, act deceitfully, be dishonest."[21] This is also preferable to Lichtenberger's proposed *abgedränkt* ("thrust aside") due to the danger of the way ("Weisheitstext," 148-49).

Line 6: "and to be separated" (ולהבדל) — See Strugnell ("Notes," 271).

Line 7: "nor gloom[. . . .] It is his [w]ill and his knowledge" — See Strugnell ("Notes," 271).

Line 8: "are you [gaining] in un[de]rstandin[g? . . .]" — See Strugnell ("Notes," 271); most of the letters in תת[בו]נג[ו] are uncertain in terms of identification.

Line 8: "Blessed is the man to whom . . ." — On the macarism form see the introduction to *Beatitudes* (4Q525) below.

Line 9: The first letters of this line are extremely difficult to read. From the faint traces available I find the reading "son of m[an]," proposed by Lichtenberger ("Weisheitstext," 130), to be possible but unlikely on a literary basis. Contra Allegro, who reads מן, "from" (DJD 5:86), I accept the reading of Strugnell, כן, "thus" ("Notes," 271), while not having a good proposal for the fol-

21. R. Payne Smith, *Thesaurus Syriacus* (2 vols.; Oxford: Clarendon, 1901), 2:3008; J. Payne Smith, *A Compendious Syriac Dictionary* (Oxford: Clarendon, 1903), 431. Michael Sokoloff, *A Syriac Lexicon: A Translation from the Latin, Correction, Expansion, and Update of C. Brockelmann's Lexicon Syriacum* (Winona Lake: Eisenbrauns and Piscataway: Gorgias, 2009), 1118, 1147.

lowing lacuna. The best reconstruction of the remainder of the phrase is still not clear to me, even though Lichtenberger's proposal to reconstruct "[. . . those who k]now" seems the best possibility to contrast the negative phrase that begins with the next word ("Weisheitstext," 130).

Line 9: "It has not been given" — Strugnell ("Notes," 271) gives this as another possible reading.

Lines 11-12: I have adopted the rather substantial revision and amendment of these two lines by Strugnell ("Notes," 271). He reads the Hebrew text as follows:

והרג שנאי]ן ח]כמ]תו. [. . .] אב]ד. . .[.]יאמר המתשבח ככה מצאנה בק]שה

ומצאה וחזק בה ונחלה ועמה] ארך י]מים ודשן עצם ושמחת לבב ע]. . .[

Aspects of this reconstruction are questioned by Lichtenberger ("Weisheitstext," 139). He offers a very tentative proposal for the beginning of line 11, "and destroyed my name in Eg[ypt]" in conjunction with 1-2i:6, 14-15. Lichtenberger is correct on paleographic grounds in the second half of line 11 when he reads, "He who glorifies her."

Line 13: "His faithfulness is eternal" — It is very hard to justify a reconstruction that connects the faithfulness of God to her youth when the common biblical idiom is to speak of God's eternal faithfulness, based on the same triliteral root, עלם.[22]

Line 13: "Blessed is the man who . . ." — On the macarism form see the introduction to Beatitudes (4Q525) below.

Lines 13-14: "and does not utter slander concerning [her;] with a spir[it] of treachery" — This is the reconstruction of Émile Puech.[23] Lichtenberger here proposes, "and does not despise her yoke" ([. . .ה]ולא יג]ע]ל עלני), presumably of wisdom ("Weisheitstext," 131, 140, 145, 150). This proposal is rejected by Goff (*Discerning Wisdom*, 139-40). While doubtful, the additional reference to this image would be significant.

Line 14: "and [hold] her [fast]" — See Strugnell ("Notes," 271).

22. Edward Cook in *DSSANT* 243. This translation demands fewer emendations than Lichtenberger's "for their people (לעמיה)" ("Mahnrede," 159).
23. "4Q525 et les péricopes des Béatitudes en Ben Sira et Matthieu," *RB* 98 (1991): 91 (also found in DJD 25:126 n. 15).

Line 15: "his [mig]ht" — See Strugnell ("Notes," 271).

Line 15: "his knowledge to her people in abundance" — This difficult fragmentary reading follows Lichtenberger ("Weisheitstext," 131, 140, 145). For a different reconstruction, "to toi[l for g]ood," see Strugnell ("Notes," 271-72).

Commentary

Line 2: The allusion to the "remnant" is interesting, but unusual in that it is tied to the phrase "for your sons after you." The remnant is an important concept in some biblical, especially postexilic, literature (see E. Jenni, "Remnant," *IDB* 4:32-33; Lester V. Meyer, "Remnant," *ABD* 5:669-71). While on the one hand the Hebrew prophets speak of the total destruction of the remnant of Israel (e.g., Jer 40:15; Ezek 9:8; 11:13, etc.), the survival of a remnant is also an important theme and a source of hope (Isa 10:20-22; Jer 23:3; 31:7; Amos 5:15; Mic 2:12; Hag 1:12-14; Zech 8:6, 11-12, etc.). The best-known usage of this theme in the Qumran materials is in CD i:4, where God preserves a remnant from destruction, out of which God brings forth a "plant root,"[24] eventually led by the teacher of righteousness and resulting in the "new covenant in the land of Damascus" (CD vi:19; viii:21). It does designate the members of the covenant in 1QM xiii:8; xiv:8-10; 1QH[a] xiv:11. The sectarian provenance of 4Q393 3:7 is less clear. A number of the sectarian scrolls use the phrase from Ezra 9:14, where the question is asked whether God has been angered to the point of destruction so that "there is no remnant or survivor." Designating total destruction, this phrase is found in 1QS iv:14; v:13; 1QM i:6; iv:2; xiv:5; 1QH[a] xiv:35. The presence in 4Q185 of this term, which links the legacy for posterity to the concept of a remnant in a context where the possibility of acquiring knowledge is identified with Torah and explicitly tied to an understanding of God's mighty acts of salvation, provides one hint of an ideological framework in the literature of Second Temple Judaism on which the sectarian adherents attested at Qumran could build their way of life and an ideology to support it.

It is also unusual to have the wisdom concept attached to the notion of posterity, "for your sons after you." The emphasis on the legacy for posterity is not evident in Proverbs. It is mentioned in the Greek text of Sir 4:16 (Crawford, "Lady," 362), but receives no mention in the Hebrew text of the corresponding verse. There is no Hebrew text for Sir 24:33, the other place where

---

24. Patrick A. Tiller, "The 'Eternal Planting' in the Dead Sea Scrolls," *DSD* 4 (1997): 312-35.

posterity receives mention in connection with wisdom. It is, however, primarily the Deuteronomic tradition that emphasizes the legacy for posterity (Deut 4:9; 6:2, 20-25; 12:12) in connection with the giving and observance of the Torah. It is this connection that the author of our text wants to consolidate in the mind of readers.

Line 3: This section begins with the wisdom introduction, "Listen to me, my sons," known from Prov 1:8; 4:10; 5:7; 7:24; 8:32 (grammatical structure varies slightly). A simple form of this injunction is also found in Sirach (Hebrew text) 31:22 and 41:15.[25] In addition to a variation of this phrase in i:13 above, it serves as an introduction to major literary sections in CD i:1; ii:2, 14; and 4Q525 2ii+3:12; 13:6; 31:1.

Line 5: "fear of him" — This common theme from wisdom literature finds its classic statement in Prov 9:10: "The fear of the Lord is the beginning of wisdom," also stated in Ps 111:10 and in Prov 1:7 (in this case using "knowledge" — see Murphy, *ABD* 6:925). In Prov 19:23 the "fear of the Lord leads to life," also found in line 2 above.

Line 5: For "the snare of the fowler" see Hos 9:8 (also found in Ps 91:3, and in 4Q175 24 and 4Q379 22ii:10 in Qumran texts); perhaps also an allusion to Isa 24:17 ("terror and the pit and the snare"), employed in CD iv:14, and also found in Jer 48:43. While in Isaiah it describes the tremendous scope of the coming judgment, in CD it describes Israel's errors during the era of the reign of Belial in Israel, actually identifying those concerns particular to the "plant root" or the "new covenant in the land of Damascus."

Line 6: "to be separated from his angels" — In 1-2i:8 a broad indictment raises the possibility that there are no human beings who are able "to endure to stand before his angels." As the focus of attention has narrowed in the progression of the document, the "sons" who "search out . . . the way to life and a highway" as well as "a pathway he inscribed for Isaac" and are spending time in "his house" now are enjoined to remain on that course so as not "to be separated from his angels." In the presence of his angels "there is no darkness or gloom." This points to the various ways in which Qumran sectarian texts express the possi-

25. Pancratius C. Beentjes, *The Book of Ben Sira in Hebrew* (VTSup 68; 1997; repr. Atlanta: SBL, 2006), 57, 72, 115; Ze'ev Ben-Ḥayyim, *The Book of Ben Sira: Text, Concordance, and an Analysis of the Vocabulary* (Hebrew, with an introduction in English; Jerusalem: Academy of the Hebrew Language/Shrine of the Book, 1973), 30 (34:22), 46 (41:14).

bility of communion with the angels through their adherence to the group and its way of life (Mach, *EDSS* 1:26-27), even though there is no evidence of the full development of this viewpoint in this text.

Lines 7-8:   The conjunction of God's will (or favor) with his knowledge and the possibility of gaining understanding suggests Prov 8:35. Both of these terms represent the breadth of meaning of Hebrew רצון. In this context the translation "will" seems to represent more adequately the use of the term in line 1 above as well as the parallel with "knowledge" suggested in this fragmentary context (*HALOT* s.v. רצון). Note already the second half of v. 32, "blessed are those who will keep my way," suggesting a broader connection of our text with this passage. While in the biblical text the subject is "wisdom" rather than "knowledge," there is adequate evidence for the presence of this theme. The use of "knowledge" as a major term for the development of wisdom topics is significant in some Qumran texts.[26]

Line 8:   A precise understanding of the relationship of the phrase, "[. . . from] his presence disaster goes out to all people," an apparent adaptation of Jer 25:32, is prohibited by the fragmentary context. The continuing integration of judgment and the acquisition of wisdom, as understood by the composition's author, is evident, an unusual conjunction in the biblical materials. In this case the unusual use of the Hebrew interrogative מה following the emphatic second person plural provides a rhetorical flourish to ask whether they are indeed gaining understanding in the context of a paragraph that warns against defying the words of Yahweh and concludes with the consequences of such a path.

Lines 8-15:   Herein are found two beatitudes, perhaps suggesting Prov 8:32-35. In the first the person who is given wisdom is blessed, in the second the person who does (or "keeps") her. This form, "blessed is . . . ," is scattered throughout the HB, most predominantly in Psalms and Proverbs; "blessed is the man who . . ." occurs exclusively in those two books (see Raymond F. Collins, "Beatitudes," *ABD* 1:629-31). A variant employing the term אנוש is found in Isa 56:2 and Job 5:17. While the "finding" of wisdom is a much more common motif in the HB than "being given" it, especially in Proverbs (see 3:13; 8:35; etc.), the latter concept is not unknown (Prov 2:6). The best-known case in the HB of being given wisdom by God is Solomon (1 Kgs 4:29; 5:12). God also gives her to "his servant Jacob" in Bar 3:36, and she is given as a gift to all the living, lavished on

---

26. W. D. Davies, "'Knowledge' in the Dead Sea Scrolls and Matthew 11:25-30," *HTR* 46 (1953): 113-39.

those who love him, in Sir 1:10. The "doing" of the law is a familiar Deuteronomic phrase (Deut 28:58; 29:29; 31:12; 32:46; Josh 1:7; 2 Chr 14:4) that is picked up in Qumran literature, most frequently in the phrase "doer(s) of the law" (1QpHab vii:11; viii:1; xii:4-5; 1Q14 8-10:8; 4Q171 1-10ii:15, 23; 4Q174 1ii+3:2; 4Q176 17:7; 4Q271 4ii:8-9; 4Q470 1:4). Its usage with regard to wisdom is comprehensible when we recall its connection with Torah, discussed in the commentary to i:13–ii:3 above.

While the division of seven lines of this text into only two beatitudes is an unusual length for representatives of this genre, it is not unprecedented (e.g., Sir 14:20-27; 4Q525 2ii:3-6). Matt 5:3-10 and Luke 6:20-26 are the best-known representatives of this genre in the NT. Note the manner in which this literary form also has been developed in a wisdom context in 4Q525. The genre is also found in apocalyptic literature, specifically related to wisdom in *1 En.* 99:10, where the blessed are those who "do [related to Hebrew עשׂה] the commandments"[27] and "walk in the path of his righteousness." In this case the beatitude is followed by a number of woes (*1 En.* 99:11-16), a feature also known from 4Q525 and Luke 6:24-26. See the introduction to Beatitudes (4Q525) below.

Line 11: "and kill those who hate [his w]isd[om . . .]" — While in Prov 8:36 we learn that "all those who hate me love death," there is no injunction that they should be killed. Assuming that this is an accurate reconstruction (see notes above on that question), this text is closer to the rhetoric of hate found in the dualistic texts, such as 1QS i:10, where inductees into the covenant are enjoined to "hate all the sons of darkness." Note also 1QS iv:1, 24; ix:16, 21; CD ii:13, 15.

Line 12: "inheritance" — See commentary on line 14 below.

Lines 13-15: On the beatitude form see commentary on lines 8-15 above. On this reading see Puech (DJD 25:124 n. 7, 126 n. 15).

Line 14-15: "Just as she was given to his fathers so he will inherit her" and "he shall give her as an inheritance to his offspring": the statements about wisdom being given for the sake of posterity have been discussed in the commentary on i:13–ii:3 above. This statement again points to the manner in which the argument for the identification of wisdom with Torah is advanced. The idea of wisdom as an inheritance is not found in Proverbs or Ben Sira. References to the strength and might of God also point to the context discussed above.

27. See E. Isaac, *OTP* 1:80 nn. v and w.

Frags. 1-2, col. iii (+frag. 3 + frag. 7)

¹toward her, for go[od . . .] ²⁻⁷[. . .] ⁸[. . . G]od will examine all the purpo[ses. . . .]
⁹He [. . .] observes the words of [his] covena[nt. . . .] ¹⁰[G]od does not [bring
judg]ment for those who turn [away . . .] ¹¹[. . . Go]d does for his house [. . .]
¹²to all the chambers of the womb. He searched out the inward parts [. . . .]
¹³tongue and knew its word. God made hands [. . .] ¹⁴holy [. . . whether] good or
evil [. . .] ¹⁵sons of his people [. . .] with the purp[oses . . .]

Notes

Line 1: "for g[ood . . .]" — See Strugnell ("Notes," 272).

Line 2: The remains of this line are too indistinct for either proposed reading
to be convincing: "and from the luminaries" (Allegro in DJD 5:86) or "from
saws" (Strugnell, "Notes," 272).

Lines 7-10: Strugnell ("Notes," 272) rightly proposes that frag. 3 in the Allegro
edition should be attached to col. iii at this point. This translation includes that
fragment as well as some additional letters from col. iii.

Line 12: "inward parts" — So Strugnell ("Notes," 272).

Line 13: "and knew" — Reading the preterite form rather than the participle
(Strugnell, "Notes," 272).

Lines 14-15: Strugnell ("Notes," 272) inserts at the beginning of lines 14 and 15
the text from frag. 7, visible on PAM 43.514 as well as on other plates with as-
sorted materials such as PAM 44.180 (the same as 44.191 [DSSCat 397]).

Commentary

Line 8: "purpo[ses . . .]" — מזמות is familiar from the HB, particularly
Psalms, Proverbs, and Jeremiah, in some cases used parallel with "knowledge,"
for example, Prov 1:4; 2:11; 3:21; 5:2; Sir (Hebrew) 44:4 (HALOT s.v. מזמה). Also
scattered throughout Qumran literature, sometimes as a synonym for מחשבות,
a ubiquitous term in Qumran literature, found within legal, blessing, and wisdom contexts. Note in particular 4Q299 3aii-6:10; 4Q402 4:13; 4Q413 1-2:1.

Line 9:   It is very doubtful that God is the subject of the sentence after the lacuna. While the column is too fragmentary to establish with any certainty, it is more likely that the addressee is similar to the "man who observes her [i.e., wisdom]" in ii:14.

Frag. 4, col. i

¹[. . .] forev[er . . .] ²[. . .] ³[. . .] holy

Col. ii

¹and to my people [. . .] ²let us contend [. . .]

Notes

Line 2:   This line is also found in 4Q299 59:7 in a very fragmentary context.

Fragments 5 and 6

Do not contain adequate material for discussion.

CryptA Words of the Maskil
to All Sons of Dawn (4Q298)

Introduction

Content

This enigmatic text has not yet received an adequate explanation as to content
and purpose. Due to its fragmentary nature speculation about its purpose most
likely will continue. Its introduction specifies that it is instruction from a sage
to all the sons of dawn. This is followed by injunctions to study and heed these
words, addressed to persons with characteristics valued by the author. We then
see hints, regrettably only fragmentary, that the knowledge to be gained from
being attached to the sons of dawn is related to a divine plan, perhaps reflected
in the structure of the universe. The virtues being developed are placed in the
context of understanding the end of the age as well as the former times, in other
words, in an eschatological context. These fragments provide only tantalizing
clues of a text that would be of tremendous interest to modern scholars wishing
to understand the development of Jewish affiliations during the Second Temple
era.

Manuscripts

There is only one extant copy of this esoteric composition. With the exception of
the title, which is written in Jewish square script, it is copied employing the
unique script that was called Cryptic A by J. T. Milik, the first scholar to decipher
it. Also copied in Cryptic A were 4Q186 (mixed), 4Q249, 4Q250, 4Q313, 4Q317,
and 4Q324c. This script was used for signs (in margins and between lines) in

several other compositions such as 1QIs[a] and 1QSa (Stephen Pfann, DJD 20:7 n. 18). Each cipher of the cryptic alphabet corresponds to one symbol in the regular Hebrew alphabet. The most developed descriptions of Cryptic Script A are to be found in the introduction to the DJD editions of this text and of 4Q249-250 (DJD 20:1-19; 36:524-33). In their introduction, Stephen Pfann and Menahem Kister have advanced the argument that this was an Essene esoteric script, written for the internal purposes of the Qumran community. In their argument it was a small scroll written for the use of the sage as he left the community to educate novices ("sons of dawn") about joining the community. The esoteric script kept it from being read by anyone except the sage (DJD 20:1-2, 17).

Adding microscopic examination of the hair follicle patterns to other methods of scroll reconstruction has permitted the detailed placement of the extant fragments into a discernible pattern that permits a more adequate reconstruction of the limited material, based on connections between fragments (DJD 20:3).

Historical Context

Paleographic analysis of the title suggests a formal script dated somewhere between the late Hasmonean and early Herodian periods (50-1 B.C.E.) (DJD 20:9). This particular copy of Cryptic A appears to be roughly contemporary to 4Q249[1] and 4Q371. The more recent carbon-14 tests date both of the latter MSS into the second century B.C.E., 4Q249 from 196-47 B.C.E. and 4Q371 from 166-48 B.C.E..[2] This accumulated evidence suggests for the editors a date of composition in the second century B.C.E.[3] Other scholars have questioned this early dating of the paleographic evidence for Cryptic A texts, however, and the date of composition may come closer to the first-century B.C.E. date proposed for the script of the title.[4]

---

1. Note the extensive fragments of 4Q249 that have been identified as part of the composition known as "Midrash Sefer Moshe," published in DJD 35:1-24. Note the further publication of fragments identified as 4Q249 published in DJD 36:515-677. Significant are the fragments of the *Rule of the Congregation* (4Q249a-i), previously available only in one MS. 4Q249-250 are papyrus rather than parchment.

2. Greg Doudna, "Dating the Scrolls on the Basis of Radiocarbon Analysis," in *The Dead Sea Scrolls after Fifty Years: A Comprehensive Assessment* (ed. Peter W. Flint and James C. VanderKam; 2 vols.; Leiden: Brill, 1998-99), 1:430-71; see charts on pp. 462, 470.

3. See DJD 36:525.

4. Charlotte Hempel, "The Groningen Hypothesis: Strengths and Weaknesses," in *Enoch and Qumran Origins: New Light on a Forgotten Connection* (ed. Gabriele Boccaccini; Grand

The structure and content of the composition point to a sectarian provenance. At this point in Qumran studies, there are no apparent exceptions to the hypothesis that MSS written in Cryptic A represent distinctly sectarian compositions. The papyrus fragments of the *Rule of the Congregation* from the collection labeled 4Q249 certainly suggest that these compositions are a significant addition to our knowledge of the history of Jewish sectarianism in the second century B.C.E. John Strugnell points out that since biblical texts do not use *maskil* ("sage") for an author, but Qumran sectarian texts often do, its use here helps to establish the sectarian provenance of this composition.[5] When compared with the archeological record, these sectarian compositions appear quite early in the history of the development of the settlement at Qumran. While there is no apparent reason to limit the interpretation of the literary evidence concerning Jewish sectarianism to the site of the Qumran settlement, it is reasonable to read these two bodies of evidence in the light of one another.

This composition is addressed to "all the sons of dawn." Pfann and Kister have proposed that this refers to the novices who are in their initial period of exploration concerning membership in the sect (DJD 20:17). The suggestion is that novices are classified as "sons of dawn" prior to their full participation in communal life as "sons of light." The two-year period of initiation and examination is described in 1QS vi:13-23. This distinct category of membership includes a prohibition against sharing in the "pure food" of the community and mixing the property of the novice with that of the full membership. Independent records of property and wealth are to be kept during this period of time.

The only other citation of this title is found in the reading of CD xiii:14-15 as proposed by Joseph Baumgarten: "any person who enters the covenant of God shall not buy or sell to the sons of dawn except hand to hand."[6] This reading has found support in some newer critical editions of this composition,[7] though even Pfann and Kister are not convinced (DJD 20:16 n. 28). If the reading is accepted, it remains difficult to interpret since it requires the hypothesis

Rapids: Eerdmans, 2005), 254; Florentino García Martínez, "Response: The Groningen Hypothesis Revisited," in *Enoch and Qumran Origins*, 314. This reference was pointed out to me by Carl Pace, a graduate student in my class at Hebrew Union College–Jewish Institute of Religion, Cincinnati.

5. John Strugnell, "The Smaller Wisdom Texts Found at Qumran: Variations, Resemblances, and Lines of Development," in *Wisdom Texts from Qumran*, ed. Hempel et al., 43.

6. Joseph Baumgarten, "The 'Sons of Dawn' in CDC 13:14-15 and the Ban on Commerce among the Essenes," *IEJ* 33 (1983): 81-85.

7. Elisha Qimron, "The Text of CDC," in *The Damascus Document Reconsidered* (ed. Magen Broshi; Jerusalem: Israel Exploration Society; Shrine of the Book, Israel Museum, 1992), 34-35.

of a connection between the limitations on commercial interactions with the sons of dawn and the prohibition against mixing the property of the novice with those of full membership. This connection is not self-evident. None of the copies of the *Damascus Document* refer to those who enter into the covenant of God as "sons of light." So there is no internal evidence within that material to suggest some contrast between the status of the sons of dawn and the sons of light. The literature that develops the dualism of the "sons of light" and the "sons of darkness," most notably the various copies of the *Community Rule*, do not lend themselves naturally to any gray areas that would suggest a gradation in the level of light. That this term was developed in relationship to the title "sons of light" is much less clear on the basis of the evidence presently available. It is much more likely that it is a designation for membership in a sectarian group.[8]

Literary Questions

This composition is the only text related to the wisdom tradition that is copied in Cryptic A script. If the hypothesis that compositions in this script are all of sectarian provenance is convincing, the presence of this text among that corpus is significant. While certain wisdom compositions among the Qumran corpus do not seem to contain evidence of sectarian ideology or social structure, this is an example of a sectarian composition solidly rooted in a wisdom tradition. In the introduction to this volume I have demonstrated that interest in eschatology is evident throughout a good deal of the wisdom literature represented in the Qumran texts. Furthermore, there is growing evidence that the genres of wisdom and apocalyptic literature cannot be as clearly delineated as once thought possible.

Bibliography

Note also the bibliography in the introduction to this volume.

Baumgarten, Joseph M. "The 'Sons of Dawn' in CDC 13:14-15 and the Ban on Commerce among the Essenes." *IEJ* 33 (1983): 81-85.

8. This is the stance of Baumgarten regarding the name ("Sons of Dawn," 81-85), and also the conclusion of Charlotte Hempel, "The Qumran Sapiential Texts and the Rule Books," in *Wisdom Texts from Qumran*, ed. Hempel et al., 292-94. Both propose that it is a synonym for "sons of light."

Kister, Menahem. "Commentary to 4Q298." *JQR* 85 (1994): 237-49.

Pfann, Stephen. "4Q298: The Maskil's Address to All Sons of Dawn." *JQR* 85 (1994): 203-35.

Pfann, Stephen, and Menahem Kister. "298. 4QcryptA Words of the Maskil to All Sons of Dawn." DJD 20:1-32.

Swanson, Dwight. "4QcrypA Words of the *Maskil* to All Sons of Dawn: The Path of the Virtuous Life." In *Sapiential, Liturgical and Poetical Texts*, ed. Falk et al., 49-61.

CryptA Words of the Maskil to All Sons of Dawn (4Q298)

Frags. 1-2, col. i

[1][Word]s of the sage that he spoke to all the sons of dawn. Pay attenti[on to me, a]ll men of understanding. [2][Pursu]ers of righteousness, gain under[sta]nding of my words. Seekers of truth, li[ste]n to my words, all that [3][iss]ues from [my] lips. [Those who] know have sou[gh]t [the]se things and m[en of] his [fav]or have turn[ed to the way of] life. [4]Etern[al peace, which is bo]undless . . .

Notes

Line 1: "[Word]s of the sage that he spoke to all the sons of dawn" — This title is the only portion of the composition that is written in the Jewish square script.

Commentary

Line 1: "sage" — See the discussion of this title and its significance in the introduction to this volume.

Line 1: "sons of dawn" — See the discussion of "Historical Context" in the introduction to this text.

Line 1: "men of understanding" — This translation more adequately conveys its sense in context than the more literal "men of heart," as also found in Job 34:10 (cf. NRSV, NJPS) and 4Q525 24ii:2.

Line 2: "[Pursu]ers of righteousness. . . . Seekers of truth, li[ste]n to my words" — See Isa 51:1. Note also CD i:1 and Isa 51:7.

Line 4: "Etern[al peace]" — A concordance search of the fragments suggests that this is a more likely reconstruction based on parallels with other texts than "eternal light" proposed by Pfann and Kister (DJD 20:19-21).

Frag. 2, col. ii

¹its roots wen[t out . . .] ²in the depths be[low . . .] ³gain in understanding [. . .]

Frags. 3-4, col. i

¹[. . .] lofty abode ²[. . .] and by what ³[. . .] dust ⁴[. . .] he gave to ⁵[. . .] in all the world ⁶[. . .] he measured their plan ⁷[. . . bel]ow there ⁸[. . .] their [p]lan to walk about ⁹[. . .] storehouse of understanding ¹⁰[. . .] my word and that [. . .]

Notes

Line 7: "there" — שׁם could also be the verb "he placed."

Commentary

Lines 6 and 8: "plan" — See the commentary on this term under 4Q415 9:6.

Line 9: "storehouse of understanding" — The plural form of "understanding" is found in the HB only in Isa 27:11. There is no apparent connection of that verse to this fragmentary reference. In the Qumran scrolls it is present in CD v:16//4Q266 (Dᵃ) 3ii:4; 1QHᵃ 10:21; 1Q29 13:2; 4Q400 1i:6; 4Q416 1:16.

Frags. 3-4, col. ii

¹[. . .] number of its boundaries [. . .] ²[. . .] without raising up [. . .] ³from [its] p[lan . . .] its boundary. Now ⁴pay attention, [men of understanding. . . .] Those who know, listen. Men of ⁵understanding, increase instruction, and seekers of

justice, walk ⁶humbly. Those who kn[ow righteousness], increase in strength and men of ⁷truth purs[ue righteousness], love kindness, increase in ⁸meekness and in[crease in the kn]owledge of the appointed [ti]mes whose ⁹interpretatio[ns I will recou]nt in order that you might gain understanding of the end ¹⁰of the ages and consider the form[er] times in order to know

Notes

Line 4:   In the lacuna in this line the editors reconstruct "the wise" (DJD 20:25-26). While this would be a convenient connection with the idea of wisdom, there is no evidence of the terms "wisdom" or "the wise" in the fragments of this composition. It is more likely that it contained one of the epithets such as "men of understanding" enumerated in frags. 1-2i:1-3 above. See commentary to 1-2i:1 above.

Line 6:   "Those who kn[ow righteousness]" — This reconstruction is based upon parallels such as CD i:1, which seems more plausible than "the way" (DJD 20:25, 27), which does not have a parallel in a text from Qumran.

Line 7:   "love" — Pfann and Kister propose a final *yod*, ואהבי, hence the participle, "those who love kindness," rather than the imperative ואהבו, which has a final *waw* (DJD 20:27). In contrast to most of the Qumran texts in square script, the cryptic script makes a clear distinction between the *yod* and *waw,* so there is no doubt about the correct reading in this copy. Were an earlier copy of this composition in the Jewish square script available to the scribe, such an error would be understandable. The evidence for such a copy is very limited.

Commentary

Lines 1-2:   "number of its boundaries . . . without raising up" — Pfann and Kister (DJD 20:27) cite 4Q405 23i:11-12 with regard to this line: "They do not run from the way or tarry away from His territory [i.e., 'boundary']. They are not too exalted [i.e., 'raised up'] for His missions, nor are [they] too lowly" (DJD 11:356-57). The term גבול designates the "territory" of "wickedness" (1QHᵃ x:10; xi:25) and of "life" (1QHᵃ xv:17-18) in the *Hodayot*. In the *Damascus Document,* however, the understanding of "boundary" is very significant with regard to the identity of those who entered into the new covenant in the land of Damascus: "In the time of wrath those who shift the boundaries arose and caused Israel to go astray" (CD v:20), based upon the use of Hos 5:10. In CD xix:15-16 the same reference is employed to designate those who had come into the covenant but then were led into error. In the further description of these traitors, the text continues: "And they rebelled with an arrogant [i.e., raised up] hand to walk in the way of the wicked" (CD xix:21). In CD i:16 the "liar" or "man of mockery" appeared to make them "turn from the paths of righteousness and to shift the boundary that the first ones had established to make a boundary around their inheritance." The "arrogant hand" is also found in CD xix:21 and xx:30, as well as in 1QS v:12; viii:17. The use of this same allusion from Hos 5:10 is found in other wisdom literature from Qumran at 4Q416 2iii:8-9; 2iv:6; 4Q418 9-9c:7; 10a,b:8. In light of the remainder of the words and allusions in this fragmentary column, these references in CD and 1QS (and parallel texts) appear to establish a better context for their meaning. Note the reference to the same term in line 3.

Line 3: "boundary" — See commentary to line 1 above.

Lines 3-4: "Now pay attention, [men of understanding. . . .] Those who know, listen" — The term האזינו ("pay attention") is not that common in the Qumran literature, found only at 4Q418 177:4 and 4Q525 24ii:2 in other wisdom texts in the corpus. However, it appears in the context of a familiar form here and in the opening title to this work (see above), with the use of the more common imperative, "listen," later in this line. If we examine the use of this form at the beginning of the *Damascus Document* we see that both "know" and "understand" are also found in the first line of a text that begins in the same manner: "*And now,* listen, all who *know* righteousness and *understand* the deeds of God" (i:1-2). The same form is used at CD ii:2-3 and ii:14-15, apparently using the model from biblical wisdom found at Prov 1:8; 4:10; 5:7; 7:24; 8:32. When combined with the commentary on line 1 above and subsequent references noted below, we see the manner in which this wisdom composition is connected with sectarian literature, particularly the *Damascus Document,* in which ample wisdom vocabulary is employed throughout the work. In the wisdom literature from Qumran it can also be found at 4Q185 1-2i:13; 4Q525 2ii+3:12; 13:6; 14ii:18; 31:1.

Lines 4-8: This list of virtues finds some resemblance in 2 Pet 1:5-8.[9] Also note the relation of the vocabulary in this section to Mic 6:8.

Line 5: "seekers of justice" — In 4Q268 (D^c) i:6 we read of "those who seek his commandments and walk in the perfection of the way."

---

9. See DJD 20:16; Swanson, "4QcrypA," in *Sapiential, Liturgical and Poetical Texts,* ed. Falk et al., 59-61.

Lines 5-6: "walk humbly" — This phrase from Mic 6:8, not found in biblical wisdom literature, is most common in the *Community Rule*: 1QS iv:5; v:3-4// 4Q256 (S[b]) ix:4//4Q258 (S[d]) i:3.

Line 6: "Those who kn[ow righteousness]" — This phrase is found at CD i:1 and parallels, as well as in 4Q270 (D[e]) 2ii:19 (see notes above). It would appear that 4Q298 parallels CD in its interest in righteousness, as evidenced in the extensive use of the term. In both compositions, "righteousness" is a central concept for describing the way of life acceptable to God, that is, the sectarian lifestyle.

Lines 6-7: "men of truth" — This designation is also found in 1QH[a] vi:13; x:16 (reconstructed); and 4Q275 2:3; all of these are assumed to be sectarian texts. It is also found in 11Q19 lvii:8, in the section entitled the "Torah of the King," one of the segments characterized as more independent in composition with regard to known biblical texts than significant portions of the remainder of the scroll.

Line 7: "purs[ue righteousness]" — See references to "those who pursue righteousness" in 1-2i:2 above, as well as in 4Q299 8:7; 4Q418 69ii:10-11; 4Q424 3:2.

Lines 8-10: "in[crease in the kn]owledge of the appointed [t]imes whose interpretation[ns I will recou]nt in order that you might gain understanding of the end of the ages" — In the *Damascus Document,* which makes extensive use of the word "knowledge," an understanding of the ages needs to be acquired by those who enter the covenant. This understanding is coupled with and integrated into the listing of the errors of the past that covenant members are enjoined to avoid. Such knowledge is at the heart of the pesher material as well as the MSS of the *Community Rule.* An understanding of the meaning of the appointed times and their significance is a necessary part of knowing how to live in a sectarian lifestyle.

Line 9: "interpretatio[ns]" (פתר[י]הם) — Most instructive for this term as well as the line in which it is located (see previous comment) is CD xiii:8. In this section of the *Damascus Document,* the rule outlining the work of the overseer specifies that he is "to recount to them what will happen in the future along with its interpretation." In other words, he is to outline the future events as well as their interpretation, in this case their significance and meaning for the nature of the sectarian lifestyle. The term "interpretations" is relatively rare, used as both verb and slightly modified noun form in the stories of Joseph's dream interpretation in Genesis 40–41. The Aramaic equivalent *(peshar)* can be found in stories about Daniel's dream interpretation in the Aramaic portions of that book.

Line 10: "form[er] times" — See Isa 43:18. The term קדמוניות or קדמניות is also found in *Instruction* (4Q418 148ii:6) in a similar wisdom context where the connection between wisdom and a knowledge of the relationship between the nature of creation and the eschatological future is being developed. Note the discussion in the commentary to that line.

Frag. 5, col. i

⁸[. . .] end ⁹[. . .] to tread

Frag. 5, col. ii

⁸the dawn and [. . .] ⁹its boundaries [. . .] ¹⁰set the boundaries [. . .]

Sapiential-Didactic Work A (4Q412)

Introduction

Content

It is difficult to establish even the main topic and genre of the fragmentary remains of this composition. The editor, Annette Steudel, states that it "seems to be a didactic collection, giving instructions for the life and behavior of a person, as well as liturgical commands."[1] Allusions from the vocabulary utilized in the first fragment in particular appear to point to similarities with compositions such as the *Hodayot*, which demonstrate a good deal of interest in knowledge and understanding integrated with theological and liturgical language. Allusions to other liturgical texts can also be identified.

Manuscripts

In the Qumran corpus only one MS is available, with at least three fragments. Based on the handwriting some question whether frag. 4 is related to this same composition (see DJD 20:163). The script is of the late Hasmonean or early Herodian type, dated to the first century B.C.E.

Historical Context

The use of the term "many" in a text that appears to be closer in vocabulary and theme to the *Hodayot* than to other Qumran wisdom texts such as *Instruction*

1. DJD 20:163.

and *Mysteries* suggests that this text should be considered among the sectarian compositions or very close to them in origin. It has been pointed out that liturgical texts tend to be more difficult to categorize with regard to this question since they employ a higher proportion of traditional language in repetitive patterns. Similarities in the literature with other liturgical texts from the Qumran corpus have been noted in the commentary. While we recognize these difficulties, the vocabulary usage and identified similarities with the *Hodayot* suggest a sectarian provenance.[2] Its fragmentary nature prohibits a definitive resolution of the question.

Literary Questions

It is significant to note that the addressee is identified in the text in the second person singular, similar to *Instruction* and some portions of the *Hodayot*.[3] The limited evidence available from this composition prohibits substantial investigation of literary questions, other than those already noted under "Content" above and discussed in the commentary to the text.

Bibliography

Note also the bibliography in the introduction to this volume.

Steudel, Annette. "412. 4QSapiential-Didactic Work A." DJD 20:163-71.

Frag. 1

[1][And yo]u, do not d[o . . .] [2][. . .] to the many, do not d[o . . . utter] [3]a defamatory rumor [about] you. Also due to iniquity to know [. . .] [4]you are confused by the words of [. . .] understanding, he utters words [. . .] [5][pl]aced a chain upon your lips [. . .] and for your tongue armo[red] doors [. . . . And now, my son, listen] [6]to me, consider righteousness in those [. . .] righteousness for those who seek [understanding . . .] [7]with all your mouth praise [. . .] your clamor [. . .] [8]give thanksgiving to his name [. . .] [9]in the assembly of the many [. . .] [10]day and night [. . .]

2. Contra John Strugnell, "The Smaller Hebrew Wisdom Texts Found at Qumran: Variations, Resemblances, and Lines of Development," in *Wisdom Texts from Qumran*, ed. Hempel et al., 38.

3. Ibid., 52-53.

Notes

Line 5: "[... And now, my son, listen]" — This reconstruction is proposed by Steudel. Note the common use of the phrase in the plural in the *Damascus Document* (CD i:1; ii:2, 14; 4Q266 2i:6; 2ii:2; 4Q268 1:9; 4Q270 2ii:19) and in 4Q525 2ii+3:12; 13:6; 14ii:18. This phrase is known from the biblical wisdom literature in Prov 1:8; 4:10; in the plural form in Prov 5:7; 7:24; 8:32.

Commentary

Line 2: "to the many" — The use of the Hebrew preposition ל ("to," "for," or "of") seems more likely than the proposed קהל, "assembly," found in DJD 20:164-65, which conflates two independent terms into one word (קהלרבים). The latter phrase is found in line 9 below as two terms. We do find this reconstruction in CD xv:8 ("of the many") and 1QS vi:9, 12-13 ("to the many"), in all cases representing the gathered membership of a sectarian community. It is not clear whether the reference in 4Q462 1:7 carries such a meaning.

Line 3: "defamatory rumor" — This apparent conflation of two terms is based in the meaning of the first part, *dibbah,* a "bad report" or "rumor." It appears only in 1QHᵃ x:13 in the Qumran corpus and rarely in the HB, where it is frequently translated as "slander."

Line 5: "[pl]aced a chain upon your lips" — On the basis of 4Q436 1a+bi:8 the Hebrew term is considered to be *moser* ("chain") rather than the more common *musar* ("instruction").

Line 5: "armo[red] doors" — In 1QHᵃ xiv:27-35 the author enters a religious space he describes as a fortified and walled city provided by God to protect him from the forces and power of Belial. This phrase is found in line 30.

Line 6: "consider righteousness" — For a similar use of this verb in the imperative, see 4Q418 43,44,45i:4, "consider the mystery of existence."

Line 6: "for those who seek [understanding . . .]" — For this phrase see 1QHᵃ vi:14.

Line 7: "your clamor" — This term appears most frequently in Ezekiel (3:12, 13; 12:18; 37:7; 38:19), but also in the other Hebrew prophets (Isa 9:5; 29:6; Jer

10:22; 47:3; Amos 1:1; Nah 3:2; Zech 14:5). The roar sometimes refers to the sound and shaking of an earthquake. The sounds related to being in the heavens approaching the divine presence are found in Ezek 3:12, 13.

Line 8: "thanksgiving" — This term, here appearing in the defective form (הדות) rather than the more common הודות, is not a biblical term but rather common in certain Qumran compositions. Elisha Qimron suggests that this is a "*hif'il* infinitive without *lamed* used as a noun, 'thanksgiving'" (*HDSS* §500.1, s.v. ידה). This latter term is very prominent in the MSS of the *Songs of the Sabbath Sacrifice* (4Q400-407, 11Q17, Masık). "Thanksgiving" in the plural also appears in that composition as well as in certain liturgical works such as 4Q502, 4Q503, and 504, as well as in the MSS of 4Q510-511. It is also found in the MSS of the *War Scroll* and the *Hodayot*. Closely related is the fundamental form, "I give you thanks," from which the MSS of the *Hodayot* get their title.

Line 9: "in the assembly of the many" — See line 2 above. The "many" is a major term used to designate the sectarian organization in the MSS of the *Community Rule*, the *Hodayot, Pesher Habakkuk,* and to a lesser extent the *Damascus Document.*

Frag. 2

²[. . .] do not [. . .] ³[. . .] three [. . .] ⁴[. . . fo]ments strife [. . .]

Commentary

Line 4: "[. . . fo]ments strife" — See Prov 6:14, 19; 16:28, where this is included among the characteristics of people not to be emulated.

Frag. 3

¹[. . .] righteous judgments [. . .] ²[. . .] concerning the words of [. . .]

Frag. 4

¹[. . .] my wealth he will give as a possession [. . .] ²[. . . according to] his will he created [. . .] ³[. . .] I will call out [. . .] ⁴[. . .] my [wo]rds and those who know [. . .] ⁵[. . .] man [. . .]

Ways of Righteousness (4Q420-421)

Introduction

Contents

This fascinating composition combines wisdom sayings with sectarian organization while also containing legislation relating to the temple. While it is difficult to determine definitively the order of the fragments, Torleif Elgvin proposes the following arrangement, based on the fragments of 4Q421:[1]

> Sectarian organization: 4Q420 1ai + 2; 4Q421 1ai
> Beginning of the wisdom sayings: 4Q420 1aii-b (+ 3?); 4Q421 1aii-b
> Scattered section of wisdom sayings in no apparent order: 4Q420 2-6; 4Q421 4-10 (with some realignment from earlier editions: frag. 5 has now become frag. 2 and frag. 4 has become frag. 3)
> The last column containing wisdom sayings: 4Q421 11
> Issues regarding temple service: 4Q421 12-13

This combination of material in one text is of great significance for our understanding of the development and nature of a trajectory of wisdom materials among the Qumran texts. In this commentary the texts of 4Q420 and 4Q421 are presented independently, with overlapping parallels noted.

---

1. DJD 20:184. I have added some of the textual references to the outline.

Manuscripts

Two copies of this composition were identified in the earlier research and form the basis for this translation. The scribe of 4Q420 wrote in a Herodian formal script, possibly dated to the turn of the era (DJD 20:174). 4Q421 is written in a developed Herodian formal script from the first half of the first century C.E. (DJD 20:185). More extensive fragments are available from the second MS, the latter portion of which is discussed with regard to 4Q264a in the following section. Overlaps between the two MSS make their identification as copies of the same composition possible. Note that in this case the text in the electronic version *(DSSEL)* has been revised from the original DJD version.

The Relationship to 4Q264a (Halakha B)

Some links between 4Q264a i and 4Q421 13 were initially recognized by Lutz Doering and noted in his dissertation, which was subsequently published.[2] Eibert Tigchelaar recognized further connections and published the results, proposing that the rule genre was predominant in this revised text.[3] In his publication of the text of 4Q264a Joseph Baumgarten noted the textual overlap with 4Q421 and used it to reconstruct what he considered a better reading of the text.[4] In a subsequent article of response Tigchelaar took issue with some details of this reconstruction based on evidence garnered from additional photographs, but then also advanced the proposition that the revised text should more likely be renamed 4QWays of Righteousness[c] and considered a third manuscript of this composition.[5] It is so limited and fragmentary that a literary classification of the evidence within the fragment itself is difficult. In reviewing this evidence John Strugnell argued that it is more likely that the fragments grouped together as 4Q421 are from two distinct works. Fragments 12-13 and presumably frag. 11 of 4Q421 are portions of the same composition of legal literature as 4Q264a.[6] While noting the manner in which frags. 12 and 13 deal with temple matters, Elgvin had argued that frag. 11 probably belongs to the section with wisdom sayings. Since

2. Lutz Doering, *Schabbat: Sabbathalacha und -praxis im antiken Judentum und Urchristentum* (TSAJ 78; Tübingen: Mohr Siebeck, 1999), 217-19.

3. E. J. C. Tigchelaar, "Sabbath Halakha and Worship in *4QWays of Righteousness: 4Q421* 11 and 13+2+8 par *4Q264a* 1-2," *RevQ* 18 (1998): 359-72.

4. DJD 35:53-57.

5. Eibert Tigchelaar, "More on *4Q264A (4QHalakha A* or *4QWays of Righteousness[c]?)*," *RevQ* 19 (2000): 453-56.

6. John Strugnell, "The Smaller Hebrew Wisdom Texts Found at Qumran: Variations, Resemblances, and Lines of Development," in *Wisdom Texts from Qumran*, ed. Hempel et al., 44-45.

these three fragments "demonstrate many similarities in their physical shape and must have been together in one wad," they represent three consecutive columns of the same composition. Hence they are all part of 4Q421.[7]

Historical Context

In this commentary I assume that we have here a composite text whose final form has been adequately outlined by Elgvin to the extent that the extant evidence permits, a subject discussed at greater length under "Literary Questions" below. While portions of it may have their origin in a presectarian priestly milieu and certain wisdom selections may go back to that same era, this composition as preserved among the Qumran holdings represents some integration of a wisdom tradition, sectarian legislation, and prescriptions concerning the temple and purity matters. From paleographic dating we know that it was copied, presumably for sectarian usage and study, by the turn of the era. That means this document was used by, and perhaps even compiled during, the sectarian phase of Qumran habitation. The representation of sectarian legislation and temple procedures in the same document is important evidence concerning the ongoing role of temple ideology within the sectarian existence of the Qumran inhabitants. The fragmentary evidence does not permit even a hypothesis concerning the performance of sacrificial and other temple procedures at Qumran. Charlotte Hempel points to the presence of overlapping terms between materials describing organizational matters in the rules and the sapiential texts, including *Ways of Righteousness*.[8] Of particular interest to her is the use of the term "sage" *(maskil)* in this text and in the well-known rules.[9] Elgvin rather uses this composition as "another indication that the *yaḥad* reflects a merger between the priestly and lay circles in the mid-second century B.C.E.,"[10] his date for the final composition of the composite work.

Literary Questions

In the research of Tigchelaar already noted, he has raised questions concerning whether this is a wisdom composition. He has proposed that it is best under-

---

7. Elgvin, DJD 20:184.
8. Charlotte Hempel, "The Qumran Sapiential Texts and the Rule Books," in *Wisdom Texts from Qumran*, ed. Hempel et al., 283-84.
9. Ibid., 286-94.
10. DJD 20:173.

stood as one of the rule compositions rather than a wisdom text.[11] Lange appears to accept this view,[12] as does Hempel.[13] I am more inclined toward the view of Elgvin, who included it within the tradition of wisdom among the Qumran texts, but noted its unique and even composite nature.[14] While its composite nature may yield evidence concerning its origins and history, the manuscript evidence does support the hypothesis that this text was available at Qumran in the form proposed by Elgvin. This means that we can read it from the standpoint of what it tells us about the nature of the collection of wisdom texts among the Qumran finds.[15]

The literary image of the two ways is important in Second Temple Judaism.[16] In this text, presumably due to its fragmentary nature, we find mention only of the ways of righteousness. With the emphasis on the ways of righteousness it follows Proverbs 1–8, where the contrast is with the wicked or the evil. In Deuteronomy 27–30 the blessings and the curses result in a choice between the ways of life and death. Elsewhere among the Qumran compositions we find 4Q473 *(The Two Ways)*, which speaks of "two ways, one good and one evil." The two very limited fragments of that composition give us little material in addition to identifying it with the story of the exodus and the blessings and curses in Deuteronomy 27–30. It is not unreasonable to think that Deut 30:15-20 was integral to both compositions: "See, I have set before you this day life and good, death and evil." In Second Temple Judaism it is developed in *1 En.* 91:3-4, 18-19; 94:1-5. Here the ways of righteousness and peace (94:4) are contrasted with the ways of violence (91:18-19), iniquity (94:1), evil, and death (94:3). In the "Treatise on the Two Spirits" (1QS iii:15–iv:26) we find the two ways theology devel-

---

11. Tigchelaar, "Sabbath Halakha and Worship," 359-72; idem, "More on 4Q264A," 453-56.

12. Armin Lange, "Die Weisheitstexte aus Qumran: Eine Einleitung," in *Wisdom Texts from Qumran,* ed. Hempel et al., 7. He cites Torleif Elgvin, "Admonition Texts from Qumran Cave 4," in *Methods of Investigation of the Dead Sea Scrolls and the Khirbet Qumran Site: Present Realities and Future Prospects* (ed. Michael O. Wise, Norman Golb, John J. Collins, and Dennis G. Pardee; Annals of the New York Academy of Sciences 722; New York: New York Academy of Sciences, 1994), 179-96, specifically pp. 179, 184-85; idem, DJD 20:173, 183. Elgvin notes the sectarian terminology present in the compositions but does not propose that they are to be considered among the Rules genre or the Halakha texts. He does note its composite nature.

13. Hempel, "Qumran Sapiential Texts," 277-95, 283-84.

14. Elgvin, "Wisdom With and Without Apocalyptic," 20-21.

15. Note also Goff, *Discerning Wisdom,* 160-61.

16. George W. E. Nickelsburg, "Seeking the Origins of the Two Ways Tradition in Jewish and Christian Ethical Texts," in *A Multiform Heritage: Studies on Early Judaism and Christianity in Honor of Robert A. Kraft* (ed. Benjamin G. Wright; Scholars Press Homage Series 24; Atlanta: Scholars Press, 1999), 95-108; idem, *1 Enoch 1: A Commentary on the Book of 1 Enoch, Chapters 1–36; 81–108* (Hermeneia; Minneapolis: Fortress, 2001), 454-56.

oped into a heightened dualism where the conflict is between the sons of light and the sons of darkness, or the sons of righteousness who walk in the light and the sons of deceit who walk in darkness. This conflict is the dominant force in creation: humankind is dominated by two spirits, the spirit of truth and the spirit of deceit, who are ruled by the Prince of Lights and the Angel of Darkness, respectively. This conflict is carried out within a universe where everything is determined under the absolute sovereignty of God.[17] Within 4Q420-421 we find vocabulary that reappears in the "Treatise on the Two Spirits," suggesting some earlier stage in this developed dualistic worldview that characterized sectarian ideology.

This tradition of the two ways is also evident in the NT. We note, for example, the imagery of Matt 7:13-14 and the two kinds of wisdom in Jas 3:13–4:10. It would also appear to be related to Paul's usage of the flesh and the spirit as found in Romans 6–8 and Gal 5:16–6:8.[18] Its best-known use in other early Christian literature is in *Didache* 1–6.

In the two ways literature we find lists of personal and ethical attributes attributed to persons associated with each path. This is apparent in 4Q420 1-2// 4Q421 1-2. Such a list would seem to be implied in the structure of the sayings of 4Q424 and related to the macarisms of 4Q525 2ii+3. A similar list is to be found in the works of the flesh and spirit in Gal 5:19-24.

Bibliography

Note also the bibliography in the introduction to this volume.

Elgvin, Torleif. "420. 4QWays of Righteousness[a]." DJD 20:173-82.

———. "421. 4QWays of Righteousness[b]." DJD 20:183-202.

———. "Admonition Texts from Qumran Cave 4." In *Methods of Investigation of the Dead Sea Scrolls and the Khirbet Qumran Site: Present Realities and Future Prospects* (ed. Michael O. Wise, Norman Golb, John J. Collins, and Dennis G. Pardee; Annals of the New York Academy of Sciences 722; New York: New York Academy of Sciences, 1994), 179-96.

———. "Wisdom With and Without Apocalyptic." In *Sapiential, Liturgical and Poetical Texts,* ed. Falk et al., 15-38.

Hempel, Charlotte. "The Qumran Sapiential Texts and the Rule Books." In *Wisdom Texts from Qumran,* ed. Hempel et al., 277-95.

---

17. Jean Duhaime, "Dualism," *EDSS* 1:215-20.

18. Note the discussion of this dichotomy in the introduction to this volume, pp. 32-33. See also Nickelsburg, "Seeking the Origins."

Strugnell, John. "The Smaller Hebrew Wisdom Texts Found at Qumran: Variations, Resemblances, and Lines of Development." In *Wisdom Texts from Qumran,* ed. Hempel et al., 44-45.

Tigchelaar, E. J. C. "More on *4Q264A (4QHalakha A* or *4QWays of Righteousness^c?),*" *RevQ* 19 (2000): 453-56.

———. "Sabbath Halakha and Worship in *4QWays of Righteousness: 4Q421* 11 and 13+2+8 par *4Q264a* 1-2." *RevQ* 18 (1998): 359-72.

Ways of Righteousness[a] (4Q420)

Frag. 1a, col. i

[4][. . . we]alth of the wicked [. . .] [5][. . . commandme]nts of God

Commentary

Line 4:   "[. . . we]alth of the wicked" — "Wicked," here in the plural, is more often translated as "evil wealth" when found in the singular. In this form it is noted in CD vi:15 and viii:5, and the problem of wealth is one of three central problems discussed throughout the *Damascus Document* with regard to the separation of those who entered the "new" covenant in the land of Damascus. These connections demonstrate the relationship of this text to the central compositions considered foundational for the life of the sect.

Line 5:   While this is a hypothetical reconstruction, it is the most likely phrase to consider given the apparent connection of the vocabulary in line 4 with sectarian compositions such as 1QS and CD and their associated MSS. This phrase is common in CD (ii:18; iii:2, 6, 12; v:21; viii:19; ix:7; xix:32) as well as in the fragments of that composition (4Q266 [D[a]] 1a-b:17; 2ii:18, 22; 3ii:8; 4Q267 [D[b]] 2:5; 9i:2; 4Q269 [D[d]] 4i:2). Those who keep "his" or "your" commandments are noted in 1QSb i:1 and 1QH[a] viii:31, 35.

Frag. 1a, col. ii-b + <u>4Q421 1a, col. ii-b</u>

[1][<u>in the ways of God to do righteousness</u>] in this way: he shall not answer before he liste<u>[ns,]</u> [2]<u>[he shall not spe]ak be[fore he understands.]</u> With patience he

shall give a reply [. . .] ³he shall utter a word [. . . he shall see]k true judgment. By seeking out righteousness ⁴he shall find [its] conse[quences. A man] who is humble and contrite in his insight shall n[o]t turn b[ack] ⁵until [. . .] a trustworthy [man] shall not turn from the ways of righteousness. [He shall set] ⁶[his heart . . .] his [bo]nes and his hands. With righteousness he is redee[med]. ⁷With understanding all [. . .] his fields, its borders [. . .] ⁸[. . .] to [do rig]hteousness [. . .]

Notes

Line 3: "he shall utter a word [. . . he shall see]k true judgment." This line is missing from the parallel text of 4Q421 1aii-b:14.

Commentary

For commentary on the text of this column see 4Q421 1aii-b.

Frag. 2

¹[. . . long] suffering [. . .] ²[. . .] joined until [. . .] ³[. . . to ad]d to their measurements [. . .] ⁴[. . .] concerning the afflictions of judgme[nt . . .] ⁵[. . .] and their seed for the consolat[ion . . .] ⁶[. . .] which he spoke [. . .] ⁷[. . .] for all who drag it away [. . .] ⁸[. . .] in its furrows he will plough and continually [. . .] ⁹[. . . the ri]ghteous [. . .] what is in the heart of [. . .] ¹⁰[. . .] for his rebuke [. . .]

Notes

Line 2: "joined" — The first letter ת proposed for this word in DJD 20:179 is very difficult to read; it could just as well be ה.

Line 7: "drag it away" — A rare word, perhaps also found in 1QpHab v:13 and 1QHᵃ xxi:35. In the latter text it is now translated "attack" (on the basis of the root גור, rather than גרר; see DJD 40:268).

Line 9: At the end of this line, Elgvin posits the reconstruction "s[ages?]" (DJD 20:179).

Commentary

The topic(s) under discussion in this column is impossible to determine. The combination of agricultural imagery and sectarian terminology does not permit easy identification. Perhaps the author is following a prophetic tradition, such as Isa 28:23-29, in which a decree for destruction is elaborated with an agricultural illustration that begins with the wisdom style injunction, "Listen and hear my voice" (DJD 20:180).

Line 2: "joined" — This verb, closely associated with the name Levi and the Levites, is used to designate those who joined the priests in leaving the land of Judah in the midrash on Ezek 44:15 found in CD iv:3, as well as similar uses in 1QS v:6; 1QH^a iv:31; 4Q169 3-4ii:9; iii:5; iv:1. We note that some of these associations are on the dark side of a dualistic worldview.

Line 4: "the afflictions of judgme[nt . . .]" — This peculiar phrase finds its closest parallels in 1QS iii:14, 23; iv:12, where it refers to the afflictions associated with the dominion of the angel of darkness and eternal damnation at the hands of all of the angels of destruction.

Frag. 3

¹[. . . ju]dgment [. . .] ²[. . .] was a measu[re of righteousness . . .]

Commentary

Line 2: "measu[re of righteousness . . .]" — This phrase also occurs in 4Q418 126ii:3. That reference appears within a column in which an all-knowing God gives wise judgment on evildoers in order to lift up the head of the poor. In 4Q418 77:3-4 the measure is something the adherent will understand and is encompassed within the mystery of existence.

Frag. 4

¹[. . .] you shall sp[eak . . .] ²[. . .] truth [. . .]

Frag. 6

¹[. . . con]cerning every wo[rd . . .] ²[. . .] to see[k . . .] ³[. . .] truth [. . .]

Notes

Line 2: "to see[k . . .]" — This reconstruction (לדרוש) seems preferable to the proposed [תם]לדרו, "for their generations" (DJD 20:181-82). This term, which in Rabbinic Hebrew becomes one of the technical terms for describing the act of interpretation, seems preferable in a column that contains "word" in the previous line. The term דרש appears 31 times in the fragments of *Instruction*.

Ways of Righteousness[b] (4Q421)

Frag. 1a, col. i

[1][. . .] with an [et]ernal enmity [. . .] [2][. . . and he shall bring all] his [wi]sdom and his knowledge and his understanding and his goodness [into the community] [3][of God . . .] to rank everyone, each man according to [his] neigh[bor] [4][. . .] the first lot [will go o]ut and then will go out [5][. . .] our words [will] be carefully observed [6][. . . h]im to admonish him [. . .] [7-14][. . .] [15][. . .] wealth

Commentary

On the basis of vocabulary and theme this column appears to be related to the *Community Rule*. The relationship between the structure of the community (of God) and the dualistic nature of the universe provides the basic conceptual framework for both compositions.

Line 1: "[et]ernal enmity" — See 1QS iv:17.

Line 2: This line is reconstructed on the basis of 1QS i:11-12. An indication of its placement within the wisdom tradition at Qumran is that only terms from the semantic domain of wisdom designate the contributions the member brings into the community, whereas in 1QS strength and wealth are also included.[19] While

19. For one recent interpretation of the community of goods see Hartmut Stegemann, *Die Essener, Qumran, Johannes der Täufer und Jesus: Ein Sachbuch* (4th ed.; Freiburg: Herder, 1994), 245-64. For the English translation of an earlier edition, see idem, *The Library of Qumran: On the Essenes, Qumran, John the Baptist and Jesus* (Grand Rapids: Eerdmans, 1998), 176-90. Explanations of the basic views concerning this subject can be found in Lawrence H. Schiffman, *Reclaiming the Dead Sea Scrolls* (Philadelphia: Jewish Publication Society, 1994), 106-10; and James VanderKam and Peter Flint, *The Meaning of the Dead Sea Scrolls* (San Francisco: HarperSanFrancisco, 2002), 246-50.

we must recognize that the text is fragmentary, hence other attributes could be included in the text, the wisdom emphasis is apparent in the list of synonyms present here that are not included in 1QS.[20]

Line 4: "lot" — גורל here means a set place or rank in the universe with a distinct order in which each person's fate or place is determined. It can also refer to the place of the individual with regard to the two portions of the dualistic structure of the universe to indicate the individual's specific allegiance. In 4Q279 5:4 it seems to refer to the assignment of rewards for the priests and Levites in the messianic age (DJD 26:218-23). According to its editors, 4Q279 may be fragments of a "Messianic Rule." The best-known Qumran composition of that nature is 1Q28a (1QSa, *Rule of the Congregation* or *Messianic Rule*). Due to the predetermined and dualistic nature of the world portrayed in the sectarian literature from Qumran, the meanings of the term outlined here are portions of one conceptual viewpoint represented throughout the *Community Rule* and the *War Scroll* as well as receiving mention in the *Damascus Document*.

Line 15: "wealth" — עשר could also be the number "ten." This is the more likely translation of עשר in 4Q421 5:2, though this text is also fragmentary.

Frag. 1a, col. ii-b + 4Q420 1a, col. ii-b

[6]rules over [. . .] [7]their times against [. . .] [8]their healing in addition to [. . .] that which [9]he declared [. . .] to bear [10]the yoke of wisd[om . . . a ma]n who is a sage and possesses understanding [11]will draw them out. He will bend down [. . .] he shall carry out the reproof [12]of the sage. A man [. . .] to walk in the ways of God [13]to do righteousness [in this way: he shall not answer before he lis]tens, he shall not speak before [14]he understands. With patie[nce he shall return a verdict and by seeking out rig]hteousness he shall find [15]its consequences. A m[an who is humble and contrite in his insight shall not tu]rn [ba]ck until [16][. . . a trustworthy man shall not turn from the ways of righteousness.] He shall set [17][his heart . . . his bones and his hands. With righteousness he is redeemed. With understand]ing all [18][. . . his fields, its borders . . .] [19][. . . to do righteousness . . .]

---

20. Note the discussion of the meaning and significance of the term סרך ("rule") in Lawrence H. Schiffman, *The Halakhah at Qumran* (SJLA 16; Leiden: Brill, 1975), 60-68.

Notes

Line 7:   "against" — The preposition עַל has a variety of meanings such as "in addition to" in the next line, also "on," "according to," and "on account of."

Lines 8-9:   "which" — The repetition of אֲשֶׁר appears to be due to dittography (Elgvin, DJD 20:188), hence it is translated only once in this text.

Line 14:   In between the phrase "[return a verdict]" and "[and by seeking out rig]hteousness," 4Q420 1aii-b:2-3 adds: "he shall utter a word [. . . he shall see]k true judgment."

Commentary

Line 10:   "yoke of wisd[om . . .]" — In Sir 51:25-26 the reader is entreated to "acquire wisdom for yourself without money" and to "put your neck under her yoke," a theme already developed in Sir 6:23-31. The connection between "yoke" and "wisdom" is more explicit in the Hebrew text of Ben Sira than in the Greek version. This relationship between the yoke and wisdom lies behind the portrayal of Jesus as wisdom in Matt 11:25-30. In the Qumran texts see also 4Q438 3:3, which states, "I have brought my neck under your yoke," even though the fragmentary state of the text does not permit us to determine the exact referent. The image of the yoke is common in rabbinic literature, with a statement of Rabbi Nechuniah (Nehunya) ben Hakanah in *m. Abot* 3:5 an important reference point: "Whoever accepts the yoke of the Torah, then the yoke of the kingdom and the yoke of daily life shall be removed from him." The yoke as symbol of a negative burden is found in Sir 28:19-20 and 2 *En.* 41:2; 48:9.

It is not clear either that the use of the phrase in this text implies a hypostatic understanding of wisdom or that it is a reference to wisdom as law as developed in Sir 24:23-29.[21] I have noted above the relative absence of references to Torah in a number of the wisdom compositions discussed in this volume, most notably *Instruction*. This has also been identified with regard to *1 Enoch*. George Nickelsburg has pointed out the all-encompassing nature of wisdom in that composition: "Law and its interpretation are embodied in the notion of revealed 'wisdom.'"[22] It may be that an understanding of wisdom de-

---

21. For the former see Elgvin, DJD 20:190; for the latter see Tigchelaar, "Sabbath Halakha," 371.

22. Nickelsburg, *1 Enoch 1*, 50. Note also his essay, "Enochic Wisdom: An Alternative to

veloped within the composition itself is the basis for the yoke underlying the rules only hinted at in the remaining fragments of this composition.

Line 10:   "sage" — The "sage" is an important figure in both sapiential and rule texts. See the introduction to this volume for a discussion of this term.

Line 11:   "will draw them out" — See Prov 20:5, where "the man of understanding will draw it [good counsel] out."

Lines 10-17:   In one of his survey articles Elgvin includes this section among the lists of virtues and vices characteristic of the wisdom genre.[23]

Line 11:   "bend down" — The Hebrew root שחח ("bow down, be humble") is the most probable basis for this translation, since the line picks up the theme of reproof after the lacuna. This term is used to describe those who go astray in CD i:15.

Lines 11-12:   "He shall carry out the reproof of the sage." In this fragmentary text it is most likely that the sage determines the reproof, the penalty, and someone else carries it out. Note 4Q477. This is a repeated theme in the wisdom texts from Qumran (see 4Q299 7:5 and 4Q300 7:2-3 above). For a more extensive discussion note 4Q417 2i:1-6 above and see commentary there. This is an important theme for the *Damascus Document* (CD vii:2-3; ix:2-8; xiv:22). For a discussion of the "sage" see the introduction to this volume.

Line 15:   "consequences" — On תוצאות see DJD 20:177-78. While in Biblical Hebrew the term is often used to indicate "boundaries" or "outer limits" as well as "source" or "origin," that usage here is only indirect. In this context it emphasizes a great deal more the results derived from having discovered the "source," "origin," or "outer limits" of thought or practice. Tigchelaar proposes "specifications."[24] Within the Qumran corpus, it is peculiar to the wisdom texts (DJD 20:177-78).

Frag. 2

[1][. . .] in [his] mouth [. . .] [2][. . .] a word to bless [. . .] [3][. . . eve]ry [m]an according to [his neighbor [. . .]

the Mosaic Torah?" in *Hesed Ve-Emet: Studies in Honor of Ernest S. Frerichs* (ed. Jodi Magness and Seymour Gitin; BJS 320; Atlanta: Scholars Press, 1998), 123-32.

23. Elgvin, "Wisdom With and Without Apocalyptic," 17 n. 8.

24. Tigchelaar, "Sabbath Halakha," 371.

Commentary

Elgvin proposes that this fragment continues the discussion of sectarian organization in 1a i (DJD 20:191).

Frag. 3

¹[. . .] concerning the conse[quences of . . .] ²[. . .] a man and those who keep [. . .] ³[. . . con]cerning its truth he shall utt[er a word . . .]

Commentary

Line 1:   "conse[quences]" — See Commentary to 1aii-b:15 above.

Frag. 4

¹[. . .] he shall keep [. . .] ²[. . .] and in his heart [. . .]

Frag. 5

¹[. . . i]f he will answer [. . .] ²[. . .] wealth, to know [. . .]

Frag. 6

³[. . .] which is not [. . .] ⁴[. . .] a man th[at . . .]

Frag. 7

²[. . .] water [. . .]

Frag. 8

¹[. . .] is reigning over [. . .] ²[. . . scr]oll of a book to read [. . .]

Commentary

Line 1:   "reigning over" — This somewhat rare term is related to למשור in 4Q416 1:4//4Q418 i:1, according to *DSSC* 2:704. See my commentary to that text above.

Line 2:   "[... scr]oll of a book to read" — This phrase is found partially reconstructed in 4Q264a 1:4 concerning a prohibition on reading, perhaps in some specific manner or for some purpose, on the Sabbath (see DJD 35:54). The "scroll of a book" is found in Jer 36:2, 4; Ezek 2:9; Ps 40:8.

Frag. 9

¹[...] he will be strong [...] ²[...] his [w]ords to strengthen the heart of [...]
³[...] to [de]stroy all the servants of e[vil ...]

Commentary

Line 2:   "to strengthen the heart of" — Antoon Schoors notes that this phrase in the HB has the negative connotations of the hardening of the heart, but that in Qumran it has a positive meaning (1QM xvi:13-14; 4Q436 1a-bi:1, 4; 4Q504 1-2v:8-9).[25]

Frag. 10

¹[... a ma]n trustworthy in al[l ...] ²[...] until [...]

Frag. 11

²[... no one should open a] sealed [vessel] to eat and to drink from it all [...]
³[...] will camp he shall not draw water from it [...] ⁴[...] for it is the work of a sl[ave. He shall not defile [...] ⁵[...] a man [...] ⁶[... a]ll [...]

---

25. Schoors, "The Language of the Qumran Sapiential Works," in *Wisdom Texts from Qumran*, ed. Hempel et al., 81. The latter reference is now listed as 4Q504 xix (1+2vi):9-10 (*DSSR* 5:254-55).

Notes

Line 2: "[. . . no one should open a] sealed [vessel]" — Note this reconstruction in *DSSEL,* based upon the text in CD xi:9.

Line 3: "will camp," חונה — Elgvin prefers to read חינם, "in vain" (DJD 20:196), a term more frequently attested in the Qumran texts, but a less likely reading on the basis of the photographs.

Commentary

Line 4: "work of a sl[ave]" — Caution should be exercised in the interpretation of the text with regard to "slave." See commentary to 12:2 below.

Frag. 12

²[. . .] neither any male nor female slave shall eat in the t[emple . . .] ³[. . .] he shall not enter into the gate of its court and into the gat[e . . .] ⁴[. . . fo]r away from its place they shall encamp. If a[n]y come [. . .] ⁵[. . .] or [. . .]

Notes

Line 4: "[. . . fo]r away from its place they shall encamp" — This reconstruction and translation is based on *DSSSE* 2:882-83.

Commentary

Both this fragment and frag. 13 deal with halakic issues regarding the temple. Their fragmentary nature prohibits definitive explanation.

Line 2: The precise nature of this prohibition is not clear from parallels in other literary sources. In Deut 16:11, 14, male and female slaves are enjoined, along with the Levites, the strangers, the orphans, and the widows, to join the remainder of the family in the celebration of the Feast of Weeks and then the Feast of Booths (Sukkot). There are no prohibitions attached to that biblical injunction. In Deut 12:18 the prohibition against eating from the tithes and firstfruits within one's town is offset by the injunction to rejoice in the eating of them in the temple. The latter again adds male and female servants along with Levites to the members of the family that should participate. Within the Qumran texts legislation concerning slaves is found in CD xi:12 with regard to work on the Sabbath and in xii:10-11 concerning their sale to gentiles. In this text the presence of slaves appears to be presumed.

While one mentions with great caution the evidence in the Greek sources concerning the Essenes, we must remember that both Josephus (*Ant.* 18.21) and Philo (*Good Person* 75) indicate that the Essenes were known for not owning slaves, a rarity during that time period.

Frag. 13

¹[. . .] except on their faces [. . .] ²[. . . a]ll the burnt offerings and the sacrifices [. . .] ³[. . .] it shall not be credited [to him . . .] ⁴[. . .] matters of holiness according to the statute [. . .] ⁵[. . .] a man shall not expose himself [. . .] ⁶[. . .] with a[l]l the sacri[fices . . .]

Commentary

Line 2: "shall not be credited" — This terminology appears in Lev 7:18 (see DJD 20:201) and often in various stipulations elaborated in Leviticus.

Line 4: "matters of holiness" — The phrase appears in 4Q418 188:7. The term דברי can also mean "words of" or "things of."

Line 5: "shall not expose himself" — The related noun ערוה, "nakedness," is much more common in usage in both the HB and the Qumran texts. In this verbal form it occurs in Isa 32:11. With regard to the sacrificial rites, persons presenting offerings are not to ascend stairs to the altar, which would permit their nakedness to be revealed (Exod 20:26). Priests are to wear linen undergarments that will cover their "naked flesh" (Exod 28:42). Closely related in terminology is the phrase "uncover the nakedness" as a euphemism for sexual relations, commonly employed in biblical usage. This is the manner in which it is employed in CD v:10 with regard to the laws of incest. In the application of the laws of holiness to the sectarian lifestyle we find in 1QS vii:13-14: "Whoever brings forth his hand [penis?] from underneath his clothing, he is so poor that his nakedness is exposed, he will be punished for thirty days."

Instruction-Like Composition B (4Q424)

Introduction

Content

This text is a collection of sayings rooted in the wisdom tradition. The majority of the sayings in the extant fragments concern the kinds of persons to be avoided if one is interested in living a life based in the pursuit of knowledge and wisdom. A longer list of the persons to be avoided is available and the implications of embracing them are spelled out in greater detail than the short account of persons with positive characteristics to be found in the last few lines of frag. 3. The literary structure of the extant text is based on a few set formulas employed throughout the composition. Fragment 1 begins with the formula, "With (עִם) one who [participle] . . ." and then changes to, "A man who (אִישׁ) . . . ," also found in frag. 3. The reader or hearer of this text is neither "to give them authority over" some persons or tasks nor "to send them" to do something. Those persons with positive characteristics are all introduced with the formula, "A man who. . . ."[1]

The obvious use of sayings from the book of Proverbs in this composition is complemented by the allusions to Deuteronomy, thereby indicating some role for legal material in the conception of wisdom spelled out herein. While we note that across the entire range of the fragments of nonbiblical compositions in the Qumran corpus Deuteronomy is the most frequently quoted biblical

---

1. John Strugnell, "The Smaller Hebrew Wisdom Texts Found at Qumran: Variations, Resemblances, and Lines of Development," in *Wisdom Texts from Qumran,* ed. Hempel et al., 46-47.

book, we have evidence of more attention to the interrelationship of law and wisdom in this composition than in some of the other wisdom works in the Qumran corpus. This is particularly evident in the scattered material available in frag. 2, which betrays hints of sacrificial law. There is no evidence that the order of the fragments is sequential, hence they are not to be interpreted in any given order. Some allusions suggest a strong connection to sectarian perceptions, particularly as they are developed in the *Damascus Document,* even though there is not enough evidence to suggest it is a sectarian composition. It does provide a rationale for a movement that stands in some judgment over mainstream Israel.

Manuscripts

Four fragments of the same manuscript are identified with this composition. Fragment 4 has so few extant letters that it does not warrant inclusion in this commentary. Fragments 5 and 6, originally identified with this composition, cannot be established with any degree of certainty as belonging to it. The scribal hand is identical to that of 4Q390 (apocrJer Cᵉ). Devorah Dimant categorizes the latter composition as representing a Herodian rustic semiformal hand dated to 30-20 B.C.E. (DJD 30:237).

Historical Context

The limited fragments available from this composition provide scant opportunity to establish historical context. The textual connections, particularly with crucial imagery related to the *Damascus Document,* suggest an early-second-century B.C.E. provenance in which divergent ideological groupings can be identified. These threads do not support an exilic date of composition, as proposed by Armin Lange.[2] In the next section, I identify connections with *Instruction.*

Literary Questions

In the description of the contents I have already discussed the particular shape of the wisdom instructions in this composition.

2. Lange, "Die Weisheitstexte aus Qumran: Eine Einleitung," in *Wisdom Texts from Qumran,* ed. Hempel et al., 26-28.

There are some particular connections between the vocabulary employed in this text and the fragments of *Instruction*. The term אט in 1:6, which I translate "inner desire," is particular to *Instruction* and *Mysteries* (see the introduction to *Instruction* for a discussion of this term). The term for "need" or "want" (מחסור in line 8) is confined in the Qumran corpus almost exclusively to *Instruction*, with 25 appearances. There is only one reference in *Mysteries* and one in the *Hodayot*. The particular use of the Hiphil form of the verb "to rule" (המשיל), which is translated "to give authority [or 'control'] over" is found 3 times in this text and at least 15 times in *Instruction*. This form of the verb is employed only 3 times throughout the entire HB. There is evidence that this text is to be located in a wisdom tradition closely related to *Instruction* and other similar texts.

Bibliography

Brin, Gershon. "Studies in 4Q424 1-2." *RevQ* 18 (1997): 21-42.
———. "Studies in 4Q424, Fragment 3." *VT* 46 (1996): 271-95.
———. "Wisdom Issues in Qumran: The Types and Status of the Figures in 4Q424 and the Phrases of Rationale in the Document." *DSD* 4 (1997): 297-311.
Tanzer, Sarah. "424. 4Q Instruction-like Composition B." DJD 36:333-48.

Frag. 1

[2][. . .] with one who divides, do [not . . .] [3][. . .] a wall he will choose for its structure and he will whitewash its surface with plaster, also it [. . . without] [4]a hiding place from a rainstorm. With a hypocrite do not share a portion, and with someone lacking conviction do not [5]enter the furnace, for like lead he will be melted and not stand before the fire[. . . .] [6]Into the hand of an indolent do not entrust an inner desire, for he will not be attentive to your business, and do not send a matter of [7]instruction [with him], for he will not make clear all of your ways. [From] a man who complains do not [8]expect to receive money for your need. Do not tru[st] a man of devious speech [. . .] [9]your judgment. He will surely be deceptive in his speech, he does not desire the truth [. . .] [10]by the fruit of his lips. Do not give a stingy man control over [your] weal[th, . . .] he will not [11]manage your balance according to your desires[. . . .] whatever remains [. . .] [12]at the time of harvest, he will be found to be fickle. [Do not . . .] short-temp[ered . . .] [13]simple, for he will surely destroy them. A man . . . .

Commentary

Line 2: "one who divides" — Tanzer proposes this reconstruction (פורס). "Simpleton" (פותה) also appears to fit the context and is just as consistent with the extant traces of the visible letters (DJD 36:337-38).

Lines 3-4: See Ezek 13:10-16. Based on that biblical reference it is evident that missing from the text is some negation of the adequacy of the structure in the face of the rainstorm.

Line 4: "With a hypocrite do not share a portion" — What more precisely is intended here is not clear. The closest parallel to this reference to the "hypocrite" occurs in Ps 26:4, but the same term appears a number of times in the *Hodayot* (1QH^a xi:29; xii:14; xv:37; 1Q35 [1QH^b] 1:8). The only parallel to the problematic phrase, "share a portion," occurs in 4Q460 9i:9, which also is fragmentary. In any case, "taking" (לקח, here translated "share") something from a hypocrite in such a manner that your welfare is linked to him or her is inadvisable.

Lines 4-5: "with someone lacking conviction" — The more literal translation here is "one who strays." The phrase "like lead he will be melted" points to Ezek 22:20-21, where all of Israel will be gathered into Jerusalem and "melted" by the anger and wrath of God, even though the listing of metals is more extensive and Israel seems to be regarded as "dross." This biblical verse lies behind CD xx:3 as well. In this case it is applied to those who have failed to follow the way of life outlined in the prescriptions of that composition for those who have entered into the new covenant. In both of the Qumran texts, the melting of Israel has been redefined to designate a more select group, perhaps still considered to be "Israel." The phrase "stand before the fire" would appear to point to judgment in the presence of God, already implied in the usage of the passage cited from Ezekiel and also suggested in the use of the phrase in instances such as 1 Sam 6:20; 2 Kgs 10:4; Ps 147:17; Dan 11:16.

Line 6: "inner desire" — On the Hebrew term אם see the discussion in the introduction to *Instruction*. For a different translation and interpretation of this term see DJD 36:339.

Line 7: "make clear all of your ways" — In Prov 5:6 the "strange woman" does not keep her paths straight or "make clear her ways." See also 3:4 below.

Line 10: "fruit of his lips" — See Hos 14:3.

Line 10:   "stingy" — Literally "man of the evil eye"; see Prov 23:6; 28:22.

Line 10:   "give . . . control over" — This Hebrew verb in the Hiphil (המשיל —
"to make rule") is almost unknown in the HB, but rather significant in this text
(see also 2:5 and 3:2) and throughout *Instruction* (at least 15 references in those
fragments).

Line 12:   "fickle" — The most common translation of חנף is "hypocrite."

Frag. 2

²[. . . be pu]rified from the guilt of the judgment of G[od] and from the
abo[minations . . .] ³[. . . a hypocr]ite, you shall not mix him in the midst of the
poo[r . . .] ⁴[. . .] and a pigeon together [. . .] a man [. . .] ⁵[. . . the po]or, do not
give him au[tho]rity [. . .] ⁶[. . .] he will n[ot] do [. . .]

Commentary

The subject of this column is hard to determine due to its fragmentary nature.
However, the vocabulary of the first line pointing to an interest in the subjects
of purity, guilt, and abomination suggests that there could be allusions to sacrificial law in this column.

Line 3:   "[. . . a hypocr]ite" — The inclusion of this term in material concerning the sin offering and the poor seems unusual. However, the reference in 1:4
proposing that the pious should not share a portion with the hypocrite points
to a line of division that could be relevant for this discussion as well. Note, for
example, 11Q19 xxxv:11-13: "for the sin offerings of the people and for their guilt
offerings, and all of them shall not be mixed one with another, for their places
shall be separated from one another so that the priests may not err with the sin
offering of the people."

Line 4:   "pigeon" — The mention of the pigeon may have relevance here since
birds could be substituted for more expensive livestock in both the burnt offering and the purification offering (Lev 5:7; 12:8; 14:21-22). The columbarium at
Mareshah in Israel and others that have been found scattered throughout the
land, including now Jerusalem, provide evidence of the rapid growth in the use
of pigeons during the Hellenistic period.

Line 5: "do not give him au[tho]rity" — See commentary to 1:10 above.

Frag. 3

¹and with a scale, he will not do his work. A man who judges before he examines and who trusts before [. . .] ²do not give him authority over those who pursue knowledge, for he will not adequately be able to discern the basis of their judgments for declaring the righteous to be righteous and the wicked to be wic[ked]. ³Also he will be despised. Do not send a man with blurred eyes to be the seer for the upright for [. . .] ⁴Do not send the hard of hearing to investigate a judgment, for a dispute between men he will not clarify, like one who scatters to the wind [. . .] ⁵that you will not separate, thus is the one who speaks to an ear that does not hear and reports to one fallen asleep, who slumbers in a spirit of [. . .] ⁶Do not send a man dull of heart to come up with thoughtful plans, for the wisdom of his heart is hidden and he has not mastered [it . . .] ⁷he has not found the skill of his hands. A man of insight will accept instruction. A man of knowledge obtains wisdom. ⁸A man of uprightness delights in justice. A man of truth rejo[ices in a pro]verb. A man of might will be zealous [. . .] ⁹and he is an adversary for all who remove the boundary. A man of compass[ion will mak]e justice for the poor [. . .] ¹⁰[. . .] He cares for all who lack wealth, the sons of righteousness [. . .] ¹¹[. . .] with all wealth [. . .]

Commentary

Line 2: "do not give him authority over" — See commentary to 1:10 above.

Line 2: "those who pursue knowledge" — See 4Q299 8:7; 4Q418 69ii:10-11. "Those who pursue righteousness" is an obvious reconstruction in 4Q298 1-2i:2 and closely related to 4Q298 3-4ii:7.

Line 2: "for declaring the righteous to be righteous and the wicked to be wic[ked.]" — See the use of this phrase in Deut 25:1, where it has a more obvious legal meaning in which the judges "acquit the righteous and convict the wicked." In Prov 17:15 the reversal of these judgments is considered an abomination to the Lord. In CD iv:7 it is listed as a characteristic of those forefathers who correctly interpreted the Torah. In the present text it appears to be more closely related to the latter meaning, indicating a level of knowledge available only to those who have developed a particular understanding of Israel. A clearly sectarian appropriation can be found in 4Q511 63iii:3-4, where we find items such as the following listed in parallel phrases: "the fulfillment of the deeds of the perfect of the way" and "to proclaim peace to all the men of the covenant."

Line 4: "clarify" — See 1:7 above ("make clear") for the use of this verb.

Line 5: "the one who speaks to an ear that does not hear" — See Isa 6:9-10. Note how this is interpreted in Matt 13:13 and Mark 4:11-12.

Line 9: "remove the boundary" — This phrase from Deut 19:14 and Prov 22:28, interpreted in the light of Hos 5:10, is employed to describe the opponents of the new covenant in the *Damascus Document* (CD i:16; v:20; xix:15-16; 4Q266 [Dᵃ] 1a-b:4). It is used to describe the manner in which the adherents of the new covenant are upholding an old standard that Israel ignored in the period of its unfaithfulness.

Beatitudes (4Q525)

Introduction

Content

This surprising text is already well known in the scholarly literature because we find near the beginning of the extant text a sequence of beatitudes (or macarisms) that are compared with those of Matthew 5. Recognized within this literary construction is the "man who has obtained wisdom" for "he has walked in the law of the Most High." While the description here focuses on wisdom, the attributes recognized are those which find their center in the study of Torah, somewhat analogous to the virtues of the study of law in Ben Sira. This thoroughgoing association of wisdom and law characterizes the first section of the composition. This initial section leads into a discussion of the pursuit of wisdom personified, analogous to 4Q185, which on the basis of the evidence in the fragments begins at 4Q525 5:5. It is the person who exhibits purity and zeal that attains her (i.e., wisdom). With frag. 10:3 the subject moves to a portrayal of judgment, presumably for those who acquiesce to the seductions of those who would pull Israelites away from wisdom, such as the seductress of 4Q184. Fragment 14 permits the contemporary reader to view the manner in which traditional wisdom formulations are interwoven with a dualistic worldview, informed by the blessings and curses of Deuteronomy. The movement to the mention of curses and a variety of serpents in frag. 15 suggests a more explicit description of judgment in the subsequent fragments, the model for which is the refining, hence purification, imagery of Ezek 22:17-22, as well as Isa 1:21-26 and other texts.

Manuscripts

There are 50 fragments from this one MS of this composition available in the Qumran corpus. Scholars interested in the NT are fortunate that one of the better-preserved portions of the MS is frags. 2 and 3, which contain the beatitudes after which the composition has been named. These fragments provide good evidence of the structure, if not all of the text, of that portion of the composition. Fragments 5, 14-15, and 23-24 provide substantive glimpses of the various sections of the material that made up this composition.

Recently Tigchelaar has identified in 5Q16 1,2,5 (previously "unidentified") a parallel text to 4Q525 15.[1] This identification provides evidence of a second MS for this composition among the Qumran finds.

Historical Context

The early Herodian or rustic semiformal script points to a paleographic date in the second half of the first century B.C.E. for the sole MS of this literary work.[2] Émile Puech proposes a date of composition prior to the Essene settlement at Qumran in the mid-second century B.C.E. after the authorship of Ben Sira and Daniel, hence 160-140 B.C.E.[3] This makes it part of a body of literature used by the sectarians at Qumran but not composed by them, hence missing some of the ideological features of those works.[4] This perspective on the Qumran wisdom literature is developed at greater length in the introduction to this volume. Counter to this view, Jacqueline de Roo has argued for its status as a sectarian document.[5] In her work we find arguments for placing this text closer to Qumran sectarian compositions than to traditional Jewish wisdom texts such as Proverbs and Ben Sira. The evidence cited in support of her hypothesis could also be used to support the viewpoint of Puech, since we do find similarities to sectarian texts in orthography, vocabulary, and teachings. While we can identify connections with the sectarian texts, there are no definitive "sectarian indicators" to mark this text as being of sectarian provenance.[6]

---

1. Tigchelaar, "Lady Folly and Her House," *RevQ* 23 (2008): 371-81.
2. Charlesworth, "Qumran Beatitudes," 14; Brooke, *Dead Sea Scrolls,* 218.
3. Note also Fabry, "Seligpreisungen," 194-95.
4. Puech, "Collection of Beatitudes," 354; DJD 25:116-19.
5. De Roo, "Is 4Q525 a Qumran Sectarian Document?"
6. See also Sidnie White Crawford, "Lady Wisdom and Dame Folly at Qumran," *DSD* 5 (1998): 355-66; Armin Lange, "Die Weisheitstexte aus Qumran: Eine Einleitung," in *Wisdom Texts from Qumran,* ed. Hempel et al., 29; Benjamin G. Wright III, "Wisdom and the Women of Qumran," *DSD* 11 (2004): 249.

Literary Questions

Title

While the macarisms of frag. 2 are the best-known portion of this text, it is not clear that they define its character as a totality. Hence the title "Beatitudes" may not be the best description of a work that is clearly a wisdom composition according to its self-description in its opening words and its content, particularly of its initial sections. As discussed below, macarisms are to be found as an integral part of wisdom literature, though they form a limited portion of the extant fragments. In an effort to describe the more extensive wisdom orientation of this work, Elisha Qimron has dubbed it "The Words of Solomon," based on the reconstruction of frag. 1, "[Words of Solomon, which he spo]ke. . . ." See the commentary to that fragment below.[7]

Biblical Wisdom Context

This composition is clearly a wisdom text. The macarism itself appears most frequently in wisdom literature, though it is not confined to that genre. Proverbs clearly provides the model (e.g., 5:7; 7:24; 8:32) for the structural features introducing sections of the composition, many of them partially reconstructed: 4Q525 1:1; 2ii+3:12; 5:5; 10:3; 13:6; 14ii:18; 31:1. The opening section of the work also appears to reflect the influence of the same biblical model.

The personification of wisdom is already found in biblical texts, most notably Proverbs 1, 8–9. In Second Temple texts it is also evident in Sirach 24; Bar 3:9–4:4; Wis 7:7–9:18; and Sir 51:13-30//11Q5 (11QPs[a]Sirach). In Qumran texts we find this feature in 4Q185, and presumably in 4Q184 and 11QPs[a] xxvi ("Hymn to the Creator").[8] In the first ten fragments of this text, Wisdom is a very lively and interactive figure. The novice desires her and seeks after her. Those who fear God will keep her ways and walk in her statutes, and also not despise her discipline.

Wisdom and Torah

The solid identification of wisdom with Torah ("law") is characteristic of extant portions of this composition. This is clear from its first preserved lines:

---

7. Qimron, "Improving the Editions," 137-38.

8. In contrast to Elgvin, I do not think it is evident in 4Q421 1aii-b:9-10 (DJD 20:190), even though he describes these texts in the context of hypostatization rather than personification. Following James Crenshaw I prefer the latter term because I think it more accurately describes the phenomenon in biblical and postbiblical Jewish literature (ABD 6:926).

"Blessed is the man who has obtained wisdom. He has walked in the law of the Most High and prepared his heart for her ways" (2ii+3:3-4). In wisdom literature the idea of "walking in the way" is a common description (Prov 1:15; 2:20), so here the wisdom phrase is applied to the law. Both of the Hebrew terms for "way" (דרך and אורח) are common descriptors of the moral dimensions of wisdom in Proverbs. The reader must interpret the third feminine singular pronoun and suffix to refer to both wisdom and Torah throughout the first section, up to 10:3. In this composition they are the same. The best-known identification of wisdom with Torah is found in Sir 24:23. This same identification in Bar 4:1 provides the climax for the wisdom poem of Bar 3:9–4:4. This identification is also evident in Ps 154:12, a sapiential hymn labeled as Syriac Psalm II, also identified in 11Q5 (Psalms[a]) xviii. The explicit identification in *Beatitudes* reflects the developing role of Torah in Second Temple Judaism.[9]

This feature is in remarkable contrast with a number of other wisdom texts in this collection that do not highlight or even mention Torah.[10] The most notable case is *Instruction,* where it does not appear. In *Mysteries* it is found only in one limited fragment that permits no interpretation of context (1Q27 5:2). There is also no reference in 4Q420-421. 4Q525 makes a connection with some traditions in Second Temple Judaism other than those represented in these compositions. John Strugnell notes, however, only the rare appearance of purity language in 4Q525, a feature often coupled with legal traditions.[11] This absence of reference to legal traditions is a feature shared with biblical wisdom texts and a number of the wisdom compositions in this collection.

The Macarism Form

The macarisms of frags. 2ii+3 are an important find for the study of the development of that genre of literature. The term "macarism" derives from Greek μακάριος, the translation of Hebrew אשרי, both meaning "happy, blessed." A particular conduct or quality of the person is mentioned that is considered praiseworthy or "blessed."[12] "Beatitude" is the more popular term that has been attached to this form, best known in Western literature from its usage in Matt

9. See de Roo, "Is 4Q525 a Qumran Sectarian Document?" 339-40.

10. In *1 Enoch* "Law and its interpretation are embodied in the notion of revealed 'wisdom'" (George W. E. Nickelsburg, *1 Enoch 1: A Commentary on the Book of 1 Enoch, Chapters 1–36; 81–108* [Hermeneia; Minneapolis: Fortress, 2001], 50).

11. John Strugnell, "The Smaller Hebrew Wisdom Texts Found at Qumran: Variations, Resemblances, and Lines of Development," in *Wisdom Texts from Qumran,* ed. Hempel et al., 50.

12. On this form see the survey article by Raymond F. Collins, "Beatitudes," *ABD* 1:629-31; Fabry, "Seligpreisungen," 189-200.

5:3-12. The HB contains forty-five macarisms, most of which are found in the Psalms and wisdom literature. These are almost all in the third person (e.g., Prov 3:13; 8:32, 34; 14:21; 16:20; 20:7; 28:14; 29:18). A similar picture emerges in Second Temple literature (note Sir 14:1, 2, 20; 25:8, 9; 26:1; 28:19; 31:8; 34:17; 48:11; 50:28). Outside the canonical literature we also find this form in apocalyptic literature (e.g., *1 En.* 58:2; 81:4; 82:4; 99:10; 103:5; *2 En.* 41:2; 42:6-14; 44:4; 48:9; 52:1-14; 61:3; 62:1; 66:7). Within the Qumran literature the form finds limited attestation outside 4Q525. It is found in a number of biblical quotations: 4Q163 23ii:9 (Isa 30:18); 4Q173 3:1 (Ps 127:5); 4Q174 1-2i:14 (Ps 1:1). All of these are interpretive texts of the pesher type. It is also found in the single fragment of 4Q528 5. Puech has proposed the reconstruction of the term אשרי in 1QH[a] vi:13-16 to make it a macarism with some similarities to both 4Q525 and Matthew 5.[13] In some text editions this is listed as vi:2-5 (e.g., *DSSSE* 1:152-53). This reconstruction does not find support in the more recent publication of the text (DJD 40:89-90). The most significant additional text employing this literary feature is 4Q185 1-2ii:8-15. In this text it also is used to describe the benefits derived from paying attention to "her," that is, wisdom.

The relationship of the macarisms in this text, 2ii+3:1-10, to Matt 5:3-12 is the question that has occasioned the most discussion of this composition. 4Q525 consists of four focused macarisms followed by a fifth lengthy concluding section that summarizes and clarifies the point of these texts, that is, that the "good life" is available to the person who has attained wisdom, who walks in the law of the Most High. Matt 5:3-12 consists of eight focused macarisms followed by a ninth that develops at greater length the point of the literary section, that the blessed are those who endure revulsion, persecution, and false testimony "on my account." Puech proposes on the basis of word count that four macarisms were present in the unpreserved bottom of frag. 2i.[14] The reconstruction of the first "blessed" does seem well informed based on its parallel structure with the following lines. However, the suggestion of George Brooke that the difference between 4 + 1 and 8 + 1 may be more a matter of poetics than distinct literary structure should be considered.[15] The parallel construction of four or eight macarisms plus in each case a lengthy concluding construction makes a more convincing case for some similarities in literary structure than the addition of four unattested macarisms. Within the NT the parallel text to Matt 5:3-12 is Luke 6:20-23 followed by the woes in vv. 24-30. The Lukan version has often been regarded as closer to the original Q version. The identification

---

13. Puech, "Hymne essénien," 59-88.
14. Puech, "Collection of Beatitudes," 361.
15. Brooke, *Dead Sea Scrolls*, 221.

of some remarkable similarities in the Matthean version to the macarisms in 4Q525 makes the hypothesis that Matthew 5 is a scribal reworking of the Lukan text much more doubtful. Whether either version is derivative directly from the other is now open to question.[16] While Sir 14:20-27 also appears in discussions of this text, it must be noted that this text is structured as one extended macarism with eight sections.

Wisdom and Apocalyptic

The foregoing discussion of the macarism demonstrates the interaction of wisdom and apocalyptic literature. Examples were cited from the books of *1 Enoch* as well as Proverbs. The literary form of the macarism is present in both bodies of literature. Within both collections of macarisms, the eschatological emphases are most evident in the extended conclusions. Within 4Q525 we see that the eschatological interests demonstrated in the fragmentary evidence for the composition after 4Q525 10:3 could suggest connections to apocalyptic literature as well as, or even more likely than, wisdom literature. This feature is particularly evident in the fragmentary remains of cols. 15 and 23, even though these themes are predominant in the vocabulary of the fragments with the section that begins with 10:3 and continues through at least frag. 28. The first few fragments of this section seem to reflect those who will be judged positively. This eschatological material in a wisdom text that continues to betray evidence of wisdom vocabulary and literary structure throughout this section reflects the innovative nature of the wisdom material from Qumran in Second Temple Judaism. The limited references in Prov 11:4 to the day of judgment and in Sir 5:7-8 to the time of vengeance and the day of wrath do not suggest that this material is at home in other Jewish wisdom literature of the era.[17]

The extended woes of *1 En.* 98:9–99:16 interspersed with a macarism in 99:10 have some similarities to the themes of 4Q525 2ii+3 and to the composition as a whole.[18] There is a good deal of emphasis on the judgment and destruction of the foolish who do not listen to the words of the wise. In this section the foolish will be delivered into the hands of the righteous, who "will cut off your necks, and they will kill you, and they will not spare you" (*1 En.* 98:12).

---

16. Ibid., 223-24.

17. De Roo, "Is 4Q525 a Qumran Sectarian Document?" 343-44. She notes that the "high concentration of eschatological elements is not typical of traditional Jewish wisdom literature" (p. 345).

18. George W. E. Nickelsburg, "The Epistle of Enoch and the Qumran Literature," *JJS* 33 (1982): 333-48; idem, "Revisiting the Rich and the Poor in *1 Enoch* 92-105 and the Gospel According to Luke," *SBLSP* 37 (2 vols.; Atlanta: Scholars Press, 1998), 2:579-95.

In contrast, the softer language of the macarism in 4Q525 2ii emphasizes "seeking" and "obtaining" wisdom, not forgetting and abandoning her, and conducting oneself according to her ways. This significant issue encountered within the trajectory of wisdom texts of the Qumran corpus is discussed at greater length in the introduction to this volume.

The literary form continues to appear in later Jewish literature. One text that is of interest to Qumran studies is the Wisdom text from the Cairo Genizah. While it has been demonstrated that it is not connected directly with the literary evidence from Qumran, it does provide examples of the continuing use of the אשרי form with the explicit connection of wisdom and Torah (3:15-16; 8:6; 9:2; 15:13).[19]

Key Terms

A number of key terms in this composition bear discussion because they represent the particular character of this composition or of its context in wisdom literature of the Qumran corpus. Note in particular the number of terms that bear similarities in usage with *Instruction*.[20]

מבין ("man of discernment")

The addressee is the מבין ("man of discernment"), the primary figure in *Instruction* as well.[21] This designation in 14ii:18 indicates this addressee with a typical wisdom form of address. The use of the phrase "and now . . . listen to me" connects it with Proverbs, though in that composition it appears in the plural (Prov 5:7; 7:24; 8:32). However, those three references within the book of Proverbs appear in the context of Proverbs 1–9, whose primary addressee is "my son" in the singular. In *Instruction* the singular term is prefaced by אתה ("you") rather than עתה ("now"), characteristic of the phrase in this composition and in Proverbs. The plural form as it is used in Proverbs can be found in 2ii+3:12 and probably in

19. G. Wilhelm Nebe, "Die wiederentdeckte Weisheitsschrift aus der Kairoer Geniza und ihre 'Nähe' zum Schrifttum von Qumran und zu Essenern," in *New Qumran Texts and Studies: Proceedings of the First Meeting of the International Organization for Qumran Studies, Paris 1992* (ed. George J. Brooke; STDJ 15; Leiden: Brill, 1994), 244. For the text see Klaus Berger, *Die Weisheitsschrift aus der Kairoer Geniza: Erstedition, Kommentar und Übersetzung* (2d ed.; TANZ 1; Tübingen: Francke, 1996).

20. For a more extensive comparison of the vocabulary of 4Q525 and *Instruction*, see Strugnell, "Smaller Hebrew Wisdom Texts," 50-52.

21. 4Q416 4:3; 4Q417 1i:1, 14, 18; 4Q418 81+81a:15; 102a+b:3; 123ii:5; 168:4; 176:3. The title appears without context in 4Q299 34:3; 4Q417 1iii:10; 4Q418 117:2; 158:4; 227:1; 273:1; 4Q418a 7:2, 3. 4Q418 17:2 may be a reference to the בן מבין ("son of discernment"). In the plural it is found in 4Q415 11:5; 4Q418 2,2a-c:8; 123ii:4; 221:3.

13:6 and 31:1. Perhaps it should also be reconstructed in 5:5. It would appear that the interchange of plural and singular, which characterizes this composition, is evident in earlier portions of the biblical wisdom tradition, such as Proverbs 1–9.[22] This interchange of number is evident in the macarisms of 2ii, where the first and the last are singular while the three in the center are plural. Note also that 10:3 is in the plural while 10:6 is singular. While 11-12:2 is in the plural, 31:2 is singular. This suggests that the "man of discernment" is the consistent addressee throughout the document, but that these instructions were written for the edification of a group of persons so designated.[23] This would mean that the נבונים ("those who have understanding") of 5:10 and 16:3 are references to the same circle of addressees. The same body of persons is addressed in 2ii-3:12 as "sons."[24] This corporate dimension to the task of acquiring and embracing wisdom seems to distinguish it from biblical wisdom as found in Proverbs. See the introduction to *Instruction* for further discussion of this term.

יחד ("together")

Another term used in a manner similar to *Instruction* is the adverb "together," the same term that in nominal form comes to designate the "community" in the *Community Rule* and its Cave 4 MSS (4Q255-264), 1QSa, and other sectarian texts.[25] It appears to be a significant term in these compositions, and perhaps in *Mysteries,* far exceeding its utilization in the HB. See DJD 34:25 and commentary to 4Q416 2iii:21. Terms such as this one suggest a particular connection between these wisdom texts from the Qumran corpus.

התהלך ("walk together")

Note the presence of this phrase in 4Q416 2iii:21 and 4Q525 14ii:15 (see 1QS 4:18). This use of the Hitpael form is characteristic of *Instruction* and this text as well as some of the rules texts. In this text it occurs at 2ii+3:3; 5:5, 9; 14ii:13, 15; 21:5; 27:2. Brooke cites the connection of the verb הלך ("walk") to halakic exe-

22. See Harrington, *Wisdom Texts from Qumran,* 68-69. He suggests that the addressee, "man of discernment," begins at least with frag. 14, rather than recognizing the interchange of singular and plural addressees throughout the composition. Note also the assumption in the statement of Strugnell and Harrington that 4Q525 is addressed to plural מבינים ("men of discernment") (DJD 34:3 n. 1).

23. On the rhetorical significance of this figure see Benjamin G. Wright III, "From Generation to Generation: The Sage as Father in Early Jewish Literature," in *Biblical Traditions in Transmission,* ed. Hempel and Lieu, 319-21.

24. For a slightly different emphasis see Goff, *Discerning Wisdom,* 208.

25. In *Instruction* it is found in 4Q415 9:7; 11:4; 4Q416 2iii:21; 2iv:5; 4Q418 103ii:9; 167a+b:5, 6; 199:1; 4Q418a 13:1. It is found in 4Q525 2ii+3:8; 14ii:9, 15, 16, 27; 22:3. See also 4Q299 20:3.

gesis, "seeking wisdom and walking in her ways."[26] See my discussion under "Key Terms" in the introduction to *Instruction*.

Bibliography

Note also the bibliography in the introduction to this volume.

Brooke, George J. *The Dead Sea Scrolls and the New Testament*, 217-34. Minneapolis: Fortress, 2005. Revised edition of "The Wisdom of Matthew's Beatitudes (4QBéat) and Mt. 5.3-12." *ScrB* 19 (1988-89): 35‐41.

Charlesworth, James H. "The Qumran Beatitudes (4Q525) and the New Testament (Mt 5:3-11, Lk 6:20-26)." *RHPR* 80 (2000): 13-35.

De Roo, Jacqueline C. R. "Is 4Q525 a Qumran Sectarian Document?" in *The Scrolls and the Scriptures: Qumran Fifty Years After.* Ed. Stanley E. Porter and Craig A. Evans, 338-67. Roehampton Institute London Papers 3; JSPSup 26. Sheffield: Sheffield Academic Press, 1997.

Fabry, Heinz-Josef. "Der Makarismus — mehr als nur eine weisheitliche Lehrform: Gedanken zu dem neu-edierten Text 4Q525." In *Alttestamentlicher Glaube und Biblische Theologie: Festschrift für Horst Dietrich Preuss zum 65. Geburtstag.* Ed. Jutta Hausmann and Hans-Jürgen Zobel, 362-71. Stuttgart: Kohlhammer, 1992.

————. "Die Seligpreisungen in der Bibel und in Qumran." In *Wisdom Texts from Qumran.* Ed. Hempel et al., 189-200.

Hengel, Martin. "Zur matthäischen Bergpredigt und ihrem jüdischen Hintergrund." In *Judaica, Hellenistica et Christiana: Kleine Schriften II* (WUNT 109; Tübingen: Mohr Siebeck, 1999), 219-92. Originally published in *TRu* 52, no. 4 (1987): 327-400.

Lichtenberger, Hermann. "Makarismen in den Qumrantexten und im Neuen Testament." In *Wisdom and Apocalypticism.* Ed. García Martínez, 395-411.

————. "Makarisms in Matthew 5:3ff. in Their Jewish Context." In *The Sermon on the Mount and Its Jewish Setting.* Ed. Hans-Jürgen Becker and Serge Ruzer, 40-56. CahRB 60. Paris: Gabalda, 2005.

Puech, Émile. "525. 4QBéatitudes." DJD 25:115-78.

————. "4Q525 et les péricopes des Béatitudes in Ben Sira et Matthieu." *RB* 98 (1991): 80-106.

————. "The Collection of Beatitudes in Hebrew and in Greek (4Q525 1-4 and Mt 5, 3-12)." In *Early Christianity in Context: Monuments and Documents.* Ed.

26. George Brooke, "Biblical Interpretation in the Wisdom Texts from Qumran," in *Wisdom Texts from Qumran*, ed. Hempel et al., 209, 218.

F. Manns and E. Alliata, 353-68. Jerusalem: Franciscan Publishing House, 1993.

———. "Un hymne essénien en partie retrouvé et les Béatitudes: 1QH[a] V 12-VI 18 (=col. XIII-XIV 7) et 4QBéat.," *RevQ* 13 (1988): 59-88.

Qimron, Elisha. "Improving the Editions of the Dead Sea Scrolls." In *Meghillot: Studies in the Dead Sea Scrolls*. Vol. 1. Ed. Moshe Bar-Asher and Devorah Dimant, vi (English abstract), 135-44 (Hebrew). Jerusalem: Bialik, 2003.

Tigchelaar, Eibert. "Lady Folly and Her House in Three Qumran Manuscripts: On the Relation between 4Q525 15, 5Q16, and 4Q184 1." *RevQ* 23 (2008): 371-81.

Viviano, Benedict. "Eight Beatitudes at Qumran and in Matthew? A New Publication from Cave Four." *SEÅ* 58 (1993): 71-84.

Text

Frag. 1

[1][. . . which he spo]ke with the wisdom that Go[d] gave to [him . . .] [2][. . . to kno]w wisdom and instru[ction], to make insightful [. . .] [3][. . .] to increase [knowledge . . .]

Commentary

Line 1:   Puech points out similarities of this opening section to Prov 1:1-4 and 7 and proposes that the line could be reconstructed on that model: "Words/proverbs of David (/Solomon, son of David,) which he spoke/wrote . . ." (DJD 25:121). This reconstruction also assumes the tradition that David and his son Solomon composed an equal number of hymnic, liturgical, and sapiential compositions, 4,050 in each case (1 Kgs 4:29-32 and 11Q5 xxvii:2-11).[27] Since neither David nor Solomon is mentioned elsewhere in the preserved text, the argument for their inclusion is not self-evident.

Line 3:   "to increase [knowledge . . .]" — See 4Q298 3-4ii:4-8, in which this infinitive is characteristic of the description of the virtues listed there.

27. Puech, "Collection of Beatitudes," 353-54; idem, DJD 25:121. The totals do not necessarily add up; see idem, "11QPsAp[a]: un rituel d'exorcismes. Essai de reconstruction," *RevQ* 14, no. 3 (1990): 399 n. 22.

Frag. 2, col. i

⁴[. . .] its [wa]ys [. . .]

Commentary

Line 4: "[wa]ys" — A significant term that establishes connection with both the wisdom tradition and descriptions of the emerging sectarian self-consciousness.

Frags. 2+3, col. ii

[Blessed is he who seeks her] ¹with a pure heart, he does not slander with his tongue. Blessed are those who hold fast to her statutes, they do not hold fast to ²the ways of injustice. Bles[sed] are those who rejoice in her, they do not spout forth the ways of folly. Blessed are those who seek her ³with pure hands, they do not search for her with a deceitful heart. Blessed is the man who has obtained wisdom. He walks ⁴in the law of the Most High and prepares his heart for her ways. He conducts himself according to her discipline and in her corrections he delights daily. ⁵He does not leave her unheeded during the afflictions of his distress, in the time of hardship he does not abandon her, he does not forget her in the days of dread, ⁶and in the affliction of his soul he does not abhor her. For on her he meditates daily and in his distress he considers [her . . . and througho]ut ⁷his living through her [he gains insight and he places her] before his eyes so as not to walk in the ways of [injustice . . .] ⁸[. . .] together and he makes his heart perfect toward her [. . .] ⁹[. . . A crown of pure g]old [she places upon] his [hea]d and with kings she se[ats him . . .] ¹⁰[with] his [sc]epter over [. . .] brothers he shall separ[ate . . .] ¹¹[. . .]

¹²Now, sons, li[sten to me and do n]ot turn asid[e from . . .] ¹³[. . .] evil [of . . .]

Notes

Line 1:   This reconstruction seems reasonable based on the form and structure of the macarism.

Line 7:   "[he gains insight and he places her] before his eyes" — For this reconstruction see Puech (DJD 25:125). The latter portion is based on Ps 101:3.

Line 10: "[sc]epter over [. . .] brothers" — Puech proposes a reconstruction in the lacuna employing the word "droiture" or "uprightness" (מישרים). While some correlation between the words שבט ("scepter") and מישר ("uprightness") can be found in Ps 45:7, this biblical text does not account for the preposition על ("over") between the two terms.

Commentary

Line 1: "[Blessed is he who seeks her] with a pure heart, he does not slander with his tongue" — This reconstruction is based on Ps 24:4-6, which refers to "clean hands and pure hearts" in v. 4, found in this macarism as a possible inclusio in lines 1 and 3. Ps 24:4 includes reference to the "deceit" found in line 3, and the two verbs used for "seek" (דרש and מבקש) are both found in Ps 24:6. Émile Puech rather points to Pss 51:12 and 15:1-2 (DJD 25:124). The reference to 4Q185 1-2ii:13-14 with regard to slander and a deceitful spirit are also of note with regard to this line. See also Ps 37:29-31, "The mouth of the righteous utters wisdom, and his tongue speaks right." While in v. 29 "the righteous shall inherit the land," in Ps 37:11 "the meek shall inherit the land," thereby pointing to Matt 5:5.

Line 1: "pure heart" — See Matt 5:8. Note also Ps 24:4, which refers both to "clean hands and pure hearts," the former found at the beginning of line 3 in this text.

Line 1: "Blessed are those who hold fast to her statutes" — See Prov 3:18. On the verb תמך ("hold fast") see also *Mysteries*: 4Q299 3aii-b:9; 6ii:4; 43:2; 4Q300 8:5; 4Q301 1:2.

Line 2: "ways of injustice" — A likely restoration in line 7 below. Hebrew עולה is also found in 5:11. The expression "ways of injustice" does not appear in the HB but is found in 1QH[a] vi:37 in the singular. "Injustice" is not a common term in the HB but is rather significant in the *Community Rule* (1QS iv:9, 17, 18, 19, 20, 23, 24; viii:10; x:20) and the *Hodayot* (1QH[a] vi:26, 36, 37; vii:38; viii:29; ix:38; x:5; xiii:10; xiv:14[?], 21[?]; xv:39; xix:25, 29; xxi:30, 35; xxiv:30; xxv:8).[28]

Line 2: "Bles[sed] are those who rejoice in her" — See Ps 1:2: "in the law of the Lord is his delight."

---

28. De Roo, "Is 4Q525 a Qumran Sectarian Document?" 348. I have edited the list of references to reflect the text of 1QH[a] in DJD 40.

Lines 2-3: "ways of folly" and "a deceitful heart" are the opposite of what emerge from the tongues and hearts of the righteous and the wise in Prov 12:5, 17, 20; 14:8, 18. "Folly" is a particular concern in *Instruction* (4Q415 9:5; 4Q416 2ii:3; 4Q417 1i:7; 4Q418 220:3; 243:2; 4Q423 5:7) and in Proverbs.

Lines 2-3: "Blessed are those who seek . . . they do not search . . ." See Matt 5:6, "Blessed are those who hunger and thirst for righteousness," which points to a similar level of desire.

Line 3: "pure hands" — This phrase can be found in 1QS ix:15 in the instructions for the sage listing the criteria by which he would judge the sons of Zadok.

Lines 3-4: "walks in the law of the Most High" — On the term "walk" see the discussion of "Key Terms" in the introduction to this text as well as in the introduction to this volume. Note the manner in which the tetragrammaton as the name for God is replaced with some alternate form of address.[29]

Lines 3-4: The identification of wisdom with law ("Torah") is discussed among the "Literary Questions" in the introduction to this text. What is noteworthy about this identification is that it is not accompanied by an interest in the details of legal literature or the purity legislation known from the biblical and postbiblical materials. In this manner it closely resembles the wisdom orientation of 4Q185 i (see the commentary to 4Q185 i:13–ii:3 above) and Ben Sira.

Line 4: "her corrections" (יסוריה) — יסורים is not biblical,[30] found elsewhere only in this composition (5:11) and in the sectarian texts in the MSS of the *Damascus Document,* the *Community Rule,* and once in the *Hodayot.* It is more common in rabbinic literature.

Line 6: "affliction of his soul" — See 1QS iii:8. The consonants ענות here can mean either "humility" (עֲנְוַת) or "affliction" (עֱנוּת), as in Ps 22:25 (BDB 776). "Humility" fits the context of 10:4 and 14ii:20 as well as probably 27:1.[31]

Line 6: "on her he meditates daily" — See Ps 1:2.

---

29. Strugnell, "Smaller Hebrew Wisdom Texts," 34-35, 38, 50-51, 53, 57; Brooke, "Biblical Interpretation," 218.

30. A word with the same letters appears in Job 40:2, but its meaning in context is hard to determine.

31. Contra de Roo, "Is 4Q525 a Qumran Sectarian Document?" 348-49 n. 27.

Line 6:   "meditates" — הגה appears in this composition at 14ii:19 as well and is also found in 4Q417 1i:6//4Q418 43,44,45i:4 with regard to the mystery of existence. It appears to reflect the same root as the חזון הגוי ("vision of insight") "for the memorial book" in 4Q417 1i:16-17, and the ספר הגוי ("book of insight") referred to in CD x:6; xiii:2; xiv:7-8; 1QSa i:7.

Line 6:   "in his distress he considers [her . . .]" — Brooke points out that this text's relationship to the response to persecution does not derive directly from a scriptural model such as Job, but is more akin to the eschatological anguish and affliction of Daniel 12.[32]

Line 8:   "together" — See discussion under "Literary Questions" in the introduction.

Line 10:   "he shall separ[ate . . .]" — הפריד appears a number of times in *Instruction*: 4Q415 11:11; 4Q416 2iv:3, 4; 4Q418 37:4; 172:8; 235:2. In most Qumran texts the concept of separation and division is rather designated through use of terms from the root בדל.

Line 12:   "Now, sons, li[sten to me]" — This wisdom injunction, found in Prov 5:7; 7:24; 8:32, is also evident in 4Q525 13:6; 14ii:18; 31:1. The indebtedness of the *Damascus Document* to this wisdom tradition is evident in CD i:1; ii:2, 14. Note the discussion of "Literary Questions" in the introduction.

Frag. 2, col. iii

[1]will compare with her. The entire day [. . .] [2]she shall not be obtained by gold o[r silver . . .] [3]with any precious stones [. . .] [4]he will be like her in the form of his face [. . .] [5]purple blossoms with [. . .] [6]scarlet with all the garments of [. . .] [7]with gold and pearls [. . .]

Commentary

Line 1:   "will compare with her" — The use of the verb שוה ("be equal to") with reference to wisdom is found in Prov 3:15 and 8:11. In both those chapters wisdom is better than silver or gold as well as pearls (or precious stones).

32. Brooke, "Biblical Interpretation," 219.

Line 3: "precious stones" — Found in Isa 54:12, this phrase also appears in the *War Rule* (1QM v:6, 9, 14; xii:13). In all instances these stones adorn objects of a protective nature, that is, walls, shields, spears, and swords.

Line 5: "purple blossoms" — This phrase suggests that this description of wisdom also finds some basis in Song of Songs imagery, since the word נצי ("blossoms") is found in the HB only in Song 2:12 (see also Song 3:10).

Line 6: While we cannot determine the full sentence here, the column continues to talk about the manner in which wisdom exceeds all human parallels and desires, a theme carried on in the following line.

Frag. 4

²[. . .] all [. . .] ³[. . .] by the priests of [. . .]

Frag. 5

²[. . .] you shall not abandon her in the time of ha[rd]sh[ip] ³[. . .] her trials [. . .] ⁴[. . .]

⁵[And now, sons, listen to me . . . in p]urity wa[lk . . .] ⁶[. . .] in tr[uth]. You shall n[ot] seek her with an ev[il] heart [. . .] ⁷her ways[. . . .] You shall not s[ee]k her with a deceitful heart and with the stat[utes . . . you shall not] ⁸[ab]andon to stra[ngers] your [port]ion nor your lot to foreigners, for the wis[e . . .] ⁹[they] will give insight with sweetness. Those who fear God will keep her ways and they will walk in [. . .] ¹⁰her statutes. Her reproofs they will not despise. Those who have understanding obtain [. . .] ¹¹those who walk perfectly turn aside injustice and her corrections they will not despise[. . . .] ¹²they will bear. The cunning will delve into her ways and in her depths [. . .] ¹³they will consider. Those who love God will be attentive to her and in the wa[ys of . . .]

Commentary

Line 2: "time of ha[rd]sh[ip]" — See 2ii+3:5 above.

Line 5: "[And now, sons, listen to me . . .]" — The change in topic and form suggests a new paragraph, which would normally be designated in this manner in this text. This is a familiar form of introduction in biblical wisdom literature (e.g., Prov 5:7; 7:24; 8:32). In the wisdom texts from Qumran we find adaptations of it (4Q185 1-2i:13; 4Q298 1-2i:2; 3-4ii:4). The form is important for the *Damascus Document* (CD i:1; ii:2, 14). In this text it can be seen in some form in 4Q525 2ii+3:12; 13:6; 14ii:18; 31:1. Note the discussion of "Literary Questions" in the introduction.

Line 5: "wa[lk...]" — On the term "walk" see the discussion of "Key Terms" in the introduction to this text as well as in the introduction to this volume.

Line 9: "sweetness" — This term, rare in both Biblical Hebrew and in the Qumran materials, applies to speech, perhaps meaning "eloquence" in Prov 16:21, and to the advice of a friend in Prov 27:9. Prov 27:9-11 concerns the value of relationships with "friends," one of the terms that applies to fellow members of the sect in the texts of the *Community Rule* and *Damascus Document*.

Line 10: "her reproofs" — In the Second Temple legal traditions, this seems to be a more appropriate translation of Hebrew תוכחת than "chastisement."[33] See also commentary to 13:3 below. For further discussion on this important topic in Qumran texts see commentary to 4Q417 2i:1-6 (see also bibliography cited there) and 4Q421 1aii-b:11-12.

Line 10: "Her reproofs they will not despise" — To despise or hate reproof is listed as a characteristic of the wicked a number of times in Proverbs (3:11; 12:1; 15:10, 32). In Prov 15:10 that person will die. In this text paying attention to reproof is a characteristic of those who walk in the way of wisdom and Torah.

Line 11: "walk perfectly" — A rare phrase in the HB, found in Prov 28:18, but rather important to sectarian compositions from Qumran. The language of perfection is common in the *Damascus Document* and pervades the *Community Rule* as well as the Cave 4 fragments of both compositions. Its presence in the *Temple Scroll*, a composition that is not necessarily sectarian, demonstrates even more clearly its centrality for the legal traditions valued in the literature of the Qumran corpus. References to the "perfect of the way," also found in Prov 11:20, and to walking in perfection appear to be significant in the *Songs of the*

33. De Roo, "Is 4Q525 a Qumran Sectarian Document?" 349-50. She also assumes this to be a construct form of תוכחה, rather than a form of the related substantive תוכחת. On this see BDB 407; and *HALOT* s.v. תוכחה and תוכחת.

Sabbath Sacrifice.[34] On the term "walk" see the discussion of "Key Terms" in the introduction to this text as well as in the introduction to the volume.

Line 11:   "injustice" — See commentary to 2ii+3:2 above.

Line 11:   "her corrections" — יסורים is not biblical, found elsewhere only in this composition (2ii+3:4) and in the sectarian texts in the MSS of the *Damascus Document,* the *Community Rule,* and once in the *Hodayot.* It is more common in rabbinic literature.

Line 12:   "delve into her ways" — See also 4Q418 55:3 for this phrase, which is not found in biblical texts.

Line 12:   "in her depths" — מעמקים is employed negatively in Ezek 27:34; Ps 69:2, 14; 130:1, all referring to the depths of the sea. In 4Q184 1:6 the "depths" are indicative of the extent of the depravity of the evil seductress as it goes on to enumerate the manner in which she is "the origin of all of the ways of perversity" (4Q184 1:8). However, this text appears to use Isa 51:10 to reverse this understanding when the question is asked, "who made the depths of the sea a way for the redeemed to cross over?"

Line 13:   "be attentive" — While the Hiphil of צנע has traditionally been translated "be humble," other meanings seem more likely (*HALOT* s.v. צנע). The more common term for humility in the Qumran scrolls, ענוה, also occurs in this composition at 10:4; 14ii:20; 27:1. See commentary to 2ii+3:6.

Frag. 6, col. ii

[1]an an[sw]er and she is zealous without [. . .] [2]not to gain understanding from a spirit that le[ads astray . . .] [3]knowledge from a weakened spirit [. . .] [4]a blessing and she causes to stumble witho[ut . . .] [5]is certain and she produces without [. . . without] [6]arrogance and she exalts without [. . .]

34. See Brent A. Strawn with Henry W. Morisanda Rietz, "(More) Sectarian Terminology in the *Songs of the Sabbath Sacrifice*: The Case of תמימי דרך," in *Qumran Studies: New Approaches, New Questions* (ed. Michael Thomas Davis and Brent A. Strawn; Grand Rapids: Eerdmans, 2007), 53-64.

Notes

None of the letters at the end of col. i make even a complete word.

Commentary

The apparent subject of this very fragmentary column is wisdom personified or a female figure. On the basis of the remainder of the composition, the former option is more likely. The fragmentary lines make more sense if a feminine subject is assumed for most of the surviving portions of this column. It appears to be some listing of the virtues of this figure, developing them in contrast to certain negative traits.

Line 2: "le[ads astray . . .]" — This term is partially reconstructed and could be from either the root תעע, "to mock," or תעה, "to go astray." The latter term is much more common throughout the Qumran scrolls, particularly in the *Damascus Document,* as well as in the fragments of that composition.[35]

Line 3: "weakened spirit" — In rabbinic literature מהל, here in participial form, comes to mean "circumcise."[36] That meaning does not seem to fit the context here but rather points to the kind of weakness that comes from mixing or dilution, as in Isa 1:22.

Frag. 7

[1][. . .] glorifi[es without . . .] [2][. . .] without being certain [. . .] [3][. . .] without [. . .] [4][. . .] from the inclination of the intentio[ns of . . .] [5][. . .] from a troubled spirit [. . .]

Commentary

This fragment appears to continue the literary pattern and content of frag. 6.

---

35. Note the discussion of this term by Nickelsburg, *1 Enoch 1,* 486-88.

36. Antoon Schoors, "The Language of the Qumran Sapiential Works," in *Wisdom Texts from Qumran,* ed. Hempel et al., 84.

Frag. 8

[1][. . .] she keeps watch without [. . .] [2][. . .] from the utterance of the spirit [her] lip[s . . .] [3][. . . judgment, destruction [. . .] [4][. . .] wealth [. . .]

Commentary

Line 2: Elsewhere in the Qumran compositions we find references to the "utterance of her lips": 1QSb iii:27; 1QH[a] xix:8; 4Q491 11i:17; 4Q511 63-64ii:4. In *Instruction* (4Q416 7:3; 4Q418 222:2) the "utterance of his lips" is directly connected with his spirit.

Line 3: "destruction" — שחת, which is in the form of a participle ("one who destroys"), also came to designate "destruction" (*HALOT* s.v. שחת). See also frag. 26:3 as well as 4Q475 5.

Frag. 9

[2][. . . from] a spirit lifted [high . . .] [3][. . .] eat wi[thout . . .] [4][. . .] roam about [. . .] [5][. . .] from a spirit [. . .]

Frag. 10

[1][. . .] from a book and there is not [. . .] [2][. . .]

[3][And now] pay [at]tention to me, all (you) sons of [. . .] [4][. . .] humility and uprightness, for sin and for perfe[ction . . .] [5][. . . judgme]nt of the enemy, the friend, and all flesh. G[od] will not justify . . .] [6][. . . i]f you do good, he will be good to you and you will n[ot] return [. . .] [7][. . .] all [Israe]l the evil of [. . .]

Commentary

This column contains hints of a universal judgment. With the beginning of the new section in line 3, wisdom is no longer the subject, even though hints of the nature of the judgment appear to be consistent with the prior section, which began at frag. 5:5.

Line 3: "[And now] pay [at]tention to me, all (you) sons of [. . .]" — See commentary to 5:5 above.

Line 4: "humility" — A valued trait in this composition and in the MSS of the *Community Rule*.

Frags. 11-12

¹[. . .] and great peace [wi]th [. . .] all blessings [. . .] ²[. . . with] a robe of splendor for a[l]l who hold fast to me [. . .] ³[. . . to all who walk] perfectly in all my ways. To a[ll . . .] ⁴[. . .] with all the spirit[s of . . .]

Commentary

While the reconstruction proposed by Puech on the basis of certain parallel vocabulary with 1QS iv:7-8 may not be convincing (DJD 25:141-42), the conceptual similarities are significant for understanding this section. This forms part of the "Treatise on the Two Spirits" (1QS iii:13–iv:26), which develops that author's particular dualistic viewpoint concerning world history and the nature of humankind. A reference to walking in perfection and the description of the spirits of humankind point to a broader similarity with that composition. Also significant for this section is the change to the first person from the third person feminine identified as Wisdom earlier in the composition (4Q525 6-9). If the theme and form of this passage are continuous from frag. 10:3, it could be argued that the speaker is the "sage" identified with other wisdom passages of this form and of the "Treatise on the Two Spirits."

Line 3: "[walk] perfectly" — See commentary to 5:11 above.

Frag. 13

¹[. . .] and from their mouths [. . .] ²[. . . you shall give as an in]heritance amid the miserly, you shall give to th[em . . .] ³[. . .] they will bear a grudge to shed blood among [. . .] ⁴[. . .] arrogance you shall inherit and in their bowels [. . .] ⁵[. . .] all who inherit it [. . .]

⁶[And now, li]sten to me, a[l]l [sons of . . .]

Commentary

Line 2: "amid the miserly" — The literal translation of ברעי עין would refer to the "evil eye," but we find references in context to this meaning in Prov 23:6; 28:22; Sir 14:3; as well as to a malevolent spirit in Deut 15:9; 28:54, 56.

Line 3: "they will bear a grudge to shed blood" — In Lev 19:16 we find the injunction: "Do not stand upon the blood of your neighbor." In these verses concerning reproof, one also is not to bear a grudge (Lev 19:15-18). The concern about the shedding of blood is evident in the wisdom tradition. See Prov 1:8-19, in which the initial topic of that composition is an injunction against joining those who shed blood, apparently in pursuit of wealth and unjust gain (see DJD 25:143). While our text appears to be the only reference that makes a direct connection between these two issues, the combination of these two significant concerns within the wisdom tradition is not surprising. In CD xii:6-7 we find an injunction against shedding the blood of a gentile for unjust gain.

Line 4: "their bowels" — The Hebrew term תכמים is found only in the Qumran texts, including 1QS iv:20, also from the "Treatise on the Two Spirits" referred to in the commentary to frag. 10 above, and in frag. 23:1 of this text as well as elsewhere.

Line 6: "[And now, li]sten to me, a[l]l [sons of . . .]" — Note the discussion of "Literary Questions" in the introduction and in the commentary to 5:5 above.

Frag. 14, col. i

²[. . . l]and [. . .] ³⁻⁷[. . .] ⁸[. . .] suddenly [. . .] ⁹[. . .] ¹⁰[. . .] your [li]fe [. . .] ¹¹[. . .] ¹²[. . .] your appearance ¹³[. . .] life [. . .] ¹⁴[. . .] ¹⁵[. . .] heart [. . .] ¹⁶⁻²⁵[. . .] ²⁶[. . .] your [inher]itance

Frag. 14, col. ii

¹[. . .] and your [in]heritance with [. . .] ²upon the throne of iniquity and upon the high places of their assembly [. . .] ³with their heart and they will raise high your head [. . .] ⁴you will praise and because of your word they will prevail [. . .] ⁵in a[l]l splendor and desirable in a[ll . . .] ⁶he has attained your ways, you shall not stagger [. . .] ⁷you shall be blessed, in the time of your reeling you shall find support [. . .] ⁸The reproach of your enemy will not reach you [. . .] ⁹together

and your enemy will lie at the threshold [. . .] [10]your heart. You shall take delight in G[od] while they defile [. . .] and he will bring you out [11]to an expansive place [for] your foot and upon the high places of your enemies you shall tread. [You shall love God with all your heart and with all] [12]your life. He will deliver you from all evil, and terror will not come to you [. . .] [13]he will give you as a possession. He will fill your days with good, and in abundant peace you [will walk . . .] [14]you shall inherit honor. When you are taken away to eternal resting places, they shall inherit [. . .] [15]in your teaching all who know you will walk together [. . .] [16]together they will mourn. By your ways they will remember you and you will be well[. . . .]

[18]Now, man of discernment, listen to me and set your heart to the say[ings of my mouth . . .] [19]Obtain knowledge for your inner parts, and with your body meditate[. . . .] [20]With righteous humility utter [your] sayings and do [no]t give [. . . do not] [21]be led astray by the words of your neighbor lest he will prepare you [. . .] [22]According to what you hear answer in accordance with what he utters. Be careful [. . . do not] [23]utter an opinion before you hear their words. Lis[ten attentively . . .] [24]greatly. First listen to what they say and then reply with [words of. . . .] With careful [25]diligence utter them and answer steadfastly in the midst of princes. In [. . .] [26]with your lips. Guard carefully against an offense of the tongue [. . .] [27]lest you will be trapped by your lips and be ensnared together with the ton[gue . . .] [28]offensive words, w[hich are abominat]ions from me. They are twisted [. . .]

Commentary

Line 5: "splendor" — The fragmentary references to "splendor" throughout this composition probably find their best explanation in frags. 11-12:2-3, "a robe of splendor for a[l]l who hold fast to me [. . . to all who walk] perfectly in all my ways." See also frag. 22:5; 26:4.

Line 9: "together" — See discussion under "Literary Questions" in the introduction.

Line 10: "You shall take delight in G[od]" — See Isa 58:14; Ps 37:4; Job 22:26; 27:10.

Lines 10-11: "he will bring you out to an expansive place [for] your foot" — Deliverance from enemies to an expansive place is the theme in 2 Sam 22:20; Ps 18:19; 31:8.

Line 15: "your teaching" — The Hebrew term *talmud* appears only two other times in the Qumran scrolls, elsewhere at 4Q169 3-4ii:8 and 1QH^a x:19 (in the most recent edition: DJD 40:132, 138).

Line 15: "walk together" — For "together" see discussion under "Literary Questions" in the introduction. On this phrase see also 4Q416 2iii:21. On the term "walk" see the discussion of "Key Terms" in the introduction to this text as well as in the introduction to this volume.

Line 16: "together" — See discussion under "Literary Questions" in the introduction.

Line 18: "Now, man of discernment, listen to me" — Concerning this phrase, note the discussion of "Literary Questions" in the introduction and in the commentary to 5:5. Note that the מבין ("man of discernment") is found once in *Mysteries* and primarily in *Instruction*. See the introduction to that text for a discussion of this term.

Lines 18-28: This section on taking care with regard to speech and the consequences of rash utterances has some remarkable similarities to 4Q420 1aii-b:1-8//4Q421 1aii-b:13-19.

Line 19: "meditate" — This verb appears in this composition at 2-3ii:6 as well and also is found in 4Q417 1i:6//4Q418 43, 44, 45i:4 with regard to the mystery of existence. It appears to reflect the same root as the חזון הגוי ("vision of insight") "for the memorial book" in 4Q417 1i:16-17, or the ספר הגוי ("book of insight") referred to in CD x:6; xiii:2; xiv:7-8; 1QSa i:7.

Line 20: "With righteous humility utter [your] sayings" — This unusual Hebrew construction finds its closest parallel in Ps 45:4, a phrase acknowledged as difficult to comprehend. "Humility" is a valued characteristic in both this composition and in the S (*Community Rule*) MSS.

Line 27: "lest you will be trapped by your lips and be ensnared together with the ton[gue . . .]" — see commentary on frag. 18:1 below.

Line 27: "together" — See discussion under "Literary Questions" in the introduction.

Frag. 15

[1][... darkne]ss falls [...] the poor gather and in storehouses [...] [2][...] vipers in [...] you shall walk to it. You shall enter [...] [3][...] serpent [walks about] and with trembling a viper will be suspended on high [...] [4][...] by it they shall stand firm. Everlasting curses and the venom of serpents [...] [5][...] poisonous snake and in it the flames of death will dart about when he enters [...] [6][... dark]ness. Its foundation is flames of brimstone and its base is fire [...] [7][...] its [do]ors are taunts of reproach, its bars are fasts of destruction [...] [8][...] they will not attain the ways of life. You shall g[o ...] [9][...] wounded by the serpent shall be put to death [...]

Commentary

This column points to the fate of those who do not follow the paths of wisdom. We find within the fragments of this column four different terms for poisonous snakes. Perhaps it is a portrait of Sheol, the habitation of the dead, developed from the curses that accrue to those who fail to follow the law at the end of Deuteronomy (see commentary on line 3 below). It does betray fragmentary evidence of a rather dramatic portrayal of the consequences of choosing the path of death rather than life, a more vivid picture than the one found in Deuteronomy 32, and reflects the manner in which those chapters provided a basis for judgments concerning the right and wrong "ways" or "paths" to life in Second Temple Judaism. Its development in a clearly sectarian text is to be found in 1QS ii:1-18.[37] While betraying some similarities with 4Q184 i, the more dramatic development in this portrait is also evident in these fragments. Qimron has related it to the description of the vile woman in Prov 2:16-19.[38]

Line 1: "poor" — The Hebrew terms רוש (verb) and ריש (noun) are found throughout *Instruction*, but this is the only other reference in the wisdom texts from Qumran. In other Qumran texts the verb occurs (1QH[a] x:36; xiii:16, 22; 4Q372 1:17). See the discussion of "Social Location" in the introduction to *Instruction*.

---

37. Note the manner in which this characterization of the material varies from that of Goff, *Discerning Wisdom*, 220-22. In his attempt to argue that this text does not reflect a "day of judgment" as in Joel 2, he fails to appreciate the dramatic nature of the judgment portrayed in these fragments.

38. Qimron, "Improving the Editions," 138-39.

Line 3: "serpent" — שרף is the same term used for the serpents in Num 21:6, 8. It is sometimes translated as "fiery serpents" because of the use of the same root as the verb "to burn." In this fragment we have four terms for poisonous snakes employed in the context of eschatological judgment: פתן ("viper," lines 2, 3), תנין ("serpent," line 4), שרף ("serpent," lines 3, 9), and צפע ("poisonous snake," line 5). Both of the first two terms are found in CD viii:9-12//xix:22-24), in the significant interpretation of Deut 32:33, "Their wine is the poison of serpents (תנינם), the cruel venom of asps (פתנים)" (NRSV), to refer to the Judean and Greek kings, respectively. The "kings of the people," also called the princes of Judah, lead the population away from the "ways" of God, so the Greek kings are the instruments of God's vengeance. The term שרף also appears in frag. 24ii:8 of this composition as well as in 4Q267 6:6, in both places meaning "burning." The last term, צפע, occurs only here in the Qumran texts and in Isa 14:29 in the HB.

Line 3: "[walks about]" — This reconstruction is based on the parallels identified by Tigchelaar in 5Q16 1, 2, and 5.[39]

Line 4: "Everlasting curses" — אררות, the term for "curses" here, is not found as a noun in the HB, hence not combined with נצח in this manner. This combination also occurs in 4Q289 1:2 and 5Q16 1:3.

Line 6: "[. . . dark]ness. Its foundation is flames of brimstone and its base is fire" — The interesting portrayal including both darkness and fire also occurs in 4Q184 i:4-7.

Frag. 16

²you have released [? . . .] ³by it the discerning go astray [. . .] ⁴and they h[id] snares [. . .] ⁵blood they di[ed . . .] ⁶with treachery and oppression [. . .] ⁷house and doo[rs . . .]

Commentary

Line 3: "go astray" — See commentary to 6ii:2 above.

39. Tigchelaar, "Lady Folly and Her House," 374.

Frag. 17

²[. . .] embers [. . .] ³[. . .] they are full of lies [. . .] ⁴[. . .] venom of the serpent consu[med . . .] ⁵[. . .] a man round about [. . .] ⁶with the brightness of light [. . .]

Frag. 18

¹[. . .] you are caught in a trap [. . .] ²with the abominations of [. . .] ³[. . .] you raise [. . .] ⁴[. . .] and with the defilement of the he[art . . .]

Commentary

Line 1:   The continuing concern of being trapped or ensnared, also found in frag. 14ii:27, is an ongoing topic in the sectarian literature of the Qumran corpus, particularly in the *Damascus Document.* Based on a commentary of Isa 24:17, CD iv:12-19 (and parallels) describes Israel as having been caught in the three nets of Belial: fornication, wealth, and defilement of the temple. These are then developed in the text, thereby providing a rationale for the formation of the new covenant in the land of Damascus. Later in CD xiv:1-2 we learn that: "All who walk in these [rules], the covenant of God stands firm for them, delivering them from all the traps of corruption." In 4Q175 23-25 an accursed man, one from Belial, will stand up or arise to be a trap for his people and ruin for all his neighbors. Those who plot deceit in 1QHᵃ xii:10-19 to catch the people of God in their nets are also considered to be doing the work of Belial. This section is built on allusions to Pss 69:23; 140:6. In the description of a weakened soul heading for destruction, 1QHᵃ xvi:35 includes a reference to the foot caught in the snare. The author of the entreaties of 1QHᵃ gives thanks that he has been protected from the "traps of the pit," set by vicious men who are of the assembly of Belial (x:22-24): "They, in the net that they spread for me, entangled their own feet and fell into the traps that they hid for me" (x:31). Similarly he thanks the Lord because "you have redeemed my life from the pit" (xi:20) and then goes on to comment, "When all the snares of the pit are opened and all the nets of wickedness and the nets of the wretched are spread upon the water, . . . a period of wrath for all who belong to Belial, when the snares of death have surrounded without escape, then the torrents of Belial will burst forth over all the high banks, like a fire that consumes all their channels, to destroy every tree, green or dead" (xi:28-31). Similar sentiments are found in 1QHᵃ xxi:11, 24, 28 (//4Q427 10:1; 11:2; 4Q428 13:4). 4Q228 1i:8 speaks of "snares of destruction." The initiate who seeks wisdom is urged in 4Q185 1-2ii:5 not to be deceived "by terror and the snare of the fowler" (see commentary to that text above).

In 1Q22 1:8 God speaks to Moses about the desertion of the Israelites from the law that was commanded, how they chose the abhorrences and abominations of the peoples around them, "and will serve idols that will become a trap and a snare." This appears to be an interpretation of Exod 34:12, also cited in 4Q368 2:4 and 11Q19 ii:5.

Line 2: "abominations" — This term שקוץ is much less common throughout the Qumran texts than תועבה, found throughout the legal section of the corpus. Within the HB the latter term is especially prominent in Deuteronomy, Ezekiel, and Proverbs, referring to those things that are counter to custom or law.

Frag. 19

¹[. . .] who are born [. . .] ²[. . . will] be joy [. . .] ³[. . .] God [. . .] ⁴[. . .] Mastemah [. . .] ⁵[. . .] con]cerning t[his] iniquity [. . .]

Commentary

Line 4: "Mastemah" — משטמה is found only twice in the HB, in Hos 9:7, 8, where it refers to persecution or hatred. In the literature of Second Temple Judaism it becomes one of the names of the opponents of the good, similar to Satan and Belial. It is used in *Jubilees* and in the Qumran fragments related to that composition. It also occurs in CD xvi:5 and parallels, 1QS iii:23, 1QM xiii:4, 11, and other scattered fragments, sometimes as an "angel of destruction," other times as the "prince of destruction," perhaps in the latter case in opposition to Michael, the chief of the angels. Where not a proper name in these contexts, "destruction" appears to be a more accurate translation.

Frag. 20

¹[. . .] with the head [. . .] ²[. . .] for those who walk in the way [. . .] ³[. . .] you shall call out [pe]ace and to procla[im . . .]

Frag. 21

¹[. . . da]rk places and I will be healed [. . .] ²[. . .] cursed of God [. . .] ³[. . . wi]cked you will proc[laim] them [. . .] ⁴[. . .] you will choose depravity [. . .] ⁵[. . .] by it they shall exalt themselves and they shall walk [. . .] ⁶[. . .] those who wallow in the dirt [. . .] ⁷[. . .] her source, the source [. . .] ⁸[. . . with the] gathering of anger and with long[suffering . . .] ⁹[. . .] be certain and curse [. . .]

Commentary

Fragments 21 and 22 are similar in vocabulary and content but are composed of a number of vocabulary items somewhat rare in the HB and the Qumran scrolls. The author of this composition has utilized prophetic texts concerning disobedience and judgment that are also related to wisdom themes.

Line 5: "walk" — On הלך see the discussion of "Key Terms" in the introduction to this text as well as in the introduction to the volume.

Line 6: "those who wallow in the dirt" — See Isa 9:4 for the use of these rare terms, even though their meaning in context there is difficult to determine. In that case they allude to the conclusion of the manifestations of military occupancy. In these two fragments they appear to be used in the description of a judgment rooted in the darkness when God felt compelled to turn his face from Israel because they relied on necromancy for teaching and instruction (Isa 8:16-22).

Line 8: "[. . . with the] gathering of anger" — For this line and for frag. 22:5, note Ezek 22:20, in which the Lord says that he will gather Israel in his anger and wrath as one gathers silver, bronze, iron, lead, and tin, and then melts them, presumably for the sake of purification as described in Isa 1:21-26. In this passage the "faithful city" is said to have become a harlot in need of purification. The harlot is a common motif in Jewish wisdom literature, hence an image that refers to both the choices involved in discerning the correct paths for wisdom and to eschatological judgment.

Frag. 22

²[. . . those who d]o depravity come to me [. . .] ³[. . .] they have dwelt together [. . .] ⁴[. . . wicked]ness they will wallow. Is it not [. . .] ⁵[. . .] in his splendor I will gather anger [. . .] ⁶[. . .] they shall return [. . .]

Notes

This fragment was originally classified as 4Q177 19, but Annette Steudel proposed a reclassification on the basis of paleographic considerations.[40]

Commentary

On content see the commentary on the previous fragment.

Line 3: "together" — See discussion in the introduction under "Literary Questions."

Line 5: "splendor" — The fragmentary references to "splendor" throughout this composition probably find their best explanation in frags. 11-12:2-3: "a robe of splendor for a[l]l who hold fast to me [. . . to all who walk] perfectly in all my ways." See also frags. 14ii:5; 26:4.

Frag. 23

¹they have grasped my bowels before God [. . .] ²I will flee and on the day which is designated [. . .] ³to descend to the furthest parts of the pit [. . .] ⁴in the furnace of wrath.

For I am wis[e . . . just as] ⁵God commanded with the men of [evil] cunning [. . .] ⁶for their sake. By knowledge, wisdom [. . .] ⁷he has changed, lest they will meditate on the words of [. . .] ⁸I have abhorred and with the scoffers [. . .] ⁹righteousness and like a rock one stum[bles over . . .] ¹⁰for God has cursed me [. . .] ¹¹[and he s]poke [. . .]

Notes

Line 11: "[and he s]poke" — Whether רב[ד] should be translated "word" or "he spoke" is impossible to determine, due to lack of context.

40. Annette Steudel, *Der Midrasch zur Eschatologie aus der Qumrangemeinde (4QMidrEschat^{a,b}): Materielle Rekonstruktion, Textbestand, Gattung und Traditionsgeschichtliche Einordnung des durch 4Q174 ('Florilegium') und 4Q177 ('Catena') repräsentierten Werkes aus den Qumranfunden* (STDJ 13; Leiden: Brill, 1994), 70, 74, 79, 112-13.

Commentary

Line 1: "bowels" — See commentary to frag. 13:4 above.

Line 4: "furnace of wrath" — This is the same furnace that is enflamed by God's wrath in Ezek 22:17-22, as referred to in frags. 21-22 above.

Line 5: "[evil] cunning" — For this reconstruction see 1QS iv:11; 4Q299 3aii-b:5.

Line 8: "scoffers" — Literally "men of scoffing." The scoffers are mentioned in Isa 28:14 and 29:20. The scoffer receives frequent mention throughout the book of Proverbs (1:22; 3:34; 9:7, 8; 13:1; 14:6; 15:12; 19:25, 29; 20:1; 21:11, 24; 22:10; 24:9; 29:8). Though not receiving excessive mention in the Qumran fragments, they are important in CD xx:11, where they spoke falsehood and despised the new covenant in the land of Damascus. In an interpretation of Isa 28:14 we find in 4Q162 ii:6, 10, that they are leaders resident in Jerusalem "who rejected the law of the Lord and mocked the word of the Holy One of Israel," thereby bringing the wrath of God against his entire people. In the singular, in CD i:14, "the scoffer" arises in opposition to the teacher of righteousness to lead Israel astray.

Line 9: "a rock one stum[bles over . . .]" — See Isa 8:14. In this same verse the Lord of hosts also is "a trap and a snare for the inhabitants of Jerusalem," continuing the theme going back at least to frag. 14ii:18.

Frag. 24, col. ii

¹[with dis]cernment you utter a saying [. . . men of] ²understanding, listen to me and dece[ption . . .] ³I have determined. They shall drink from [. . .] ⁴my house is a house [. . .] ⁵my house. The one who dwells in [. . .] ⁶forever they shall tread [. . .] ⁷those who gather it will coll[ect . . .] ⁸burn and all those who dri[nk . . .] ⁹well from the waters of a spr[ing . . .]

Commentary

Line 1: "you utter a saying" — In contrast to Goff (*Discerning Wisdom*, 216), I do not think that this should be translated as a feminine form, "she utters a saying," on the assumption that this is a wisdom poem uttered by Lady Wisdom. It is my judgment that we are past the point in this composition where wisdom is the subject.

Lines 1-2: "[... men of] understanding" — אנשי לבב could also be translated "men of heart," but my translation more adequately conveys its meaning in context, as also in Job 34:10 (NRSV, NJPS). This reconstruction is based on parallels with Job 34:10 and 4Q298 1-2i:1.

Line 4: While the inclination is to reconstruct this line on the basis of Isa 56:7, "for my house will be called a house of prayer for all the nations," Puech suggests that the trace of ink on the fragment for the following letter does not support that hypothesis (DJD 25:164).

Frag. 25

²[... so]ns of Bel[ial ...] ³[... those who g]row old you will walk [...] ⁴[... you shall not be a glutton or a drunk]ard with noth[ing in your purse ...]

Commentary

Line 4: This reconstruction is based on the Hebrew text of Sir 18:33. In the advice to the son in Prov 23:21, the result of being a "glutton and drunkard" is impoverishment. "Glutton and drunkard" are characteristic descriptions of the rebellious son in Deut 21:20 and 11Q19 lxiv:4-5. It is with reference to wisdom that the accusation against Jesus about being "a glutton and a drunkard" appears in the NT: "Yet wisdom is vindicated by her deeds" (Matt 11:19 NRSV); "Nevertheless, wisdom is vindicated by all her children" (Luke 7:34-35 NRSV).

Frag. 26

²[. . .] suddenly [. . .] ³[. . .] destroys as one who does vio[lence . . .] ⁴[. . . neck]laces of splendor [. . .] ⁵[. . .] sash of li[nen . . .]

Commentary

Line 4: "splendor" — The fragmentary references to "splendor" throughout this composition probably find their best explanation in frags. 11-12:2, "a robe of

splendor for all who hold fast to me . . . to all who walk perfectly in all my ways."
See also frags. 14ii:5; 22:5.

Frag. 27

¹[. . .] humility [. . .] ²[. . .] you will walk around [. . .] ³[. . .] and not [. . .] ⁴[. . .]
men of perfection [. . .]

Commentary

Line 1: "humility" — This is a valued characteristic both in this composition
and in the MSS of the *Community Rule*.

Line 2: "walk" — On הלך see the discussion of "Key Terms" in the introduction to this text as well as in the introduction to this volume.

Frag. 28

¹[. . .] to cleanse [. . .] ²[. . .] like the waters of a rock [. . .] ³[. . . ha]nd stronger
than [. . .] ⁴[. . . ir]on and lead [. . .] ⁵[. . .] return injustice [. . .]

Commentary

Line 4: "[. . . ir]on and lead" — This appears to be an allusion to Ezek 22:20, already cited as the potential context in 21:8 and 22:5 above. The verb שוב ("turn"
or "return") in the following line also occurs in 22:6. Such references point to the
continuing concern over the purification of Israel, which "did not distinguish
between the holy and the common or make known the difference between the
impure and the pure" (Ezek 22:26). This passage is utilized twice in the *Damascus Document* (CD vi:17-18; xii:19-20), thereby pointing to its centrality for the
various versions of that composition. This distinction also provides the ideological foundation for other compositions such as 4QMMT and the *Temple Scroll*,
quite evident in the vocabulary employed throughout the works.

Frag. 29

²foot, and they shall remain firmly resolute [. . .] ³in the dwelling places of G[od
. . .]

Frag. 30

¹with all [. . .] ²testimony [. . .] ³with loving-kindness [. . .] ⁴to all gener[ations . . .]

Frag. 31

¹[And now . . . li]sten to my words [. . .] ²[. . .] fullness [. . .] ³[. . . with]out interest [. . .]

Commentary

Line 1:   "[And now . . . li]sten to my words" — Note the discussion of "Literary Questions" in the introduction and the commentary to 5:5.

Line 3:   "interest" — That is, usury or profit.

Frag. 32

²[. . .] transgression and you will deliver us [. . .] ³[. . .] from death [. . .]

Frag. 33

¹[. . .] you will inherit [. . .] ²[. . .] you will [no]t be afraid [. . .]

Frag. 35

²[. . .] I have mixed [. . .]

Frag. 36

²[. . .] what [. . .]

Frag. 38

²[. . .] the day [. . .]

Frag. 39

[1][. . .] formerly [. . .] [2][. . .] th[is . . .]

Frag. 40

[2][. . .] was [. . .]

Frag. 42

[1][. . .] act unjustly [. . .]

Frag. 43

[2][. . . in ord]er that he will kee[p . . .]

Frag. 47

[1][. . .] spirit [. . .]

The Wisdom of Ben Sira (Sirach)

Introduction

This composition has been considered part of the deuterocanonical tradition in the Western church, hence included in the Apocrypha of the Protestant canon. Within the Jewish tradition it has been regarded as one of the ספרים חיצונים ("outside books"). Hebrew copies of this composition, already known in Latin and Greek translation, were found among the MSS from the Cairo Genizah in 1896. Limited fragments of this composition in Hebrew have been found among the scrolls from Qumran and Masada. In the Greek texts this composition frequently bears the name "The Wisdom of Jesus Son of Sirach," and in Latin versions it is "Ecclesiasticus." The Wisdom (or Book) of Ben Sira has been its most common name in the Jewish tradition. We do not have the first page or cover of a Hebrew MS to determine the title given in those copies. The subscription at the end of MS B reads, "The Wisdom of Yeshua son of Eleazar son of Sira."

Content

This composition is one of the best-known examples of wisdom literature related to the Hebrew Scriptures, together with Job, Proverbs, Qohelet (Ecclesiastes), and the Wisdom of Solomon. As is true of some other wisdom literature, a systematic outline of the contents is not apparent, so a relative scholarly consensus on that issue is not available. As a compendium of instructions and proverbs, it most resembles the biblical book of Proverbs. The nature of wisdom itself as well as issues such as theodicy common to wisdom literature are explored. A distinguishing feature of this composition is the section from Sir 44:1–50:21, which begins in the Greek, "Let us now sing the praises of famous men."

As one would expect, the Hebrew MSS have no evidence of the Prologue written by the grandson, who translated the work into Greek.

Text and Manuscripts

The first copies of the Hebrew text were found in the collection from the Cairo Genizah in 1896. Eventually six Hebrew MSS (MSS A-F) were identified from those finds, the most recent published in 1988 and 2008. These MSS are dated to the tenth through the twelfth centuries c.e. They contain evidence of two textual traditions along with some medieval retroversions from the Syriac and/ or Greek texts. These MSS do provide the basis for a good deal of the reconstruction of the Hebrew text that is translated in this commentary. Two major critical editions of the Hebrew text are available for study (see Ben-Ḥayyim and Beentjes in the bibliography to this chapter). The only complete edition is the electronic version by Martin G. Abegg Jr., available in the relevant module from Accordance Bible Software (see Abegg in the bibliography to this chapter). Where these versions differ in the placement of fragments in relationship to the Greek text, I have followed the reconstruction of Beentjes. In this commentary only those sections partially represented by MSS from the Dead Sea are included. Not included in this volume is the text of 11Q5 (Ps^a Sirach) (col. xxi:11-17; xxii:1 = Sir 51:13-20, 30). It is discussed elsewhere in this series in conjunction with the publications of the *Psalms Scroll*.

The two fragments of 2Q18 provide limited evidence of Sirach 6 and perhaps a portion of Sirach 1. If they are fragments of a text that originally encompassed all or at least a majority of the composition, then frag. 1 is more likely to be from Sir 6:14-15. If, however, it was a compilation of texts, such as MS C of the texts from the Cairo Genizah,[1] then it could just as well be from 1:19-20. In this case both fragments are drawn from that limited body of passages in the third feminine singular in which wisdom is personified. Only traces of four letters can be found on frag. 1. Epigraphic analysis of this text by its editor points to a date in the second half of the first century b.c.e. in the transitional period from the Hasmonean to the Herodian scripts, resembling 1QIsa^b (DJD 3:75).

The Masada text appears to be the earliest extant copy of the text, de-

---

1. Referred to as a florilegium by Patrick Skehan and Alexander Di Lella, *Wisdom of Ben Sira*, 52.

scribed by Yigael Yadin as written in a middle or late Hasmonean script, hence in the first half of the first century B.C.E.[2] In a footnote he ascribes the date of 100-75 B.C.E. to Frank Moore Cross. The extant text covers Sir 39:27–43:30 and is remarkably similar to the Cairo Genizah versions of this section. It was found in Casemate 1109 of the eastern wall. Yadin concluded that the piece of scroll from which these fragments came had originally been torn from the main body and thrown onto the floor, presumably when the remainder was tossed out by Roman soldiers and lost.[3] The extant fragments are stichometrically arranged, that is, they are written in two columns or divided into hemistichs, separated by narrow margins.

The Hebrew texts cover a period of more than a millennium. The MSS from the Dead Sea represent a textual tradition that most likely precedes the Greek translation of the text in addition to the later copies from the Cairo Genizah. Unless noted, the proposed reconstructions of these texts in this commentary are based on the MSS from the Cairo Genizah. This translation follows the order of the primary Hebrew text for the relevant section but identifies the lines according to the Greek MSS, which provide the basis for the verse structure in modern translations.

Historical Context

According to the Prologue to the Greek version the grandson began work on the translation of the text into Greek after his move to Egypt in 132 B.C.E. In 50:27 the author of the original Hebrew composition describes himself as Jesus son of Eleazar son of Sirach of Jerusalem. This suggests a date of composition around 180 B.C.E. or slightly earlier, almost certainly after the Seleucid monarchs had seized control of the area from the Ptolemies and before the immediate succession of events under Antiochus IV Epiphanes leading up to the Maccabean revolt.

The modern authors of most commentaries place a good deal of emphasis on the Hellenistic aspect of Ben Sira. This is a feature that certainly distinguishes it from Proverbs, Qohelet, and Job. However, all of the wisdom compositions at Qumran originate from the Hellenistic era, providing a different framework for analysis.

---

2. Yadin, *Ben Sira Scroll*, 4.
3. Ibid.

Literary Questions

The composition of Ben Sira is remarkable for its use of the HB. Already upon the initial publication of the Hebrew text from the Cairo Genizah, Solomon Schechter pointed out the extensive use of biblical material, suggesting that the author was a conscious imitator of the HB, particularly the book of Proverbs.[4] These connections are developed at length in the commentary by Skehan and Di Lella.[5] It is this extensive connection with Proverbs that makes it appear such a natural part of the biblical wisdom tradition, even though it is developed in a manner considerably different from those other biblical texts.

More central to this composition than to Job, Proverbs, and Qohelet is the role of the law. While we read in Prov 1:7 and 9:10, "The fear of the Lord is the beginning of wisdom ('knowledge' in 1:7)," and in Sir 1:14, "To fear the Lord is the beginning of wisdom," the contexts of the phrase in the two compositions vary greatly, demonstrating some basic differences between them. While the fundamental appeal to the "fear of the Lord" is characteristic of the wisdom taught in both documents, in Ben Sira this is developed into a connection with the law, as can been seen in Sir 2:16: "Those who fear the Lord seek to please him, and those who love him are filled with his law"; or 19:20: "The whole of wisdom is fear of the Lord and in all wisdom there is fulfillment of the law."[6] The centrality of the law for the understanding of wisdom is elaborated in chap. 24, the very center of the book, in which wisdom is a female figure. Sir 24:1-22 is sometimes termed in Greek MSS "The Praise of Wisdom," in which personified wisdom is developed in a manner already familiar from Prov 1:20-33 and 8:1-36, as well as Egyptian wisdom material. This is then followed by the section in 24:23-34, which begins: "All this is the book of the covenant of the Most High God, the law that Moses commanded as an inheritance for the congregations of Jacob." The emphasis on the law is also noted in the last line of the Prologue when the grandson identifies the purpose of the work. This connection between wisdom, law, and "fear of the Lord" distinguishes Ben Sira from Proverbs and a number of other wisdom compositions in the HB, as well as some other works represented in the collection of wisdom materials from Qumran. Most commentators understand this emphasis on the law in wisdom materials as a response to the demands of Hellenism. In her dissertation Sarah Tanzer noted the manner in which wisdom becomes less universal as we move from Proverbs to the particular iden-

---

4. Schechter and Taylor, *Wisdom of Ben Sira*, 12-25.
5. See Skehan and Di Lella, *Wisdom of Ben Sira*, 40-45, for initial comments.
6. See Sir 2:15-18; 15:1; 19:20; 23:16-27; 32:24–33:3.

tification of wisdom with Torah in Ben Sira, a particularization developed even further in the sectarian literature from Qumran.[7]

Bibliography

Note also the bibliography in the introduction to this volume.

Abegg, Martin G., Jr., with the assistance of Casey Towes. "The Grammatically Tagged Hebrew Text of Ben Sira Based on Manuscripts from the Cairo Geniza, Masada, and Qumran (BENSIRA-C/BENSIRA-M)." Altamonte Springs: OakTree Software, 2009. Abegg et al. *DSSB,* 597-606.

Baillet, Maurice. "Ecclésiastique." DJD 3:75-77.

Beentjes, Pancratius C. *The Book of Ben Sira in Hebrew.* VTSup 68. 1997. Repr. Atlanta: SBL, 2006.

———, ed. *The Book of Ben Sira in Modern Research: Proceedings of the First International Ben Sira Conference, 28-31 July 1996, Soesterberg, Netherlands.* BZAW 255. Berlin: de Gruyter, 1997.

Ben-Ḥayyim, Ze'ev, ed. *The Book of Ben Sira: Text, Concordance, and an Analysis of the Vocabulary* (Hebrew with an English summary). Jerusalem: Academy of the Hebrew Language/Shrine of the Book, 1973.

Corley, Jeremy. "Sirach." *NIDB* 5:285-94.

Crenshaw, James L. "The Book of Sirach: Introduction, Commentary, and Reflections." In *NIB* 5:601-867.

Di Lella, Alexander A. "Wisdom of Ben Sira." *ABD* 6:931-45.

Egger-Wentzel, Renate. "Ein neues Sira-Fragment des MS C." *BN* 138 (2008): 107-14.

———, ed. *Ben Sira's God: Proceedings of the International Ben Sira Conference, Durham — Ushaw College 2001.* BZAW 321. Berlin/New York: de Gruyter, 2002.

Elizur, Shulamit. "A New Hebrew Fragment of Ben Sira (Ecclesiasticus)." *Tarbiz* 76 (2008): 17-28 (Hebrew).

Schechter, Solomon, and Charles Taylor. *The Wisdom of Ben Sira: Portions of the Book of Ecclesiasticus from Hebrew Manuscripts Presented to the University of Cambridge by the Editors.* Cambridge: Cambridge University Press, 1899.

Skehan, Patrick W., and Alexander A. Di Lella. *The Wisdom of Ben Sira.* AB 39. New York: Doubleday, 1987.

Wright, Benjamin G. *No Small Difference: Sirach's Relationship to Its Hebrew Parent Text.* SBLSCS 26. Atlanta: Scholars Press, 1989.

7. Sarah Tanzer, "The Sages at Qumran: Wisdom in the *Hodayot*" (Ph.D. diss., Harvard University, 1987), 162.

Yadin, Yigael. *The Ben Sira Scroll from Masada: With Introduction, Emendations and Commentary.* Jerusalem: Israel Exploration Society/Shrine of the Book, 1965.

2Q18 (Sir)

Frag. 1, option 1 *(Sir 1:19-20)*

[19][She pours forth insight and knowledge, she raises high the glory of those who] ho[ld her fast.] [20][The fear of the Lord is the root of wisdom and] her [branches are] long [life.]

Notes

Since there is no copy of another extant Hebrew text for this portion of the composition, Maurice Baillet proposed a reconstruction on the basis of the Greek text translated into Hebrew (DJD 3:76). The present translation is based on that text.

Commentary

This reconstruction appears in the context of the opening praise of wisdom (vv. 1-20). The subject here is wisdom as a female figure, even though in the immediate context she is manifested in the fear of the Lord, since Sir 1:18 reads: "The fear of the Lord is the crown of wisdom, making peace and perfect health to flourish" (NRSV). Within the broader context of the remainder of Ben Sira it is "wisdom" that is personified and referred to using the feminine personal pronoun.

Frag. 1, option 2 *(Sir 6:14-15)*

[14][A faithful friend is a friend of] str[ength, whoever finds him finds value.] [15][For a faith]ful [friend] is beyond [value, there is no price for his goodness.]

Notes

On the two options for the placement for this fragment see the discussion of "Text and Manuscripts" in the introduction to this chapter.

Verse 14: "[friend of] str[ength]" — The Greek translation here is "mighty shelter." This text is based on Genizah MS A. In the fragment from MS C published in 2008, this phrase reads "shield of strength."[8]

Commentary

These lines fall within a section that stresses the importance of friendship and gives advice concerning the use and cultivation of it. These verses form the center of the literary unit, 6:5-17, which has already enumerated examples of friends who are not faithful. Despite the NRSV translation, both the Hebrew and the Greek texts are constructed in the singular.

Frag. 2 (Sir 6:20-31)

[20][She appears deceptive to the simple and he who has no sen]se [will not persevere with her]. [21][She will be like a heavy stone to him and he will not hesitate to cast it away.] [22][For the discipline is just like her name, and she is not access]ible [to the many. . . .] [23-24][. . .] [25][Extend your shoulder and bear her. Do not be frightened by her direction.] [26][Draw near to her with all your soul, and keep] her [ways with all your might.] [27][Examine and search, seek and find, you will take hold of her and not let her] go. [28][For afterward you will find the rest she brings and it will be changed for you into plea]sure. [29][Her net will be for you a foundation of strength and her snare] garments of gold. [30][Of gold is her yoke and her fetters a cord of pur]ple. [31][You will wear her as garments of glory] and put her on [as a crown] of splendor.

Notes

The reconstruction is based upon MS A with a few parallels from MS C.

Verses 23-24: There are no traces of the letters for these lines on 2Q18 2 and they are absent from MSS A and C.

Verse 27: "[you will take hold of her]" — While Baillet reconstructs this verb

---

8. Elizur, "New Hebrew Fragment," 23; Egger-Wentzel, "Neues Sira-Fragment," 109. I thank Martin G. Abegg Jr. for drawing these publications to my attention.

in the Hitpael form, both Ben-Ḥayyim and Beentjes show that in the only other extant copy of this Hebrew text, Genizah MS A, the Hiphil form is employed.[9]

Verse 28: "[the rest she brings]" — Literally "her rest" (*DSSB* 600).

Commentary

This section in which wisdom is personified as a female figure characterizes the first portion of Ben Sira. This is the earliest composition in which the correlation of wisdom with Torah is firmly held (Sir 24:23-29). The connection between wisdom and law is noted in v. 37 of this chapter, after the conclusion of the fragment under discussion. For introductory comments on the personification of wisdom, see the discussions above under the "Literary Questions" in the introductions to 4Q185 and 4Q525.

Verses 20-22: These verses are the conclusion of a section that stresses the necessity of the exercise of discipline for the acquisition of wisdom.

Verse 21: "[like a heavy stone]" — The comparison is used to illustrate its impact on one who is unwilling to accept its discipline.

Verse 22: "[discipline]" — This verse contains a play on the Hebrew term for "discipline" or "instruction", מוסר, based on the root יסר ("instruct"); מוסר can also be taken to be the Hophal participle of סור, to "turn aside" or "withdraw."

Verse 22: "[access]ible" — נכוחה also can mean "plain" and is found in Prov 8:9: "All are *straightforward* to the intelligent man" (NJPS, emphasis mine).

Verse 25: "[Extend your shoulder and bear her]" — This continues the image of the "yoke of wisdom" developed on the basis of the comparison between the acquisition of wisdom and plowing known from the Greek text. The term "yoke" is found in v. 30 in the Hebrew text, but not in the Greek. The image of the yoke is also found in 4Q421 1aii-b:10 and is discussed at greater length there (see commentary to that text). Both the weight of wisdom, noted in v. 21, and the imagery of the "yoke" are brought together in the portrayal of Jesus as wisdom in Matt 11:28-30.

9. Ben-Ḥayyim, *Book of Ben Sira*, 8; Beentjes, *Book of Ben Sira*, 134.

Verse 26: The reference to "[all your soul]" and "[all your might]" suggests Deut 6:5.

Verse 27: "[Examine]" — This term (דרש) appears throughout *Instruction* as well as in the sectarian texts of S and D, and became a basic term for the rabbinic exegetical method.

Verses 28-30: These verses describe the reward for the effort expended in the acquisition of wisdom. The "yoke" in this case becomes an adornment upon her neck. The idea that wisdom brings "rest" is developed in Matt 11:29. In Matt 11:30 it is "pleasant." See v. 25 above.

Masıh (Sir)

Col. i (Sir 39:27–40:10)

²⁷[All these things will be good for the good, yet for the evil] they are tur[ned] into loathing. ²⁸[. . .] they will [remo]ve [moun]tains [. . .] they will calm. ²⁹[Fire and hail, misfortune and plague, also these are cre]ated [for judgment].

Notes

Verse 27: "loathing" — Genizah MS B reads רעה, "evil," which adds to the symmetry of the stich. Yadin reads זרה, "loathing," based on Num 11:20 and a marginal reading in MS B (*Ben Sira Scroll*, 12, 39). The term could also be translated "harlotry," with reference to the "strange woman" (Prov 2:16; 5:3, 20; 7:5; 23:27; Sir 9:3), though that does not fit the context of this section of Ben Sira. On the "strange woman" see 4Q184 above.

The remainder of this column is too fragmentary to permit any meaningful reconstruction and comment.

Col. ii (Sir 40:11–41:1)

⁴⁰:¹¹All things from [the earth will return to the earth and whatever is from the heights returns to the heights.]

¹²All that is from a br[ibe . . .] ¹³Wealth from in[iquity . . .] ¹⁴With its elevation rock[s are rolled away . . .] ¹⁵A shoot borne of violence will not [. . .] ¹⁶Like a reed upon the river bank [. . .] the grass is extinguished. ¹⁷Kindness like eternity will not be cut off and [right]eousness will be established forever.

¹⁸A life of excess and wealth is sweet, but better than both of them is find[ing a treasure.] ¹⁹Having children and [founding a city will estab]lish a name, but better than both of them is the find[ing of wisdom. Calves and seedlings will make] a kinsman [prosper, but better than both of them is a devoted wife. . . .] ²⁰⁻²⁵[. . .] ²⁶[power and might make the heart proud, but better than both] of these [is the fear of the Lord. There is no want in the fear of the Lord] and with it there is no need to seek for support. ²⁷[The fear of the Lord is a blessing like Eden] and it covers everything with gl[ory.]

²⁸[My son, do not live the life of a beggar.] Better is the one who is dead than one who is importunate. ²⁹[The man who gazes upon the table of the stranger, his life is not] considered to be a life. A repudia[tion of life are its delicacies for the] man who kno[ws] internal discipline. ³⁰In the mouth of a bold man [the request is sweet, but within] him it burns as a fire.

⁴¹˸¹O D[eath, how bitter is the mention of] you for the man who is peaceful in his dwelling place, [a man] at ease and suc[cessful] in everything, who even has the strength to enjoy luxury.

Notes

Verse 40:14:   In Genizah MS B this verse reads: "as he raises his hands he re-joices."

Verse 16:   In Genizah MS B this verse reads: "Like axes upon the river bank be-fore all the rain, they disappear."

Verse 19:   "kinsman" — This is the only extant term from this line in the frag-ment, so the line is reconstructed from Genizah MS B, which repeats the term "name" from the first line in this verse. On this basis we cannot eliminate the possibility that this entire line had a different reading in our text.

Verse 26:   "[make the heart proud]" — This line is reconstructed on the basis of Genizah MS B, which also is fragmentary. On the basis of Ezek 28:5 I have chosen to reconstruct that text with this phrase rather than "gladden the heart."[10]

Verse 28: "[My son]" — This reading is based on the textual note in Genizah MS B.

Commentary

Verse 40:11: This verse concludes a section that dwells on the fate of the wicked.[11] Their only relief comes at the point of death. For a similar interpretation of Gen 2:7 and 3:19, see Eccl 12:7. The breath of life is from above, from God, and that is where it returns. This speaks to the end of life, rather than constituting any reference to immortality of the soul, or the resurrection of the body. Note the contrast in the conclusion of this section with the end of the next paragraph in v. 17: "Kindness like eternity will not be cut off and [right]eousness will be established forever."

Verses 12-17: In this section we observe considerable differences in the imagery employed in the Greek texts and extant portions of the Hebrew MSS, but the thematic emphasis on the superiority of a life of kindness and righteousness over injustice is characteristic of both versions.

Verses 18-27: This section is made up of ten "better than" sayings in the Greek text, a structure rooted in the Hebrew as attested in the extant portions of those MSS.[12] This poetic structure is employed to demonstrate the superiority of a life of wisdom for living the truly good life.

Verse 26: "no want . . . no need to seek for support" — The Hebrew term מחסור occurs only here in the extant fragments of Ben Sira, but is very common in *Instruction*. Within Proverbs it is used to designate the poverty that results from laziness or excessive living (6:11; 14:23; 21:5, 17; 22:16; 24:34). Note my discussion of the word among the "Key Terms" in the introduction to *Instruction*.

---

10. This is the reconstruction proposed in *DSSB* 601.

11. This is in contrast to Skehan and Di Lella (*Wisdom of Ben Sira,* 470-71), who consider this to be the first verse of the following section.

12. Skehan and Di Lella, *Wisdom of Ben Sira,* 471-73; Crenshaw, "Sirach," 823-24.

Verses 26-27:   The repetition of the "fear of the Lord" in these verses reinforces this basic theme of wisdom, beginning with Prov 9:10: "The fear of the Lord is the beginning of wisdom."

Verse 28:   "importunate" — חצף does not appear in the HB. Yadin notes that the construction is rabbinic (*Ben Sira Scroll*, 16).

Verses 28-30:   These verses discuss the indignity of begging for sustenance, also found in 29:24-28.

Verse 29:   The second line is very similar to 1QS ii:26 (and parallel texts in other S MSS), where the initiate is refused admission to the community (*yaḥad*) "because his soul has rejected the discipline of knowledge." See also 4Q266 11:7; 4Q504 1-2vi:7; 4Q525 2ii+3:6; 11Q19 lix:19.

Verse 41:1:   See the following section for commentary.

Col. iii (Sir 41:2-21)

²[Ha]il to death, how good is [your decree for] the one who is without might and lacks strength, a man who stumbles and becomes entangled in [all manner of things], without sight and for whom hope is destroyed. ³Do not fear death, your decree; remember those before and those after are with you. ⁴This is the end of all [flesh determined by God. Why should you despise the law of] the Most High? Whether for ten, a [hund]red, or a thousand years [there are no re-proaches concerning life in Sheol.]

⁵De[scend]ants of evil are despised offspring [and the progeny of fools are . . . wi]cked. ⁶[For children of perversi]ty dominion is destroyed [. . .] reproach daily. ⁷A child will curse [an evil father for] they will suffer contempt because of him. ⁸[Woe to you,] men of perv[ersity], who have abandoned the law of the Most High. ⁹[If . . . by calamity], if you beget them, it results in sighing. If you stumble it is the occasion for lasting joy, if you die it is for a curse. ¹⁰[All that is from] nothing, to nothing it will return. Thus the godless, from emptiness to emptiness. ¹¹A man is vain with regard to his body, only a trustworthy name will not be cut off. ¹²[Be fearful concerning] a name, for it will accompany you better than thousands of artful treasures. ¹³The [go]od life is of limited duration, but a good [name] has no limit.

[14]Hidden [wi]sdom and secret treasure, what do you produce with either of them? [15][Be]tter is the man whose [fool]ishness is hidden rather than his wisdom. Children, heed instruction about shame and [hu]mi[lia]tion according to my statutes. [16]For it is not proper to feel shame for every shame, nor is every humiliation to be preferred. [17]Be ashamed before a father and mother for being insolent, before a prince and ruler for [lying], [18]before a master or mistress for deceit, before an assembly or a people for transgression, before a companion or a friend for treachery, in the place where you reside for theft, [19]for breaking an oath and covenant, for extending the elbow for bread, for withholding a gift when asked, for turning away from your kin, [20]for concealing the distribution of a portion, for being silent when receiving a greeting,

Notes

Verse 8: "[Woe to you]" — This expression (either אוי — or more likely הוי — לכם) is reconstructed on the basis of the presence of the terms οὐαί ὑμῖν in the Greek MSS. This is the reconstruction also followed by Yadin (*Ben Sira Scroll*, 41).

Verse 9: "if you beget them" — The evidence suggests that this first line is related to children who are born of "men of perversity."

Verses 10-12: These lines stress the lasting value of a good reputation, presumably established through a life of piety based on following the law, already noted in vv. 4 and 8, and rooted in an understanding of the fear of the Lord. In this case the lesson emerges from the encounter with the possible meaninglessness of life upon the acknowledgment of human mortality, already mentioned in vv. 1-4, and known to us from other wisdom passages such as Eccl 3:20: "All [both man and beast] come from the dust and all return to dust." In the case of the text from Ben Sira, it is from "nothingness" (אפס) and "emptiness" (תהו), the "formlessness" of Gen 1:2, from which "all" come and to which they return. These two Hebrew terms are found together only in Isa 40:17: "as nothingness and emptiness they [i.e., the nations] are considered by him [i.e., God]." The term "emptiness" is used in the Deuteronomic and prophetic traditions (particularly Isaiah) much more widely than in the wisdom literature; the term "nothingness" is most common in Isaiah. In this section we see a text with an identifiable literary connection to an issue in wisdom literature using vocabulary that brings in the theme of judgment from Deuteronomy and Isaiah justifying a standpoint important within Ben Sira, that is, the meaning and significance of "a good name."

Verses 14-16: The order of the hemistichs in these verses is somewhat differ-ent in the Greek MSS. In Genizah MS B there also is evidence of erasure and correction. As indicated in the introduction to this section, the Hebrew MSS reflect earlier textual traditions.

Verse 17: "being insolent" — Genizah MS B here reads זנות ("fornication"), one of the topics of discussion in Second Temple texts, including the polemical approach in CD iv–v.[13]

Verse 18: "for theft" — The Hebrew text is difficult to determine at this point; it would literally read "for [your] hand." Note 42:6, "for a place of many hands a key."[14]

Verses 19-21: The order of these lines is different in the Greek MSS (which form the basis for the identification of verses) from our text and from the Genizah MSS.

Commentary

Verses 1-4: Death is more welcome for the weak and disheartened than for the vigorous and healthy, but it comes to all with an equal inevitability. Note the re-lief for the wicked that comes with death in 40:11 above (see commentary there).

Verse 2: "[Ha]il" — This mode of address is used for God in Pss 47:1; 66:1; 81:1; 95:1, 2; 98:4; 100:1.

Verse 2: "the one who is without might and lacks strength" — For this phrase see Isa 40:29: "to the one without might he increases strength."

Verse 3: "those before and those after" — See Isa 43:18. Genizah MS B reads ראשנים ואחרנים ("the first and the last"), which can refer to the entire spec-trum of people or events ("from the first to the last"), such as in 1 Chr 29:29;

---

13. For a study of this term see John Kampen, "The Matthean Divorce Texts Reexam-ined," in *New Qumran Texts and Studies: Proceedings of the First Meeting of the International Or-ganization of Qumran Studies, Paris, 1992* (ed. George J. Brooke; STDJ 15; Leiden: Brill, 1994), 149-67.

14. See Skehan and Di Lella, *Wisdom of Ben Sira*, 482.

2 Chr 9:29; 12:15; 16:11. It also refers to earlier and later revelation in texts such as *Jub.* 1:4, 26 (see also 1QS ix:10; CD xx:8-9, 31).

Verse 4: "end" — Genizah MS B uses Hebrew חלק ("portion, lot") rather than the term employed here, קץ, which is closer to the language of the biblical prophets.

Verse 4: "[law of] the Most High" — See the discussion of the law in the "Literary Questions" of the introduction to this composition.

Verse 4: "[there are no reproaches concerning life in Sheol]" — There is no concept of reward in the afterlife in Ben Sira. Life ends at death and all people went to Sheol, the netherworld, a dark and dismal place. Within this viewpoint reward and punishment take place in this life. Ben Sira's instructions about the nature of the good life lived on the basis of the Torah concern life in this world.[15]

Verses 5-13: The concern about death, the end of life, turns here to the manner in which life continues: through children and a good reputation. "The men of perversity, who have abandoned the law of the Most High," do not leave a good legacy for their children.

Verses 5-6: "offspring" (נין) and "[progeny]" (נכד) — These terms occur only as a pair in the HB (Gen 21:23; Job 18:19; Isa 14:22). The two terms are also paired in Sir 47:22.[16] "Children of perversity" (בני עול) occurs only in 1QS iii:21 setting out the dualism developed in the "Treatise on the Two Spirits" and 4Q468a-c b:5 in the context of a small fragment that deals with the radiance of the divine and the corresponding holiness in which there is some division between the "children of perversity" and the "children of righteousness." The feminine form of this same term, עולה, has more frequent references in the HB (2 Sam 3:34; 7:10; Ps 89:22; 1 Chr 17:9). It appears even more frequently in Qumran fragments (4Q174 1-2i:1; 4Q265 7:10; 4Q418 69ii:8; 201:2; 4Q429 1i:3; 4i:5; 4Q511 1:8). The nature and scope of these appearances suggest it was one of the terms used to designate one side of the polarity in the growing dualism evident in this literature.

Verse 8: "law of the Most High" — See the discussion of the law in the "Literary Questions" of the introduction to this composition.

15. See ibid., 83-87.
16. Ibid., 474.

Verses 14-15: "Hidden [wi]sdom and secret treasure" — There are repeated injunctions against hiding wisdom throughout this composition. A parallel to these two verses is found in 20:30-31. Some references appear to be very straightforward statements concerning the futility of wisdom that is not shared (4:23-24). There are also injunctions against secret and/or speculative knowledge. Whether these injunctions are directed against proponents of Greek speculation of a cosmogonic character or certain Hebrew apocalyptic traditions is hard to determine (3:22-23).

Col. iv (Sir 41:21–42:14)

^{41:21}for gazing at [a man's wife,] for directing one's attention to prostitutes, ²²for exploiting your [maid] and for violating her bed, for words of abuse for a friend, for a taunt following a gift, ^{42:1}for repeating a w[or]d that you hear, for baring any word of secret counsel. Then you [will] truly show shame and find grace within the eyes of all the living.

Concerning these things do not endure shame and do not show favor and thereby sin. ²Concerning the law of the Most High and the statute and the judgment to acquit the wicked, ³of reckoning with a partner and traveler, and of dividing an inheritance or property, ⁴concerning layers of dust on a balance or scale, of polishing weights and measures, concerning a purchase whether great or small, [and concerning] the price in a sale with a merchant, ⁵[. . .] and concerning an evil servant who walks with a limp, ⁶[for an untrustworthy w]ife a seal and for a place of many hands a key, ⁷[for a place of] deposit a number, for trade let everything be in writing, ⁸concerning the in[struction of the si]mple and the foolish, and the tottering old man preoccupied with fornication, then you will be truly observant and humble before all life.

⁹[A daughter] is a dec[eptive] treasure to a father, [concern for her keeps] away slumber, lest she will be rejected in her youth and lest she [. . .] in her days, ¹⁰lest she be defiled in her virginity and with regard to her husband she has gone astray, lest she bear a child in the house of her father, or [her] husband[. . . .] ¹¹[. . .] keep watch over a strong daughter [le]st [. . .] hearsay in the city and in the assembly of the people[, . . .] in the place where she lodges there should not be [a window, or a house in which she can observe the entrance. . . .] ¹²She shall not show off her beauty to any male, [or have ongoing conversation with married women], ¹³for from a garment a moth comes forth and [from a wom]an the evil of a [wo]man. ¹⁴Better is the wickedness of a man than the goodness of a woman and a daughter who is fearful of reproach.

Notes

Verse 21: "[a man's wife]" — This reconstruction is based on the Greek MSS.

Verse 22: "[maid]" — This reconstruction is based on the Greek MSS.

Verse 9: "[daughter]" — The fragmentary letters at this point in our text do not permit a firm reading, but this reconstruction is supported by Genizah MS B and the Greek MSS.

Verses 11-12: While fragmentary for this section of the text, Genizah MS B permits the proposed reconstructions.

Commentary

Verses 41:21–42:8: These verses continue a section on shame that begins in the Greek text at 40:14, opening with a list of items to be ashamed about, and then in 42:1 changes to items that one should not be ashamed of. The negatives to be avoided include sexual sins as well as relational issues such as lying and cheating. The positive injunctions are more practical, related to taking good care of one's relationships and business dealings.

Verse 2: "law of the Most High" — See the discussion of the law in the "Literary Questions" of the introduction to this chapter.

Verse 4: See Isa 40:12, 15.

Verses 9-14: The concern about the daughter here is based in the reputation of the "house," that is, the extended family and its patriarch. The daughter could bring public disgrace on the family by putting herself in a situation whereby she was subject to the penalties the community was to impose on a woman guilty of fornication or adultery (e.g., Lev 18:20; 20:10-21; Deut 22:13-29). See also the following commentary on v. 10.[17]

Verse 10: "with regard to her husband she has gone astray" — See Num 5:11-31 for the priest's administration of the rite of the bitter waters for the unfaithful wife.

---

17. This is noted by Eileen Schuller, "The Apocrypha," in *The Women's Bible Commentary* (ed. Carol A. Newsom and Sharon H. Ringe; Louisville: Westminster/John Knox, 1992), 237.

Verse 11: "assembly" (קהלה) — This concept is important in Second Temple literature, even though this formulation of the term is not that common. In the Hebrew fragments of Ben Sira this term appears elsewhere only in 7:7; in the HB it occurs only in Deut 33:4 and Neh 5:7. Much more frequent and significant is the term קהל, with roughly the same meaning. In the various MSS of the Hebrew fragments of Ben Sira it is found in 16:6; 15:5; 31:11 (not clear in the text [Genizah MS B], but see Ben-Ḥayyim, *Book of Ben Sira,* 29, on 34:11); 33:19 ([Genizah MS E]; see Ben-Ḥayyim, *Book of Ben Sira,* 26, on 30:27); 44:15; 46:7; 50:13, 20. Note that the references in chap. 50 are to the "whole assembly of Israel" over which the high priest Simon presides. While קהל is translated consistently as ἐκκλησία in the Greek MSS of Ben Sira, קהלה does not yield a consistent term. Throughout the LXX, קהל is translated either as ἐκκλησία or as συναγωγή. These are the terms that come to designate "church" and "synagogue" in the Christian and Jewish traditions, respectively.

Verses 12-14: These lines are some of the evidence used when arguing that Ben Sira had a pronounced misogynistic tendency.

Verse 14: "reproach" — The sense of "shame" implied in the use of this term as the basis for ethical action is an important descriptor signifying the nature of the sanctions valued for community maintenance.

Col. v (Sir 42:15–43:8)

42:15Let me recollect the deeds of God. This that I have seen I shall recount. By the word of the Lord are his works, and through the activity of his will is his instruction. 16The sun shines over all that is revealed, the glory of the Lord fills all his works. 17The holy ones of God are too weak to recount all of his wonders. The Lord has strengthened his host to stand steadfast before his glory. 18He searches out the deep and the heart, and has understanding into their essence, for he knows that which is highest of all [. . .] and he sees the signs for eternity. 19He makes known the changes [in what will be] and he reveals the meaning of the mysteries. 20From him insight is not lacking, and [n]othing is lo[st] to him. 21The strength of [his] wisd[om . . .] He is one for eternity. Nothing can be added [or taken away,] and he has no need of any sage. 22Are not all of his works desirable, even a spark and a fleeting vision? 23All live and endure forever, [for] all are necessary and all are preserved. 24All of them are pairs, one corresponding to the other, and he made none of them [in vain]. 25They exceed one another in their good, so who could get enough of beholding their splendor?

⁴³:¹The form of the heights and the clear vault of the sky, the heaven itself [dem-onstrates] its majesty. ²The sun, when it appears, shines with full radiance, an awesome vessel of the works of the [Most] High. ³When it shines, it scorches the earth, and before its heat who can endure? ⁴A glowing furnace made of cast metal, the ra[ys from the su]n [kindle the mountains]. A tongue from the lumi-nary finishes off the land and the light burns the eye. ⁵For great is the Lord who made it, and [his] w[ords make the powerful shine].

⁶It is the [m]oon that travels through the seasons, governing the times and their signs forever. ⁷The sea[sons] belong to it and from it come the festivals. [The seasons take pleasure in their appointment]. ⁸The new moon according to its name is [renewed, how awesome it is in its changing].

Notes

42:18: "their essence" — Literally "their nakedness."

43:1: "[demonstrates]" — The limited remains of this word in Genizah MS B make reconstruction difficult. I follow Yadin's hypothesis as to the original meaning of the term based on Hebrew מראה.

Verse 3: "When it shines" — בהצהירו can also designate "at noon."[18] I have chosen to translate it here with the broader meaning.

Commentary

This section extols the wonders of God's creation, especially the work of God as creator. Creation as an action carried out at the word of God is already found in Genesis 1. It is also found in 2 Esd 6:38 and Jdt 16:14. In Wis 9:1-2 creation by word is also connected with wisdom. Through this word God knows every-thing in time and space, hence creation is evidence that God has a deep under-standing of all aspects of creation, and knowledge of the future in addition to the past. The capacity to understand all of this is beyond the subordinate heav-enly beings, hence also of human beings. However, God can strengthen the heavenly beings so that they can endure the majesty of all of this beauty, hence gain knowledge. By implication the writer appears to suggest that this is then

18. So Yadin, *Ben Sira Scroll*, 45; and Skehan and Di Lella, *Wisdom of Ben Sira*, 485.

possible for human beings as well. Wisdom is also an activity of God, hence accessible if God wills it. The wonder and majesty of creation is evidence that there is wisdom that is made accessible by the will of God.

The authors of the sectarian texts from Qumran could have found support in such a theology. The emphasis on "seeing" with regard to creation is found in both *1 Enoch* and Ben Sira.[19] The framework of creation is also important in portions of *Instruction*.[20] The lowliness of the human being described in 1QS and 1QH can be advanced under the canopy of the God described in this section. It may be that sections of Ben Sira that root wisdom in the act of creation by an omnipotent and omniscient God were valued by the authors of sectarian texts and the leaders of communities that lived according to those principles.[21]

42:21: "He is one for eternity" — The concept of God as "one" is fundamental for the monotheism of the HB as well as for subsequent Judaism and Christianity. The most significant reference to this concept is in Deut 6:4, "Hear, O Israel, the Lord is our God, the Lord is one," the first line of the Shema, a central prayer of Jewish synagogue liturgy and individual piety.

Verse 24: "All of them are pairs, one corresponding to the other" — Note that this construction also appears in Sir 33:15 (Genizah MS E; see Ben-Ḥayyim, *Book of Ben Sira,* 34, on 36:15). Here it is meant to convey the parallelism and order of the universe, night and day, light and darkness, cold and hot, and so on. This sense of parallelism is in marked contrast to the dualism that underlies many of the sectarian texts from Qumran. It is quite possible, however, that sectarian readers of this text may have interpreted these lines of the Hebrew text as justification for their dualistic viewpoint.

43:2: "an awesome vessel of the works of the [Most] High" — This line continues to demonstrate the manner in which creation is the result of the work of God (see also v. 5). In these lines we also see that creation is witness to its own splendor and magnificence. The role of wisdom in creation is analogous; it testifies to both its integral relation to the Creator and its self-validating nature within creation.

19. Randal A. Argall, *1 Enoch and Sirach: A Comparative Literary and Conceptual Analysis of the Themes of Revelation, Creation and Judgment* (SBLEJL 8; Atlanta: Scholars Press, 1995), 99-164.
20. Matthew J. Goff, "The Mystery of Creation in 4QInstruction," *DSD* 10 (2003): 163-85.
21. See Daniel J. Harrington, "Creation," *EDSS* 1:155-57.

Verses 6-8:   — The role of the moon in determining time and its signs is evidence of a lunisolar calendar, in contrast to the solar calendar described and mandated in the Qumran scrolls and *Jubilees*. The 364-day solar calendar was based on a perfect cycle of 3 months, each comprising 30 days, along with one day for a total of 91 days. This cycle is repeated four times to complete the solar cycle of 364 days. *Jubilees* 6:32-38 warns against the corruption of this calendar ordained by God. It also is described in the Astronomical Book (or Book of the Luminaries) of *1 Enoch* 72–82.[22]

Verse 8:   "The new moon according to its name is [renewed]" — חדש can mean "new moon" or "month" since the month begins with the new moon.

Col. vi (Sir 43:8-25)

[8]A vessel of the host of the clouds on high, br[ightenng the vault of the heavens with its shining].

[9]The beauty of the heavens and the majesty of the star adorn and inflame the heig[hts of God]. [10]By the word of the Lord it remains in its prescribed place, and it does not sink during their watch. [11]See the rainbow and bless the one who made it, for it is v[e]ry majestic [. . .] [12][It encircles] the ordered hea[ven] with its glory, [and] the hand of God stretched it out with mi[ght.] [13]His rebuke marks the hail and illuminates the meteors of judgment. [14]For his own purpose he releases the storehouse and the clouds soar like birds of prey. [15]His might sustains the clouds and cuts up the hail[stone]s. [16]The sound of his thunder makes the earth tremble, and by his strength the mountains shake. His word impels the south wind, in addition to the whirlwind and the gale. [17]Like a plague his snow springs forth, and like locusts settling is its descent. [18]The glare of its whiteness blinds the eyes, and from its fall the heart is terrified. [19][Also fros]t he pours out like salt, and he sprouts flowers like a briar bush. [20][The cold wind from the no]rth he sends and the spring freezes solid. He covers every pool of water[. . . .] [23][. . .] islands. [24][. . .] our ears hear we are amazed. [25][. . .] might of Rahab.

---

22. For a more extensive discussion, see Shemaryahu Talmon, "Calendars and Mishmarot," *EDSS* 1:108-17; James C. VanderKam, *Calendars in the Dead Sea Scrolls: Measuring Time* (London: Routledge, 1998).

Commentary

This column continues with the theme of creation and the role of the word of the Lord from the previous section.

Verse 8: "clouds on high" — Literally "the jars of heaven"; cf. Job 38:37.

Verse 10: The orderliness of the heavens is asserted in Second Temple literature to attest to the structure that undergirds the earth as well as to the nature of its Creator. A good example of this assertion is found in the Book of the Luminaries in *1 Enoch* 72–82. While the detailed description focuses on the sun and the moon, the stars are included as an integral part of the structure of the cosmos (*1 En.* 72:1; 75:1-3; 79:1-6; 82:9-20). Note the parallels with 1QH^a ix discussed in vv. 12 and 14 below. Note also Job 38:29 and 37.

Verse 11: "majestic" — The word נהדר in this text is not as common in the HB or in the texts from Qumran as the term נאדר ("glorious") found in Genizah MS B.

Verse 12: "[It encircles] the ordered hea[ven] with its glory, [and] the hand of God stretched it out with mi[ght.]" See 1QH^a ix:11-12 along with the references noted in vv. 10 and 14.

Verse 13: "meteors" — While the term זיקות (Isa 50:11; Prov 26:18[זקים]) refers to flaming arrows in Biblical Hebrew, it includes shooting stars and meteors in rabbinic literature (Jastrow, 395-96), as well as in 1QH^a ix:14; 4Q286 3:4.

Verse 14: "For his own purpose, he releases the storehouse" — The heavens are referred to as the treasure house of the Lord in Deut 28:12 and 32:34, from which the wind, snow, and hail come (Job 38:22; Ps 135:7; Jer 10:13; 51:16). In 1QH^a ix:13-15 the storehouses have a place in the design along with other heavenly constellations such as the luminaries, the stars, the wind, and lightning.

Verse 18: In context this verse suggests the continuing metaphors of judgment carried out by a powerful God who has the full force of nature at his command. In this sense portions of this verse are closer to the "confusion of heart" in Deut 28:28 than to the beauty of creation, found in the translations of the Greek text. The phrase "blinds the eyes" is suggested by *HALOT* s.v. הגה II. Note also the Piel form, "to pierce, sting," cited in Jastrow, 331.

Verse 25: "Rahab" — The name of a mythological sea serpent or dragon similar to Leviathan. While these lines appear to be dependent on Pss 104:25-26 and 107:23-24, the vanquishing of Rahab in creation is suggested in Ps 89:10; Job 9:13; 26:12; Isa 51:9 (John Day, "Rahab [Dragon]," *ABD* 5:610-11). It also is sometimes used as a metaphorical name for Egypt.

Col. vii (Sir 44:1-17)

[1][Let me praise the] pious [men, our] father[s in their generations.] [2]Much honor the Most High has apportioned and greatness from [the days of old], [3]advisors with their discernment and seers with their prophecy, [4]leaders of the people with their prudence and governors with [their] decree[s], thoughtful sages with their literary expertise, [5]composers of musical psalms and authors of [written] prove[rbs], [6]men of wealth who possess power, sec[ure in their dwelling place.] [7]All these were honored in their generation [and in their days possessed distinction.] [8]Some of them have left a name [to rely on in their inheritance.] [9]Some of them receive no mention [and they came to an end when they perished.] They became as though they had not been [and their sons after them.] [10]However, these are pious men[. . . .] [11]Their good remains with their descendants and [their] inher[itance. . . .] [12]Their descendants stand in their covenant and their offspring[. . . .] [13]Their descendants will stand forever, and their glory will not be an[nihilated]. [14]Their bo[dies] will be buried in peace, but their name lives throughout every generation. [15]The assembly [repeats their wisdom], and the congregation recounts their praise[. . . .] [17]Noah the righteous was found perfect[. . . .]

Notes

Verse 3: — Prior to the line cited in the text, Genizah MS B records: "Rulers of the earth with their dominion, men of repute with their valor."

Verse 11: "with" — Through scribal error the first word in this verse is אם ("if"), rather than עם.

Commentary

This column begins the best known and final major section of Ben Sira, entitled "Praise of the Fathers of Old" in Genizah MS B and "Praise of the Ancestors" in most Greek, Latin, and Syriac texts. We see in the Hebrew text a greater emphasis on piety in contrast to the fame and power accentuated in the LXX.

Verse 1: "[in their generations]" — This implies a historical recital similar to the genealogies of Gen 2:4; 5:1; 11:10, and so on, even though the term used in the first four books of the Pentateuch and the books of Chronicles is תולדות rather than the more common דור.

Verse 6: "men of wealth who possess power" — The most common translation of חיל is "might," though we find in the LXX version of this verse ἄνδρες πλούσιοι ("rich men"), evidence that the term also designated wealth in Second Temple Judaism. Hence the Hebrew text here appears to refer to men who possessed wealth as well as political and perhaps some military power. Note that in the second century B.C.E. these were the men who were secure in their homes.[23]

---

23. John Kampen, *The Hasideans and the Origins of Pharisaism: A Study in 1 and 2 Maccabees* (SBLSCS 24; Atlanta: Scholars Press, 1988), 97; see pp. 95-107 for the more general discussion of this translation.

Index of Modern Authors

Index of Scripture and Other Ancient Texts